THE FUTURE OF CROSS-BORDER INSOLVENCY

The Future of Cross-Border Insolvency

Overcoming Biases and Closing Gaps

IRIT MEVORACH

OXFORD
UNIVERSITY PRESS

OXFORD
UNIVERSITY PRESS

Great Clarendon Street, Oxford, OX2 6DP,
United Kingdom

Oxford University Press is a department of the University of Oxford.
It furthers the University's objective of excellence in research, scholarship,
and education by publishing worldwide. Oxford is a registered trade mark of
Oxford University Press in the UK and in certain other countries

Published in the United States of America by Oxford University Press
198 Madison Avenue, New York, NY 10016, United States of America

British Library Cataloguing in Publication Data
Data available

Library of Congress Control Number: 2018930534

ISBN 978–0–19–878289–6

Printed and bound by
CPI Group (UK) Ltd, Croydon, CR0 4YY

Preface

Cross-border (international) insolvency law attempts to regulate the treatment of financial and economic distress of debtors who have presence in or connection to more than one country. In recent decades, particularly following the 2008 global financial crisis, the challenges of addressing cross-border insolvency effectively have been highlighted in domestic, regional, and international policy considerations and reform agendas. Considering the cross-border insolvency of both commercial entities and financial institutions, this book explores the key theoretical and practical developments in this field from a broad inter-disciplinary perspective to provide insights about the future of cross-border insolvency and how the system can be improved going forward.

This book is the outcome of a few years of research on issues and challenges concerning the theory and practice of cross-border insolvency. It is also a result of my involvement in standard setting and policy work, through roles in the World Bank Group Insolvency and Creditor/Debtor Regimes Initiative, participation in the United Nations Commission on International Trade Law (UNCITRAL) Working Group V, and in the Financial Stability Board (FSB) Resolution Legal Expert Group, and through technical assistance and capacity building in several emerging and developing jurisdictions. While these experiences left me optimistic about the ability of legal systems to improve and to cooperate across-borders, they also opened my eyes to persisting problems.

In my earlier research on cross-border insolvency, especially empirical studies, I was able to highlight the success of existing cross-border insolvency instruments, including the way courts have interpreted and applied them—in general, with a universalist spirit. In that research, I focused much on the glass half-full. This book explores the other—bleaker—half as well, with the aim of continuing to strengthen the system. It seeks to address pressing questions regarding the sort of future we may envisage for cross-border insolvency: Is a pure universalist system the ultimate aim? What holds universalism back? Should we at some stage replace model laws with treaties as the governing instruments in this field? Can trust be required of participants in cross-border insolvency? Should we employ sanctions or other forms of incentives to promote compliance with cross-border insolvency instruments? Why has the cross-border insolvency of multinational financial institutions not yet been addressed in a comprehensive framework, notwithstanding lessons from the 2008 global financial crisis? What is the right instrument for these institutions?

The book addresses these and related questions, and, in the process, provides a normative framework that can guide reform. That framework is built primarily on the theory and practice of cross-border insolvency; yet it is also informed by, and makes connections with, public international law and the international law-making process, as well as behavioural international law and economic insights. Thus, it ventures outside the insolvency and cross-border insolvency silo to look at issues more broadly. The approach is also holistic in its attempt to address the variety of business structures, including both single entities and groups, and it makes associations between cross-border insolvency regimes for commercial entities and for multinational financial institutions.

The book is divided into seven chapters. *Chapter 1* depicts the current state of affairs of cross-border insolvency, specifically of what is called 'modified universalism'. Modified universalism has translated the theoretical model of universalism—where one law governs, and one forum presides in cross-border insolvency cases—to concrete and more nuanced emerging norms that are fit for the real-world and real business structures. It is, however, still held back where it is regarded as a trend and an interim solution in the context of an aspiration for pure universalism. Consequently, one of the challenges confronting the universalist approach, in its various forms, is that even though it is generally beneficial, it is not universally adopted. *Chapter 2* then explores, by drawing on behavioural international law and economics, what the reasons for deviating from modified universalism in practice may be. It argues that certain decision-making biases may play a role in cross-border insolvency and can explain both negative inclinations and instances of lack of cooperation, as well as the relative success of modified universalism. The chapter's key argument is that instead of yielding to territorial inclinations, cross-border insolvency law has a debiasing role to play. It should attempt to align choices with optimal solutions, overcoming biases, and should also close gaps in the cross-border insolvency system in line with modified universalism. Following this rationale, *Chapter 3* suggests that modified universalism's emerging norms should transform into customary international law (CIL), and shows how CIL can be a debiasing tool that can also close gaps in the system. In this respect, the chapter highlights the prominent international role of private international law and, thus, the role of actors and participants in international insolvencies as creators and guardians of international law. *Chapter 4* considers which type of written international instrument could best serve a system based on modified universalism. Drawing on international law and practice, and economic and behavioural perspectives, it questions the predisposition in favour of a treaty as the ultimate solution and argues that while a treaty has potential benefits, it also entails important drawbacks. This chapter also shows the importance of instrument design and how it may promote effective implementation. *Chapter 5* provides the normative framework for promoting broad compliance of countries and implementing institutions with the cross-border insolvency system. It thus elucidates the role of incentives and of mutual trust, the type of harmonization that can support compliance, the role of forum shopping in view of gaps and deficiencies in domestic legal systems and institutional frameworks, and the benefits and drawbacks of attempting to delegate implementation roles to external bodies to bridge capacity gaps and to overcome biases. Against this normative backdrop, *Chapter 6* assesses existing instruments for cross-border insolvency as they apply to commercial entities or to financial institutions, and unearths issues regarding gaps and biases in those instruments. The focus is on the global instruments; however, for comparison, this chapter also refers to the regional EU cross-border insolvency regime, which has significantly influenced global developments. When this book went to print, UNCITRAL Working Group V was developing new instruments concerning the insolvency of multinational groups and the enforcement of insolvency-related judgments; thus, this chapter also provides tentative insights concerning these developments. *Chapter 7* provides concluding remarks regarding the future of cross-border insolvency.

This book, and the research and thinking it required, could not have come about had I not had the benefit of discussions with colleagues, co-thinkers in the field of international insolvency, including in debates and conversations during sessions of the World Bank Global Task Force on Insolvency (Washington/New York, 2013–15) and of UNCITRAL (since 2005). Within the UK delegation to UNCITRAL I had stimulating conversations in recent years, particularly with Dean Beale, Mark Smith, and Riz Mokal. I benefitted too from discussions of issues concerning international solvency with colleagues at the World Bank, especially: Vijay Tata, Leif Clark, Adolfo Rouillon, Mahesh Uttamchandani, and Antonia Preciosa. Specifically, I owe gratitude to readers of parts and drafts of the book at different stages of its development for their invaluable comments: Ian Fletcher, Janis Sarra, Adrian Walters, Ignacio Tirado, Jenny Clift, Ted Janger, Steven Schwarcz (and research assistant Miata Eggerly), John Pottow, and Jay Westbrook. I also benefited immensely from discussions, and comments on drafts, from colleagues at the Nottingham International Law and Security Centre: Dino Kritsiotis, Daria Davitti, Marko Milanovic, and Sandesh Sivakumaran. Additional thanks go to Tomer Broude and Carmel Mevorach for feedback, and to the participants in the following events where aspects of the book, or the research leading to it, were presented: the Insolvency Law Association (ILA) conference in London in March 2017, especially the discussant, David Chivers QC; the panel on 'Financial Institutions Failure' at the International Insolvency Institute's Annual Meeting (London, 2017), especially the panel chair, Don Bernstein; the Brooklyn Journal of Corporate, Financial & Commercial Law Symposium on 'The Treatment of Financial Contracts in Bankruptcy and Bank Resolution' (Brooklyn Law School, New York, 2015); the Brooklyn Journal of Corporate, Financial & Commercial Law Symposium on 'Choice of Law in Cross-Border Insolvency Cases' (Brooklyn Law School, New York, 2014); and the UNCITRAL Fourth Colloquium on International Insolvency Law (Vienna, 2013). I am also grateful for help with access to materials, especially to my colleagues Stephan Madaus, Rodrigo Rodriguez, Janis Sarra, Monica Marcucci, Andre Boraine, and Sanam Saidova. Finally, I thank Aysenaz Tahmaz, Bojan Bajalovic, and Roni Mevorach for research and other assistance, and the production team at Oxford University Press, especially Eve Ryle-Hodges, Jamie Berezin, Vignesh Kannan, and Allan Hoyano for their invaluable support. Interactions and discussions with my students in the module 'International

Aspects of Corporate Law and Insolvency' have also influenced my thinking. Of course, any mistakes in this book are my own, and the views expressed are solely mine and do not represent the views of any of the abovementioned organizations.

Irit Mevorach

School of Law
Faculty of Social Sciences
University of Nottingham
September 2017

Contents

Table of Cases

Table of Cases

Table of Statutes and Other Instruments

Table of International Instruments

List of Abbreviations

ALI	American Law Institute
BRRD	Bank Recovery and Resolution Directive
CIL	customary international law
CJEU	Court of Justice of the European Union
CLOUT	Case Law on UNCITRAL Texts
COMI	centre of main interests
EIR	(EU) Regulation on Insolvency Proceedings (2000)
EMCA	European Model Company Act
EMEA	Europe, the Middle East, Africa
EU	European Union
FINMA	(Swiss) Financial Market Supervisory Authority
FSB	Financial Stability Board
G-SIFI	Global systemically important financial institution
HCCE	Hague Conference on Private International Law
IAIR	International Association of Insolvency Regulators
ICJ	International Court of Justice
ICR	Insolvency and Creditor-Debtor Regimes
IBA	International Bar Association
ILA	International Law Association
ILC	International Law Commission
ILO	International Labour Organization
IMF	International Monetary Fund
IO	international organization
IOSCO	International Organization of Securities Commissions
ISDA	International Swaps and Derivatives Association
JIN	Judicial Insolvency Network
MFI	multinational financial institution
MLCBI	(UNCITRAL) Model Law on Cross-Border Insolvency
MLCBI GEI	MLCBI Guide to Enactment and Interpretation
MLG	(UNCITRAL draft) model provisions/law on cross-border insolvency of groups
MLJ	(UNCITRAL draft) model law on the recognition and enforcement of insolvency-related judgments
MOU	memorandum of understanding
NAFTA	North American Free Trade Agreement
NGO	non-governmental organization
NPL	non-performing loan
OECD	Organisation for Economic Co-operation and Development
Recast EIR	Recast EU Regulation (2015)
ROSC	Report on the Observances of Standards and Codes
SADC	Southern Africa Development Community
SIFI	systemically important financial institution
SPOE	single point of entry

SRM	Single Resolution Mechanism
TLAC	total loss absorbance capacity
UIA	Union Internationale des Avocats
UNCTAD	United Nations Conference on Trade and Development
UNCTIRAL	United Nations Commission on International Trade Law
UNIDROIT	International Institute for the Unification of Private Law
WTO	World Trade Organization

1

Modified Universalism to Date

1.1 Introduction

This chapter depicts the current position of cross-border insolvency and, specifically, of what is called 'modified universalism'—the prevailing approach for addressing cross-border insolvency cases, which is emerging from the theory of 'pure universalism' to suit the real-world circumstances. The chapter considers in this regard the treatment of multinational commercial entities (or enterprise groups comprising several entities) as well as multinational financial institutions (MFIs) in cross-border insolvency.[1] It also synthesizes the different aspects of modified universalism into a set of emerging norms for the governance of such cross-border insolvencies, concerning jurisdiction, choice of law, recognition, assistance, and cooperation, accompanied by global duties and safeguards. It shows how these norms can increase global welfare by preserving cross-border links for the benefit of the stakeholders as a whole, matching cross-border insolvency solutions with the economic reality of businesses and financial institutions. In the process this chapter also suggests that, contrary to prevailing views, modified universalism is not a compromise or a manifestation of concessions to countries' territorial inclinations until the ideal of pure universalism can be implemented. Rather, the correct understanding of modified universalism is as an approach that, if followed uniformly, can produce optimal results in cross-border insolvencies.

---

[1] Namely, entities (or enterprises) of whatever form engaged in economic activities that have presence in or connections to multiple jurisdictions, eg through the location of their head office, registered office, assets, creditors, activities, or affiliates, or because of cross-border relocation before insolvency proceedings commence. 'Cross-border Insolvency' (or international insolvency) means here any form of process or solution concerning such entities (also referred to as 'debtors'), including liquidation or forms of reorganization or restructuring processes. 'MFIs' include both banks and other non-bank financial institutions with presence in or connections to more than one country as noted above. Banking may be the main activity of financial institutions, or their activities may extend beyond simple deposit-taking and lending, covering a full range of non-bank financial activities. 'Cross-border insolvency' in the financial institutions' context also refers to any form of solution that may be employed to resolve the distress of the MFI, including liquidation, reorganization, or the use of various resolution measures. The problem of coordinating resolution action across borders raises similar issues with respect to both bank and non-bank financial institutions and many 'systemically-risky international financial groups are, at their core, investment banks and broker-dealers' (International Monetary Fund, 'Resolution of Cross-Border Banks—A Proposed Framework for Enhanced Coordination' (11 June 2010) <https://www.imf.org/external/np/pp/eng/2010/061110.pdf>).

This chapter also admits the vulnerability of modified universalism. Conceptually, modified universalism is still held back where it is regarded as a trend and an interim solution. The survey of practice across legal systems also shows mixed success, whereby modified universalism is prevalent, yet is not fully universal, complete, and consistently applied. Territorial inclinations certainly persist and have been particularly pronounced during the global financial crisis of 2008 ('the global financial crisis'), where there have been notable instances of discrimination or non-cooperation in cross-border insolvencies. So far, scholars are divided on how they view the reality of cross-border insolvency, where some focus on the 'glass half-full' and others on the 'glass half-empty'. This chapter seeks to break with that division and portray a more objective picture. The aim, however, is not to undermine (modified) universalism,[2] but rather to be realistic about its current status in order, in subsequent chapters, to contemplate ways to strengthen the system of cross-border insolvency going forward.

The chapter proceeds as follows. Section 1.2 reviews the debate between universalism and territorialism. It explains each approach and its underlying philosophy and highlights the supremacy of universalism as a theoretical model for international insolvencies. Modified universalism is a derivative of the model of pure universalism. Section 1.3 describes the evolution of modified universalism, understood so far as the best interim solution. It delineates the key emerging norms, which, it is submitted, can be followed in the real world of cross-border insolvency. These norms are based on the universalist philosophy, yet accommodate nuanced solutions that take account of different business and financial institution structures. Modified universalism also does not rely on full convergence, harmonization, and the establishment of an international court or conclusion of a treaty. Section 1.4 describes, however, the scepticism concerning the feasibility of forms of universalism. It also depicts the reception and application of modified universalism in practice, revealing mixed success, whereby modified universalism is dominant yet not universally and consistently applied. Section 1.5 provides summary conclusions.

1.2 Pure Universalism: The Theoretical Paradigm

Solutions for cross-border insolvency have been considered against the backdrop of the theoretical debate between two polarized schools of thought, universalism and territorialism, linked to the antithetical principles of unity and plurality.[3] This section describes these principles and the position of each approach. It portrays the supremacy of universalism as a theoretical model for the resolution of multinational default, where it is based on the preservation and maximization of the debtor value for the benefit of the stakeholders as a whole.

---

[2] cf LM LoPucki, 'Cooperation in International Bankruptcy: A Post-Universalist Approach' (1999) 84 Cornell L Rev 696, 762 (who suggested 'to recognize that universalism is the problem, not the solution, and to put universalism behind us').

[3] IF Fletcher, *Insolvency in Private International Law* (OUP 2005) 11.

1.2.1 Universalism: a model based on the principles of unity and universality

Under the unity principle applied to cross-border insolvency, debtors should be subject to a single and unified insolvency process encompassing all assets and claims.[4] The resultant principle of universality addresses the effect of opening the unified single process and suggests that such proceedings will have a worldwide effect over all property and interests of the debtor, wherever located.[5] In accordance with these principles, universalism proposes that cross-border insolvencies should be unitary and universal.[6]

More specifically, universalists have sketched a model of pure universalism, contemplating how, ideally, the cross-border insolvency system would look if we were to fully adopt the unity and universality principles.[7] That model envisages a system whereby a single court administers the multinational case and applies a single insolvency law.[8] Thus, all aspects of the multinational debtor's insolvency, including the treatment of creditors' claims, the administration and distribution of assets, all substantive and procedural legal issues, and all decisions would be conducted in one single proceeding and would be effective in all countries where assets or other aspects of the debtor are located.[9] The same model would apply in regard to cross-border insolvency of MFIs, whereby one single jurisdiction is in charge of the insolvency proceedings and is responsible for the resolution of all domestic and cross-border activities of the failing institution.[10]

Universalism foresees a global, multinational convention that will create such a system based on universality and unity in cross-border insolvency.[11] The global regime which such a convention would introduce would be equivalent to federal systems' statutory structures. In those structures, even where state laws govern various commercial aspects, the federal insolvency law allows for the insolvency process to cover all assets and govern the interests of all stakeholders throughout the national market.[12] Similarly, on the global level, an international convention would create a global structure for worldwide insolvency proceedings under a single law with universal effect. Ideally, a single forum would be created under

---

[4] ibid.   [5] ibid 11–13.

[6] ibid. See also R Bork, *Principles of Cross-Border Insolvency Law* (Intersentia 2017) 28–29.

[7] JL Westbrook, 'A Global Solution to Multinational Default' (2000) 98 Mich L Rev 2276, 2293–94.

[8] ibid 2292 (noting regarding the 'two elements necessary to an international convention for international bankruptcy: a single law and a single forum' that: 'These two elements are distinct and need not necessarily be conjoined in an international bankruptcy system, although ideally they would be').

[9] B Wessels, *International Insolvency Law* Part I (Wolters Kluwer 2015) 9.

[10] RM Lastra, 'International Law Principles Applicable to Cross-Border Bank Insolvency' in RM Lastra (ed), *Cross-Border Bank Insolvency* (OUP 2011) 166.

[11] Westbrook, 'A Global Solution to Multinational Default' (n 7) 2287 (noting that the international convention may not create an entire international commercial system). See also K Anderson, 'The Cross-border Insolvency Paradigm: A defence of the Modified Universal Approach Considering the Japanese Experience' (2000) 21 U Pa J Intl Econ L 679, 682 (noting that: 'universalism in its pure form was not feasible without an international convention …').

[12] Westbrook, 'A Global Solution to Multinational Default' (n 7) 2284, 2287 (mentioning eg the USA, Canada, Mexico, and Germany).

this system through establishing a single international system of bankruptcy courts, thus attaining benefits such as those achieved under a single national bankruptcy law.[13] The insolvency representative or the manager of a reorganization would report to this single court system.[14] The single international forum would apply a single bankruptcy law, preferably a supranational law on all insolvency-related matters, including the order of priorities and rules for voidable transactions.[15]

1.2.2 Territorialism: the traditional approach based on plurality and territoriality

The principle of plurality, on the other hand, envisages multiple proceedings opened in different countries regarding the same debtor, namely a divided administration of the debtor's insolvency.[16] The corollary principle of territoriality confines the effects of insolvency proceedings to the jurisdiction where proceedings are opened; that is, there should be no extraterritorial (outbound) effect to proceedings opened within the country, and a country need not give (inbound) effect to proceedings opened elsewhere.[17] Plurality and territoriality correspond with the traditional notions of state sovereignty and vested rights, namely the conviction that the laws of one sovereign state cannot, of themselves and as of right, produce effects within the territory of another sovereign and independent jurisdiction. Thus, in insolvency, the law of the sovereign is imposed on all within its territorial reach, and that law grants vested rights in assets situated therein at the time an insolvency proceeding is begun.[18]

In line with these principles, and in opposition to universalism, under territorialism legal action may be taken against the debtor and its assets independently in the different countries where the property is located at the time of the insolvency filing. Such property may be seized by the courts of the jurisdiction where it is found for the benefit of local creditors; thus, in negative terms, territorialism is also called the 'grab rule'.[19] Administration of aspects of the insolvency is confined to each territorial jurisdiction, and each jurisdiction may apply its own law with little or no regard for foreign proceedings regarding the same debtor. Foreign proceedings may not have any effect on portions of the debtor and its assets located in other jurisdictions.[20]

---

[13] ibid 2292–94 (noting that the single system may include more than one court and may be comprised of courts in different regions and of courts devoted to cases centred in large economics. In the absence of unified international institutions, the application of such regime could be achieved by harmonizing the private international law rules pertaining to insolvency, but Westbrook considers such solution to be much less predictable).

[14] ibid 2293.   [15] ibid.

[16] Fletcher, *Insolvency in Private International Law* (n 3) 11; Bork, *Principles of Cross-Border Insolvency Law* (n 6) 21–22.

[17] Fletcher, *Insolvency in Private International Law* (n 3) 13.

[18] LM LoPucki, 'The Case for Cooperative Territoriality in International Bankruptcy' (2000) 98 Mich L Rev 2216, 2218; F Tung, 'Fear of Commitment in International Bankruptcy' (2001) 33 Geo Wash Intl L Rev 555, 561; JJ Chung, 'The New Chapter 15 of the Bankruptcy Code: A Step Toward Erosion of National Sovereignty' (2007) 27 Nw J Intl L & Bus 89, 93. See also Fletcher, *Insolvency in Private International Law* (n 3) 13.

[19] LA Bebchuk and AT Guzman, 'An Economic Analysis of Transnational Bankruptcies' (1999) 42 JL & Econ 775, 777.

[20] LoPucki, 'Cooperation in International Bankruptcy' (n 2) 725–55.

Similarly, in the context of cross-border insolvency of MFIs, under a territorialist system, the MFI in distress would be de-globalized; that is, proceedings may be opened in multiple jurisdictions where the institution has realizable assets, and each jurisdiction may separately treat that portion of the institution as if it were a stand-alone branch or subsidiary.[21]

1.2.3 Supremacy of universalism as the theoretical model

The opposing principles of unity/universality and plurality/territoriality in cross-border insolvency have created a 'historic struggle' that 'has been unusually intense'.[22] In the process, territorialism evolved and challenged universalism, pointing to significant issues in the purist model.[23] These problems include: the reliance of pure universalism on full convergence of laws or the creation of supranational law, which may not be achievable;[24] its inadequacy for business structures such as some forms of enterprise groups that comprise separate and independently controlled entities;[25] and its disregard of the possible disadvantaged position of creditors where the process takes place in a foreign country.[26] Yet, territorialism, including its modern version, called 'cooperative territoriality',[27] by adhering to a solution based

---

[21] Lastra, 'International Law Principles Applicable to Cross-Border Bank Insolvency' (n 10) 170. See also International Monetary Fund, 'Resolution of Cross-Border Banks—A Proposed Framework for Enhanced Coordination' (11 June 2010) 15 <https://www.imf.org/external/np/pp/eng/2010/061110.pdf>.

[22] Fletcher, *Insolvency in Private International Law* (n 3) 11. See eg LoPucki, 'The Case for Cooperative Territoriality in International Bankruptcy' (n 18) 2216; Tung, 'Fear of Commitment in International Bankruptcy' (n 18) 561; F Tung, 'Is International Bankruptcy Possible?' (2002) 23 Mich J Intl L 31; Chung, 'The New Chapter 15 of the Bankruptcy Code' (n 18) 89; AM Kipnis, 'Beyond UNCITRAL: Alternatives to Universality in Translational Insolvency' (2008) 36 Denv J Intl L & Pol'y 155; S Franken, 'Cross-border Insolvency Law: A Comparative Institutional Analysis' (2014) 34 OJLS 97. cf eg Westbrook, 'A Global Solution to Multinational Default' (n 7); Anderson, 'The Cross-border Insolvency Paradigm' (n 11) 679; AT Guzman, 'International Bankruptcy: In Defence of Universalism' (2000) 98 Mich L Rev 2177; Bork, *Principles of Cross-Border Insolvency Law* (n 6) 28.

[23] Although, the critique often confuses pure universalism with modified universalism. For example, the claim of territorialists that universalism cannot produce a workable jurisdiction test (LoPucki, 'Cooperation in International Bankruptcy' (n 2) 713 ff) concerns *modified* universalism, as under pure universalism the establishment of an international court provides a solution.

[24] LoPucki, 'The Case for Cooperative Territoriality' (n 18) 2217. See also Chapter 5, section 5.3.2.

[25] It has been argued that territorialism fits better with the way enterprises normally operate, namely as distinct entities, incorporated in each country where the debtor is doing business (LoPucki, 'Cooperation in International Bankruptcy' (n 2) 750).

[26] ibid 734 ff (expressing concern about expectations of creditors regarding where an insolvency case will be held and under which laws); Chung, 'The New Chapter 15 of the Bankruptcy Code' (n 18) 120 ff (noting the problem of employees treated differently in different countries); Tung, 'Fear of Commitment in International Bankruptcy' (n 18) 578 (noting that local creditors may be disadvantaged because they are not 'on the ground' when a process takes place in a different country).

[27] Under cooperative territorialism, each country would administer the assets located within its own borders as separate estates and would determine whether to reorganize or liquidate the estate and how to conduct a distribution, according to local laws. Yet, countries may enter into treaties to allow for mutually beneficial cooperation (LoPucki, 'Cooperation in International Bankruptcy' (n 2) 742–43). Thus, cooperative territorialism is grounded in territoriality (Kipnis, 'Beyond UNCITRAL: Alternatives to Universality' (n 22) 159, explaining that: 'Cooperative territoriality is very similar to classic territoriality in that it provides for separate proceedings to occur in each country in which the debtor has assets';

on splitting the case between jurisdictions and disregarding foreign stakeholders, cannot provide a regime that promotes the goals of insolvency when insolvency happens across legal systems.[28]

1.2.3.1 Universalism promotes the goals of insolvency law

The universalist approach, on the other hand, offers a solution for global insolvencies in designing a model that, in theory, achieves the fundamental goals of insolvency laws.[29] Insolvency law aims to promote the procedural goal of efficiency to achieve the substantive goal of fairness.[30] Thus, wealth should be maximized, and waste minimized. In insolvency, this may require that the race of creditors to collect their claims and grab assets be stopped and replaced by mandatory collective procedures and that the process be subject to possible alternative arrangements such as reorganization or restructuring mechanisms.[31] It also requires that insolvency law is predictable, thus allowing relevant stakeholders to calculate and adjust to the risk of granting credit and of transacting with businesses.[32] Insolvency law should also ensure that creditors are treated equitably through equal treatment of similarly situated creditors as well as through

---

Westbrook, 'A Global Solution to Multinational Default' (n 7) 2302, noting that '... the inevitable consequence is that real cooperation in a territorial system is necessarily very limited ...').

[28] Fletcher, *Insolvency in Private International Law* (n 3) 14 (noting regarding cooperative territorialism that 'the theory encounters the serious objection that it gives rise to the consequence that creditors' expectations of recovery would be affected by the chance location of the debtor's assets at the moment of bankruptcy, which may bear no relation to the pattern of pre-bankruptcy conduct of the debtor through which the debts and liabilities have arisen ...'); Westbrook, 'A Global Solution to Multinational Default' (n 7) 2308 (arguing that territorialism's 'fundamental flaw is that no national bankruptcy law is symmetrical with a global market ... no system of managing a general default can be effective unless it is symmetrical with the market ...').

[29] An alternative approach is 'contractualism' (R Rasmussen, 'A New Approach to Transnational Insolvencies' (1997) 19 Mich J Intl L 1) under which companies would select, at the time of their formation, the jurisdiction and applicable insolvency law. This approach has been criticized for failing to appreciate the multiparty nature of insolvency regimes and the divergent claimants (see eg Westbrook, 'A Global Solution to Multinational Default' (n 7) 2303 ff; E Warren and JL Westbrook, 'Contracting Out of Bankruptcy: An Empirical Intervention' (2005) 118 Harv L Rev 1197, 1201; Fletcher, *Insolvency in Private International Law* (n 3) 14–15). However, aspects of contractualism support universalism, including: 'ad hoc contractualism' where parties in the course of insolvency agree eg to defer to a single jurisdiction (I Mevorach, 'Towards a Consensus on the Treatment of Multinational Enterprise Groups in Insolvency' (2010) 18 Cardozo J Intl & Comp L 359, 385 ff), or 'cross-border recognition clauses' in financial contracts that enhance certainty about the cross-border application of stays of termination rights (see Chapter 6, section 6.3.2). Contractual solutions cannot offer a complete solution for global default, however, as it is not possible in this way to reach the level of completeness and global obligation required (see Chapter 4, section 4.4 and Chapter 6, section 6.3.3).

[30] RJ Mokal, *Corporate Insolvency Law: Theory and Application* (OUP 2005) 24–25; DA Farber, 'What (if Anything) Can Economics Say about Equity?' (2003) 101 Mich L Rev 1791, 1821.

[31] TH Jackson, *The Logic and Limits of Bankruptcy Law* (Harvard University Press 1986) chs 1–2; see also Fletcher, *Insolvency in Private International Law* (n 3) 9 (noting that 'at least one fundamental principle appears to command universal acceptance ... This may be termed "the principle of collectivity", and amounts to a recognition that insolvency constitutes an example of the so-called "common pool problem" ...').

[32] Guzman, 'International Bankruptcy: In Defence of Universalism' (n 22) 2181.

considering the need to protect vulnerable parties to promote deep, not merely flat, equality.[33]

Universalism envisages such a type of collective process on the global level, namely one that is symmetrical with the market it covers, thus encompassing all stakeholders whose interests are implicated (without discriminating against foreign creditors) and all assets wherever located.[34] The links between the aspects of the business are preserved and it is possible to consider the interests of all stakeholders related to that business, allowing maximal value for the benefit of the stakeholders as a whole. Issues of debtor liability and transactions which prefer some creditors (foreign or local) at the expense of the general body of creditors, including diversion of assets across borders, can be addressed under this model.[35] *Ex post* efficiency is further increased by avoiding duplicative proceedings and allowing a more expeditious and efficient administration of the estate.[36] *Ex ante* efficiency increases as well where credit providers can structure loans or agree on debt workouts with greater certainty of the outcome in the event of insolvency because they can rely on a single, supranational legal system.[37] Additionally, the prospect of an insolvency process that can preserve and maximize value can induce investment and reduce the cost of capital.[38]

Certainly, to promote efficiency and fairness under the universalist model, countries must surrender sovereignty in international insolvency cases. Thus, they must agree to lose some power and control over local constituencies, businesses, and stakeholders, and defer to an international system of insolvency.[39] In return, however, the stakeholders as a whole should benefit under this model from a value-maximizing solution, and the interests of all should be adequately taken into account, thus also inducing access to credit and investment, domestic and foreign.

---

[33] R Dworkin, *Sovereign Virtue: The Theory and Practice of Equality* (Harvard University Press 2000) 11. See also E Warren, 'Bankruptcy Policy' (1987) 54 U Chi L Rev 775, 778; V Finch, *Corporate Insolvency Law* (CUP 2002) 32–33; RJ Mokal, 'On Fairness and Efficiency' [2003] MLR 452, 459.

[34] Westbrook, 'A Global Solution to Multinational Default' (n 7) 2283; Anderson, 'The Cross-border Insolvency Paradigm' (n 11) 681; U Drobnig, 'Secured Credit in Cross-Border Insolvency Proceedings' (1998) 33 Tex Intl L J 27, 66. See also G McCormack, 'Universalism in Insolvency Proceedings and the Common Law' (2012) 32(2) OJLS 325, 328 (noting that: 'National chauvinism is especially unappealing if it overtly discriminates against foreign creditors').

[35] JL Westbrook, 'Choice of Avoidance Law in Global Insolvencies' (1991) 17 Brook J Intl L 499.

[36] Wessels, *International Insolvency Law* (n 9) 9; Bork, *Principles of Cross-Border Insolvency Law* (n 6) 28.

[37] Westbrook, 'A Global Solution to Multinational Default' (n 7) 2286, 2294 (also noting though that high levels of predictability are never likely to be achievable as general default produces considerable chaos). See also Bebchuk and Guzman, 'An Economic Analysis of Transnational Bankruptcies' (n 19) 775 (arguing, based on theoretical economic analysis, that territorialism can distort investment decisions, while universalism avoids such distortion and leads to a more efficient allocation of capital); Bork, *Principles of Cross-Border Insolvency Law* (n 6) 28.

[38] JAE Pottow, 'Greed and Pride in International Bankruptcy: The Problems of and Proposed Solutions to "Local Interests"' (2006) 104 Mich L Rev 1899, 1927–28.

[39] Bork, *Principles of Cross-Border Insolvency Law* (n 6) 16 (noting that: 'States accept constraints on their sovereignty insofar as they acknowledge the principles of unity and universalism of cross-border insolvency proceedings (i.e. that there will be only one set of proceedings with worldwide effect)'). The loss of control and of sovereignty may have important effect on countries' choices and may lead to the adoption of territorialism, as discussed in detail in Chapter 2, but it does not mean that territorialism is the better choice.

It is true that in the specific case, local constituencies may possibly profit from territorialism where there are sufficient local assets to grab to satisfy the local debts.[40] Yet,
in the absence of knowledge of what the asset/debt ratio will be in each case in the
jurisdictions involved, and importantly, the going-concern value and other potential advantages of reorganization or of global integrated sales, a universalist system
should be countries' preferred model because it can increase welfare for the benefit
of stakeholders as a whole.[41] Thus, as a theoretical model, universalism can increase
global welfare, which is also in line with country welfare, where the country's interest
is to maximize value for stakeholders within its borders and ensure their equitable
treatment and the inducement of investment in local businesses.[42]

It is the essence of universalism that it resolves the collective action problem
that creates a 'prisoners' dilemma'[43] and a race to collect, translating the insolvency
principle of collectivity to the global level.[44] Generally, a system based on a universalist model works where there is full coordination and asset grabbing is restricted,
namely where the common pool problem of insolvency is controlled on a global
scale and countries and their implementing institutions have regard to the effects
of their actions on proceedings and stakeholders in other countries.[45] Proponents

[40] This pure universalist model needs, however, to be translated to real-world circumstances. For
example, non-discrimination of creditors under the universalist model must take account of possible
locations of creditors in remote jurisdictions hence the need to ensure that equal treatment is real and
takes account of such circumstances and other vulnerabilities; the concentration of the process needs
to be based on a jurisdiction test that is generally ascertainable by third parties, etc. (see section 1.3.2).

[41] Anderson, 'The Cross-border Insolvency Paradigm' (n 11) 699 (noting with reference to
examples, and in response to territorialist assertions that territorialism is more consistent with creditors'
expectations, that parties dealing with multinationals also often extend credit based on an assumption
about worldwide assets rather than on the basis of local assets). See also regarding MFIs, JL Westbrook,
'SIFIs and States' (2014) 49(2) Tex Intl L J 329, 337–38 (noting how host countries suffered serious
losses and how their economies were damaged during the global financial crisis where home countries
failed to address bank failures collectively by taking a global approach).

[42] It has been argued that countries may prefer territorialist approaches as they would be able to
attract firms to their regime if they favour local creditors, where such preference presumably results
in reduced interest rates on loans (Bebchuk and Guzman, 'An Economic Analysis of Transnational
Bankruptcies' (n 19)). This argument is based on certain assumptions regarding the availability of
assets in the territorial state and the preferences of debtors to invest abroad. Debtors, however, may
prefer to avoid a territorial system that splits the business in the event of insolvency; creditors too, not
knowing in advance which assets will be available in each country at the time of insolvency, and what
will be the going concern value of the business, may prefer a universalist system that maximizes business
value. It has also been argued that less dominant countries are disadvantaged by universalism as they
are less likely to host multinational firms (Tung, 'Fear of Commitment in International Bankruptcy'
(n 18) 576 ff) and it is less likely that the professionals in the country will gain from localization of proceedings (LoPucki, 'Cooperation in International Bankruptcy' (n 2) 713). While it is true that 'interest
groups such as lawyers and other insolvency professionals might be engaging in rent-seeking behaviour'
(S Gopalan and M Guihot, 'Recognition and Enforcement in Cross-Border Insolvency Law: A Proposal
for Judicial Gap-Filling' (2015) 48 Vand J Transnat'l L 1225, 1274), what should matter is whether
debtors and stakeholders can take part in value-maximizing processes wherever these processes are
centralized, not that the professionals can benefit from local proceedings.

[43] Where parties might not act collectively even though cooperation is in their best interests (see in
the context of insolvency, eg TH Jackson and RE Scott, 'On the Nature of Bankruptcy: An Essay on
Bankruptcy Sharing and the Creditors' Bargain' (1989) 75(2) Vand L Rev 155).

[44] JL Westbrook, 'Theory and Pragmatism in Global Insolvencies: Choice of Law and Choice of
Forum' (1991) 65 Am Bankr L J 457, 465–66.

[45] Such other-regarding considerations may be perceived as requiring a sacrifice in the specific case,
namely a form of altruism (Westbrook, 'Theory and Pragmatism in Global Insolvencies' (n 44) 466;

of territorialism have argued that universalists have not provided proof of these proclaimed benefits of universalism.[46] Yet this argument is weak. It implies that an insolvency system that is primarily based on individual, separate (country-by-country) enforcement of debt might be superior to a system based on collectivity, equitable treatment of creditors, and advancement of reorganization of viable businesses. It ignores the fact that universalism is premised on such fundamental notions of insolvency that are shared among legal systems.[47]

1.2.3.2 Universalism responds to modern developments

The attractiveness of universalism is also attributed to its relevance to the modern global economy. The need to respond to the fact of global default is not new, and universalism has old roots.[48] Certainly, with increased economic integration and globalization, and the movement from sovereign states to cross-national markets,[49] universalism has become the more relevant theoretical model for cross-border insolvency, compared with territorialism.[50] Even essentially domestic enterprises, incorporated and doing business in a single country, often now have creditors in other jurisdictions or assets in more than one country. Entities may also attempt to move their operations or certain assets from one jurisdiction to another in the course of business or prior to insolvency.[51]

1.2.3.2.1 Multinational enterprise groups
The rise of multinational enterprise groups since the end of the nineteenth century has increased the impact of global businesses, including their insolvency.[52] Even

see also Chapter 5, section 5.2.4). However, under a universalist model, the rights of stakeholders are considered regarding the global enterprise. Stakeholders can enjoy the benefits ensuing from the preservation of business value. Therefore, they cannot at the same time enjoy rights pursued separately on a territorial basis.

[46] Chung, 'The New Chapter 15 of the Bankruptcy Code' (n 18) 110 ff.

[47] See key insolvency objectives proclaimed in the UNCITRAL Legislative Guide on insolvency law (Legislative Guide), pt one, paras 4–14, recs 1–5. See also I Mevorach, *Insolvency within Multinational Enterprise Groups* (OUP 2009) 119 ff.

[48] It is associated with long-standing concepts such as 'international comity' (section 1.4.3).

[49] R Michaels, 'Private and Public International Law: German View on Global Issues', (2008) J Priv Intl L 121, 130.

[50] See also Lord Neuberger, 'The International Dimension of Insolvency' [2010] Insolv Int 42 (noting that: 'One thing which the credit-crunch and its after effects have highlighted is that, as we all really knew, the world we live in today is truly borderless, at least where business is concerned ... In such a world it seems to me, and I am not alone in this, that we must do everything we properly can to ensure that such cross-border insolvencies are capable of being administered seamlessly across those very borders').

[51] Such international mobility has become more plausible and more frequent with the development of integrated markets. See eg in Europe, the Treaty on the Functioning of the European Union arts 49 and 54, providing freedom of movement and establishment, including to companies and firms. See also Case C-212/97 *Centros Ltd v Erhvervs- og Selskabsstyrelsen* [1999] ECR I-1459.

[52] Multinational enterprises in their modern sense began to appear in the nineteenth century with the growth of world trade and industrial production and the simultaneously growing importance of technological know-how. The pressure to find affiliates increased, due to the need to open up new, attractive markets and to secure access to raw materials. Independent agents still played a major role in this regard but, as they were often unreliable, they were replaced more and more by directly controlled affiliates (M Wilkins, *The Emergence of Multinational Enterprises: American Business Abroad*

though enterprise groups are legally split into separate entities, they are often economically, administratively, or financially integrated. Thus, the group entities' activities may be operated via product lines rather than divided by entity, or even where
activities are divided by entity, they may be economically interlinked. Management
may be intertwined through cross directorships, or financial interdependence may
result from significant cross guarantees. Therefore, such enterprises require a global
approach.[53] Only where the insolvency process imitates the commercial reality of integration and allows the group or its relevant parts to be kept together is it possible to
restructure the group as a whole or apply other group-wide solutions that can maximize value. In the absence of a global approach, there is a risk of fragmentation of
the business, including premature liquidation of entities to satisfy creditors' claims
in jurisdictions where the entities operate or have assets.[54]

1.2.3.2.2 Small- and medium-sized enterprises with international elements
Multinational businesses, particularly groups, may be large and comprise hundreds
of entities.[55] However, smaller businesses, too, may have international elements,
assets, creditors, or even a branch abroad, and they may also operate through group
structures with affiliates in several countries. In the absence of an effective system that
takes account of the cross-border aspects of the business, such entities and groups
may suffer even more (compared to larger enterprises) because they might not have
the financial means to resolve the issues through ad hoc cooperative solutions.[56]

1.2.3.2.3 Multinational financial institutions
Financial institutions, too, often span borders, particularly, but not only, the systemically important financial institutions (SIFIs),[57] which tend to be complex and
have a significant degree of cross-border presence.[58] The cross-border insolvency of
MFIs in distress raises specific issues and concerns, and may be different in fundamental ways from the insolvency of commercial entities.[59] Failures of MFIs often

---

from the Colonial Era to 1914 (Harvard University Press 1970) Part Two; V Bornschier and H Stamm,
'Transnational Corporations' in S Wheeler (ed), *The Law of the Business Enterprise* (OUP 1994) 340. See
also Mevorach, *Insolvency within Multinational Enterprise Groups* (n 47) 10–13.

[53] See Mevorach, *Insolvency within Multinational Enterprise Groups* (n 47) 153 ff; J Sarra, 'Oversight
and Financing of Cross-Border Business Enterprise Group Insolvency Proceedings' (2009) 44 Tex Intl
L J 547, 550–51.

[54] Mevorach, *Insolvency within Multinational Enterprise Groups* (n 47) 153 ff.

[55] The notable example of a collapse of such a group is the insolvency of Lehman Brothers in 2008.

[56] Bebchuk and Guzman, 'An Economic Analysis of Transnational Bankruptcies' (n 19) 776, referring to various examples of such cases.

[57] 'A financial institution or group that, because of its size, complexity and systemic interconnect-
edness, would, in the view of the relevant authorities, cause significant disruption to the domestic
or broader financial system and economic activity if it were to fail in a disorderly manner' (Financial
Stability Board, 'Key Attributes of Effective Resolution Regimes for Financial Institutions, Second
Thematic Review on Resolution Regimes Peer Review Report' (18 March 2016) 3 <http://www.fsb.org/
2016/03/second-thematic-review-on-resolution-regimes/>).

[58] Lastra, 'International Law Principles Applicable to Cross-Border Bank Insolvency'(n 10) 162.

[59] Banks and financial institutions may be subject to a special resolution regime, separate and distinct
from the general insolvency regime. Alternatively, the insolvency law may apply to banks as *lex generalis*,
while special rules (*lex specialis*) or exemptions from the general regime may apply where called for by

have significant implications for the entire market, and, therefore, their resolution requires special consideration of the public interest. Hence, financial institutions, particularly banks, are usually heavily regulated.[60]

Insolvency regimes for financial institutions may focus on the provision of speedy measures for quick resolution to ensure stability and contain losses.[61] Other distinct features of bank resolution may include the involvement of bank supervisors and the deposit protection agencies.[62] However, there are also important common grounds with the general problems which cross-border insolvencies bring about. The cross-border insolvency of MFIs, as well, is prone to conflicts where multiple national authorities or courts are involved, and assets, liabilities, collateral, financial contracts, or entities are subject to different governing laws. Without a global perspective and a timely, close coordination of the process across the countries where the institution operates, asset maximization, avoidance of loss to stakeholders, and effective resolution of the ailing institution may be significantly undermined.[63] In both restructurings and liquidations, a global approach could be crucial to containing a systemic impact of a bank failure and realizing coordination benefits.[64] A holistic, consolidated view of the international institution can be paramount in the banking sphere, where ring-fencing creates significant uncertainties that can accelerate liquidity problems.[65]

1.2.3.3 Universalism promotes rescues

The growing emphasis on rescuing viable businesses and *avoiding* insolvency, including the proliferation of preventive measures and pre-insolvency restructuring processes,[66] further highlights the supremacy of universalism as a model for cross-border insolvency. A rescue requires having regard for the business as a whole, or for coherent segments of it, or for certain classes of its debts, which may be located

---

the specifics of bank insolvency (EHG Hüpkes, 'Insolvency: Why a Special Regime for Banks?' (2005) 3 Current Dev in Monetary and Fin L, International Monetary Fund 1, 12).

[60] FM Song and L Li, 'Bank Governance: Concepts and Measurements' in JR Barth et al (eds), *Research Handbook on International Banking and Governance* (Edward Elgar Publishing 2012) 17, 22.

[61] Speed is crucial in many insolvency scenarios where it is important to avoid dissipation of asset value or attempt to turn around a business but, in a bank context, a failure to resolve the institution's distress speedily may also impose risks to financial stability.

[62] Hüpkes, 'Insolvency: Why a Special Regime for Banks?' (n 59) 13.

[63] Westbrook, 'SIFIs and States' (n 41) 345 (noting that: 'It seems almost unnecessary to argue that resolution of SIFIs will require a high level of coordination among national regulators and international institutions given that virtually all experts around the world take this view' (footnote omitted)).

[64] International Monetary Fund, 'Resolution of Cross-Border Banks—A Proposed Framework for Enhanced Coordination' (June 11, 2010) 1 <https://www.imf.org/external/np/pp/eng/2010/061110.pdf>. The report mentions the cases of Fortis and Lehman Brothers that demonstrated how the existing territorial approach had failed to realize coordination benefits.

[65] JL Bromley and T Phillips, 'International Lessons from Lehman's Failure: A Cross-Border No Man's Land' in RM Lastra (ed), *Cross-Border Bank Insolvency* (OUP 2011) 443; See also Lastra, 'International Law Principles Applicable to Cross-Border Bank Insolvency' (n 10) 162 (noting that: 'We need to move from consolidated supervision to consolidated resolution').

[66] See in particular in Europe, the proposal of a Directive on preventive restructuring frameworks (Chapter 5, n 149, and accompanying text).

or relate to creditors situated in more than one country. Handling indebtedness or the deterioration in business operations often needs to be done speedily because time is of the essence in rescue processes. A prolongation of the process is likely to deteriorate the financial position of the debtor to a point where a rescue is no longer a feasible solution. The business may need to be under common control on a global basis to be able to operate as a going concern for the needed period and to coordinate the reorganization plan for the business. The stakeholders negotiating a reorganization plan will also require the assurance that the plan will thereafter bind the collective body of creditors, wherever located.[67] The business may also need a 'breathing space' to be able to reorganize or to be sold as an operating entity. Thus, a moratorium on individual collection, as well as measures to control the termination of relevant contracts, may be needed, but may work effectively in support of a rescue only if applied simultaneously across the relevant countries where the business, assets, or creditors are located. Pre-insolvency mechanisms that are contractual or semi contractual[68] would also take place more effectively and fairly under the umbrella of a universalist system that imposes a global approach.[69] Under such a system, for example, pre-insolvency transactions and financing arrangements, including cross-border ones, could be protected if agreed in good faith as part of the negotiations, or later avoided when detrimental. In other circumstances, it would be possible to address holdouts in the negotiations, including by foreign creditors, for example through voting mechanisms in restructuring processes that are applied on a worldwide basis.

1.3 Modified Universalism: Norms for Real-World Cross-Border Insolvencies

From pure universalism developed what is called modified universalism.[70] This section describes the evolution of this approach. It also describes the emerging norms of modified universalism and highlights their normative strength. Modified universalism is normatively desired as it is in line with the universalist model and the unity/universality principles, but, at the same time, it avoids a one-size-fits-all solution

---

[67] Westbrook, 'A Global Solution to Multinational Default' (n 7) 2285.

[68] eg workouts, which may include the agreement among all creditors on a 'stand-still' whereby creditors agree not to pursue their claims individually (INSOL International, Statement of Principles for a Global Approach to Multi-Creditor Workouts II (2nd edn, INSOL International 2017).

[69] See also Anderson, 'The Cross-border Insolvency Paradigm' (n 11) 726 (noting that 'decisions made by actors in private agreements will reflect the options available in, and the likely results of, formal proceedings').

[70] The label 'modified universalism' was introduced by Professor Westbrook (Westbrook, 'Choice of Avoidance Law in Global Insolvencies' (n 35) 517). In the MFIs' context, the term 'middle ground' approach is often used, which is 'between full universality which would require a binding international treaty and de-globalization of financial institutions' (Lastra, 'International Law Principles Applicable to Cross-Border Bank Insolvency' (n 10) 165; see also I Mevorach, 'Beyond the Search for Certainty: Addressing the Cross-Border Resolution Gap' (2015) 10(1) Brook J Corp Fin & Com L 183, 209).

and, thus, it fits real-world circumstances. As such, modified universalism provides a realistic and indeed optimal approach for cross-border insolvency, not merely for the interim but for the long term as well.

1.3.1 Evolution of modified universalism

Modified universalism has been contemplated as an interim solution pending movement to true universalism. As it has been acknowledged that pure universalism may not be achievable in the foreseeable future, modified universalism has emerged as a solution as close as possible to universalism. It has been explained that, 'The most difficult problem is fashioning an interim solution pending movement to true universalism'.[71] Notwithstanding the development of modified universalism, pure universalism continues to be viewed as an ideal[72] that should not be abandoned.[73]

In truth, however, what universalism in its pure form has provided is a theoretical model. That model neatly transforms a collective local insolvency case into a global one. Yet, this transformation cannot match real-world circumstances without modifications.[74] In the real world, the global economy operates within nation states whose laws, cultures, institutional frameworks, and institutional capacities are different.[75] The world cannot be equated to a federal nation with a federal government controlling the states.[76] Legal systems may at times converge, and at other times may develop new processes that have not yet spread into other jurisdictions.[77] The ability

---

[71] Westbrook, 'A Global Solution to Multinational Default' (n 7) 2277.

[72] See eg Fletcher, *Insolvency in Private International Law* (n 3) 12 ('While it may be conceded that this appears to represent the ultimate ideal towards which we should be progressing, present reality suggests that its implementation would give rise to major difficulties, and real injustice').

[73] Bork, *Principles of Cross-Border Insolvency Law* (n 6) 28 (noting that: 'For the time being, exceptions to the principle of universalism ... must be tolerated, yet there is no need to lose sight of the final goals of global implementation of this principle with as few exceptions as possible'); JAE Pottow, 'Beyond Carve-Outs and Toward Reliance: A Normative Framework for Cross-Border Insolvency Choice of Law' (2014) 9(1) Brook J Corp Fin & Com 197, 198 (suggesting that modified universalism is at present an independent normative approach, though considered an incremental step towards pure universalism); LoPucki, 'The Case for Cooperative Territoriality' (n 18) 2217 (LoPucki, a leading proponent of (cooperative) territorialism for cross-border insolvency, notes that he agrees with Professor Westbrook, the key proponent of universalism, that eventually the world will be ripe for an ideal universalism: 'That may take decades, however, or even centuries. The issue is what to do while we are waiting for the "new world" society—essentially, a world government—to arrive ... Responding to the universalist ideal, some bankruptcy judges already surrender assets to "home country" courts ... '). cf Anderson, 'The Cross-border Insolvency Paradigm' (n 11) 686; EJ Janger, 'Universal Proceduralism' (2007) 32 Brook J Intl L 819; G McCormack, 'Universalism in Insolvency Proceedings' (n 34) 325; A Walters, 'Modified Universalisms & The Role of Local Legal Culture in the Making of Cross-Border Insolvency Law' Am Bankr L J (*forthcoming*) available at SSRN: <https://papers.ssrn.com/sol3/papers.cfm?abstract_id=3084117>.

[74] Kipnis, 'Beyond UNCITRAL: Alternatives to Universality' (n 22) 173 (noting regarding pure universalism that: 'This idyllic proposal is recognized, even by its proponents, as unworkable in the current world circumstances ... ').

[75] See Chapter 5, sections 5.3.1 and 5.3.2.

[76] Janger, 'Universal Proceduralism' (n 73) 834.

[77] Fletcher, *Insolvency in Private International Law* (n 3) 1 (noting in 2005 that the convergence of insolvency systems is not within reach as 'the dissimilarities are so numerous, and so substantial, as to oblige the realist to accept that the world essentially consists of separate, self-contained systems').

to predict the level of convergence at a given point in time is limited, but in any event, an expectation of full harmonization seems unrealistic.[78] Cross-border insolvencies can also benefit from the variations in legal systems where these can generate constructive competition.[79] At the same time, that variety requires safety valves in a universalist system to avoid submission to laws or systems that deviate from fundamental standards of procedural and substantive justice.

Regions also differ in such areas as degree of homogeneity or market integration.[80] Different regions engage in varying levels of unity or pooled sovereignty. Globalization is not a given state of affairs, the continuation of which is always predictable.[81] Even if globalization in the long run continues, the global market remains widespread and distanced. Furthermore, businesses and financial institutions in the global economy, within regions and internationally, use different structures and often operate as enterprise groups with different levels of integration and central control, meaning that different levels of centralization, of forum and of law, or co-operation may be warranted in the event of general default.[82] Modified universalism is evolving as a set of norms that derive from the universalist paradigm but are more nuanced and flexible and thus fit different levels of convergence, globalization, homogeneity, and integration.[83] As such, modified universalism enables optimal solutions and not just transitory mechanisms.

1.3.2 Emerging norms of modified universalism

Modified universalism at its core uses private international law rules and shapes them to fit the goals of global insolvency in line with the universalist theory, to provide a global collective process that is fair and efficient.[84] Typical rules of private

---

[78] The prospects and problems of harmonization are discussed in detail in Chapter 5, section 5.3.2.
[79] ibid.   [80] ibid.
[81] See also Walters, 'Modified Universalisms' (n 73) (noting that 'as deglobalization takes hold in the post-2008 world, notably in the West, global markets and free trade are increasingly under attack').
[82] It has been noted in regard to cross-border insolvency of banks that: 'To some extent, the discussion about territoriality and universality is somewhat theoretical, since—as the Basel March 2010 report states in paragraph 55—both principles are "entity-centric and do not address the many complexities that arise in the resolution of cross-border financial groups consisting of multiple interconnected legal entities in many jurisdictions"' (Lastra, 'International Law Principles Applicable to Cross-Border Bank Insolvency' (n 10) 165).
[83] There is often confusion between pure and modified universalism, including in terms of their legal status (see Bebchuk and Guzman, 'An Economic Analysis of Transnational Bankruptcies' (n 19) 778 (noting that: 'Both terms [universalism and territorialism] are sometimes used to refer to arrangements that lie between these two poles'). See also Bork, *Principles of Cross-Border Insolvency Law* (n 6) 42, 44, 163–64 (referring variably to aspects of universalism as 'principles', 'manifestations', or 'features'). Modified universalism is, however, fundamentally different from pure universalism. The latter is a theoretical model based on the fundamental building block principles of unity and universality, while the former is emerging as a set of rules that, when fully endorsed, can be binding and operational (cf the discussion of principles of cross-border insolvency in Bork, *Principles of Cross-Border Insolvency Law* (n 6) 12 ff). See also Chapter 3 for a discussion of the possible transformation of modified universalism into international binding norms.
[84] See on the objectives of modified universalism, Westbrook, 'A Global Solution to Multinational Default' (n 7) 2299 ff; Anderson, 'The Cross-border Insolvency Paradigm' (n 11) 679; Pottow, 'Beyond Carve-Outs and Toward Reliance' (n 73) 197; G Moss, '"Modified Universalism" and the Quest for the

international law, such as the presence of a defendant or submission to a forum that provides a basis for jurisdiction, are adjusted by modified universalism to provide an optimal system for transnational insolvency. Private international law concepts are also complemented by additional norms concerning assistance, support, duties, and safeguards to provide a workable scheme for the administration of cross-border insolvencies in a manner as centrally controlled as is optimal in the circumstances. Modified universalism necessitates a certain degree of loss of control and sovereignty by countries to achieve a global perspective over multinational default, in line with the universalist theory. Yet, it accommodates a toolkit of solutions, which takes into account world realities, and it also guarantees a certain retention of control by the other jurisdictions involved in the process.[85] The norms seek collectivity and equitable treatment in the real global market and aim to promote optimal results such that value is maximized for the stakeholders as a whole. The norms are also flexible in accommodating changing conditions, as well as differences between regions, where they may be applied with some modifications within different transnational settings. They are discussed below, starting with the outbound aspects, which focus on the role and scope of the main insolvency process and the law that applies, followed by inbound mechanisms, which recognize and support this process, and finally the safeguards contemplated by modified universalism.

1.3.2.1 *Jurisdiction: efficient levels of centralization*

Although compliance with modified universalism may be enhanced through some degree of delegation of certain functions to international bodies,[86] modified universalism does not require that a supranational tribunal be established. Rather it relies primarily on the existing domestic system (the courts or other administrative or resolution bodies) within which the proceedings will take place. As such, modified universalism is in line with the reality wherein insolvencies, contrary to the usual resolution of disputes, may, in many instances, require long-term supervision of a business, complex implementation of resolution or insolvency solutions, and overseeing a process that affects multiple groups of stakeholders. Such supervision often would most efficiently take place within the territory where the business has been active or has been controlled. Cross-border insolvency cases are also numerous and of different sizes and objectives, and the cross-border insolvency element may or may not be critical to the case; thus, directing all such cases to international tribunals or to an international system of courts is impractical.[87]

Golden Thread' (2008) 21 (10) Insolv Int 145. In the context of MFIs, see eg Westbrook, 'SIFIs and States' (n 41) 329; I Mevorach, 'Beyond the Search for Certainty' (n 70) 183.

[85] See also A Godwin, T Howse, and I Ramsay, 'The Inherent Power of Common Law Courts to Provide Assistance in Cross-Border Insolvencies: From Comity to Complexity' (2017) 26 Intl Insolv Rev 5, 14 ('The doctrine of "universalism"—or "modified universalism" as it has come to be regarded in its more limited form—is the principle that insolvency proceedings should be dealt with under a single, unified system, with appropriate safeguards to avoid manifestly unfair outcomes').

[86] See Chapter 5, section 5.3.3.

[87] This may be the case even in regions such as the European Union eg where the institutional framework provides for a semi-federal system with international institutions. Even then, the operation or

Modified universalism prescribes the centralization of the process as the presumptive solution, namely a 'single forum' approach, where one of the countries where the entity has presence has international jurisdiction and presides over the entire estate worldwide, allowing the design of a global solution and avoiding costs of multiple proceedings.[88] That country and its implementing institutions would have international jurisdiction reaching beyond its borders. This is, therefore, an outbound aspect of modified universalism,[89] which prescribes the global authority of the main forum. The relevant authorities in that country should be empowered to make decisions on the implementation of appropriate tools and procedures regarding the entity as a whole, fundamentally deciding whether the entity or parts thereof should be reorganized or liquidated.[90] This norm also provides that all stakeholders should have access to and participate in the process, and that this process covers the entire pool of claims and assets, wherever located, for the purpose of worldwide distribution or other global insolvency solutions.[91]

Often centralization would be optimal because it can avoid duplication and costs of coordinating solutions between multiple processes, and because it can minimize conflicts and inconsistencies.[92] Even for enterprise groups with distinct entities, centralization of the proceedings regarding the group as a whole is often the optimal solution.[93] Frequently groups, especially the relatively smaller ones, operate a single business in much the same way as a company with branches, and large enterprises as well are often centrally controlled from the group's head office. Therefore, as a matter of economic realities, all entities, or a certain part of the group, are connected to a central jurisdiction.[94] In such cases, both in terms of transparency of the jurisdiction and administration of the process, central control of the proceedings could lead

---

implementation of insolvency proceedings, and the enforcement of orders and judgments rely on the domestic system. See the role of the Court of Justice of the European Union (CJEU), which ensures that EU law is interpreted and applied consistently by member states, and that member states and EU institutions abide by EU law. See also the Single Resolution Mechanism (SRM), the central institution for managing bank failures in Europe. The SRM leaves 'an important role to the national resolution authorities. This is due to the nature of the EU in which different national legal systems and traditions co-exist' <http://europa.eu/rapid/press-release_MEMO-14-295_en.htm>.

[88] Anderson, 'The Cross-border Insolvency Paradigm' (n 11) 690, 772; R Goode, *Principles of Corporate Insolvency Law* (Sweet and Maxwell 2011) 786; Bork, *Principles of Cross-Border Insolvency Law* (n 6) 31.

[89] Or 'outgoing universalism' (Bork, *Principles of Cross-Border Insolvency Law* (n 6) 26).

[90] Goode, *Principles of Corporate Insolvency Law* (n 88) 786 (noting that a feature of modified universalism is the overall control of the insolvency process by the insolvency representative in the main liquidation or reorganization proceedings).

[91] Bork, *Principles of Cross-Border Insolvency Law* (n 6) 31–32 (noting that under universalism the main proceedings have worldwide effect and the insolvency practitioner in the main proceedings must have control over all creditor–debtor relationship and all assets).

[92] cf the experience of administering the *Nortel* cross-border insolvency in parallel in Canada and the United States. The court eventually managed to reach a global solution for the enterprise group, yet the process was not always smooth and that result was achieved after years of expensive litigation (JAE Pottow, 'Two Cheers for Universalism: Nortel's Nifty Novelty' in JP Sarra and Justice B Romaine (eds), *Annual Review of Insolvency Law* (Carswell 2015) 351 ff; see also on the complexities at the appeal stage DJ Miller and M Shakra, 'Nortel: The Long and Winding Road' in JP Sarra and Justice B Romaine (eds), *Annual Review of Insolvency Law* (Carswell 2015) 306 ff).

[93] Mevorach, *Insolvency within Multinational Enterprise Groups* (n 47) 175 ff.

[94] eg in *Nortel* nineteen subsidiaries that operated in Europe, the Middle East, and Africa (EMEA) were headed by the UK holding company and in the event of insolvency were centralized in that

to optimal group-wide solutions, including application of preventive mechanisms such as schemes of arrangement or homologations.[95]

Such concentration does not undermine the legal separateness between the entities in group structures if, in considering global solutions, the fact that each entity is distinct is properly taken into account. Only in limited circumstances, where the enterprise group was heavily integrated, more complex solutions, such as a pooling of assets and a pro rata distribution may be necessary.[96] More often, though, it will suffice to utilize some form of procedural consolidation to coordinate a group solution,[97] without interfering with assets/liabilities segregation. Additionally, when considering solutions for a group, it is possible that entities that could have done better in a separate process or that incur additional costs if they cooperate, for example, because they possess most of the information that other companies require, be compensated within the coordinated solution, to respect entity separateness.[98]

Even in cases of globally decentralized commercial or financial groups,[99] the centralization of the insolvency process or the minimization of proceedings[100] can be fair and efficient.[101] The concentration of proceedings and of decision-making can reduce the number of proceedings and allow the formulation of solutions, such as a package sale or group restructuring, for the benefit of the enterprise's stakeholders,[102]

---

jurisdiction, where decisions concerning the process were taken centrally (see *Re Nortel Networks UK Ltd & others* [2015] EWHC 2506 (Ch)).

[95] See eg *In re AXA Insurance UK Plc* et al, Nos 07-B-12110–07-B-12113 (Bankr SDNY 2007) where a US court granted recognition to UK main proceedings of three of the four group entities and to French non-main proceedings of the French subsidiary. Subsequently, the court enforced a UK scheme of arrangement regarding all entities; *In re Abengoa* et al *SA*, Nos 16-10754 (Bankr Del 2016), where a US court recognized the foreign proceedings concerning the parent company and several subsidiaries that were subject to insolvency homologation proceedings in Spain (see also F Garcimartin, 'Universal Effects of European Pre-Insolvency Proceedings: a Case Study' in R Parry and P Omar (eds), *Re-imagining Rescue* (INSOL Europe Technical Series 2016) 77 ff).

[96] See the circumstances in *Nortel* described in Miller and Shakra, 'Nortel: The Long and Winding Road' (n 92) 281). See also the pooling of assets and debts in the insolvency of the BCCI Banking Group (in *re Bank of Credit & Commerce International SA* (No.10) (1997) 2 WLR 172 (Ch 1996) where the court referred to the UK court hearing of the winding-up petition of 2 December 1991 and noted 'the truly gargantuan task of preserving and realising assets of BCCI worldwide'.

[97] A tool available in various jurisdictions in legislation or as a matter of practice, as described in the Legislative Guide, pt three, 27 ff.

[98] Mevorach, *Insolvency within Multinational Enterprise Groups* (n 47) 187–89, 240–44; Goode, *Principles of Corporate Insolvency Law* (n 88) 788–90.

[99] Paradigmatic examples include the insolvencies of Lehman Brothers and Nortel. Within such large groups, certain parts may be centrally controlled while the group as a whole is more spread out and decentralized.

[100] See eg the circumstances of the BCCI banking groups (*Re Bank of Credit & Commerce International SA* (No 10) (1997) 2 WLR 172 (Ch 1996)). The group had operations (through subsidiaries and branches) in many countries. Liquidators were appointed in more than fifty different jurisdictions, yet at least it was possible to globally coordinate the process through three main proceedings in London, Luxemburg, and the Cayman Islands from where BCCI was ultimately regulated.

[101] Mevorach, *Insolvency within Multinational Enterprise Groups* (n 47) 153 ff. Regarding MFIs, see Westbrook, 'SIFIs and States' (n 41) 332, 343, 345 ff (stressing the need for agreement on the single jurisdiction in cases of resolution of SIFIs that will take the role of the centre of a coordination effort).

[102] In some group circumstances, there might not even be a local capability to deal with local subsidiaries, which may have limited assets to cover the costs of a process if it is delinked from a global approach.

again without unduly undermining the corporate form. In cases of MFIs, depending on the institutions' structure, a resolution process may take place, for example, on a 'single point of entry' (SPOE) basis.[103] It may also be found, however, especially in a more decentralized enterprise or financial institution, when taking such a global perspective, that interests are not aligned across the entities or that interlinks between the entities are not significant, and thus it is most efficient to proceed separately.[104] Modified universalism's jurisdiction norm can adjust to this diversity of circumstances. It is wedded to a global approach, but recognizes that the ultimate solution may require some separation where certain entities may not take part in a uniform centralized solution.[105] The point is that the home or host jurisdiction makes the determination based on efficiency and commercial reality rather than based on sovereignty and vested rights.

Centralization is efficient only up to a point in an international (regional or global) setting, and even in single-entity cases. The size of the market that the universalist theoretical model covers has required modifications of the single-forum model. There are practical difficulties, including language barriers, in dealing with an insolvency case from a central forum, notwithstanding advances in technology. Differences between legal systems, specifically in the insolvency laws and other laws relevant to the insolvency process, may also be such that it is difficult to extend the effect of the home country's laws or it is more efficient to conduct local proceedings based on local laws. Thus, in certain circumstances, the general body of stakeholders may be better off where more than one proceeding is opened.[106] In other circumstances, additional proceedings would be efficient to aid the main

---

[103] A strategy that has been developed by the US Federal Deposit Insurance Corporation, under which the resolution takes place at the top tier parent company while the operating subsidiary remains open (Fed Deposit Ins Corp & the Bank of England, 'Resolving Globally Active, Systemically Important, Financial Institutions' (2012) <https://www.fdic.gov/about/srac/2012/gsfi.pdf>). This strategy might not work in all circumstances, and it also requires a parent–subsidiary structure where the parent is not a significantly important entity (J Crawford, ' "Single Point of Entry": The Promise and Limits of the Latest Cure for Bailouts' (2014) 109 Nw U L Rev Online 103, 107).

[104] International Monetary Fund, 'Cross-Border Bank Resolution: Recent Developments' (2 June 2014) 10, 22 <https://www.imf.org/external/np/pp/eng/2014/060214.pdf> (explaining how in certain circumstances of MFIs in resolution, a multiple point of entry (MPOE) or a hybrid approach, where certain operating affiliates 'are resolved separately in different jurisdictions by the respective resolution authorities' may be appropriate, and that: 'When the operations of a cross-border institution are of systemic importance in a host country, but immaterial to the G-SIFI as a whole, it may not be realistic to expect an alignment of interests between jurisdictions').

[105] Anderson, 'The Cross-border Insolvency Paradigm' (n 11) 772 (noting that while the presumption under modified universalism is centralization, modified universalism can also apply to more complex, centreless cases, where it may be possible to opt out from a unified approach).

[106] Fletcher, *Insolvency in Private International Law* (n 3) 16, 17 (explaining that 'if the logical conclusion, derived from an assessment of the pattern of dispersal of assets and claims and also of the complexity of the administrative process, is that the goals of convenience and efficiency will best be realized through plural administrations, then this should be preferred, subject to the proviso that the laws of the States concerned are furnished with provisions to enable proper coordination and communication ... '); Bork, *Principles of Cross-Border Insolvency Law* (n 6) 23 (giving the following example as a reason for opening more than one proceedings in international insolvency: 'another reason may be that the debtor's affairs in state B are too complex to simply include them in the proceedings opened in state A. Under such circumstances it may be reasonable—despite the additional costs—to permit the commencement of additional proceedings in state B alongside those opened in state A ... ').

proceedings, for example in the collection of assets.[107] Still, at least in single-entity cases, additional proceedings yield to the 'main' proceedings. Depending on the circumstances, such proceedings may be 'secondary' or just limited 'ancillary' proceedings (see section 1.3.2.3), but even secondary proceedings under modified universalism cannot be used to segregate assets in favour of local claims. Rather, under the norm, secondary proceedings would be subject to a global collective process of collection and distribution. In enterprise groups, the need for hierarchy, giving primacy to one forum, would depend on the group structure and the need for a closely coordinated solution. Insofar as the determination whether to open additional proceedings is made from a global perspective and is not aimed at asset ring-fencing, the opening of proceedings, or non-pursuit of a fully centralized or coordinated process, is not a concession to territorialism but rather an optimal modified universalist approach.[108]

Centralization under modified universalism is, in principle, in a jurisdiction representing the home country of the debtor.[109] Modified universalism is not wedded to a specific jurisdiction test, however, but rather to placing the case in a forum that allows a collective process for the benefit of the stakeholders as a whole. In principle, this approach requires a real connection to the forum because it would usually be more efficient, transparent, and predictable to globally administer the case where the enterprise actually carries on its business. In the commercial context, such a place is termed the debtor's 'centre of main interests' (COMI).[110] Modified universalism also requires that the rule which applies is uniform, so that it can lead parties to the single forum and avoid jurisdictional conflicts.[111]

Sticking to the single-entity home country rule may, however, impede jurisdictional centralization or coordination in certain enterprise structures.[112] In group

[107] JL Westbrook, 'Multinational Enterprises in General Default: Chapter 15, The ALI Principles, and The EU Insolvency Regulation' (2002) 76 Am Bankr L J 1, 10–12.
[108] The decision needs to be made by the relevant body presiding over the global (main) process or in the relevant circumstances through cooperation between the main and the additional proceedings, or if that is not appropriate in the circumstances, by the local courts taking a global perspective themselves, rather than by sections of the enterprise and courts in the territory focusing on local interests.
[109] Westbrook, 'Theory and Pragmatism in Global Insolvencies (n 44) 461. See also Fletcher, *Insolvency in Private International Law* (n 3) 12 (noting that 'it is an inherent part of the doctrine of Unity that the process is opened at the place with which the debtor's affairs, interests and general circumstances have their closest affinity, and that the administration is conducted in accordance with the insolvency law of that place ... ').
[110] JL Westbrook, 'Universalism and Choice of Law' (2005) 23 Penn St Intl L Rev 625, 634 ('The emerging international rule in multinational bankruptcy cases focuses on the center of the debtor's main interests'). COMI may require a certain factual assessment as the debtor may have close connections, eg through incorporation or the location of the head office, to different jurisdictions (see further on the definition and application of COMI under existing frameworks in Chapter 6, section 6.2.2.). In the case of banks, the identification of the 'home country' is often more straightforward as banks are usually required to have their head office and place of registration in the country that granted them the authorization to carry on the business.
[111] McCormack, 'Universalism in Insolvency Proceedings' (n 34) 328 (noting that: 'If one state purports to exercise universal bankruptcy jurisdiction on the basis of tenuous links with that state then other states with superficially stronger links to the insolvent debtor may cry foul').
[112] Advocates of territorialism have argued that universalism is not workable in enterprise group cases because a group does not have a home country (LoPucki, 'The Case for Cooperative Territoriality' (n 18) 2229 ff. Modified universalism, however, is flexible to accommodate group structures.

structures, a global solution contemplated on a group level from a single location might be difficult to plan unless the home country happens to be the same for all entities. Such concentration of entities' home countries (home country grouping, or 'group COMI') is indeed more likely when the notion of home country is based on the location of the place of central administration and control of the entities,[113] which may lead the process to where the enterprise's, often the parent company's, headquarters is located.[114]

The jurisdiction norm which is based on the location of the debtor home country requires further modifications, however. Even when using central administration as the key connecting factor, if the group was decentralized in the course of business, the reality may be that several jurisdictions have been the home countries of entities belonging to the same integrated group.[115] Modified universalism's emergent jurisdiction norm is still in rather early stages with regard to corporate, and even more so financial, groups.[116] Yet in principle, and subject to modifications of the choice of law norm, discussed in section 1.3.2.2, it can accommodate such structures by allowing coordination from a single jurisdiction. An example is one of the entities' home countries or the place of the institution's ultimate headquarters, even where that forum does not correspond with each entity's separate home country.[117] The norm is also flexible enough to accommodate the real-world fact of diversity as well as inequality between legal systems and, as a result, situations where a shift of the

---

[113] Compared with connecting factors such as place of incorporation, assets, or operations that would likely exist in different places (I Mevorach, 'The Home Country of a Multinational Enterprise Group Facing Insolvency' (2008) 57 ICLQ 427, 442. See also Sarra, 'Oversight and Financing of Cross-Border Business Enterprise Group Insolvency Proceedings' (n 53) 558–61).

[114] See eg the concentration of the *Nortel* proceedings in the United Kingdom (n 94), which was the forum of the holding company of nineteen Nortel subsidiaries that were incorporated and operated in different countries in the EMEA region.

[115] Mevorach, 'The Home Country of a Multinational Enterprise Group' (n 113) 446 ff.

[116] The academic thinking as well as the international efforts to design frameworks for cross-border insolvency have focused initially on the cross-border insolvency of single, commercial, entities. See also Chapter 6, sections 6.2.4 and 6.3.

[117] See eg Mevorach, 'The Home Country of a Multinational Enterprise Group' (n 113) 446 ff (proposing that proceedings concerning groups may be centralized in the headquarters from where the group was coordinated and that this forum can assume a role of a coordinating proceeding); Westbrook, 'Multinational Enterprises in General Default' (n 107) 38 (referring to a solution proposed in Principles developed by the American Law Institute (ALI) under which subsidiaries should be able to open proceedings at the jurisdiction of the parent company); UNCITRAL draft model provisions, which address the insolvency of multinational groups, provide for central coordination at the jurisdiction where a main proceeding is opened concerning one of the entities that is an integral part of the group and in which other members participate (see in detail Chapter 6, section 6.2.4). The Basel Committee envisions the possibility that MFI groups will be centralized at their headquarters for the purpose of resolution (Bank for International Settlements, Basel Committee on Banking Supervision, 'Report and Recommendations of the Cross-Border Bank Resolution Group' (2010) para 70 www.bis.org/publ/bcbs169.pdf); the Financial Stability Board (FSB) has defined 'home jurisdiction' as 'the jurisdiction where the operations of a financial group are supervised on a consolidated basis' (Financial Stability Board, Key Attributes of Effective Resolution Regimes for Financial Institutions, Second Thematic Review on Resolution Regimes Peer Review Report (18 March 2016) 3 <http://www.fsb.org/2016/03/second-thematic-review-on-resolution-regimes/>).

forum ('forum shopping') from the original COMI may benefit the general body of stakeholders.[118]

Thus, the concentration and coordination of the proceedings is to some extent fact-specific under modified universalism. This flexibility of the jurisdiction norm fits with the complexity of real-world business and financial institution structures and the differences between legal systems. Indeed, modified universalism has been strongly challenged for its indeterminacy concerning the jurisdiction test it employs and how it is applied in different structures, especially groups.[119] Yet this elasticity and practicality enshrined in modified universalism has also had its strong proponents.[120] Optimal approaches for multinational default inherently require non-neat, non-one-size-fits-all solutions because that is the reality of the global market and the businesses and institutions operating within it.

1.3.2.2 *Choice of law: the law of the main forum with limited exceptions*

Another outbound aspect of modified universalism, which complements the jurisdiction norm, is the norm concerning the choice of law, namely the law that should apply, in cross-border insolvency. Modified universalism, in line with the universalism theory, in principle relies on the *lex fori concursus* private international law rule, namely the application of the law of the insolvency forum to all insolvency-related matters.[121] This way, a single law applies and there is minimum fragmentation of the

---

[118] Particularly where the insolvency objective is a more limited restructuring—compared with a continued long-term running of the business which may be more efficiently conducted in the original forum—or where no party has attempted to open such proceedings in that forum. See also A Walters, 'United States' Bankruptcy Jurisdiction over Foreign Entities: Exorbitant or Congruent?' (2017) Journal of Corporate Law Studies 1, 26 ff (contrasting the case of *Avianca* (*In re Aerovias Nacionales de Colombia SA Avianca* (2003) 303 BR 1) where the US court opened Chapter 11 proceedings against a company whose economic centre was Columbia where no proceedings were opened in Columbia and where the Chapter 11 procedure provided the most effective tool in the circumstances, with the case of *Northshore Mainland* (*In re Northshore Mainland Services, Inc* (2015) 537 BR 192) where the US court dismissed the request to open proceedings against Bahamian companies in circumstances where the case mainly concerned real estate assets which implicated powerful Bahamian national interests). The problems and prospects of forum shopping as a tool for promoting compliance with a cross-border insolvency system are discussed further in Chapter 5, sections 5.3.1 and 5.3.2.

[119] LoPucki, 'The Case for Cooperative Territoriality' (n 18) 2226 ff.

[120] See commentary cited in nn 113, 117–18.

[121] JL Westbrook, 'International Arbitration and Multinational Insolvency' (2011) Penn St Intl L Rev 635, 649 (noting regarding modified universalism that: 'The logic of that approach . . . leads almost always to the conclusion that the law of the main insolvency proceeding should be chosen to govern the various legal issues that may arise concerning the debtor and its assets'); Goode, *Principles of Corporate Insolvency Law* (n 88) 786 (noting that one of the features of universalism is the application of the *lex concursus* of that state to govern the effects of the opening of those proceedings); LC Ho, *Cross-Border Insolvency: Principles and Practice* (Sweet & Maxwell, 2016) 270 (arguing that 'the choice of law rules should be generally in service of the theory of universalism: that all bankruptcy assets and claims should be administered in the debtor's "home country" under the laws of that country . . . '). See also Westbrook, 'Universalism and Choice of Law' (n 110) 634; JL Westbrook, 'Locating the Eye of the Financial Storm' (2007) 32 Brook J Intl L 1019, 1021–22; JL Westbrook, 'Breaking Away: Local Priorities and Global Assets' (2011) 46 Tex Intl L J 601; LM Clark and K Goldstein, 'Sacred Cows: How to Care for Secured Creditors' Rights in Cross-Border Bankruptcies' (2011) 46 Tex Intl L J 513; Bork, *Principles of Cross-Border Insolvency Law* (n 6) 31.

process. The collection of assets, distribution, and consideration of solutions for the multinational default are conducted and contemplated collectively under uniform laws for the benefit of the creditors as a whole.[122] This outcome is achieved without reliance on full convergence of the laws of different systems.[123]

Notwithstanding dispersal of creditors across nations, creditors' expectations are not undermined by this norm where the applicable law is of a forum representing the entity's home country, which is transparent and ascertainable by creditors.[124] In other words, the emerging choice of law norm is linked to the choice of forum norm, that in turn takes due account of creditors' expectations and more generally of the objectives of international insolvency. The choice of law norm is in a more developing stage compared to the jurisdiction (choice of forum) norm, especially where the United Nations Commission on International Trade Law (UNCITRAL) Model Law on Cross-Border Insolvency (the MLCBI[125]), the global cross-border insolvency instrument, does not explicitly address the choice of law problem.[126] It is in the essence of modified universalism, however, that it can accommodate special protections granted domestically to certain stakeholders,[127] including for reasons of social policies.[128] Thus, the *lex fori concursus* rule is not absolute under modified universalism. Modifications of the rule may vary between regions and globally, taking into account different levels of dissimilarities between insolvency laws in the relevant grouping of states.[129] Thus, the guiding rule is deference to the

[122] Westbrook, 'Choice of Avoidance Law in Global Insolvencies' (n 35); JL Westbrook, 'Avoidance of Pre-Bankruptcy Transactions in Multinational Bankruptcy Cases' (2007) 42 Tex Intl L J 899.

[123] Indeed, modified universalism has been formulated in response to a conviction that convergence is likely to be a slow process (Westbrook, 'A Global Solution to Multinational Default' (n 7) 2319). Some degree of targeted harmonization would, however, promote compliance with cross-border insolvency system based on modified universalism (see Chapter 5, section 5.3.2).

[124] Westbrook, 'Theory and Pragmatism in Global Insolvencies' (n 44) 478.

[125] United Nations Commission on International Trade Law, UNCITRAL Model Law on Cross-Border Insolvency (1997) with Guide to Enactment and Interpretation with Guide to Enactment and Interpretation (2013) <http://www.uncitral.org/uncitral/en/uncitral_texts/insolvency/1997Model.html>.

[126] Westbrook, 'Universalism and Choice of Law' (n 110) 634 ('The emerging international rule in multinational bankruptcy cases focuses on the center of the debtor's main interests. Up to now, that standard has been adopted primarily as a choice-of-forum rule rather than a choice-of-law rule, but it is necessary to use it for both purposes to achieve the goals of universalism'). See also Chapter 6, section 6.2.5.

[127] DT Trautman et al, 'Four Models or International Bankruptcy' (1993) 41 Am J Comp L 573, 579 (noting that: 'If cases should arise where the reasonable expectation of unsophisticated creditors . . . might suffer unfairly, there is no reason a special rule cannot be applied in such cases').

[128] Pottow, 'Beyond Carve-Outs and Toward Reliance' (n 73) 218. See also The American Law Institute and the International Insolvency Institute, 'Transnational Insolvency: Global Principles for Cooperation in International Insolvency Cases, Annex: Global Rules on Conflict-of-Laws Matters in International Insolvency Cases' (2012) (B Wessels and IF Fletcher, Joint Reporters) <https://www.iiiglobal.org/sites/default/files/alireportmarch_0.pdf>, r 19–21 ('Based on perceived impressions of the importance of certain social policies and on several high-profile court cases, the Reporters believe that a rule of global application should be proposed with regard to current contracts of employment in case of the insolvency of the employer').

[129] Territorialism proponents have claimed that the choice of law norm of modified universalism is indeterminate as it is tainted with exceptions (LoPucki, 'Cooperation in International Bankruptcy'

law of the main forum, unless international insolvency objectives require giving effect to local protections because of recognized public policies or the need to protect certain parties, including when they actually relied on the local law and can demonstrate that the application of the home country law would contradict their legitimate expectations.[130]

The choice of law norm of modified universalism must also accommodate the flexibility of the jurisdiction norm where the opening of local insolvency proceedings pursuant to domestic law, in addition to a main proceeding, is more efficient; where the main forum has shifted to benefit the stakeholders as a whole; and where in more decentralized group structures, a group coordinating process may take place in a forum other than that of a participating entity's home country.[131] In such cases, local laws other than the law of the main or coordinating forum should be taken into account to ensure efficiency of the process and the equitable treatment of stakeholders.[132] Still, a main proceeding or a coordinating proceeding even where they take place in parallel to additional local processes or require accommodating certain local rights, may take place according to the procedures and tools available in the main or coordinating forum, and a wholesale importation of the procedures of local laws may not be necessary.[133]

(n 2) 700). It is, however, in the nature of insolvency, which deals with different types of stakeholders, and of international insolvency, which governs processes that take place within a global market, that solutions must be nuanced as they aim to achieve fine balances (see also AL Gropper, 'The Curious Disappearance of Choice of Law as an Issue in Chapter 15 Cases' (2014) 9(1) Brook J Corp Fin & Com L 151).

[130] Pottow, 'Beyond Carve-Outs and Toward Reliance' (n 73) 205 ff. See also Clark and Goldstein, 'Sacred Cows' (n 121) 513. More controversial is the treatment of rights *in rem* (security interests), which may receive special and different protections in different legal systems. In principle, recognition of local protections of such rights should not undermine a global collective process and thus it follows that it should be possible for the main forum to impose a limited moratorium on the exercise of foreign rights *in rem* (Pottow, 'Beyond Carve-Outs and Toward Reliance' (n 73) 217–18). More generally, rights *in rem* may yield to the law of the forum unless this law's treatment of the security interest is inconsistent with recognized standards, namely, with the general safeguard of public policy. Treatment may not be identical, but if eg the law of the forum disregards the security interest, deference to this law may be denied (Clark and Goldstein, 'Sacred Cows' (n 121).

[131] See section 1.3.2.1.

[132] Such a solution has been applied under the EU insolvency regime to address the problem of the opening of disruptive secondary proceedings and has been termed 'synthetic secondary proceedings'; see eg *Re Collins & Aikman Europe SA* [2006] EWHC (Ch) 1343; *Re Nortel Networks SA & ORS* [2009] EWHC (Ch) 206 where local priorities, mainly concerning employees and other preferential creditors, were taken into account. This approach was adopted in the Recast EU Regulation of 2015 (Recast EIR) (see Chapter 6, section 6.2.2) and is also being utilized in the development of new mechanisms to facilitate the cross-border insolvency of multinational enterprise groups (Chapter 6, section 6.2.4).

[133] A commercial group may eg be resolved through a scheme of arrangement or some other restructuring process, where such a procedure is available in the presiding forum (see eg the Da Movo, IMO car wash and Wind Hellas enterprises that migrated to the United Kingdom in order to take advantage of its pre-pack strategy; for further detail see I Mevorach, 'Forum Shopping in Times of Crisis: A Directors Duties Perspective,' (2013) ECFR 523, 525). In a resolution process, the coordinating forum may use eg the SPOE strategy where such is available in the jurisdiction (n 103). See also I Mevorach, 'Cross-Border Insolvency of Enterprise Groups: The Choice of Law Challenge' (2014) 9(1) Brook J Corp Fin & Com L 105, 238 ff.

1.3.2.3 *Recognition, assistance, and cooperation: universal effect of a global approach*

Recognition, assistance, and cooperation are additional aspects of modified universalism that mirror and complement the jurisdiction and choice of law norms. Thus, to ensure that a central forum can address the cross-border case collectively, or to achieve a common resolution strategy in case of the multinational default of a MFI, modified universalism requires that these proceedings or the measures taken in such proceedings be recognized, supported, and given effect (enforced) by courts or authorities in other countries. This is an inbound aspect of modified universalism,[134] focusing on the role of the host countries where the debtor has some form of presence (eg assets, branches, or subsidiaries) or impact (eg impact on local stakeholders with whom the debtor had dealings) or where the debtor is engaged in local proceedings. It requires a certain surrender of sovereignty and control, and deference to a main forum.[135]

Recognition of proceedings or certain forms of measures may be specifically time sensitive. Generally, because an insolvency process starts when the debtor is suffering financial difficulties, it is important that it proceed speedily if value is to be preserved, and often it requires an immediate stop to individual collection or other quick measures.[136] Therefore, recognition and assistance under modified universalism are meant to be swift measures, as the case may require, which avoid delays and are not conditioned by the similarities of the laws of the host and home country or other forms of reciprocity.[137] Recognition and its effect in host jurisdictions may not even require a court decision as a matter of course.[138] Modified universalism is flexible and can accommodate different institutional settings (eg integrated regions

---

[134] Or 'incoming' universalism (Bork, *Principles of Cross-Border Insolvency Law* (n 6) 27).

[135] See eg Goode, *Principles of Corporate Insolvency Law* (n 88) 786 (noting recognition and the provision of assistance as elements of modified universalism); Bork, *Principles of Cross-Border Insolvency Law* (n 6) 32 (noting that recognition, enforcement, cooperation, and assistance are essential elements of universalism); Westbrook, 'SIFIs and States' (n 41) 329 (arguing that 'no resolution system for global institutions will be workable unless regulators are prepared to give deference and cooperation to one national regulator as the leader of the global effort'); EHG Hüpkes, 'Allocating Costs of Failure Resolution: Shaping Incentives and Reducing Moral Hazard' in RM Lastra (ed), *Cross-Border Bank Insolvency* (OUP 2011) 124 (noting that to make resolution possible in a cross-border context, close cooperation and coordination among national authorities is essential and that it is also required that the legal status of actions taken are recognized by foreign courts or authorities).

[136] In the context of cross-border insolvency of MFIs, for example, it is often required to impose a temporary stay on exercising early termination and cross-default rights in financial contracts that arise by reason of a firm's entry into resolution, to avoid close-out in volumes that would disrupt orderly resolution (Key Attributes, s 4).

[137] Many agree that identical laws should not be a precondition to recognition or assistance (Bork, Principles of Cross-Border Insolvency Law (n 6) 41). See also *In re Metcalfe & Mansfield Alt Inv* 421 B.R. 685, 697 (Bankr SDNY 2010) (where the court stated that 'relief granted in the foreign proceeding and the relief available in a US proceeding need not be identical. A US bankruptcy court is not required to make an independent determination about the propriety of individual acts of a foreign court. The key determination required by this Court is whether the procedures used in Canada meet our fundamental standards of fairness' (footnotes omitted)). cf *In re Qimonda* (2013) 737 F3d 14.

[138] Bork, *Principles of Cross-Border Insolvency Law* (n 6) 53 (arguing that requiring a court decision as a precondition for recognition is not efficient).

versus the global setting) and the level of coherency of the cross-border framework at different stages.[139] Yet in any event, under modified universalism, recognition and relief should be at least 'quasi automatic'—the foreign bodies seeking it should be able to easily access the host country process and, subject to clear criteria,[140] should be provided with the required support promptly.

The modified universalism norm of recognition, assistance, and enforcement is also meant to capture the various orders and judgments emanating from the proceedings; importantly, included are those judgments related to the estate, such as avoidance of pre-insolvency transactions or contributions from directors, as well as the decision to complete the process and discharge the debtor.[141] Assistance by local courts includes the recovery of assets and pursuit of claims by the insolvency representative[142] in the main proceedings, or recognition and effectuation of resolution tools employed by the presiding forum. Thus, local (host country) courts should in relevant circumstances act as ancillary courts to either an entity's home country's court or a court that coordinates a group process,[143] and give up control of domestic assets and interests for the benefit of a foreign insolvency.[144] They should also refrain from ascertaining jurisdiction, or be able to stay proceedings, when, in taking a global approach, it appears that full deference to a centralized process is more efficient. Typical private international law rules, such as submission to, or presence in a forum, may not apply, because what matters is that orders, judgements, or other actions derive from the collective insolvency process, and thus the corresponding local support would benefit the general body of stakeholders, in line with global insolvency goals.[145]

Assistance may also be granted to home proceedings by aiding the local stakeholders in host jurisdictions for whom travelling to the home country may be too burdensome. Generally, modified universalism is not indifferent to inherent

---

[139] eg where proceedings are opened by countries that are not party to a uniform framework, recognition of such proceedings may require a certain process in the host country.

[140] Thus, for example, if recognition is sought concerning a debtor whose home country is elsewhere, or if there has been fictitious or abusive forum selection, recognition may not be granted (see eg the decisions in *re Bear Stearns High-Grade Structured Credit Strategies Master Fund Ltd* 374 BR 122 (Bankr SDNY 2007) affirmed, 389 BR 325 (Bankr SDNY 2008); *in re Creative Finance Ltd* (In Liquidation) BL 8825 (Bankr SDNY Jan 13 2016)). See also Chapter 5, section 5.3.2.

[141] See eg regarding the recognition of foreign discharge, JL Westbrook, 'Chapter 15 and Discharge' (2005) 13 Am Bankr Inst L Rev 503; Fletcher, *Insolvency in Private International Law* (n 3) 209–10. In the MFIs' context, effect may need to be given, for example, to resolution orders such as the stay of exercising early termination rights in financial contracts or to bail-in powers or to transfers orders (a transfer of assets and liabilities from a failing to a healthy bank) issued by the home resolution authority (see the resolution powers delineated in the Key Attributes, s 3).

[142] 'Insolvency representative' mean the insolvency professional, also often called insolvency office holder, liquidator, administrator, or trustee, who is appointed (including on an interim basis) to administer the debtor proceedings, which may include seeking assistance abroad (see also Chapter 6, n 40).

[143] Mevorach, *Insolvency within Multinational Enterprise Groups* (n 47) 169 ff.

[144] Anderson, 'The Cross-border Insolvency Paradigm' (n 11) 690–91.

[145] See the approach of the UK court in *Cambridge Gas Transp Corp v Official Comm of Unsecured Creditors* [2006] UKPC 26, [2006] 3 WLR 689, contrasted with the approach in *Rubin and another v Eurofinance SA and others* and *New Cap Reinsurance Corporation (in Liquidation) and another v AE Grant and others* [2012] UKSC 46 (n 202).

disadvantages of foreign creditors or other stakeholders and is also adaptable to changing conditions, including possible advancement in communication technologies. Thus, local courts may assist the foreign court's attempt at a global approach by entertaining requests for relief by local stakeholders, making determinations regarding such requests through full cooperation with the main forum and subject to its process and law.[146]

Where local insolvency proceedings are required from an efficiency perspective, the local courts in host countries where the entity has branches will conduct what may be called 'non-main' or secondary proceedings.[147] These proceedings may also require recognition and assistance in other countries. Importantly, in these circumstances as well, under modified universalism, the additional process yields to the main proceedings and should cooperate with them fully in terms of, for example, the conduct of the proceedings, the use of assets, which, under modified universalism, should not be ring-fenced, and the sharing of information.

Modified universalism also accommodates the circumstance where it is more efficient to conduct parallel proceedings, again taking a global approach, rather than designate one forum as leader. Still, if an enterprise-wide solution is beneficial, it should be achieved through cooperation: for example, the initiation of cross-border insolvency agreements (protocols)[148] or joint hearings and communication.[149] Cooperation tools should also assist in coordinating a more centralized solution that still requires several processes to take place simultaneously. Or, in other circumstances, it should precede a centralized approach, where through negotiations and cooperation the needed level, and manner, of centralization is determined. Thus, cooperation should take place promptly and as early as required in the circumstances. Often the parties and even insolvency representatives are conflicted in a cross-border default scenario, and thus the role of courts and other authorities is paramount in pursing court-to-court active, often multilateral, cooperation and

---

[146] Such concerns regarding the costs to local employees of pursuing claims abroad were expressed eg in *Sanjel* (*In re Sanjel USA Inc* et al [July 28 2016] No 16-50778-CAG), where a US court modified a stay to allow local creditors to pursue their claims locally; however, in this case the court only aided the local creditors and not through cooperation with the foreign court and insolvency representative. cf *Nortel* (*In re Nortel Corp* WL 6053845 (Bankr D Del 2013)) where a Delaware court considered that relief should be sought from the main court exclusively.

[147] In the sense that an actual process may take place locally.

[148] PH Zumbro, 'Cross-Border Insolvencies and International Protocols—An Imperfect but Effective Tool' (2010) 11 Business Law International 157; JL Westbrook, 'International Judicial Negotiations' (2003) 38 Tex Intl L J 567, 571–73; JS Ziegel, 'Corporate Groups and Crossborder Insolvencies: A Canada–United States Perspective' (2002) 7 Fordham J Corp & Fin L 367, 369. See eg the use of protocols in *Federal Mogul* (*In re T&N Ltd and Others* [2004] EWHC 2361 (Ch)); *In re ICO Global Communications Servs Inc*, No 99-2933 (Bankr D Del 1999); *In re Global Crossing Ltd* No 02-40188 (REG) (Bankr SDNY 2003); *In re Maxwell Communications Corp*, [1993] 1 WLR 1402 (Ch); *In re Inverworld* 267 BR 732, 740 No 10 (Bankr WD Tex 2001); *In re Smouha* 136 BR 921 (Bankr SDNY 1992); *In re Loewen Group Intl Inc*, No 99-1244 (Bankr D Del 1999); *In re Enron*, No 01-16034 (Bankr SDNY Dec. 10, 2001); *In re Singer Company NV,* 262 BR 257 (Bankr SDNY 2001).

[149] See eg the group-wide solution contemplated in *Nortel* through cooperation between the Canadian and US courts and a joint trial (for a description see Miller and Shakra, 'Nortel: The Long and Winding Road' (n 92) 281).

communication.[150] Such cooperation may result, in appropriate circumstances, in deference to foreign courts, ensuring though that the foreign court that administers a centralized process adheres to global duties and responsibilities.[151]

1.3.2.4 *Duties and safeguards: global responsibility and residual territorial control*

Modified universalism as a norm based on the principles of unity and universality, but shaped to fit with real-world circumstances—relying on domestic systems' mechanisms—requires that stakeholders are not discriminated against in any of the jurisdictions involved in the process.[152] More so, in particular, a main forum presiding over a centralized or centrally coordinated process would need to take extra care of foreign stakeholders, considering their possible disadvantaged position.[153] That forum has a global responsibility and, thus, a duty to level the playing field between foreign and local stakeholders in terms of their ability to access and participate in the process, ensuring that due process and equitable treatment are real and taking into account the distance and language barriers.[154]

The courts, or other bodies, under modified universalism again mirror the different solutions envisaged by the jurisdiction and choice of law norms for different types of entities and enterprise structures. Thus, for example, where a multinational group process is placed in a single forum, that forum should be concerned with the position of the independent but implicated entities and their stakeholders.[155] For another example, if a multinational banking group is to be resolved through concentration at the group's head office, the coordinating jurisdiction should have specific responsibilities, including consideration of foreign depositors and, more generally, of the impact of solutions contemplated in the

---

[150] In cases of MFIs, especially SIFIs, regulatory or resolution authorities are often best placed to cooperate with foreign regulators at an early stage. See the critique of the US Financial Institutions Bankruptcy Act 2017 under which the bankruptcy system and courts may be used to resolve MFIs, in JN Gordon et al, 'Financial Scholars Oppose Eliminating 'Orderly Liquidation Authority' As Crisis-Avoidance Restructuring Backstop' (May 23, 2017 letter to Congress) 5 <https://www.law.columbia.edu/sites/default/files/microsites/law-economics-studies/scholars_letter_on_ola_-_final_for_congress.pdf>. The letter notes the important role of regulators observing their 'prior understandings with foreign regulators . . . ' (ibid 3) and noting that: 'These prior understandings also bring the benefits of international coordination, which will be needed for the many complex aspects of the failure of a massive global financial firm' (ibid 3). See also Chapter 5, section 5.3.1 for a discussion of the effect of institutional incapacity on compliance with the cross-border insolvency system.
[151] Westbrook, 'International Judicial Negotiations' (n 148) 567, 568, 579 ff.
[152] Goode, *Principles of Corporate Insolvency Law* (n 88) 787 (noting that: 'Hand in hand with the concepts of unity and universality goes the principle of non-discrimination against foreign creditors'). See also in the context of MFIs, Lastra, 'International Law Principles Applicable to Cross-Border Bank Insolvency' (n 10) 171.
[153] I Mevorach, 'Centralizing Insolvencies of Pan-European Corporate Groups: A Creditor's Dream or Nightmare?' [2006] JBL 468, 484–85.
[154] ibid, 484–85 (arguing that relevant bodies presiding over a centralized process should provide adequate notifications to foreign creditors and even consider their position when they cannot be present physically).
[155] Mevorach, *Insolvency within Multinational Enterprise Groups* (n 47) 259 ff.

home jurisdiction on host countries.[156] Host countries involved in a cross-border insolvency process, as well, need to consider the effect of solutions and decisions on countries and stakeholders outside their borders and adhere to commitments and agreements. Solutions involving cooperation and communication, including between courts, should be subject to proper safeguards as well, ensuring due process and considering any restrictions concerning confidentiality of information.[157]

Modified universalism also accepts both the role of sovereign states as ultimate custodians of the welfare of their inhabitants,[158] and the differences among legal systems and cultures.[159] Therefore, modified universalism also guarantees a certain level of sovereign control to any country implicated in the process. Thus, a country may refuse to defer to a foreign process or implement the decisions or actions taken in that forum, and it may instead take local actions, in circumstances where duties concerning standards of fairness, non-discrimination, and due process are breached. Such circumstances can be grouped under the notion of 'public policy',[160] informed as well by recognized standards regarding insolvency and resolution.[161] This safeguard is, however, limited and concrete under modified universalism to ensure certainty and avoid reverting to ring-fencing.[162] It does not accept refusal of recognition or other forms of support on the basis that laws are not identical.[163] This notion would, however, require some variation with respect to the type of entity. Thus, for example, in the MFIs context, public policy would also specifically refer to adverse effects of foreign measures on the financial stability of local markets or to material adverse fiscal implications.[164]

---

[156] Hüpkes, 'Allocating Costs of Failure Resolution' (n 135) 125 (noting that host countries may recognize the rulings of home resolution authorities where they are reassured that the interests of the host jurisdiction will be adequately protected). See also Lastra, 'International Law Principles Applicable to Cross-Border Bank Insolvency' (n 10) 169. Specific arrangements would also be needed regarding burden-sharing (see Chapter 6, section 6.3.3).

[157] Westbrook, 'International Judicial Negotiations' (n 148) 581.

[158] Bork, *Principles of Cross-Border Insolvency Law* (n 6) 40.

[159] See also Chapter 5, sections 5.3.1 and 5.3.2.

[160] See the leading decision on the public policy safeguard under the EIR, Case C–341/04 *In re Eurofood IFSC Ltd* [2006] ECR I–03813 para 66. See also eg the order of the UK court *In re Dalnyaya Step LLC* [2017] EWHC 756 (Ch) granting security for costs from the liquidator where there was a public policy argument against the recognition of the foreign Russian proceedings; or the decision of a US court *In re Vitro SAB de CV* [2012] 701 F 3d 1031 where the court refused to enforce a Mexican reorganization plan that sought to deviate from fundamental standards of fairness.

[161] The Insolvency Standard and the Key Attributes (section 1.4.4). See also Chapter 5, section 5.3.2.4.

[162] Bork, *Principles of Cross-Border Insolvency Law* (n 6) 37 ff.   [163] See n 137.

[164] The need to ensure that foreign resolution powers taken by the home jurisdiction sufficiently consider the impact on host countries' financial stability is recognized in recommendations and standards regarding resolution, see Key Attributes, s 7.3. See also International Monetary Fund, 'Cross-Border Bank Resolution: Recent Developments' (2 June 2014) 23 <https://www.imf.org/external/np/pp/eng/2014/060214.pdf> (noting how especially small host jurisdictions impacted by an insolvency of an MFI may have to prioritize domestic financial stability); M Peihani, 'Crisis Management and Orderly Resolution of Banks in Canada and Internationally: A Perspective on Reforms and Challenges' in JP Sarra and Justice B Romaine (eds), *Annual Review of Insolvency Law* (Carswell 2015) 614 (noting that the failure of branches of foreign banks can cause systemic risk when they perform systemically important operations, and therefore, it is important that host countries retain resolution powers over such branches).

1.4 Reception of Modified Universalism: The Glass Half-Full/Half-Empty

Notwithstanding the attractiveness of modified universalism, territorialists have been sceptical about the desirability and feasibility of any form of universalism, importantly because of persisting territorialist inclinations of countries. Universalists too, indeed for similar reasons, express various levels of disbelief about the feasibility of optimal universalism in the foreseeable future. In practice, we see that a significant portion of modified universalism norms is generally dominant to date, but it is certainly vulnerable and encounters setbacks. This section considers the reception of modified universalism in national and international cross-border insolvency law and practice. It does not purport to provide precise findings or detailed analysis of international instruments.[165] Instead, it shows the general trend whereby modified universalism is leading, although it is not fully and consistently endorsed. Notwithstanding its emergence as an approach attuned to the reality of distinct systems, it has been difficult to commit to modified universalism abundantly.

1.4.1 Scepticism and claims about countries' territorial preferences

Territorialism proponents generally observe that countries would not agree, and do not currently agree, to universalist norms, at least not in sufficient numbers.[166] Countries' preference, so the argument goes, is to control what is within their borders and not submit to foreign proceedings, laws, and policies,[167] especially as the law of insolvency is considered a 'meta-law'.[168] Countries will not agree to lose such control, limit their sovereignty, and disempower their local courts.[169] They may be willing to apply their own laws beyond their borders, but would strongly prefer to

---

[165] See Chapter 6 for an analysis of the global frameworks.

[166] See eg F Tung, 'Is International Bankruptcy Possible?' (n 22) 31, 33, 84 (arguing that universalism is 'politically implausible and likely impossible', and that: 'When we move to a world with many states, "numbers problems" arise. Even if bilateral universalism was not difficult enough to realize, multilateral universalist cooperation is even less tractable'); Kipnis, 'Beyond UNCITRAL: Alternatives to Universality' (n 2) 173 (observing that: 'Desire to protect sovereignty leads countries— even those with universalist leanings— to adopt limits on their cooperation with foreign proceedings, much like the United States did before the adoption of the UNCITRAL Model Law, and continues to do today').

[167] LoPucki, 'The Case for Cooperative Territoriality' (n 18); RS Avi-Yonah, 'National Regulation of Multinational Enterprises: An Essay on Comity, Extraterritoriality, and Harmonization' (2003) 42 Colum J Transnat'l L 5, 8–9, 12; Tung, 'Is International Bankruptcy Possible?' (n 22) 54 ff; Chung, 'The New Chapter 15 of the Bankruptcy Code' (n 18); Franken, 'Cross-border Insolvency Law' (n 22). See also Fletcher, *Insolvency in Private International Law* (n 3) 12–13.

[168] Tung, 'Fear of Commitment in International Bankruptcy' (n 18) 566 ff.

[169] ibid 573 (Tung seems to agree with the universalist goals but considers them unachievable where they require turning over local assets and surrender of sovereignty, noting that: 'Westbrook eschews conventional conflicts analysis as "unsuited to current realities" of modern multinational enterprise regulation. He may be right in terms of his universalist goals, but as long as states care about their "prickly rights of sovereignty," universalism has some conventional jurisdictional obstacles to overcome' (footnotes omitted)).

do so unilaterally only, and not let other countries' procedures and laws affect assets and stakeholders in their territory.[170]

Even where, as a second preference, so the argument goes, countries would have theoretically opted for mutual universalism over mutual territorialism, they would be caught in a prisoners' dilemma and would not be able to agree to mutual universalism, which requires loss of control and deference to a foreign system.[171] Thus, countries would fear that the other countries would not commit to mutual universalism and, therefore, would choose defection, concerned that they would otherwise end up with the worse possibility of being committed to submit to the systems of other countries which do not reciprocate. Such commitment cannot be assured on the international level in the absence of an authority that can enforce countries' promises. Countries cannot guarantee the future performance of other countries, particularly where countries in given cases may be better off grabbing assets for the benefit of local creditors.[172]

Scholars of the territorialist camp have generally pointed to countries' inclination to exercise jurisdiction and control within their borders and protect local constituencies, implying that any system based on unity and universality is doomed to fail.[173] It has been argued that even where countries and implementing institutions seem to adopt modified universalism frameworks, they do so reluctantly, and in practice they take territorial approaches.[174] Countries and implementing institutions are arguably hesitant to provide assistance to support foreign proceedings and will, therefore, find ways to refuse to cooperate, such as by citing vague standards which may attempt to specify when cooperation is required, and construing those standards in a way that would prevent deferral.[175] Universalists have also acknowledged countries' territorial inclinations.[176] These tendencies have been viewed as the reason for the need for concessions, hence the current stance of basing cross-border insolvency law on modified, rather than pure, universalism, where modified universalism

---

[170] Tung, 'Is International Bankruptcy Possible?' (n 22) 54 ff; Franken, 'Cross-border Insolvency Law' (n 22) 99.

[171] Tung, 'Is International Bankruptcy Possible?' (n 22) 60 ff.

[172] ibid 64 (noting the prisoners' dilemma that universalism attempts to resolve). See also Chapter 5 for a discussion of enforcement on the international level and generally on compliance challenges.

[173] Kipnis, 'Beyond UNCITRAL: Alternatives to Universality' (n 22) 173; Chung, 'The New Chapter 15 of the Bankruptcy Code' (n 18) 93.

[174] LoPucki, 'Cooperation in International Bankruptcy' (n 2) 700 ('although courts and lawyers have continually given lip service to universalism in resolving multinational bankruptcy cases, they increasingly have found nonuniversality solutions to multinational problems ...'). See also LoPucki, 'The Case for Cooperative Territoriality' (n 18); RS Avi-Yonah, 'National Regulation of Multinational Enterprises' (n 167) 8–9, 12.

[175] LoPucki, 'Cooperation in International Bankruptcy' (n 2) 730.

[176] See eg Bork, *Principles of Cross-Border Insolvency Law* (n 6) 256 (noting regarding the prospect of harmonization in insolvency that 'the disparity of the interests involved, local interests, territorial motives and mistrust of foreign law will disturb negotiations at least somewhat, and will hamper agreement on a principled solution' (footnotes omitted)); Fletcher, *Insolvency in Private International Law* (n 3) 12 ('Above all, it must be recognized that States are averse to allowing foreign laws to operate with extraterritorial effect in relation to property located within their jurisdiction ... therefore, the pragmatic attractions of plurality are likely to prevail over the more idealistic claims of the principle of Unity').

is understood as deviation from optimal solutions (purer forms of universalism) and as requiring exceptions.[177]

The normative conclusions of each school of thought have been quite different. Universalism proponents often suggest that universalism should be pursued through incremental and interim solutions, or ultimately through agreeing on treaties.[178] Territorialists, on the other hand, propose to abandon universalism and to limit any solution to cooperative versions of territorialism.[179] A framework for cross-border insolvency must be such, it has been argued, that countries will be willing to accept; and, therefore, it should not impose cooperation or other universalist characteristics beyond what is in the interests and tendencies of countries.[180] The prediction of each camp is also different. Universalists generally believe that, through the incremental approach, purer forms of universalism will emerge.[181] Territorialists, on the other hand, predict general failure: 'Territoriality will remain the dominant approach in international bankruptcy for the foreseeable future and maybe forever.'[182]

1.4.2 The traditional territorialist practice

It is indeed the case that countries have traditionally followed territorialism.[183] In particular, countries have been reluctant to acknowledge the effects of foreign insolvency proceedings conducted under the laws of a foreign country, at least not freely and unilaterally.[184] Countries and implementing institutions have been specifically

---

[177] See eg Bork, *Principles of Cross-Border Insolvency Law* (n 6) 27–28 (noting that 'universalism in its current form does not come without exceptions. It is because of these exceptions that the current stance of cross-border insolvency law is termed "modified universalism"; universalism is not implemented in a pure manner but rather with concessions to states' wishes for some elements of territorialism' (footnote omitted)). See also arguments of universalists, based on theoretical economic analysis, that even though territorialism is inefficient and reduces global welfare, each country acting individually is likely to adopt territorialism (Bebchuk and Guzman, 'An Economic Analysis of Transnational Bankruptcies' (n 19) 780).

[178] See eg Bebchuk and Guzman, 'An Economic Analysis of Transnational Bankruptcies' (n 19) (suggesting that universalism may be achieved through reciprocal agreements or treaties). See also Chapter 4, section 4.2.

[179] See eg LoPucki, 'Cooperation in International Bankruptcy' (n 2); Tung, Is International Bankruptcy Possible?' (n 22).

[180] Kipnis, 'Beyond UNCITRAL: Alternatives to Universality' (n 22) 155 (noting that 'any proposed regime must be sufficiently attractive to sovereign actors for adoption, and actually become widely adopted, if it is to become a genuine international regime. To that end, it must allow sovereign actors to satisfy the needs of their own domestic public policy if they are to cooperate').

[181] Janger, 'Universal Proceduralism' (n 73) 821 (noting that universalists hope the world will eventually be ready for true universalism). See also section 1.3.1.

[182] Tung, 'Is International Bankruptcy Possible?' (n 22) 102.

[183] ibid 34; Bebchuk and Guzman, 'An Economic Analysis of Transnational Bankruptcies' (n 19) 781–82. An example of a country that used to firmly restrict the effect of its insolvency proceedings to their own territory is Japan, though its position has changed, especially after 2010 when it adopted the MLCBI.

[184] Fletcher, *Insolvency in Private International Law* (n 3) 13 (noting that 'the notion of territoriality is applied towards foreign proceedings involving debtors with property or other interests which lie within the jurisdiction of the State in question: by denying the capability of the foreign proceedings to produce any effects regarding that part of the debtor's patrimony, the way is left open for local actions to be taken by any party with standing to exercise rights over it' (footnote omitted), referring as examples to the private international law regimes of the Netherlands and of Sweden).

disinclined to subscribe to norms concerning recognition and relief to foreign proceedings regarding assets of the debtor located within the country's jurisdiction.[185]
Countries have also manifested various forms of favouritism towards local creditors,
for example requiring the satisfaction of local debts from local assets before a turnover,[186] or providing assistance only if it does not prejudice their citizens, thus benefiting local creditors by giving them the advantage of either the foreign law or the
local law.[187]

In the context of MFI cross-border insolvency, the traditional approach has also
been territorial.[188] Thus, each country has imposed its own regulation and resolution
processes upon international banks operating within its borders.[189] Even with some
increase in international coordination among domestic regulators and supervisors
following the crises in the twentieth century, regulation as well as resolution of financial institutions in distress remained primarily territorial.[190]

1.4.3 Modified universalism gaining impetus

Notwithstanding the traditional territorialist approach of countries, modified universalism is considered the leading approach to date.[191] Forms of universalism have
been customarily more prevalent in common law-dominant jurisdictions, which
have generally accepted the notion that insolvency should have a worldwide effect
and that courts or other bodies should cooperate with and aid foreign courts.[192]
Courts in the United Kingdom, for example, have considered non-discrimination

---

[185] Fletcher, *Insolvency in Private International Law* (n 3) 13. The willingness of countries to surrender control over assets located in their territory and avoid protectionism of local creditors is arguably
'[t]he true test of universality ... ' (Bebchuk and Guzman, 'An Economic Analysis of Transnational
Bankruptcies' (n 19) 782).

[186] Bebchuk and Guzman, 'An Economic Analysis of Transnational Bankruptcies' (n 19) 783, referring to *In re Lineas Areas de Nicaragua* 10 BR 790 (SD Fla 1981) at 791.

[187] Bebchuk and Guzman, 'An Economic Analysis of Transnational Bankruptcies' (n 19) 783, referring to *In re Cunard* 773 F2d 452 (2d Cir 1985).

[188] Lastra, 'International Law Principles Applicable to Cross-Border Bank Insolvency' (n 10) 170–71.

[189] Westbrook, 'SIFIs and States' (n 41) 336.

[190] ibid, noting the case of the Bank of Commerce and Credit in 1991. In this case, a number of
countries, including the United States, in which the group had subsidiaries or branches, ring-fenced
assets and insisted on giving priority to local claims against local assets with little regard to proceedings
taking place elsewhere, despite the fact that the group's funds were extensively commingled (see also *In re
Bank of Credit & Commerce International SA* [1997] No 10 2 WLR 172, where the UK court applied its
national concepts of *pari passu* in regard to the doctrine of set-off notwithstanding the ancillary nature
of the UK proceedings in this case).

[191] See eg Anderson, 'The Cross-border Insolvency Paradigm' (n 11) 691–92 (Anderson had noted
already in the early 2000s regarding modified universalism that 'the approach benefits from the fact that
it is, or is becoming, the most common international system'); Bork, *Principles of Cross-Border Insolvency
Law* (n 6) 41 (noting that 'modern cross-border insolvency regimes are coined by the principle of
(modified) universalism ... '); Gopalan and Guihot, 'Recognition and Enforcement in Cross-Border
Insolvency Law' (n 42) 1268 (noting that: 'The debate on this topic appears to have settled for now. The
universalists have "won" the debate in that many parts of the economically powerful world have now
adopted a modified universalist approach').

[192] Fletcher, *Insolvency in Private International Law* (n 3) 18–19 (referring to the case of *Odwin v
Forbes* from 1814 where a court in Demerara and Essequibo gave recognition and international effect
to a foreign discharge, on the basis of comity. The judgment was later confirmed by the Privy Council).

towards creditors as a basic principle of cross-border insolvency and have recognized that local creditors should not be favoured and assets should not be ring-fenced.[193] Similarly in the United States, courts have accepted the obligations, resulting from the worldwide effect of insolvency, not to discriminate towards foreign creditors[194] and to defer to and assist foreign courts in facilitating a centralized insolvency based on the law of the debtor's home country.[195] The importance of cooperation has been highlighted in many UK cross-border insolvency cases. For example, in *Banque Indosuez SA v Ferromet Resources Inc.*, the UK court stated that it 'will do its utmost to co-operate with the US Bankruptcy Court and avoid any action which might disturb the orderly administration of [the company] in Texas under ch 11'.[196]

Assistance and cooperation have been provided by courts in the United States and the United Kingdom, albeit with limitations, both via statutory provisions, such as former section 304 of the US Bankruptcy Code,[197] or section 426 of the UK Insolvency Act,[198] and by the general application of common law and international comity.[199] Modified universalism has been referred to as the 'golden thread running through English cross-border insolvency law since the eighteenth century'.[200]

---

[193] *In Re BCCI* [1997] No 10 Ch 213, 239–40.

[194] *Felixtowe Dock and Railway Co v U S Lines Inc* [1989] QB 360 at 368 (which includes extracts from an opinion about the US bankruptcy law explaining that: 'The intended scope of bankruptcy and reorganization jurisdiction extends beyond the border of the United States ... The broad scope of bankruptcy jurisdiction under United States law is intended to permit similarly situated creditors, regardless of where they are located, to be treated equally in a bankruptcy or reorganization case. Discrimination on the basis of citizenship is not permitted ... '). See also Goode, *Principles of Corporate Insolvency Law* (n 88) 787 (noting that the position is the same under UK insolvency law).

[195] See eg *In Re Hamilton* 240 F 3d 148, 153 (2d Cir 2001).

[196] *Banque Indosuez SA v Ferromet Resources Inc* [1993] BCLC 112, 117. In *Credit Suisse Fides Trust v Cuoghi*, the court more generally noted the understanding of national courts around the world of the necessity of cooperation: 'It is becoming widely accepted that comity between the courts of different countries requires mutual respect for the territorial integrity of each other's jurisdiction, but that this should not inhibit a court in one jurisdiction from rendering whatever assistance it properly can to a court in another in respect of assets located or persons resident within the territory of the former' ([1998] QB 818, 827 (per Millett LJ)).

[197] Which made available a broad range of types of assistance that may be given to foreign proceedings and insolvency representatives without the need to open formal bankruptcy proceedings locally. This section has been described as representing 'a benchmark in terms of the liberal, universalist approach to the problems posed by multi-jurisdictional insolvencies' (Fletcher, *Insolvency in Private International Law* (n 3) 247 ff). The section was later replaced by Chapter 15 of the US Bankruptcy Code that enacted the MLCBI.

[198] Section 426 of the UK Insolvency Act empowers courts in the United Kingdom to give international assistance to certain qualifying countries and territories (Fletcher, *Insolvency in Private International Law* (n 3) 227 ff). Courts have also exercised discretion under this section to reach universalist solutions under the EIR. For example, *In re Integrated Medical Solutions Limited and Ors* [2012] BCC 215, following the receipt of a letter of request from the foreign court, the a UK court denied a petition for the opening of secondary proceedings in the United Kingdom following the opening of main proceedings against the same company (including other companies of the same group) in Ireland. This allowed achieving a unified group-wide solution via the Irish examinership regime.

[199] Comity generally refers to the established tradition among judges within the common law legal tradition to cooperate and assist foreign jurisdictions (Fletcher, *Insolvency in Private International Law* (n 3) 17). In the United States, the requirement of comity was incorporated into the text of Chapter 15 of the Bankruptcy Code that enacted the MLCBI (11 USC, s 1507). See also Chapter 3, section 3.4.1.

[200] *In re HIH Casualty and General Insurance Ltd* [2008] UKHL 21, [2008] 1 WLR 852, para 30 (per Lord Hoffmann).

It has been recognized that modified universalism requires cooperation with foreign courts, particularly with the court in the country where the main proceedings take place.[201] Generally, courts in these jurisdictions have shown increased flexibility in interpreting their inherent powers to promote universalism and comity.[202]

In Australia too, courts have entertained requests for assistance from foreign courts and insolvency representatives, including requests under statutory provisions.[203] Canada, as well, has taken an activist approach and has provided assistance and relief based on discretionary common law, comity principles,[204] and statutory powers.[205] Canada has acknowledged the notion of modified universalism as requiring the court to recognize main proceedings in one jurisdiction, while allowing the recognition of non-main proceedings in other jurisdictions, to advance international comity and cooperation.[206]

The notion of assistance, cooperation, and effect given to foreign proceedings has also been applied in proceedings involving smaller and offshore jurisdictions. For example, in the case of *Al-Sabah*, it was found that the Grand Court of the Cayman Islands has jurisdiction under statute[207] to confer additional powers on a Bahamian trustee in bankruptcy pursuant to a letter of request issued by the Bahamian Grand Court.[208] In *Picard v.*

---

[201] ibid.

[202] See eg *Cambridge Gas Transp Corp v Official Comm of Unsecured Creditors* [2006] UKPC 26, [2006] 3 WLR 689, where the Privy Council recognized a chapter 11 plan confirmed by a New York court against a group of companies, notwithstanding opposition of the principal shareholder of the parent company. The court stated that at common law 'the domestic court must at least be able to provide assistance by doing whatever it could have done in the case of a domestic insolvency' so as to avoid the need for parallel proceedings. This approach was rejected, however, in later cases insofar as it purported to provide a broad source of authority circumventing domestic private international law rules (*Rubin and another v Eurofinance SA and others and New Cap Reinsurance Corporation (in Liquidation) and another v AE Grant and others* [2012] UKSC 46, at 132); *McGrath and another v Riddell and others* [2008] UKHL 21, where the House of Lords ruled, based on s 426 of the UK Insolvency Act 1986, that the UK assets of the HIH group of companies were to be remitted to the Australian liquidators to be distributed in accordance with Australian law; In *Maxwell Communication Corp. plc v Societe Generale* 93 F 3d 1036 (2nd Cir 1996), where a US court deferred to UK courts and laws based on the doctrine of international comity; *In re Multicanal, SA*, 314 BR 486 (Bankr SDNY 2004), where a US court recognized an Argentine pre-packaged plan, preventing parallel proceedings from taking place in the United States); *In re Bd of Dirs of Telecom Arg SA* (2d Cir NY May 29 2008), where a US court recognized an Argentine restructuring plan despite differences between Argentine Insolvency Law and the US Bankruptcy Code. See also A Walters, 'Giving Effect to Foreign Restructuring Plans in Anglo-US Private International Law' (2015) 3 NIBLeJ 37.

[203] Section 581 of the Australian Corporations Act 2001. This statutory regime requires mandatory assistance to designated countries, and assistance on a discretionary basis regarding other countries (Fletcher, *Insolvency in Private International Law* (n 3) 262 ff, noting the cautious approach of Australian courts to the giving of assistance in the absence of evidence that the foreign laws are broadly like those of Australia). The regime has been enhanced, however, after the enactment of the MLCBI in Australia in 2008.

[204] *In re Babcock & Wilcox Canada Ltd* [2000] CanLII 22482 (ON SC), 18 CBR (4th) 157 and *Lear Canada, Re* [2009] CanLII 37931 (ON SC), 55 CBR (5th) 57.

[205] J Sarra, 'Northern lights, Canada's version of the UNCITRAL Model Law on Cross-Border Insolvency' (2007) 16 Intl Insolv Rev 19, 24 (noting that Canada follows a system of modified universalism). See also Fletcher, *Insolvency in Private International Law* (n 3) 265 ff.

[206] *In re MtGox Co Ltd* [2014] ONSC 5811.

[207] The English Bankruptcy Act 1914 s 122.

[208] *Al-Sabah v Grupo Torras SA* [2005] UKPC 1.

Primeo,[209] a Cayman Islands court applied its discretionary powers under common law to provide assistance to US bankruptcy proceedings, allowing the foreign insolvency representative to pursue proceedings directly in the Cayman Islands.[210]

In Hong Kong, courts have noted that recognition and assistance applications have become 'increasingly common in recent years'.[211] As a result, courts have developed a standard order for applications of this sort,[212] noting that the order provides a stay on proceedings against the company in Hong Kong, as well as a variety of powers afforded to foreign liquidators, including the power to protect, secure, and take into their possession assets, books, papers, and records of the debtor.[213]

The practice and acceptance of modified universalism norms reach beyond common law countries. Many legal systems have generally accepted the idea that an insolvency process should include all assets and that the law of the forum should apply.[214] Countries' domestic private international laws related to insolvency usually afford insolvency proceedings a universal effect, even in the absence of a treaty,[215] and countries also often accept certain constraints on their sovereignty.[216] Even legal systems associated with the civil law tradition (Germany for example), originally being less universalist, have developed rules that generally follow modified

---

[209] *Irving H Picard and Bernard L Madoff Investment Securities LLC v Primeo Fund* [16 April 2014] Cayman Islands Court of Appeal.

[210] ibid. The court found, however, that common law powers did not allow the court to apply the law of the home country, rather the foreign representative must apply Cayman Islands (avoidance) law.

[211] *In the Matter of Rennie Produce (Australia) Pty Ltd (In liquidation)* [2015] FCA, in the High Court of the Hong Kong, Special Administrative Region Court of First Instance, Miscellaneous Proceedings No 1640 of 2016.

[212] *In re Centaur Litigation SPC (In Liquidation)* HCMP 3389/2015 (unreported, 10 March 2016).

[213] ibid. See also *Joint Provisional Liquidators of BJB Career Education Company Limited (in provisional liquidation) v Xu Zhendong* [2016] HKCFI 1930 [3]; M Michaels, 'Hong Kong court sets standard order for recognition applications', *Global Restructuring Review* (27 September 2016).

[214] Fletcher, *Insolvency in Private International Law* (n 3) 13 (noting that: 'The more usual approach however has been one whereby the State regards its own, domestic bankruptcy laws as producing universal effects ... '); Bork, *Principles of Cross-Border Insolvency Law* (n 6) 27 (noting more generally that 'almost all modern cross-border insolvency laws follow the principle of universalism, even though this is heavily criticized by those scholars who prefer territorialism (albeit a cooperative version thereof) or a contractual approach' (footnotes omitted)).

[215] Fletcher, *Insolvency in Private International Law* (n 3) 13 (noting that this is particularly the case where the debtor's relationship with the country is a close one, which enables the case to be classified as a 'domiciliary' proceeding). There is, however, still some confusion, even in leading jurisdictions, regarding the scope of extraterritoriality of the home country laws, specifically regarding the extraterritoriality of avoidance powers. See eg the approach that is in line with modified universalism in the United Kingdom: *Jetivia v Bilta* [2015] UKSC 23; *Official Receiver v Norris* [2015] EWHC 2697 (Ch); and in the United States: *Weisfelner v Blavatnik (In re Lyondell)* 543 BR 127 (Bankr SDNY 2016); *Sec Investor Prot Corp v BLMIS (In re BLMIS)* 513 BR 300 (SDNY 2014); *French v. Liebmann*, 440 F 3d 145 (4th Cir 2006). cf in the United Kingdom, *In re MF Global UK Limited* [2015] EWHC 2319 (Ch) and in the United States, *SIPC v Bernard L Madoff Inv Sec* LLC, 480 BR 501 (Bankr SDNY 2012); *Barclay v Swiss Fin Corp Ltd*, 347 BR 708 (Bankr CD Cal 2006); *Societe Generale plc v Maxwell Commc'n Corp plc* 186 BR 807 (SDNY 1995); *Spizz v Goldfarb Seligman & Co (In re Ampal-Am Israel Corp)* 562 BR 601 (Bankr SDNY 2017).

[216] Bork, *Principles of Cross-Border Insolvency Law* (n 6) 41.

universalism, including inbound aspects that require recognition and assistance to foreign proceedings.[217]

Certain countries that were formerly cautious about universalism have become strong enthusiasts of this approach, notably Singapore. Mistrust and concern about universalism were expressed until fairly recently. For example, a Court of Appeal in Singapore in the *Beluga* case stated as follows:[218]

We would observe however that the commencement of legal proceedings against a defendant foreign company or an attempt to levy execution against its assets is not precluded by the mere fact that insolvency proceedings have been commenced against the company in another jurisdiction.

The court did note, however, that a universal approach to collection and distribution of assets is fair and desirable, although it may only ever be adopted as a broad statement of principle.[219] By 2017, the Singaporean government passed a bill adopting the MLCBI,[220] and, more generally, support of modified universalism has been strongly expressed by Singapore courts in more recent decisions.[221]

Various countries have introduced, or are in the process of introducing, more modern legislation on cross-border insolvency, even where they have not yet been ready to adopt the MLCBI. To mention a few examples, the Bahamas enacted new legislation in 2011, which allows granting recognition and assistance to designated countries.[222] In Eastern Europe, Hungary in 2017 passed a new act on private international law that provides a framework for choice of applicable law in cross-border cases, including recognition of foreign insolvency proceedings and enforcement of foreign judgments.[223] Switzerland announced a revision project of its private international law in 2015, which was submitted to its parliament in 2017, regarding the recognition and coordination of foreign insolvency proceedings.[224] The new proposals aim to streamline the recognition and assistance process, more in line with modified universalism, removing conditions (such as proof of reciprocity) and

---

[217] See German Insolvency Statute of 5 October 1994 (Federal Law Gazette I page 2866), as last amended by Art 19 of the Act of 20 December 2011 (Federal Law Gazette I page 2854); Bork, *Principles of Cross-Border Insolvency Law* (n 6) 29 (noting that: 'Today, German national cross-border insolvency law is firmly based on the principle of universalism for domestic as well as for foreign insolvency proceedings ... ').

[218] *Beluga Chartering GmbH v Beluga Projects (Singapore) Pte Ltd* [2014] SGCA 14.

[219] ibid.

[220] The MLCBI was finally implemented in Singapore on 23 May 2017, through the Companies (Amendment) Act 2017.

[221] See eg *Pacific Andes Resources* Development Ltd and other matters [2016] SGHC 210.

[222] Bahamian Companies Winding-Up Amendment Act 2011 ss 253–56. Liquidation Rules from 2016 designated 142 countries for this purpose.

[223] J Barton, 'Regulatory round-up: Hungary Snubs the Model Law' *Global Restructuring Review* (20 April 2017).

[224] Present law restricts recognition, including by requiring reciprocity, namely that the decision was rendered in the country of the debtor's domicile or registered seat and that it is enforceable in the country where it was rendered. After recognition, ancillary proceedings must be opened in Switzerland even when there is no need for local assistance (N Meier and R Rodriguez, 'Recast of the Swiss International Insolvency Law' in *Yearbook of Private International Law*, Vol 17, 2015/2016 (De Gruyter 2016) 355–69).

obstacles (such as a mandatory ancillary process), allowing swifter recognition, including of orders issued at the debtor's COMI, and enhancing cooperation and coordination in cross-border insolvency.[225] India introduced in 2016 provisions on cooperation in cross-border insolvency, although these are based on entering into reciprocal arrangements.[226]

Cooperation and assistance have also emerged through the growing use and approval of protocols, importantly, to address insolvencies of enterprise groups. Protocols have enabled insolvency representatives to run concurrent insolvency proceedings in different countries in a coordinated manner, and have even addressed deferral to foreign courts, resulting in greater centralization in accordance with modified universalism. Protocols have often been used together with the appointment of examiners or foreign representatives by the courts involved.[227] Other mechanisms being used include court-to-court communication and joint hearings.[228]

For cross-border insolvencies of MFIs, various systems, such as those of the United Kingdom and Luxembourg, follow in principle the jurisdiction norm of modified universalism, whereby banks are administered from the home country as one entity. Thus, the insolvency process should encompass all branches and worldwide creditors, and the duty not to discriminate against foreign creditors should be observed.[229] Regulation and preplanning of resolution of financial institutions generally increased after the global financial crisis, including the use of mechanisms such as 'living wills',[230] and requirements regarding loss-absorbing and recapitalization capacity.[231] Certain countries have developed specific statutory mechanisms concerning the cross-border aspects of MFI insolvency.[232] For example, Singapore included in legislation certain forms of support for foreign resolution actions.[233] The

---

[225] ibid.

[226] India's Code also provides that the National Company Law Tribunal may authorize issuing a letter to authorities in other countries to seek information or request action in relation to the assets of a debtor located abroad (India Insolvency and Bankruptcy Code 2016 ss 234–35).

[227] See examples in n 148.

[228] See eg court-to-court communication *In re Cenargo International Plc* [2003] 294 BR 571; and the communication that took place in *Nortel* (n 149). See also the enhancement of such mechanisms through soft law techniques (nn 261–62 and accompanying texts).

[229] Lastra, 'International Law Principles Applicable to Cross-Border Bank Insolvency' (n 10) 166–67 (though Lastra notes that in practice home countries 'are likely to obtain control only of assets located within their jurisdiction and foreign assets that are located in jurisdictions where they can obtain recognition').

[230] Resolution plans that state the way the firm may be resolved in the event of failure (J Meyerowitz et al, 'A Dodd-Frank Living Wills Primer: What you Need to Know Now' (2012) 31 Am Bankr Inst J 34).

[231] See eg the Dodd-Frank Act 2010 in the United States, and the Financial Stability Board, 'Principles on Loss-absorbing and Recapitalisation Capacity of G-SIBs in Resolution, Total Loss-absorbing Capacity (TLAC) Term Sheet' (9 November 2015) <http://www.fsb.org/wp-content/uploads/TLAC-Principles-and-Term-Sheet-for-publication-final.pdf>.

[232] Financial Stability Board, 'Resilience through resolvability—moving from policy design to implementation' 5th Report to the G20 on progress in resolution (18 August 2016) 21–22 <http://www.fsb.org/wp-content/uploads/Resilience-through-resolvability-%E2%80%93-moving-from-policy-design-to-implementation.pdf>.

[233] Financial Stability Board, 'Principles for Cross-Border Effectiveness of Resolution Actions' (3 November 2015) 18–19<http://www.fsb.org/wp-content/uploads/Principles-for-Cross-border-Effectiveness-of-Resolution-Actions.pdf>.

Swiss regulator, as well, in 2008 introduced provisions for recognition and assistance to foreign resolutions.[234] Under that legislation, recognition and assistance depend on reciprocity, namely an examination as to whether the foreign jurisdiction would recognize a Swiss insolvency judgment under similar circumstances. Yet experience has shown a rather relaxed application of the reciprocity restriction. For example, assistance was provided to Dutch proceedings even though the Netherlands lacked similar legislation.[235]

1.4.4 Development of international instruments and standards

Importantly, regional and international initiatives have been taken in recent decades, to regulate cross-border insolvency through various forms of international instruments and frameworks, even though cross-border insolvency treaties have had limited success.[236] These instruments generally, though not fully, follow modified universalism.[237]

Regionally, Europe has been the most advanced in the development of both institutional and regulatory frameworks for cross-border insolvency, in line with its agenda to create an integrated market.[238] Following previous failed attempts to ratify a treaty, a regulation addressing cross-border insolvency was enacted in 2000 and later revised in 2015. The European Union (EU) Regulation on Insolvency Proceedings (2000) (EIR) and the Recast EU Regulation (2015) (Recast EIR)[239] generally follows the modified universalist approach.[240] It provides a comprehensive framework, directly applicable in member states' systems, covering the range of private international law related to insolvency. It contemplates the centralization of the main proceedings in a single forum that applies its laws and the recognition and effect of these proceedings in the other member states.[241] The EU cross-border insolvency

---

[234] ibid.

[235] The Swiss Financial Market Supervisory Authority (FINMA) had given an order on 8 November 2011 regarding Van der Moolen Effecten Specialist BV registered and headquartered in Amsterdam for which resolution, recognition, and assistance was sought in Switzerland. The assistance was provided based on 'a result-oriented (*ergebnisorientierten*) comparison of both legal systems' (see B Wessels, 'Is Switzerland opening up for cross-border insolvency?' (*Leiden Law Blog*, 7 May 2012) <http://leidenlawblog.nl/articles/is-switzerland-opening-up-for-cross-border-insolvency>).

[236] Treaties concerning cross-border insolvency have mainly succeeded thus far between specific countries but not on a global level (see Chapter 4, section 4.2.1).

[237] Goode, *Principles of Corporate Insolvency Law* (n 88) 785–86 (noting that: 'The current trend, as exemplified by the UNCITRAL Model Law ... and the EC Insolvency Regulation ... is clearly in favour of a modified universalist approach, albeit with rather more territorial elements than may have been envisaged by the proponents of that approach').

[238] See eg recital 3 of the Recast EIR, which states that: 'The proper functioning of the internal market requires that cross-border insolvency proceedings should operate efficiently and effectively. This Regulation needs to be adopted in order to achieve that objective, which falls within the scope of judicial cooperation in civil matters within the meaning of Article 81 of the Treaty.'

[239] Council Regulation 1346/2000, of 29 May 2000 on Insolvency Proceedings, 2000 OJ (L 160) 1 (EC); Regulation 2015/848, of the European Parliament and of the Council of 20 May 2015 on Insolvency Proceedings, 2015 OJ (L 141) 19. The Recast EIR entered into force on 26 June 2017. The regime applies directly to all EU member states, except Denmark, which opted out.

[240] It is noted in the regulation that full universalism is not feasible (recitals 22 and 23 of the Recast EIR, replacing recitals 11 and 12 of the EIR).

[241] See generally Fletcher, *Insolvency in Private International Law* (n 3) ch 7.

regime is also based on EU uniform concepts and interpretations, including referral of issues to the Court of Justice of the European Union (CJEU).[242] Additional issues, notably the cross-border insolvency of groups, have been addressed in the Recast EIR by providing mechanisms for cooperation and coordination in such cases.[243] The EU regime has been generally a success as a framework for reaching solutions along the lines of modified universalism. The rule it prescribes for identifying the debtor's home country (the debtor's COMI) has usually been workable. As a home country rule based on the real seat of the debtor, it has not been wholly unpredictable, as feared,[244] and it allowed centralizations, including in group cases.[245] In certain circumstances, disruptive secondary proceedings could be avoided, for example, through assurances that specific protections of local creditors would be considered in the main forum.[246]

Specific European instruments have been designed for the cross-border insolvency of MFIs. A directive on the reorganization and winding-up of credit institutions (the EU Winding-up Directive)[247] created a regime largely in line with modified universalism, whereby the home country of the institution presides over its liquidation or reorganization in accordance with the home country's laws, subject to exceptions, and the measures it applies have universal effect.[248] In 2014, driven by lessons from the financial crisis, the regime was expanded to address more complex resolution tools and institution structures through the adoption of a Bank Recovery and Resolution Directive (BRRD).[249] More generally, the EU has moved towards greater centralization through the single supervisory and single resolution mechanisms.[250]

Notably, in the late 1990s, UNCITRAL adopted a global framework for cross-border insolvency in the form of a model law (the MLCBI) which also includes a

---

[242] See <https://europa.eu/european-union/about-eu/institutions-bodies/court-justice_en>.

[243] Ch V of the Recast EIR.

[244] See eg LoPucki, 'Cooperation in International Bankruptcy' (n 2) 713–18.

[245] I Mevorach, 'Jurisdiction in Insolvency: A Study of European Courts' Decisions' (2010) 6(2) Journal of Private International Law 327. See also Chapter 6, section 6.2.4.

[246] See the approach applied in *Collins & Aickman* and *Nortel* (n 132). See also cases such as *Trillium (Nelson) Properties Ltd v Office Metro Ltd* [2012] EWHC 1191 (Ch) where secondary proceedings were not opened in the absence of establishment, but the court held that there would have been little purpose in making a winding-up order even if there had been an establishment in the United Kingdom.

[247] Council Directive 2001/24/EC of the European Parliament and Council on the Reorganization and Winding-up of Credit Institutions 2001 OJ (L 125) 15.

[248] See generally A Campbell, 'Issues in Cross-Border Bank Insolvency: The European Community Directive on the Reorganisation and Winding-Up of Credit Institutions' <https://www.imf.org/external/np/leg/sem/2002/cdmfl/eng/campb.pdf>. See eg the application of the EU Winding-up Directive in accordance with modified universalism in *Tchenguiz & ors v Kaupthing Bank HF* [2017] EWCA Civ 83 CA.

[249] Directive 2014/59 of the European Parliament and of the Council, of 15 May 2014 Establishing a Framework for the Recovery and Resolution of Credit Institutions and Investment Firms and Amending Council Directive 82/891/EEC, and Directives 2001/24/EC, 2002/47/EC, 2004/25/EC, 2005/56/EC, 2007/36/EC, 2011/35/EU, 2012/30/EU, 2013/36/EU, and Regulations (EU) No 1093/2010 and (EU) No 648/2012, of the European Parliament and of the Council, 2014 OJ (L 173) 190. The BRRD establishes a common EU-wide regime for the recovery and resolution of credit institutions and investment firms in distress across all member states.

[250] See the explanation on the European Commission website: <https://ec.europa.eu/info/business-economy-euro/banking-and-finance/banking-union_en>.

Guide to Enactment and Interpretation (MLCBI GEI).[251] The MLCBI contains uniform rules concerning large portions of modified universalism norms, specifically regarding recognition of main, as well as non-main, proceedings, a range of relief that should be provided to foreign proceedings, assistance to foreign courts and foreign representatives, and mechanisms to enhance cooperation and coordination between courts and insolvency representatives.[252] Even compared with the relatively advanced statutory approaches such as the old section 304 of the US Bankruptcy Code, the MLCBI and its enactment in the United States has been considered 'far more expansive', thus placing 'the United States farther along the path toward universality'.[253] Additional instruments are being designed to close gaps in the MLCBI, importantly concerning groups and the enforcement of insolvency-related judgments.[254]

A few years after the adoption of the MLCBI, UNCITRAL also concluded the UNCITRAL Legislative Guide on Insolvency Law (Legislative Guide),[255] which, together with the World Bank Principles on Creditor–Debtor Regimes (World Bank Principles),[256] constitutes the international best-practice standard for insolvency regimes (the Insolvency Standard).[257] The Insolvency Standard is generally dedicated to standardization and modernization of insolvency laws,[258] yet it also recognizes the need for a global cross-border insolvency framework and recommends that countries adopt the MLCBI.[259] It also contains certain recommendations on cross-border insolvency, which are generally in line with modified universalism.[260] Various other soft law mechanisms have been developed, such as non-binding rules for cross-border court-to-court cooperation in insolvency cases and other cooperation methods.[261]

---

[251] The MLCBI GEI was revised in 2013.

[252] See in more detail Chapter 6, section 6.2.2.

[253] Kipnis, 'Beyond UNCITRAL: Alternatives to Universality' (n 22) 163. See also Godwin et al, 'The Inherent Power of Common Law Courts' (n 85) 14 ('"Modified universalism" is widely recognized and is "strongly embodied" in the UNCITRAL Model Law on Insolvency'); G McCormack, 'US Exceptionalism and UK Localism? Cross-border Insolvency Law in Comparative Perspective' (2016) 36(1) Legal Stud 136 (referring in fn 17 to Franken (Franken, 'Cross-border Insolvency Law' (n 22) 104) 'who argues the Model Law embodies an approach of "cooperative territorialism", but she does not address any analysis or judicial pronouncements to the contrary').

[254] See Chapter 6, sections 6.2.3 and 6.2.4.

[255] The first two parts were concluded in 2004. Additional parts were added in 2010 and 2013 (United Nations Commission on International Trade Law, UNCITRAL Legislative Guide on Insolvency Law, parts one and two, 25 June 2004; part three, 1 July 2010; part four, 18 July 2013 <http://www.uncitral.org/uncitral/en/uncitral_texts/insolvency/2004Guide.html>).

[256] World Bank Principles for Effective Insolvency and Creditor/Debtor Regimes (2016) <http://documents.worldbank.org/curated/en/518861467086038847/pdf/106399-WP-REVISED-PUBLIC-ICR-Principle-Final-Hyperlinks-revised-Latest.pdf>.

[257] The insolvency standard is one of several such standards recognized by the FSB to be 'broadly accepted as representing minimum requirements for good practice that countries are encouraged to meet or exceed' (see <http://www.fsb.org/what-we-do/about-the-compendium-of-standards/key_standards/>).

[258] See Chapter 5, section 5.3.2.   [259] Legislative Guide, pt one, para 14, rec 5.

[260] See Chapter 6, section 6.2.1.

[261] See eg the EU Cross-Border Insolvency Court-to-Court Cooperation Principles and Guidelines (2014) <http://www.tri-leiden.eu/uploads/files/EU_Cross-Border_Insolvency_Court-to-Court_Cooperation_Principles.pdf> (discussed in B Wessels, 'Towards a Next Step in Cross-Border Judicial Cooperation' (2014) 27 Insolv Int 100); The American Law Institute (ALI), 'Principles of Cooperation Among the NAFTA Countries Transnational Insolvency' (2003); The American Law Institute (ALI) and

A notable initiative of judges is the establishment in 2016 of a judicial insolvency network (JIN) from several jurisdictions to encourage communication and cooperation among national courts.[262]

Important developments also took place globally regarding MFIs, particularly following the global financial crisis. Leading international organizations (IOs) put forward recommendations for the development of effective mechanisms for the resolution of MFIs. The Basel Committee,[263] in a 2010 report, advocated for enhanced coordination among resolution authorities as a middle-ground approach (between territorialism and universalism). While the report acknowledged the legitimacy of ring-fencing 'in the current context',[264] at the same time it envisioned an alternative approach based on a more universal framework, which would be set out in a binding instrument or treaty and would accord primacy to the resolution of all domestic and cross-border activities of a failing financial group by the jurisdiction in which the institution is headquartered or possibly by a supranational entity.[265]

Most significantly, the Financial Stability Board (FSB),[266] in cooperation with the International Monetary Fund (IMF) developed an international standard on resolution in the form of the Key Attributes of Effective Resolution Regimes for Financial Institutions (Key Attributes).[267] This instrument is primarily a measure for standardization of resolution regimes,[268] but it also contains specific recommendations on the cross-border aspects of SIFIs' insolvency.[269] Along the lines of modified universalism, it recommends, inter alia, non-discrimination towards creditors with regard to nationality, and contemplates measures for recognition and support to give effect to foreign resolution measures.[270] Additional instruments have since been developed, especially to enhance the recognition of certain resolution tools.[271]

---

the International Insolvency Institute, 'Transnational Insolvency: Global Principles for Cooperation in International Insolvency Cases' (2012) (Wessels, B, and Fletcher, IF, Joint Reporters) <https://www.iiiglobal.org/sites/default/files/alireportmarch_0.pdf>. See also the discussion of tools for enhancing trust among participants in cross-border insolvency in Chapter 5, sections 5.2.5 and 5.3.1–5.3.2.

[262] The JIN has developed 'Guidelines for Communication and Cooperation between Courts in Cross-Border Insolvency Matters', which were formally adopted by courts in several jurisdiction, including Singapore, England and Wales, Bermuda, Southern District of New York, Delaware, and the BVI (Guidelines for Communication and Cooperation between Courts in Cross-Border Insolvency Matters (as promulgated by the Judicial Insolvency Network Conference 10–11 October 2016) <https://www.gov.uk/government/uploads/system/uploads/attachment_data/file/612376/JIN_Guidelines.pdf>).

[263] The Basel Committee 'provides a forum for regular cooperation on banking supervisory matters. Its objective is to enhance understanding of key supervisory issues and improve the quality of banking supervision worldwide' (<https://www.bis.org/bcbs/>).

[264] Bank for international Settlements, Basel Committee on Banking Supervision, 'Report and Recommendations of the Cross-Border Bank Resolution Group' (March 2010) para 67 <http://www.bis.org/publ/bcbs169.pdf>.

[265] ibid para 70 ff.

[266] The FSB is a non-governmental body of regulatory experts created under the auspices of the G20.

[267] Financial Stability Board, 'Key Attributes of Effective Resolution Regimes for Financial Institutions' (2011), revised in Financial Stability Board, 'Key Attributes of Effective Resolution Regimes for Financial Institutions' (2014) <http://www.fsb.org/what-we-do/policy-development/effective-resolution-regimes-and-policies/key-attributes-of-effective-resolution-regimes-for-financial-institutions/>.

[268] See Chapter 5, section 5.3.2.   [269] Key Attributes, 12 ff.

[270] See in more detail, Chapter 6, section 6.3.   [271] ibid.

It is difficult to assess the precise take-up of the international aspects included in the insolvency and resolution standards and other documents that provide high-level guidelines, standards, or recommendations.[272] However, the adoption of the MLCBI, which is intended for enactment in a more or less complete manner, is monitored by UNCITRAL, and this record shows that it has already been enacted in legislation by more than forty countries.[273] More countries are in the process of adoption of the MLCBI,[274] and it has also influenced reform in other systems.[275] Adopting countries include both common law and civil law jurisdictions, small and large countries, dominant and less developed regimes. The enactment of the MLCBI has largely been consistent in that leading jurisdictions adopting it have generally followed its provisions rather than create significantly different versions.[276] A few empirical studies, mainly but not solely focused on the Unites States' application of the MLCBI, have also shown that the MLCBI has been generally implemented by courts in line with the modified universalist approach. Thus, recognition under the MLCBI has usually been speedily granted and has become a standard practice.[277] That practice has also extended, to some extent, to circumstances where members of enterprise groups commenced proceedings jointly in the same jurisdiction.[278] The public policy safeguard has not been overused,[279] and courts have tended to provide a range of assistance and relief to foreign courts and insolvency representatives tailored to the specific case, including the more 'universalist relief' of turnover of local assets.[280]

---

[272] Implementation of the resolution standard in domestic systems has proved challenging, though, particularly the cross-border aspects (see Chapter 6, section 6.3.2).

[273] To date, forty-five jurisdictions have enacted laws based on the MLCBI according to the list maintained by UNCITRAL (http://www.uncitral.org/uncitral/en/uncitral_texts/insolvency/1997Model_ status.html).

[274] eg Israel is currently in the process of enacting the MLCBI.

[275] eg it has been noted that the new Swiss proposals on cross-border insolvency have been influenced by the MLCBI (Meier and Rodriguez, 'Recast of the Swiss International Insolvency Law' (n 224) 355–69).

[276] eg the United Kingdom, United States, New Zealand, and Australia adopted the MLCBI almost verbatim. Though, see some important deviations noted in section 1.4.5.

[277] I Mevorach, 'On the Road to Universalism: A Comparative and Empirical Study of UNCITRAL Model Law on Cross-Border Insolvency' (2011) 12 EBOR 517, 533 ff (a study that looked at the application of the MLCBI in eight jurisdictions); JL Westbrook, 'An Empirical Study of the Implementation in the United States of the Model Law on Cross Border Insolvency' (2013) 87(2) The American Bankruptcy Law Journal 247, 254 ff (a study that focused on the application of the MLCBI in the United States). Westbrook also refers to findings by Dawson (A Dawson, 'Offshore Bankruptcies' (2009) 88 Neb L Rev 317) showing lesser recognition by US courts of requests from offshore jurisdictions, explaining this result by the rejection of forum shopping in circumstances where proceedings were opened on the basis of a thin connection to the country); J Leong, 'Is Chapter 15 Universalist or Territorialist? Evidence from United States Bankruptcy Cases' (2011) 29 Wis Intl L J 110, 123 (a study that also focused on the application of the MLCBI in the United States). See also Walters, 'Modified Universalisms' (n 73), mentioning another unpublished study by Alix Partners, which covers all US chapter 15 cases up to September 2016 and confirms similar patterns of smooth recognition.

[278] Mevorach, 'On the Road to Universalism' (n 277) 537 ff; Westbrook, 'An Empirical Study of the Implementation' (n 277) 265 ff.

[279] It has been rarely invoked and rarely applied (Mevorach, 'On the Road to Universalism' (n 277), 537).

[280] ibid 517, 543 ff; Westbrook, 'An Empirical Study of the Implementation' (n 277) 260 ff (Westbrook refers to contrary findings in a study by Leong, but notes certain problems with that study,

1.4.5 Incompleteness, limitations, and pushbacks

The foregoing discussion reflects the 'glass half-full', showing progress and movement towards the universal application of modified universalism. However, modified universalism is generally regarded as merely a trend or broad principle, even when invoked in systems that largely follow this approach, such as the United Kingdom and the United States, and whether its application is based on statutory provisions, a global framework, or common law.[281]

Modified universalism has also suffered some notable pushbacks with regard to important aspects of its emerging norms, particularly by the decision in *Rubin v Eurofinance*, where the UK Supreme Court refused to enforce a judgment of the main proceedings under common law or the British version of the MLCBI;[282] and subsequent cases such as *Singularis,* where the Privy Council stated that 'the principle of modified universalism is part of the common law, but it is necessary to bear in mind, first, that it is subject to local law and local public policy and, secondly, that the court can only ever act within the limits of its own statutory and common law powers'.[283] Generally, even in regimes regarded as universalist such as the United Kingdom, there may be discrepancies and '… a want of symmetry between the international effects claimed by English law for insolvency proceedings which take place in this country, and the effects which will be accorded in England to proceedings opened in other countries'.[284]

---

specifically the way requests for relief and the subsequent court orders have been coded: see J Leong, 'Is Chapter 15 Universalist or Territorialist?' (n 277)).

[281] See eg the references of the UK court in *In re HIH Casualty and General Insurance Ltd* [2008] UKHL 21, [2008] 1 WLR 852 (paras 7 and 30) to a 'principle rather than a rule', an 'aspiration' and a 'thread'; or the reference of the US court *In re Nortel Networks, Inc*, 532 BR 494 (Bankr D Del 2015) 111 to 'terms such as "universalism" '. See also Chapter 3, section 3.6.1.

[282] *Rubin and another v Eurofinance SA and others* and *New Cap Reinsurance Corporation (in Liquidation) and another v AE Grant and others* [2012] UKSC 46. See also *Pan Ocean* [2014] EWHC 2124 (Ch). Rubin has been considered a setback or even a decision that 'killed' universalism. See eg H Rajak, 'Modified universalism in international insolvency and the Rubin case: one step backwards?' (2014) 350 Company Law Newsletter 1; C Webber, 'Universalism? Not in my backyard' (2013) 47 Com Litigation J 6; McCormack, 'Universalism in Insolvency Proceedings' (n 34) 336 ff.

[283] *Singularis Holdings Limited (Appellant) v PricewaterhouseCoopers (Respondent)* [2014] UKPC 36, para 33. Thus, the Privy Council refused to grant a disclosure order at the request of the liquidators as such relief was not available before the courts in which the foreign insolvency proceedings had been opened. In *Hooley Ltd v Titaghur plc, The Samnugger Jute Factory and The Victoria Jute Co Ltd* [2016] CSOH 141, a Scottish court refused to defer to proceedings held in India where three group companies incorporated in Scotland did their business and had their assets, and instead allowed a Scottish insolvency parallel process to continue, referring to the restricted application of modified universalism in the cases of *Rubin* and *Singularis*. See also Godwin et al, 'The Inherent Power of Common Law Courts' (n 85) 6 (noting regarding the use of common law inherent powers to assist foreign courts that: 'Recent English cases have seen a refinement of the power but also caused considerable confusion and raised additional questions about the scope and continuing utility of the power').

[284] Fletcher, *Insolvency in Private International Law* (n 3) 225. A durable manifestation of this asymmetry is the 'Gibbs rule' (*Gibbs and Sons v La Societe Industrielle* [1890] 25 QBD 399 (CA) 406), which allows suing in the United Kingdom based on a contract governed by English law even where the debt has been discharged in foreign liquidation in the debtor home country. It has been observed that: 'The Gibbs doctrine belongs to an age of Anglocentric reasoning which should be consigned to history' (Fletcher, *Insolvency in Private International Law* (n 3) 130; see also *Global Distressed Alpha Fund 1*

Countries' domestic legislation, even when it contains mechanisms for recognition and assistance for foreign proceedings, often includes conditions and constraints, such as reciprocity,[285] or procedural burdens such as a requirement to enter into agreements to operationalize the cross-border regime,[286] or they lack sufficient detail to provide a complete system based on modified universalism.[287] Generally, domestic systems of private international law concerning insolvency lack uniformity, especially when they do not follow a more harmonized, global framework.[288] Some countries do not have any special provisions regulating cross-border insolvency proceedings, which usually means that the general private international laws apply. In Turkey, for example, issues arising in cross-border cases are addressed through concepts such as reciprocity, and execution or recognition of foreign judgment processes.[289] Under Russian law, judgments related to insolvency may be recognized and enforced in Russia only based on treaties, otherwise the principle of reciprocity applies.[290] In Hong Kong, despite many calls for reform, the cross-border insolvency legislation has remained inadequate.[291] It was noted above that recognition and relief have become standard in Hong Kong. However, at the same time, concerns have been raised that the lack of legislation may result in restrictive application of common-law powers to assist foreign courts and insolvency representatives.[292]

Regionally, for example within the EU, the cross-border insolvency regime is uniform and based on EU-wide norms.[293] Yet territorial elements in the regime, for example the exceptions to the universal effect of the main process when secondary proceedings are opened, threaten to swallow the rule.[294] Furthermore, the regime only applies within the EU and does not regulate relations with third countries.

The MLCBI has attempted to create a uniform global framework, but has not addressed all modified universalism aspects fully, and it deviates from modified universalism in some respects, notably where it allows a certain degree of local favouritism.[295] Importantly, it has not been adopted universally. Notable countries that have not enacted the MLCBI include significant European economies such as France, Germany, Spain, and the Netherlands, as well as offshore jurisdictions that

---

Ltd Partnership v PT Bakrie Investindo [2011] EWHC 256 (Comm), [2011] 1 WLR 2038; LC Ho, 'Recognising Foreign Insolvency Discharge and Stare Decisis' (2011) 26 JIBLR 266).

[285] See eg the recognition regime under the 2017 Hungarian legislation (n 223 and accompanying text), that is conditional upon reciprocity.

[286] See the Indian regime (n 226 and accompanying text).

[287] See eg the assistance provision under UK law (s 426 of the Insolvency Act 1986) (see also n 198).

[288] Fletcher, *Insolvency in Private International Law* (n 3) 7.

[289] Pursuant to the Turkish Act on Private International and Procedural Law (Act No 5718).

[290] Art 1(6) of the Russian Insolvency Law, 2002.

[291] Godwin et al, 'The Inherent Power of Common Law Courts' (n 85) 21–22.

[292] *Joint Official Liquidators of A Co v B* [2014] 4 HKLRD 374 [11].

[293] The concepts contained in the EIR (and now the Recast EIR) have an autonomous meaning (Case C-341/04 *In re Eurofood IFSC Ltd* [2006] BCC 397).

[294] McCormack, 'Universalism in Insolvency Proceedings' (n 34) 339 (noting that: 'There are, however, so many exceptions in the EU Regulation eating away at the universalist principle … '). See eg *Alitalia Linee Aeree Italiane spA, Re* [2011] EWHC 15 (Ch) [2011] 1 ELR 2049, where the UK court felt it had to follow the EIR and allow the segregation of assets subject to secondary proceedings and apply the local law regarding their disposal, even though it was the less efficient and fair approach.

[295] See Chapter 6, sections 6.2.2 and 6.2.5.

are significant players in cross-border insolvencies, such as the Cayman Islands, and large economies, including China, Russia, India, and Brazil.[296] Some commentators have considered the limited adoption of the MLCBI as a sign of lack of enthusiasm,[297] and it has also led to discussions in international forums about the possibility of transforming the MLCBI to a treaty.[298]

Some countries that have adopted the MLCBI have deviated from its modified universalist provisions, as contemplated in the model, in some important ways. For example, several countries have included a reciprocity requirement,[299] or a broader public policy safeguard.[300] Even between regimes of countries such as the United States and the United Kingdom, which enacted the MLCBI almost verbatim, divergences are apparent in implementation and interpretation.[301] Generally, the

[296] In Brazil, a working group has been convened to consider reform of the bankruptcy regime, including the possible adoption of the MLCBI or a modified version thereof (G Colombo et al, 'Potential Reforms to Brazilian Bankruptcy Law—Getting Closer to UNCITRAL Model Law on Cross-Border Insolvency' <http://www.insol.org/emailer/July_2017_downloads/Doc1.pdf> noting that a reform of the law is expected by end of 2017).

[297] See eg S Chandra Mohan, 'Cross-Border Insolvency Problems: Is the UNCITRAL Model Law the Answer?' (2012) 21 Int Insolv Rev 199. Arguably, territorial tendencies explain why the MLCBI has not been adopted more widely (see concerns about sovereignty, reciprocity, and subordination of national interest to foreign influence noted in the context of the MLCBI and international attempts at harmonization, in the Asian Development Bank, 'Technical Assistance Completion Report' (TA 5975—REG: Promoting Regional Cooperation in the Development of Insolvency Law Reforms' (2009) <https://www.adb.org/sites/default/files/project-document/64987/34496-reg-tcr.pdf>).

[298] See Chapter 4, section 4.2.2.

[299] See eg Romania (Law 85/2014 on insolvency prevention procedures and insolvency proceedings, art 289); South Africa (Cross-Border Insolvency Act 42 of 2000, s 2); Mauritius (Insolvency Act 2009, s 366).

[300] See Romania Law 85/2014 on insolvency prevention procedures and insolvency proceedings, art 278. Other notable deviations include the non-adoption of the notion of the automatic stay upon recognition of main proceedings by the Republic of Korea (see ch 5 of the Republic of Korea Debtor Rehabilitation and Bankruptcy Act 2005 with effect from 1 April 2006. See also S Oh, 'An Overview of the New Korean Insolvency Law' (2007) 16 Norton Journal of Bankruptcy Law and Practice 5). Japan too deviated from the MLCBI in significant ways, including imposing more onerous conditions for recognition (Japanese Law for Recognition and Assistance to Foreign Insolvency Proceedings, with effect from 1 April 2001. See also K Yamamoto, 'New Japanese Legislation on Cross-Border Insolvency as Compared to the UNCITRAL Model Law' (2002) 11(2) Int Insolv Rev, 67. Canada made some significant modifications including the non-adoption of the provision limiting the scope of opening concurrent proceedings following recognition of a foreign proceeding (Statute of Canada ch 47; Sarra, 'Northern lights, Canada's version of the UNCITRAL Model Law' (n 205) 40). See also Mevorach, 'On the Road to Universalism' (n 277) 528; Chandra Mohan, 'Cross-Border Insolvency Problems' (n 297) 208–15.

[301] Importantly, in terms of the relief available following recognition, including the scope of the stay, the enforcement of judgments, and the deference to foreign law (McCormack, 'US Exceptionalism and UK Localism?' (n 253)). The UK approach seems to have been more constrained in some important ways (see notably *Rubin v Eurofinance* and *Pan Ocean* (n 282)). Yet, there have been deviations from modified universalism by US courts as well. See eg *In re Elpida Memory, Inc*, No 12-10947 (D Del Nov 16 2012), where the court applied domestic rules concerning assets sales even though the transaction had been approved already in the main proceedings, and *In re Qimonda* (2013) 737 F3d 14 where the court refused to defer to German law which permitted the cancellation of US patent licences, even though the German bankruptcy system was considered in line with fundamental fairness standards. See also, *In re Barnet*, 737 F.3d 238 (2d Cir. 2013) where a Court of Appeal in the United States applied a constrained approach concerning recognition and held that recognition of foreign proceeding requires, in addition to the conditions set out in Chapter 15 of the Bankruptcy Code (the US version of the MLCBI), that the debtor has a residence, domicile, place of business, or assets in the United States, thus adding an obstacle to recognition. cf *In re Bemarmara Consulting a.s.,* Case No 13-13037 (KG) (Bankr D Del Dec 17, 2013). See also Lord Neuberger, President of the Supreme Court, 'The Supreme

use of the MLCBI in cross-border insolvency cases is not always consistent and fully in line with modified universalism.[302] The empirical findings about the positive operation of the MLCBI in the practice, as well, are not conclusive: they have focused mostly on the MLCBI's application in leading jurisdictions and mainly in the United States, where the jurisprudence has developed most rapidly. They have also revealed certain limitations in the operation of the global framework.[303] One study also reached very different results, arguing that the US courts have behaved in a territorial manner when applying the MLCBI.[304] Certainly, it seems that the MLCBI and, generally, cooperation in cross-border insolvency work more smoothly between certain neighbouring countries, and when countries more familiar with the ideas of comity and coordination are involved.[305] Indeed, mechanisms such as the use of protocols and communication between courts have worked well mostly between close-neighbour countries, such as the United States and Canada.[306]

Regarding MFIs, especially the Global systemically important financial institutions (G-SIFIs), it has so far not been possible to agree on a global comprehensive and uniform framework specific to such institutions, beyond high-level principles.[307] Where countries have attempted to provide assistance measures in domestic laws, these are often lacking uniformity and consistency.[308] In this regard, the following has been

Court, the Privy Council and International Insolvency', Keynote speech at the International Insolvency Institute Annual Conference (2017, London) para 26 ('The extent to which the Model Law promotes substantive universalism (i.e. the application of the law governing the foreign insolvency proceeding) appears to be answered differently in different jurisdictions. Thus, the US courts seem to have adopted a rather more universalist approach than the courts of the UK').

[302] See the examples mentioned in n 301. See also robust deviation from the notion of centralization in the COMI jurisdiction enshrined in the MLCBI, in *Hooley Ltd v Titaghur plc, The Samnugger Jute Factory and The Victoria Jute Co Ltd* [2016] CSOH 141. As mentioned in n 283, the court in this case refused to give supremacy to Indian proceedings regarding companies that were incorporated in Scotland, but who conducted their businesses in India. The court noted that the UK Supreme Court and Privy Council did not recognize modified universalism other than in circumstances where the proceedings took place at the jurisdiction where the company was incorporated.

[303] Mevorach, 'On the Road to Universalism' (n 277) 537 ff, 543 ff (showing that recognition of proceedings opened jointly against companies belonging to the same enterprise group has not been always smooth and that there has been some reluctance to invoke and grant discretionary relief). See also JL Westbrook, 'Chapter 15 Comes of Age' in JP Sarra (ed), *Annual Review of International Law* (2013) 173.

[304] J Leong, 'Is Chapter 15 Universalist or Territorialist?' (n 277) 136.

[305] Mevorach, 'On the Road to Universalism' (n 277) 540–41.

[306] Lord Neuberger, 'The international Dimension of Insolvency' [2010] Insolv Int 42, 45 (referring to comments by Chief Justice Brenner of the British Columbia Supreme Court in (2009) 83 ALJ 290).

[307] Despite proposals to pursue such an approach, eg by UNCITRAL (United Nations Commission on International Trade Law, Insolvency Law: Possible Future Work: Addendum, Proposal by the Delegation of Switzerland for Preparation of a Study on the Feasibility of an Instrument Regarding the Cross-Border Resolution of Large and Complex Financial Institutions, A/CN.9/WG.V/WP.93/Add.5 (2010); United Nations Commission on International Trade Law, Insolvency Law: Insolvency of Large and Complex Financial Institutions, Note by the Secretariat, A/CN.9/WG.V/WP.109 (2012); United Nations Commission on International Trade Law, Insolvency Law: Background Information on Topics Comprising the Current Mandate of Working Group V and Topics for Possible Future Work, Note by the Secretariat, A/CN.9/WG.V/WP.117 (2013) <http://www.uncitral.org/uncitral/en/commission/working_groups/5Insolvency.html>). The MLCBI applies to debtors and entities generally, yet it allows countries to exclude entities such as banks, which are subject to special regimes (see Chapter 6, section 6.3.3).

[308] Under Swiss legislation, for example, following the recognition of foreign bank insolvency proceedings or measures, concurrent proceedings may be opened in Switzerland or assets may be transferred to the home jurisdiction, subject to certain safeguards. On the other hand, Singapore's framework

noted: 'Recognition of the legal status of action by foreign courts or authorities has long been a feature of judicial and supervisory cooperation. Yet, with a few exceptions ... it requires formal recognition procedures that involve reciprocity and public interest considerations.'[309] To some extent, domestic legislation concerning insolvency of financial institutions seems to be going in a territorialist direction where there is lack of sufficient regard to cross-border aspects and to the interests of foreign stakeholders.[310] Notwithstanding certain existing agreements (eg memorandums of understanding (MOU)), the level of coordination during the global crisis has been limited.[311]

Even within Europe, despite the existence of the Winding-up Directive, deviations from commitments and from modified universalism have been significant (eg during the collapse of the Icelandic banks) where governments took unilateral decisions based on territorial interests and failed to cooperate, resulting in overall loss of value.[312] Post-crisis, while there has been immense improvement of the regime, territorial tendencies may not have disappeared, as demonstrated, for example, in the *Novo Banco* case, in which the UK court refused to give direct effect to the ruling of the Bank of Portugal pursuant to the relevant provision of the BRRD,[313] though this decision was eventually reversed.[314] Beyond Europe, the collapse of Lehman Brothers in 2008, in particular, exhibited a large degree of non-cooperation and a focus on local interests.[315] Notwithstanding important developments post-crisis, especially in increased regulation and resolution preplanning measures,[316] significant challenges remain.[317]

supports only certain foreign measures, and provides for a limited form of assistance. It also requires Ministerial approval to exercise the power of transfer of shares (Financial Stability Board, Cross-Border Recognition of Resolution Action: Consultative Document 7 (29 September 2014) <http://www.financialstabilityboard.org/wpcontent/uploads/c_140929.pdf>).

[309] Hüpkes, 'Allocating Costs of Failure Resolution' (n 135) 124–25.

[310] Westbrook, 'SIFIs and States' (n 41), 346 (noting the example of the United States where in response to the crisis, regulators adopted rules that denied insurance to deposits payable in branches outside of the country and limited availability of insurance to deposits of foreign banks payable in the United States, also noting that similar measures have been enacted in other countries as well).

[311] ibid 347. See also Peihani, 'Crisis Management and Orderly Resolution of Banks in Canada and Internationally' (n 164) 614.

[312] See eg the collapse of Landsbanki financial group, where the Icelandic authorities breached commitments concerning foreign depositors, including in the United Kingdom, resulting in a British government attempt to freeze assets located in the United Kingdom; or the territorial resolution of Fortis, which was broken up along national lines when it collapsed (JM Edwards, 'A Model Law Framework for The Resolution of G-SIFIs' (2012) 7 Cap Mkts L J 122, 131–33; Lastra, 'International Law Principles Applicable to Cross-Border Bank Insolvency' (n 10) 176; PL Davies, 'Resolution of Cross-Border Banking Groups' in M Haentjens and B Wessels (eds), *Research Handbook on Crisis Management in the Banking Sector* (Research Handbooks in Financial Law Series 2015) 263).

[313] BRRD, art 66. See *Goldman Sachs International v Novo Banco SA* [2015] EWHC 2371 (Comm) (Hamblen J, 7 August 2015).

[314] *Guardians of New Zealand Superannuation Fund & Ors v Novo Banco SA* [2016] EWCA Civ 1092. See also: A Gardella, 'The Court of Appeal Rules in Favor of Mutual Recognition and Rescues Cross-Border Resolution' (2016) <https://www.law.ox.ac.uk/business-law-blog/blog/2016/11/court-appeal-rules-favor-mutual-recognition-and-rescues-cross-border>.

[315] Davies, 'Resolution of Cross-Border Banking Groups' (n 312) 263–64.

[316] See n 230 and accompanying text.

[317] Peihani, 'Crisis Management and Orderly Resolution of Banks in Canada and Internationally' (n 164) 615. See also the analysis of the international instruments for cross-border insolvency of MFIs, developed following the global financial crisis, in Chapter 6, section 6.3.

1.5 Conclusion

To date, modified universalism is the leading approach for cross-border insolvency. This chapter argued that modified universalism is also not a concession compared to an ideal of pure universalism; rather, it is the optimal approach for global insolvency driven from a theoretical paradigm of universalism. It is evolving from the pure theory of universalism as a set of norms that are fit for real-world circumstances. Large portions of these emerging norms are followed in practice, where many countries have introduced legislation to address the inbound and outbound aspects of modified universalism, and where courts and other bodies have developed means for cooperating and communicating to achieve global, coordinated solutions for multinational defaults. International instruments have also been developed, largely along the lines of modified universalism.

Yet modified universalism is still generally recognized as merely a broad principle or trend. There are also important gaps in international instruments, such as in terms of their adoption, application, and coverage. Domestic laws in turn, where they do not follow international frameworks, tend to be incomplete or lacking uniformity. Countries and implementing institutions show territorial inclinations when they refrain from adopting international frameworks, or adopt them only partially, or where in actual cases requested relief is denied, or where otherwise there is lack of support, even when the conditions for the application of safeguards are not present in the circumstances.

The scepticism of the territorialist school of thought about the ability of modified universalism to become fully endorsed, and concerns of universalists about the possibility to achieve optimal solutions in cross-border insolvency, are therefore grounded in the reality of cross-border insolvency practice and its current state of affairs. This situation raises a couple of related questions: Is the lack of full universality of modified universalism due to the actual preferences of countries? What holds modified universalism back, and from the glass half-full perspective, what has contributed to modified universalism becoming widespread? These questions are addressed in Chapter 2.

2

The Debiasing Role of the Cross-Border Insolvency System

2.1 Introduction

The previous chapter has shown how modified universalism is emerging from the universalist theory as a set of norms of cross-border insolvency that fit with the reality of multinational businesses and financial institutions operating through different structures and across distinct legal systems. Modified universalism adjusts universalism to such a reality, thereby facilitating optimal solutions in cross-border insolvency cases that preserve value for the benefit of stakeholders, considered from a global perspective. A system based on modified universalism requires complete coordination between countries and institutions where asset grabbing is restricted, namely where the common pool problem of insolvency is controlled on a global scale and countries have regard to the effects of their actions on operations and stakeholders in other countries. As such, modified universalism is normatively desired. It has also been quite dominant in practice, although not completely and not fully universally.

This chapter explores the possible reasons why regardless of the benefits of modified universalism, there are notable deviations in its practice by countries and their implementing institutions. The focus is on decision-making and choices on the 'macro' (country and institution) level. The micro-level decisions, namely the actions of firms and creditors involved in the cross-border insolvency case, intersect with and may influence institutional behaviour, for example, when creditors attempt to grab assets in the territory, or when firms and even insolvency representatives refuse to cooperate. Courts, for example, may then be inclined to fulfil local demands. However, on the 'micro' level, parties are often conflicted and long-term welfare implications are not relevant considerations. At the country and institution levels, on the other hand, decision-making independence is expected and therefore it should be possible, in principle, to opt for solutions in the general interests of stakeholders to create a system that is fair and effective over time, both at the stage of enacting frameworks (eg adopting a model law or a treaty) and at the stage of implementing the regime. Therefore, this chapter considers what may affect defection from a global system based on modified universalism by countries' policy makers and regulators as well as by judges and other authorities in charge of interpreting and applying

The Future of Cross-Border Insolvency: Overcoming Biases and Closing Gaps. Irit Mevorach.
© Irit Mevorach 2018. Published 2018 by Oxford University Press.

cross-border insolvency law; it also considers what factors may have driven modified universalism's relative success.

Certainly, part of the inconsistency and incompleteness of modified universalism is inherently because its norms are still evolving.[1] Problems also derive from domestic regimes' inequality, which also affects the level of trust in foreign systems and thus cooperation in cross-border insolvency.[2] However, the question is whether in addition to being in the developmental stage, there may be a deeper problem with universalism that prevents it from reaching its full potential or that suggests a vulnerability in its claimed normative supremacy. The debate regarding which approach, universalism or territorialism (including in their different variations), is more desirable has not been conclusively resolved,[3] resulting in calls to abandon universalism altogether or seek more compromises to take account of territorialistic needs and inclinations.[4] Specifically, it has been territorialism's main critique of the universalist approach that it has failed to take sufficient account of countries' real-world reluctance to adhere to internationalist solutions and their actual preference of territorialism.[5]

Thus, whilst the situation in practice seems generally positive, an appreciation of the motives for deviations from modified universalism as well as what incentivizes adherence can assist in understanding the nature of persisting weaknesses of modified universalism and possibly contribute to maximizing the system's potential in the future. In particular, the question is whether most manifestations of territorialism must represent actual preferences of countries, suggesting that territorialism ultimately is a more desirable approach, at least for some countries, or whether there are also other factors likely contributing to a territorialist inclination that the international system may be able to address. Relatedly, it might be that countries simply cannot cooperate fully, where they are caught in a prisoner's dilemma and fear non-compliance by other countries.[6]

Such further investigation of countries' preferences and the resultant feasibility and desirability of modified universalism can have important implications regarding the goals, roles, and design of the cross-border insolvency system. It requires having due regard to what influences choices in the real world, particularly in the contexts of international law and international relations. Therefore, this chapter considers economic theories concerning choices, namely the expected utility theory and its assumptions about people's choices and preferences, but also the theories and experiments that have shown bounds on decision-making in real-world circumstances.

The chapter draws on cognitive psychology theories of decision-making and particularly the 'prospect theory' initially developed by Kahneman and Tversky,[7] which

---

[1] See Chapter 1, section 1.3.2.   [2] See Chapter 5, section 5.3.
[3] See Lord Neuberger, President of the Supreme Court, 'The Supreme Court, the Privy Council and International Insolvency, Keynote Speech' (International Insolvency Institute Annual Conference 2017, London, 19 June 2017) para 10 (noting the 'perennial debate between territorialism and universalism').
[4] See Chapter 1, section 1.4.1.   [5] ibid.   [6] ibid.
[7] A Tversky and D Kahneman, 'Judgment under Uncertainty: Heuristics and Biases' (1974) 185 Science 1124; D Kahneman and A Tversky, 'Prospect Theory: An Analysis of Decisions under Risk' (1979) 47 Econometrica 263. See detailed discussion in section 2.3.

revealed certain robust cognitive biases that can affect choices. This chapter also takes account of bounds on willpower as well as the peer effect on people's choices and the limitations to assumptions about people's self-serving inclinations. It is not the intention, however, to provide a full description and complete explanation of what shapes behaviour and affects choices. Rather, the aim is to point to certain universal biases and bounds on decision-making that could also explain behaviour in the context of cross-border insolvency.

Interestingly, and more recently, it has also been shown that extant bounds on decision-making and other biases can be in operation regarding international law issues, thus bringing the cognitive insights closer to the realm of cross-border insolvency, where countries and implementing institutions make decisions and choices along the spectrum between universalism and territorialism. This chapter, therefore, draws from 'behavioural international law' scholarship,[8] which has brought together economic analysis of international law, behavioural economics, and political psychology in international relations, to shed light on behavioural constraints in addressing problems on the international level.

In view of these insights, this chapter considers the inferences for cross-border insolvency and the universalism versus territorialism debate. It argues that extant bounds on decision-making and bounds on willpower provide a probable explanation for territorialist behaviour, more probable than the possibility that territorialism is always a choice based on a pure calculation of expected utility. Thus, the fact that countries and implementing institutions might be inclined to adopt territorialist solutions in certain circumstances could be attributed, at least to some degree, to bounds on decision-making rather than a choice for the most welfare-increasing approach. At the same time, certain limitations to the expected utility model suggest that cooperation, even concerning complex matters that require multilateral coordination, is feasible, and can explain the growing dominance of modified universalism. These assertions are further supported by examples from actual case law and by considering the way countries have thus far addressed cross-border insolvency issues.

The normative implication is that the cross-border insolvency system, rather than yielding to territorialism or attempting to reach compromises, should strengthen modified universalism as its underlying fundamental norm, and should continue to address extant gaps and design its system in a way that is compatible with modified universalism's emerging norms. Cross-border insolvency law and the system supporting cross-border insolvencies have a 'debiasing' role.[9] That is, it should attempt to address and reduce the effect of biases to align behaviour with normatively desired choices. It should also attempt to exploit and enhance those biases that can foster compliance and cooperation.

---

[8] See section 2.4.1.

[9] See generally C Jolls and CR Sunstein, 'Debiasing Through Law' (2006) 35 J Legal Stud 199, and in the context of international law, A van Aaken, 'Behavioral International Law and Economics' (2014) 55(2) Harv Intl L J 421, 449 (arguing that insights from behavioural economics can help better design international law as a fundamental debiasing mechanism).

The chapter proceeds as follows. First, section 2.2 considers the possibility that territorialism is the actual preference of countries or a choice that is a result of the impossibility of cooperating in multinational insolvencies, taking account of the expected utility model of decision-making. The discussion is then expanded in section 2.3 by considering the limitations on this model's assumptions, overviewing key biases revealed by the prospect theory and by further experiments. Next, section 2.4 outlines the way these biases and preferences may manifest themselves in international law contexts, as highlighted in behavioural international law scholarship. Section 2.5 shows how these biases and effects on decisions may explain behaviour in international insolvency. Against this backdrop, section 2.6 considers the policy implications in terms of the choice of modified universalism as the desired norm and the debiasing role of the cross-border insolvency system. Section 2.7 provides summary conclusions.

2.2 Territorialist Preferences and Standard Economic Presumptions

Modified universalism requires taking a global approach to multinational default, demanding a level of unity/universality alongside adequate safeguards and due regard to differences in business structures and insolvency scenarios. As a solution driven by the theory of pure universalism, it is based on the shared philosophy of collectivity of the insolvency proceedings to achieve fair and efficient results. Thus, in the long run, the expected utility from modified universalism is larger than the expected utility from territorialism. Not knowing where assets and creditors will be located in future cross-border insolvency cases, and taking account of the interdependence and integration of global businesses, all countries and their implementing institutions should prefer the modified universalist norm over a territorialist system.[10]

Nonetheless, not all countries have adopted modified universalist frameworks. Where they have, implementing institutions sometimes deviate from modified universalist solutions.[11] The existing cross-border insolvency frameworks themselves to some extent exhibit indeterminacy about the adoption of modified universalism, perhaps demonstrating the difficulties in reaching optimal solutions among representative decision makers.[12] Proponents of territorialism have stressed that universalism is not feasible, and that territorialism is the preferred option of countries. They have pointed to persistent inaction in response to international initiatives, lack of political will to follow universalist frameworks, and the ingrained tendency of national systems to grab assets in multinational insolvency cases. Moreover, they have argued that countries and implementing institutions give lip service to

---

[10] As explained in Chapter 1, both global and country welfare is increased by modified universalism. Although local insolvency professionals might, to some extent, be disadvantaged, the policy makers and implementers in countries should focus on the pursuance of insolvency objectives, specifically ensuring debtors and stakeholders participation in the value-maximizing process, wherever it is centralized, and not on how the professionals can benefit from local proceedings (see Chapter 1, n 42).

[11] See Chapter 1, section 1.4.5.

[12] See Chapter 6 for an assessment of the key international instruments.

universalism.[13] Namely, even where they adopt and seem to follow or to design universalist frameworks, countries do it hesitantly and will look for opportunities to apply the frameworks in territorialistic ways in practice. The conclusion of proponents of territorialism is to follow these inclinations and adhere to a territorialist, country-by-country, approach for cross-border insolvency.[14]

This conclusion may seem logical. If countries do not really and willingly embrace modified universalism, then this approach should be either abandoned or at least it should accommodate more compromise solutions fitting the territorialist tendencies. Countries and implementing institutions' choices are for solutions that would increase, rather than decrease, welfare. If they prefer territorialist solutions, and such preferences are based on calculation of expected utility, then cross-border insolvency frameworks should be designed in a manner that reflects this choice, or at least it should accommodate the wishes of those countries that express territorial preferences. As well, if cooperation of the sort envisaged by modified universalism is not feasible then pursuing it is arguably pointless.

Standard economic models of choices and decisions support such assertion about following territorialist inclinations. Thus, the rational choice model presumes that decision makers evaluate risks accurately, and that accordingly, they are able to maximize their expected utility, making choices based on probability calculations. It is assumed that preferences of actors are separate from circumstances and are motivated by self-regarding interests. Preferences are expected to be stable and well defined, and actors are presumed to make choices consistent with those preferences.[15] Initial assignments of resources or entitlements do not affect final decisions, according to this model, because actors make decisions based on perfect efficiency calculations regardless of starting points.[16]

International law issues have been analysed extensively from an economics perspective, using the rational choice paradigm and expected utility theory.[17] Assumptions about behaviour based on this model have been thus ascribed to individuals as well as to collective actors, such as international organizations (IOs) and countries,

---

[13] See Chapter 1, section 1.4.1.   [14] ibid.

[15] GS Becker, *The Economic Approach to Human Behavior* (University of Chicago Press 1976) 14.

[16] This is based on the Coase theorem (RH Coase, 'The Problem of Social Cost' (1960) 3 J L & Econ 1. See also T Broude, 'Behavioral International Law' (2015) 163 U Pa L Rev 1099, 1115).

[17] Using tools such as game theory, collective action theory, externalities, and common goods. See eg JL Goldsmith and EA Posner, *The Limits of International Law* (OUP 2005); AT Guzman, 'Saving Customary International Law' (2005) 27 Mich J Intl L 115; R Scott and P Stephan, *The Limits of Leviathan: Contract Theory and The Enforcement of International Law* (CUP 2006) 9, 59–60; AT Guzman, *How International Law Works: A Rational Choice Theory* (OUP 2008); EA Posner and AO Sykes, *Economic Foundations of International Law* (Harvard University Press 2013); JL Trachtman, *The Economic Structure of International Law* (Harvard University Press, 2008). A rational choice assumption also underlies other approaches to international law and international relations, including institutionalism and constructivism (van Aaken, 'Behavioral International Law and Economics' (n 9) 435–36). See also J Galbraith, 'Treaty Options: Towards a Behavioral Understanding of Treaty Design' (2013) 53 Va J Intl L 309, 310–11 (noting that a rational choice assumption also implicitly underlies Louis Henkin's analysis of international law-making in *How Nations Behave* (L Henkin, *How Nations Behave* (Columbia University Press 1979) 36).

supposing such behaviour on the aggregate level.[18] Under this standard assumption of choice theory, countries and decision makers are expected, for example, to enter into international agreements if they consider that the utility is higher from cooperation than from non-cooperation.[19] Actors will consent to international legal obligations and make choices regarding the preferred source of international law, its design, and their level of compliance based on a comparison of the expected values of available options. They will consider the final states of wealth and welfare that their choice is likely to generate and will choose the option that is in their best interests.[20]

Accordingly, it would be expected that in the international insolvency context, international frameworks or other solutions based on modified universalism would be adopted by all and be implemented consistently if they can increase expected utility. Countries, their negotiators, and implementing institutions should be able to ascertain that solutions based on modified universalism will increase welfare and will advance their interests because they are the fairest and most efficient notwithstanding any degree of loss of sovereignty that such solutions entail. Countries should be able to reach the conclusion, based on expected utility calculus, that the expected costs they might endure because of the constraint on sovereignty will not exceed the expected net benefits from cooperation. Consequently, if they decide to take a different approach, this choice should be followed, as it is implied that this choice must be the desirable option.

Alternatively, it can be argued that even if modified universalism is desired in theory, it is not possible to pursue it because of the complexity of addressing the multinational insolvency collective action problem where stakeholders in different jurisdictions have rights over the same finite fund and where countries cannot trust that other countries will adhere to mutual universalism.[21] Expected utility theorists have been generally sceptical about the ability of international frameworks (eg treaties) to deal with complex coordination issues especially regarding global commons and problems involving the prisoner's dilemma.[22] The prediction under the standard economic theory is of inefficient excess appropriation of common pool resources.[23] Each party involved in a commons situation may rationally pursue its

---

[18] C Engel, 'The Behavior of the Corporate Actors: How Much Can We Learn from the Experimental Literature?' (2010) 6 J Inst Econ 445, 446.

[19] On the normative level, decision theory suggests that those negotiating contracts should compare the expected value of agreement with the expected return of non-agreement and make a decision accordingly. On the positive level, arguably negotiators make choices consistent with the normative models, namely they draw accurate conclusions from relevant information and select the option that maximizes their expected utility (R Korobkin and C Guthrie, 'Heuristics and Biases at the Bargaining Table' (2004) 87 Marq L Rev 795, 795–96).

[20] AT Guzman, 'Against Consent' (2012) 52 Va J Intl L 747, 758.

[21] See Chapter 1, section 1.2.3 (regarding the collective action problem in international insolvency), and section 1.4.1 (noting the claim that countries, even *ex ante* through treaties and even if they value mutual cooperation over mutual territoriality, will not be able to agree to a universalist approach because they will be faced by a prisoner's dilemma).

[22] Posner and Sykes, *Economic Foundations of International Law* (n 17) 231–32 (noting the example of treaties on climate change); Guzman, 'Against Consent' (n 20) 764–65 (noting generally the difficulty in addressing international problems involving the prisoner's dilemma). On the rational choice view of the commons problem see G Hardin, 'The Tragedy of the Commons' (1968) 162 Science 1243.

[23] van Aaken, 'Behavioral International Law and Economics' (n 9) 469.

own self-interest while disregarding others who will pursue their own self-interests in a similar manner, resulting in a loss to everyone in terms of receiving a share in the collective resource.[24]

All in all, as modified universalism, notwithstanding its general pervasiveness, is not fully consistently chosen and applied across the board, arguably the claim of universalists about its utility is, at least to some extent, misconceived. However, the descriptive account of decision theory that asserts that actors make choices in line with the normative model has been substantially criticized. Decision-making in the real world is complex and may be influenced by various factors. Specifically, behavioural psychology has demonstrated through experimental manipulations that decision-making is bounded.[25] The assumptions about self-regarding behaviour that arguably makes it impossible to cooperate and to resolve complex coordination problems have also been qualified.

2.3 Real-World Decision-Making

Kahneman and Tversky developed in the 1970s what is called the prospect theory and introduced the notion of heuristics[26] and biases in judgment and decision-making.[27] The prospect theory has attempted to model real-life choices rather than optimal decisions and provide a more accurate description of decision-making between probabilistic alternatives, compared to the expected utility doctrine. Through careful experimentation, behavioural sciences researchers have shown that decision-making is significantly bounded, and human action is affected by various psychological constraints.[28] People's preferences in making decisions systemically violate the axioms of expected utility theory as decision makers frequently deviate in predictable ways from economically optimal behaviour.

---

[24] ibid. It has been acknowledged that the problem of lack of cooperation may be mitigated to some extent where there is a chance for repeated interactions (see eg R Axelrod and RO Keohane, 'Achieving Cooperation Under Anarchy: Strategies and Institutions' in KA Oye (ed), *Cooperation under Anarchy* (Princeton University Press 1986)).

[25] Korobkin and Guthrie, 'Heuristics and Biases at the Bargaining Table' (n 19) 796.

[26] Namely, rules of thumb or mental shortcuts relied upon by people in making judgements or choices (Tversky and Kahneman, 'Judgment under Uncertainty' (n 7) 1124; D Kahneman, 'Maps of Bounded Rationality: Psychology for Behavioral Economics' (2003) 93 Am Econ Rev 1449, 1450).

[27] Tversky and Kahneman, 'Judgment under Uncertainty' (n 7); Kahneman and Tversky, 'Prospect Theory' (n 7); A Tversky and D Kahneman, 'Advances in Prospect Theory: Cumulative Representation of Uncertainty' (1992) 5(4) Journal of Risk and Uncertainty 297; Kahneman, 'Maps of Bounded Rationality' (n 26) 1450. See also G Gigerenzer and PM Todd, *Simple Heuristics that Make Us Smart* (OUP 1999); G Gigerenzer and DG Goldstein, 'Reasoning the Fast and Frugal Way: Models of Bounded Rationality' (1996) 103 Psychol Rev 650; G Gigerenzer and R Selten (eds), *Bounded Rationality: The Adaptive Toolbox* (The MIT Press 2002). See also previously HA Simon, 'A Behavioral Model of Rationale Choice' (1955) 69 Q J Econ 99.

[28] F Parisi and VL Smith, 'Introduction' in F Parisi and VL Smith (eds), *The Law and Economics of Irrational Behavior* (Stanford University Press 2005) 1–2 (noting that human action 'is highly affected by people's endogenous preferences, knowledge, skills, endowments, and a variety of psychological and physical constraints' (footnote omitted)).

Some of these key biases that have been found to exist in actual decision-making and that could shed important light on choices in cross-border insolvency, are overviewed in this section. Particularly, the focus is on bounds on decisions and choices revealed by prospect theory, generated from loss aversion, status quo, framing, and endowment effects. Additional empirical findings regarding bounds on willpower, the limitations on assumptions about self-interested behaviour, and the influence of peer effect on choices are considered. The exposition of biases in this section is based on experiments that focused on individuals' behaviour (in various settings), yet as discussed in the next section, behavioural international law reveals that these biases can be relevant in international law contexts as well.

2.3.1 Loss aversion and the framing effect

Prospect theory has shown that people have asymmetrical attitudes towards gains and losses, and their perceived utility is increased less by gains than by averted losses (the subjective impact of losses is roughly twice that of gains; this is the notion of 'loss aversion'). Thus, when in a loss frame (a 'negative domain'), people tend to be more risk seeking. Specifically, they will prefer to take a risk for a loss that is merely probable over a smaller loss that is certain. The reverse effect is observed in a gain frame, where people refrain from taking a risk for a greater probable gain, tending to choose a sure option over a gamble option.[29] In other words, people are more keen to avoid what they perceive as a loss than to pursue greater gains.[30] Choices are also not purely consistent across decisions, but instead are influenced by the manner in which available choices are presented (the 'framing' effect). For example, framing a sure option as a loss biases people to avoid that sure option and choose a gamble instead.[31]

The choice process involves two phases, editing and evaluation, where in the editing phase people normally denote a 'reference point' and perceive outcomes as gains or losses relative to this point rather than as final states of wealth or welfare. The reference point usually corresponds to the current asset position (the status quo), and gains/losses are deviations from the reference point. Again, the exact position of the reference point and the consequent perception (coding) of outcomes as

---

[29] Kahneman and Tversky, 'Prospect Theory' (n 7) 265–69.

[30] Furthermore, people do not objectively weigh outcome probabilities as assumed by the expected utility theory, but rather they underweight outcomes that are merely probable in comparison with outcomes that are certain, contributing to risk aversion in choices involving sure gains and to risk-seeking in choices involving sure losses (Kahneman and Tversky, 'Prospect Theory' (n 7)). A further development and variant of prospect theory was later introduced in Tversky and Kahneman, 'Advances in Prospect Theory' (n 27), where weighting was applied to cumulative probability rather than the probability of individual outcomes to demonstrate overweighting of extreme events, which occur with small probabilities, instead of overweighting of all small probability events.

[31] Choices between options are also influenced by other factors such as ambiguity. Thus, decision makers are more risk averse when probabilities are not clearly defined (D Ellsberg, 'Risk, Ambiguity and the Savage Axioms' 75 Q J Econ 643; A Tversky and CR Fox, 'Ambiguity, Aversion and Comparative Ignorance' (1995) 110(3) Q J Econ 585; HJ Einhorn and RM Hogarth, 'Decision Making under Ambiguity' (1986) 59(4) J Bus 225).

gains or losses can be affected by the formulation of the offered prospects. In any event, values are attached to changes rather than to final states, and the perception of changes is also affected by past and present context of experience.[32]

The existence of loss aversion and the effect of framing have been observed in a wealth of empirical research, including neurobiological experiments that showed that this pattern of behaviour (responding differently to perceived losses as opposed to perceived gains) is tied to the brain's greater sensitivity to potential losses than to gains.[33] Other experimental studies have shown that loss aversion has a specific effect when considering avoiding an option versus actively approaching an option.[34] Thus, people choose risky options with losses more frequently when such a choice is related with no action ('no-Go') than when it is associated with active action ('Go').[35]

2.3.2 The endowment effect

The Coasean assumption that items have equal worth whether gained or lost has been qualified by many experiments showing that initial assignments in fact significantly influence people's decisions. Thus, the disutility of giving up (losing) an endowment is greater than the utility associated with acquiring it; namely, loss aversion is linked to an 'endowment effect'.[36] People demand more to give up something than they would be willing to pay to get it, and are generally reluctant to part with their endowment. Kahneman et al referred in this respect to US Supreme Court Justice Oliver Wendell Holmes, who in 1897 noted this principle in his statement that:

It is in the nature of a man's mind. A thing which you enjoyed and used as your own for a long time, whether property or opinion, takes root in your being and cannot be torn away without

---

[32] Kahneman and Tversky, 'Prospect Theory' (n 7) 274, 277 (noting that this assumption is compatible with basic principles of perception and judgement, as people are attuned to the evaluation of changes or differences rather than of absolute magnitudes). See also, A Tversky and D Kahneman, 'The Framing of Decisions and the Psychology of Choice' (1981) 211 Science 453, 455; A Tversky and D Kahneman, 'Rational Choice and the Framing of Decisions' (1986) 59 J Bus 251, 255–62; D Kahneman, 'A Perspective on Judgment and Choice: Mapping Bounded Rationality' (2003) 58 Am Psychol 697, 703.

[33] See eg B De Martino et al, 'Frame, Biases, and Rational Decision-Making in the Human Brain' (2006) 313 Science 684; M Tom et al, 'The Neural Basis of Loss Aversion in Decision-Making Under Risk' (2007) 315 Science 515.

[34] ND Wright et al, 'Manipulating the Contribution of Approach-Avoidance to the Perturbation of Economic Choice by Valence' (2013) 7 Frontiers in Neuroscience 1; ND Wright et al, 'Approach-Avoidance Processes Contribute to Dissociable Impacts of Risk and Loss on Choice' (2012) 32(20) J Neuroscience 7009.

[35] Wright et al, 'Manipulating the Contribution of Approach-Avoidance to the Perturbation of Economic Choice by Valence' (n 34); Wright et al, 'Approach-Avoidance Processes Contribute to Dissociable Impacts of Risk and Loss on Choice' (n 34).

[36] D Kahneman, JL Knetch, and R Thaler, 'Anomalies: The Endowment Effect, Loss Aversion and Status Quo Bias' (1991) 5(1) J Econ Perspectives 193; D Kahneman and A Tversky, 'Choices, Values and Frames' (1984) 39 Am Psychologist 341; JL Knetsch and JA Sinden, 'Willingness to Pay and Compensation Demanded: Experimental Evidence of an Unexpected Disparity in Measures of Value' (1984) 99 Q J Econ 507; D Kahneman, JL Knetsch, and R Thaler, 'Experimental Tests of the Endowment Effect and the Coase Theorem' (1990) 98 J Pol Econ 1325.

your resenting the act and trying to defend yourself, however you came by it. The law can ask no better justification than the deepest instinct of man.[37]

2.3.3 The status quo bias

People on average have a strong preference for the current state of affairs; that is, they have a 'status quo bias' and rely on this heuristic when making decisions.[38] Thus, the status quo bias is another robust anomaly affecting choices, contradicting the assumptions about stability and symmetry, as experiments have shown that the disadvantages of a change loom larger than its advantages.[39] Accordingly, adherence to the status quo may be preferred over any change from the status quo even where the status quo is not objectively superior to other options. Thus, the status quo bias can lead to decisions that depart from the normative model of choice.[40]

The role of the status quo and of entitlements and expectations has been shown to be of huge importance when considering what factors influence judgments and choices in the real world. Consistent with extant loss aversion as well as the effect of framing, evidence of the status quo bias shows that decision makers' choices may depend on how they perceive the status quo (which can be affected by the formulation of options and of the current state of affairs). Thus, it is more probable that decision makers will accept the status quo and refrain from taking actions when selecting an option that could increase gains, or when the result of taking the action is framed as an increase in gains rather than an avoidance of loss.[41] Yet, the status quo bias also has a separate effect, and it persists even in the absence of gain/loss framing for a range of other possible reasons, such as psychological commitment.[42]

2.3.4 Bounded willpower

Experimental studies have also documented bounded willpower in behaviour of individuals, which also contradict the standard assumptions about what drives choices.[43] Thus, studies in cognitive psychology have shown that people often act in ways that conflict with their own long-term interests.[44] Notwithstanding awareness of the possible damage of certain behaviour, people may be tempted to act in a destructive manner. For example, they may continue smoking even if expressing

---

[37] D Kahneman, JL Knetch, and R Thaler, 'Anomalies' (n 36).   [38] ibid.

[39] W Samuelson and R Zechhauser, 'Status Quo Bias in Decision Making' (1988) 1 Journal of Risk and Uncertainty 7 (demonstrating the status quo effect by using a questionnaire in which participants faced a series of hypothetical decision problems, which were framed to be with and without a pre-existing status quo position. On aggregate, across all problem scenarios, people tended to select options when they reflected the status quo). See also D Kahneman, JL Knetch, and R Thaler, 'Anomalies' (n 36).

[40] Korobkin and Guthrie, 'Heuristics and Biases at the Bargaining Table' (n 19) 803; R Korobkin, 'The Endowment Effect and Legal Analysis' (2003) 97 Nw U L Rev 1227, 1231–42.

[41] See section 2.3.1.

[42] Samuelson and Zechhauser, 'Status Quo Bias in Decision Making' (n 39) 7 (showing that, for example, when participants were asked to choose the colour of their new car, they tended towards one colour that was arbitrarily framed as the status quo).

[43] van Aaken, 'Behavioral International Law and Economics' (n 9) 431.

[44] C Jolls et al, 'A Behavioral Approach to Law and Economics' (1998) 50 Stan L Rev 1471, 1479.

an interest in quitting, or may under-save despite knowing that such behaviour has long-term negative implications.[45] Behaviour apparently tends to be inconsistent as time passes, as people tend to discount future costs and rewards.[46] This problem of bounded willpower has been observed in legal contexts too or in areas relevant to law, for example with regard to criminal behaviour.[47]

2.3.5 Bounded self-interest and peer effect

It is also the general assumption of the standard expected utility theory that people are solely motivated by self-regarding interests, usually material interests.[48] Experimental studies show, however, that people may care about others in certain circumstances and may take deliberate actions contrary to their own self-interest for reasons of fairness to others. Self-interest is not the only interest that may influence decisions, because it is qualified by fairness preferences ('bounded self-interest').[49] People can be strongly motivated by other-regarding preferences in a broad range of settings.[50] They may also develop an expectation of fair treatment from others. Furthermore, preferences do not only depend on material gains, but also on the understanding and perceptions of others' intentions, namely the perception of the reasons for the types of action taken by the other parties.[51] The notion of reciprocity is extended to consider not only the promotion of self-interest through mutual favours, which is the standard rational choice model of reciprocity, but also the response to how actions and intentions of others are perceived. Experiments show that such perceptions significantly influence behaviour and can foster cooperation.[52] In particular, experiments concerning common pool resources have shown that allowing for informal sanctions and communication reduces excess appropriation

---

[45] See eg JQ Wilson and A Abrahamse, 'Does Crime Pay?' (1992) 9 Just Q 359, 368–71.

[46] T O'Donoghue and M Rabin, 'Doing it Now or Later' (1999) 89 Am Econ Rev 103. See also van Aaken, 'Behavioral International Law and Economics' (n 9) 431–32.

[47] Wilson and Abrahamse, 'Does Crime Pay?' (n 45) 368–71.

[48] van Aaken, 'Behavioral International Law and Economics' (n 9) 432.

[49] Jolls et al, 'A Behavioral Approach to Law and Economics' (n 44) 1479. Experiments also show that this bounded self-interest is both a social phenomenon and an aspect of human rationality (BA Mellers et al, 'Group Report: Effects of Emotions and Social Processes on Bounded Rationality,' in Gigerenzer and Selten (eds), *Bounded Rationality, The Adaptive Toolbox* (n 27) 263; J Henrich et al, 'Group Report: What Is the Role of Culture in Bounded Rationality?' in Gigerenzer and Selten (eds), *Bounded Rationality, The Adaptive Toolbox* (n 27) 343).

[50] Jolls et al, 'A Behavioral Approach to Law and Economics' (n 44) 1479 (noting that 'in many market and bargaining settings (as opposed to nonmarket settings such as bequest decisions), people care about being treated fairly and want to treat others fairly if those others are themselves behaving fairly. As a result of these concerns, the agents in a behavioral economic model are both nicer and (when they are not treated fairly) more spiteful than the agents postulated by neoclassical theory'). See also E Fehr and KM Schmidt, 'The Economics of Fairness, Reciprocity and Altruism—Experimental Evidence and New Theories' in S Kolm and JM Ythier (eds), *Handbook of the Economics of Giving, Altruism and Reciprocity* (Science Direct 2006) 621.

[51] A Falk et al, 'Testing Theories of Fairness—Intentions Matter' (2008) 62 Games & Econ Behav 287.

[52] ibid.

of the resource and results in greater contribution to public goods.[53] It has also been shown in experiments testing group pressure or peer effect on individual decision-making that choices of people are influenced by the choices of others in the group they are in.[54] People on average seem to benefit socially and psychologically from meeting the expectations of the group.[55]

2.4 Behavioural Perspectives in the International Law Context

The emerging field of behavioural international law provides theoretical grounds and indicative studies that show that bounds on decision-making may operate when actors in international law make decisions concerning international law issues. These studies could, therefore, shed light on decision-making in the field of international insolvency, where countries and implementing institutions (such as bankruptcy courts, authorities, or regulators) make decisions regarding adoption and implementation of universalist solutions.

2.4.1 Behavioural international law

Behavioural international law draws on prospect theory and additional empirical findings regarding biases in decision-making, and asserts the relevance of behavioural insights to international law issues.[56] More broadly, it brings together economic analysis of international law, behavioural economics, and political psychology in international relations, to provide insights for international law.[57] As such, it enhances, complements, and sometimes qualifies economic analysis of international law.[58] The

---

[53] A Falk et al, 'Appropriating the Commons: A Theoretical Explanation' in E Ostrom et al (eds), *The Drama of the Commons* (The National Academies Press 2002).

[54] See eg I Ayres et al, 'Evidence from Two Large Field Experiments that Peer Comparison Feedback Can Reduce Residential Energy Usage' [2009] Natl Bureau of Econ Research, Working Paper No 15386 noted by Galbraith, 'Treaty Options' (n 17) 351. See also E Asch, 'Effects of Group Pressure upon the Modification and Distortion of Judgments' in H Guetzkow (ed), *Groups, Leadership and Men; Research in Human Relations* (Carnegie Press 1951).

[55] R Goodman and D Jinks, 'How to Influence States: Socialization and International Human Rights Law' (2004) 54 Duke L J 621, 640–41.

[56] Behavioural international law as a method for systematically analysing international law issues is a relatively recent endeavour. See eg Galbraith, 'Treaty Options' (n 17); LNS Poulsen and E Aisbett, 'When the Claim Hits: Bilateral Investment Treaties and Bounded Rational Learning' (2013) 65 World Pol 273; LNS Poulsen, 'Bounded Rationality and the Diffusion of Modern Investment Treaties' 58(1) (2013) Int Stud Q 1; EM Hafner-Burton et al, 'Decision Maker Preferences for International Legal Cooperation' (2014) 68 Intl Org 845 <http://fowler.ucsd.edu/decision_maker_preferences_for_international_legal_cooperation.pdf>; van Aaken, 'Behavioral International Law and Economics' (n 9); Broude, 'Behavioral International Law' (n 16). See also, in the context of human rights law, R Goodman and D Jinks, 'How to Influence States' (n 55); R Goodman and D Jinks, *Socializing States: Promoting Human Rights through International Law* (OUP 2013); AK Woods, 'A Behavioral Approach to Human Rights' (2010) 51 Harv J Intl L 51.

[57] van Aaken, 'Behavioral International Law and Economics' (n 9) 424.

[58] Behavioural international law does not purport, though, to provide a 'theory of everything', or a complete theory of international law. Rather, it seeks to add an important methodology to the analysis of international law (Broude, 'Behavioral International Law' (n 16) 1136).

aim is to contribute to a more refined understanding of behaviour and choice in the context of international law by asking whether and to what extent countries and institutions likely act and make decisions based on utility calculus when they 'interact with each other in the process of making international law, abiding by it, violating it, and enforcing it'.[59]

2.4.2 Behavioural biases ascribed to international law actors

A key objection to the behavioural approach to international law is that behavioural theory and empirical experiments focus on the individual, while in international law the country and other group actors are the key players.[60] Arguably, such actors may not be subject to the same cognitive biases as individuals when they make decisions and choices, or the processes on the collective and country level will correct any imperfections in decision-making processes. However, the same criticism regarding ascribing assumptions about choices to collective actors applies to the traditional expected utility analysis, which assumes the country and relevant institutions can be regarded as a unitary actor and decision maker.[61]

Furthermore, on the international level as well, different groups of individuals play a role and may be the decision-making unit.[62] Thus, actors such as judges or elite decision makers interact with international law or make decisions regarding it.[63] In these cases, the behavioural economic analysis concerning the behaviour of individuals applies.[64] Cognitive biases can also be ascribed to collective actors directly, including states as well as non-state actors that make decisions in international law (such as IOs and non-governmental organizations (NGOs)). Experiments in the field of company law, for example, show the existence of biases in corporate actors via the notion of 'attribution'.[65] Behavioural international law scholars observed that it is reasonable to assume that similar biases would be in operation in any corporate actor including a state.[66] Political psychologists have also challenged assumptions that countries maximize power, wealth, or utility and have proposed

---

[59] Broude, 'Behavioral International Law' (n 16) 1104.
[60] J Galbraith, 'Treaty Options' (n 17) 354–55; Broude, 'Behavioral International Law' (n 16) 1121–22; van Aaken, 'Behavioral International Law and Economics' (n 9) 439–41.
[61] Broude, 'Behavioral International Law' (n 16) 1122.
[62] van Aaken, 'Behavioral International Law and Economics' (n 9) 442.
[63] ibid 441–49.
[64] Although elite decision makers may be less prone to biases compared to other individuals as they may be less averse to loss and be more willing to cooperate, they may still be influenced by bounds on rationality (van Aaken, 'Behavioral International Law and Economics' (n 9) 445). See also Galbraith, 'Treaty Options' (n 17) 354–55 (noting, as an example, executives making decisions about treaty options who may be biased towards the status quo written into the treaty, or the head of a state who may opt for the default option assuming that the domestic public will be concerned about losses).
[65] This research has shown that companies take higher risk when they are in a loss frame (ie where their industry performs poorly compared to other industries), namely that they are subject to loss aversion (van Aaken, 'Behavioral International Law and Economics' (n 9) 444).
[66] ibid.

to take cognitive, as well as social, biases into account and include them in inter-national relations theories.[67]

Surely, the application of behavioural insights to countries and other collective actors relevant to international law is more complex, and it is not asserted that any bias found in an individual decision-making context will necessarily apply in the same manner to country (*qua* country) and other institutions' decisions.[68] Countries' choices are shaped through dynamic, evolving, and not necessarily uni-form processes.[69] Yet that complex process may not necessarily result in countries' approaches to international law matters that conform with a perfect utility calcu-lation. Generally, behavioural psychology does not claim that bounds on decision-making manifest themselves in the same manner in all decision makers and in all circumstances, but rather reveal that people on average have certain robust ten-dencies and biases when making judgements and choices.[70] Similarly, on the inter-national level, biases will not necessarily appear equally across countries (in fact it is the prediction that the effect of bounds on decision-making will vary across coun-tries).[71] In addition, within the country, different types of institutions and actors (eg decision makers, regulators, or judges) may be affected by biases and bounds on decision-making in different ways. The 'country approach' may, therefore, be an accumulation of diverging attitudes of institutions within the country where the legislator, for example, may be more conservative and averse to change compared with, for example, the judiciary.[72]

2.4.3 Bounds on decision-making in legal contexts and in international law

Bounds on decision-making have been primarily considered in relation to individuals' choices and judgments in a variety of settings. Thus, many types of decisions made by individuals—concerning investments, retirement plans, buying or selling of property, and the like—are influenced by loss aversion, the endowment effect, and related biases whereby people are usually more concerned about losing than gaining assets.[73]

---

[67] See eg R Jervis, *Perception and Misperception in International Politics* (Princeton University Press 1976); J Gross Stein, 'Psychological Explanations of International Conflict' in W Carlsnaes et al (eds), *Handbook of International Relations* (Sage Publishing 2002).

[68] Broude, 'Behavioral International Law' (n 16) 1124.

[69] ibid 1125 (noting that 'state behavior with respect to international law is the outcome of intricate social, political, administrative, and legislative processes that take place within the state').

[70] Broude, 'Behavioral International Law' (n 16) 1114.

[71] Galbraith, 'Treaty Options' (n 17) 355 (observing that countries have heterogeneity in their interests as well as different levels of susceptibility to various cognitive biases).

[72] Another example is where treaty ratifiers may be more concerned about deviations from the status quo compared with the treaty negotiators who typically are experts in the treaty's subject matter and may therefore have a better understanding of the merits of new concepts and mechanisms (see Chapter 4, section 4.5.3).

[73] Tversky and Kahneman, 'Advances in Prospect Theory' (n 27); Tversky and Kahneman, 'Prospect Theory' (n 7).

Yet evidence about deviations from choices based on the expected utility model has also been taken into account in considering various legal contexts, including tort law, contract law, criminal law, and risk regulation.[74] It has also been shown that legal developments in various fields are often constrained by path dependency, namely the strong influence of history over institutions, which may follow established patterns of behaviour and be resistant to change. Indeed, the idea of path dependency acknowledges the power of the status quo on legal development.[75]

Behavioural international law scholars have observed that countries and other actors in international law as well may be subject to bounds on decision-making, for example endowment dispositions where they need to make decisions involving a change in position or loss of an item of political importance, for example a resource or a territory.[76] Consent to international agreements may not be solely based on objective judgments. Thus, for example, a study that looked at the adoption of bilateral investment treaties by developing countries had found that adherence to such treaties could be explained by bounds on decision-making. It was suggested that adoption of the treaties, which provided investors greater protection compared with the previously applicable rules, was likely based on cognitive faults, specifically the neglect of low probability events even though such events entail high-impact risks.[77]

Decisions may differ depending on whether countries and implementing institutions are in a loss or gain frame and whether a decision requires a change in the status quo. Specifically, the power of the status quo may impede agreements to new concepts on the international level, and actors may tend towards the current state of affairs even if it does not represent the most beneficial approach. Additionally, the way options are presented, and the initial assignments of legal entitlements, may affect the perception of what is fair and may drive decisions whether to take on options in international agreements or whether to dispense with an entitlement.[78]

---

[74] See eg T Kuran and CR Sunstein, 'Availability Cascades and Risk Regulation' (1999) 51 Stan L Rev 683; E Guttel and A Harel, 'Matching Probabilities: The Behavioral Law and Economics of Repeated Behavior' (2005) 72 U Chi L Rev 1197, 1199; Wilson and Abrahamse, 'Does Crime Pay?' (n 45). See also on the application of bounded rationality to various legal problems, Jolls et al, 'A Behavioral Approach to Law and Economics' (n 44); Jolls and Sunstein, 'Debiasing Through Law' (n 9); DC Langevoort, 'Behavioral Theories of Judgement and Decision Making in Legal Scholarship: A Literature Review' (1998) 51 Vand L Rev 1499; CR Sunstein, *Behavioral Law and Economics* (CUP 2000); R Korobkin and TS Ulen, 'Law and Behavioral Science: Removing the Rationality Assumption from Law and Economics' (2000) 88 Calif L Rev 1051, 1055; R Korobkin, 'The Status Quo Bias and Contract Default Rules' (1998) 83 Cornell Law Rev 608; O Ben-Shahar and JAE Pottow, 'On the Stickiness of Default Rules' (2006) 33 Fla St U L Rev 651.

[75] OA Hathaway, 'Path Dependency in the Law: The Courts and Pattern of Legal Change in a Common Law System' (2001) 86 Iowa L Rev 601; Korobkin, 'The Status Quo Bias and Contract Default Rules' (n 74) 608.

[76] Broude, 'Behavioral International Law' (n 16) 1115.

[77] Poulsen and Aisbett, 'When the Claim Hits' (n 56); Poulsen, 'Bounded Rationality and the Diffusion of Modern Investment Treaties' (n 56). See also van Aaken, 'Behavioral International Law and Economics' (n 9) 459.

[78] Galbraith, 'Treaty Options' (n 17) 309; van Aaken, 'Behavioral International Law and Economics' (n 9) 463–68.

Thus, a study that combined empirical observations with behavioural insights and looked at adherence to options in treaties could show the possible effect of biases on decision-making on the international level. It was found that ratifying countries have accepted dispute resolution mechanisms in treaties (the jurisdiction of the International Court of Justice (ICJ)) at much higher rates when presented with opt-out (default) clauses than with opt-in clauses.[79] On average, where countries had the implied authority opt out of the ICJ jurisdiction, 95 per cent continue to accept it; where countries had the explicit right to opt out, 80 per cent continue to accept it. In contrast, where countries could explicitly opt in to ICJ jurisdiction, only a mere 5 per cent did so on average.[80] These findings correlated with the experiments showing that individuals tend to be biased in favour of whatever option is framed as the status quo,[81] and thus could be explained by the powerful effect of framing and the overwhelming preference of default options.[82] The findings rebut the assumption that people always make choices that advance their interests, and thus that framing should not matter and default rules should not affect choices. Importantly, these results are consistent with the prospect theory and show the apparent operation of biases in actions concerning international law.

Loss aversion can also explain issues related to compliance with international law. Thus, it has been observed that countries may care more—or less—about their reputation depending on whether they are in a loss or gain frame and whether loss of reputation is considered certain, affecting the extent to which they may be willing to cooperate with other countries and comply with international norms. Specifically, it was observed that the fact of dearth of treaty exits can be explained by loss aversion, namely the tendency to want to prevent a decline in reputation more than there may be an interest in increasing (ie gaining) more reputation.[83]

2.4.4 Bounded willpower and short-term policies

The application of bounded willpower on the international level and generally to collective actors is not as straightforward as in the case of individuals taking day-to-day actions and decisions. However, it has been observed that functionally equivalent issues of short-termism, time inconsistency, and difficulty in making credible and long-term commitments arise also in the context of decision-making relevant to international law and international relations.[84]

---

[79] The study investigated opt-in clauses and optional protocols, which allow countries to opt in to additional commitments, and opt-out clauses, which allow countries to opt out of certain commitments (Galbraith, 'Treaty Options' (n 17) 313).

[80] ibid 314.

[81] EJ Johnson and D Goldstein, 'Do Defaults Save Lives' (2003) 302 Science 1338. See also Chapter 3, section 3.3.1 where the effect of default rules is considered regarding the choice of sources for international law.

[82] Galbraith, 'Treaty Options' (n 17) 349, 352–53. As will be discussed in section 2.4.5, a peer effect may have also contributed to these robust results.

[83] van Aaken, 'Behavioral International Law and Economics' (n 9) 477. Compliance issues are discussed in detail in Chapter 5.

[84] van Aaken, 'Behavioral International Law and Economics' (n 9) 431–32.

Behavioural international law scholars note as an example the possible problem of governments exploiting their power for their own gains, such as re-election, following short-term policies in conflict with long-term, more optimal, solutions.[85] Thus, in the real world, actors in the international realm might not cooperate and might take actions that serve short-term interests even though such actions do not reflect the desired solution that is in the countries' and relevant stakeholders' best long-term interests, including the risk of decline in reputation and the possible retaliation by other countries as a response to the lack of cooperation. In this regard, behavioural insights enrich the expected utility theory. As was noted above, that theory has led scholars to observe that the resolution of global commons situations on the international level is insurmountable. However, behavioural international law also points to the effect of bounds on self-interest inclinations (discussed next) that can contribute to an effective resolution of complex coordination problems.

2.4.5 Bounded self-interest and the peer effect on international cooperation

The assumption of expected utility theory is that standard self-regarding preferences guide countries and other actors in making choices related to adherence to treaties, treaty design, international cooperation, compliance with international law, and so forth.[86] Yet experiments show that self-interest is qualified by fairness preferences. Such preferences may not be simply assumed regarding countries *qua* countries.[87] Countries as such cannot care or act altruistically; yet, it has been observed that a country may expect fair treatment or act altruistically towards other countries as a result of the country's internal mechanisms. For example, decision makers within the country may act in ways that manifest other-regarding inclinations and such acts may be attributed to the country; or preferences of individuals within the country may influence the country's choices.[88]

Other-regarding preferences can specifically explain approaches to collective action, multilateral cooperation, and global commons problems, which are at the core of international law.[89] It has been observed that countries and implementing institutions can develop fairness preferences and expect adherence to certain behaviour by others, at which point a more altruistic multinational cooperation by participating actors can be expected.[90] Not only does the outcome of others' behaviour play a role, but also the perception of the legitimacy and fairness of the action.[91]

In the international context, too, cognitive pressures can result in an inclination of countries to conform their behaviour to community expectations.[92] The

---

[85] ibid 431–32.   [86] ibid 431.

[87] Broude, 'Behavioral International Law' (n 16) 1124.

[88] van Aaken, 'Behavioral International Law and Economics' (n 9) 470.

[89] ibid 469–70.   [90] ibid 470.

[91] A Falk et al, 'Testing Theories of Fairness' (n 51); A Falk and U Fischbacher, 'A Theory of Reciprocity' (2006) 54 Games & Econ Behav 293.

[92] Goodman and Jinks, 'How to Influence States' (n 55) 640–41.

empirical research noted above concerning adherence to options in treaties showed, for example, how the peer effect likely exacerbated the operation of other robust biases affecting the level of adherence to the options. It was found in that study that countries seem to have been significantly influenced by the way options were presented, which could be explained by the robust impact of the status quo bias and the effect of framing.[93] The peer effect provided an additional explanation for the robustness of the results. Because information about participation was readily available, it was likely that the fact that certain countries early on followed the option (perceived as the status quo), resulted in more countries taking the same route.[94]

2.5 Decision-Making Biases Affecting Choices in Cross-Border Insolvency

The behavioural perspective concerning decision-making processes highlights the fact that choices and decisions in real world circumstances are subject to biases. Behavioural international law shows that cognitive biases may also play a role regarding international law. Actors on the international level making choices concerning international law issues may be affected by loss aversion, by the tendency to prefer things to stay as they are, by the way options are framed, and by perception of entitlements. They may also act with short-term considerations in mind and may find it difficult to cooperate when multiple interests are at stake. At the same time, actors may not always act self-servingly, and they may be positively affected by the behaviour of others.

The existence of cognitive biases and the fact that they can influence choices related to international law—particularly where international law attempts to address complex coordination issues, where contemplated solutions generate long-term benefits, and where they involve a degree of sovereignty loss—suggests that such biases could be crucial in understanding the international insolvency choices. Specifically, loss aversion, status quo and related effects, as well as short-termism may explain territorialist tendencies of countries and different implementing institutions. Thus, choices of territorialism might reflect bounds on decision-making and might not necessarily represent what is most desirable. At the same time, the ability to develop fairness preferences and the peer effect support the contention that modified universalist solutions are feasible and that such existing preferences by important actors have likely contributed to the emergence of modified universalism as a dominant approach.

---

[93] See also Chapter 4, section 4.5 for a discussion of the design of options in treaties and other instruments.
[94] Galbraith, 'Treaty Options' (n 17) 353–54.

2.5.1 Loss aversion, status quo, and perceived endowments in cross-border insolvency

Loss aversion can be a plausible explanation for why certain countries have not yet adopted more modified universalist approaches, and why implementation of universalist aspects in existing frameworks might be slower, or not fully consistent, or involve some degree of lip service. Adherence to modified universalism solutions requires a certain loss of sovereignty and of control over locally registered companies, locally situated stakeholders, or local assets, including where modified universalism requires deference to foreign law, or the transferring of domestic assets to foreign jurisdictions, to achieve a global collective process.[95]

Such expected outcomes of modified universalism may be perceived as a sure loss, thus exacerbating the inclination to guard against it. Even if modified universalism is understood as potentially resulting in gains, countries and their implementing institutions may be less inclined to take risks to make more gains. As we have seen, people generally have asymmetrical attitudes towards gains and losses, and their perceived utility is increased less by gains than by losses averted, especially as the gains from cooperation and from modified universalism solutions may also seem uncertain and ambiguous. The gains from cooperation may be less vivid compared with the perceived losses. For example, a court in a host country that is asked to turn over assets to a main process abroad, to the frustration of a local creditor, may observe a concrete loss today, while the benefits in terms of increased international trade, certainty, and so forth are more difficult to appreciate.

A negative perception of modified universalism is expected particularly where the country's reference point is a state of affairs that is generally territorialist: namely, if the country does not have an established internationalist approach in its domestic methods for addressing cross-border insolvency. Because utility is driven more by relative change than by the final states of welfare, and is also affected by context and experience, loss of sovereignty and control might loom larger for countries with a territorialist history. Thus, to avoid the perceived certain loss of ability to control and protect local interests, countries may prefer passing the opportunity that their stakeholders will benefit from global beneficial solutions in future cases and that the economy in general will benefit from increased international trade and investment. Especially where adherence to modified universalism requires taking an action such as signing an agreement or joining a new global framework,[96] countries perceiving modified universalism as involving a change and a loss may avoid this option and stick with the current situation.

In addition, countries may be strongly influenced by their legal history and tend to perpetuate the status quo, exacerbating the difficulty of shifting to more universalist approaches. There is some indication that countries associated with the civil law tradition or that have been traditionally more territorially oriented (and even if economically influential) have also been relatively slow in adapting to new universalist frameworks. Although countries such as The Republic of Korea and Japan have

---

[95] See Chapter 1, sections 1.2.3 and 1.3.2.   [96] See also Chapter 4, section 4.3.4.

adopted the global cross-border insolvency framework developed by the United Nations Commission on International Trade Law (UNCITRAL), the Model Law on Cross-border Insolvency (the MLCBI), which is generally associated with modi-fied universalism,[97] some important aspects of that model were not adopted in these jurisdictions. In both Japan and The Republic of Korea, new legislation replaced a previous territorialist regime. Yet the new legislation was more constrained compared with the MLCBI, for example where it imposed more onerous conditions on recognition and relief.[98] There is also indication of a territorial tendency in the application of the MLCBI in these countries and a general concern or even 'fear' of universalism.[99] The reluctance of other countries at different stages to enact the MLCBI was noted earlier in Chapter 1: for example, Singapore, which has had (in the recent past) territorialist elements embedded in its legislation.[100] The movement from an existing territorial approach to a more universalist solution can be diffi-cult, considering behavioural constraints, even if utility calculation suggests that it is most desirable.[101] Such movements do take place, though, as can be seen in the relatively large number of civil law jurisdictions that have adopted the MLCBI.[102]

---

[97] See Chapter 1, section 1.4.4 and the detailed assessment in Chapter 6, section 6.2.2.

[98] See Chapter 1, section 1.4.5.

[99] I Mevorach, 'On the Road to Universalism: A Comparative and Empirical Study of UNCITRAL Model Law on Cross-Border Insolvency' (2011) 12 EBOR 517, 549; M Han, 'Recognition of Insolvency Effects of a Foreign Insolvency Proceeding: Focusing on the Effect of Discharge' in MP Ramaswamay and J Ribeiro (eds), *Trade Development Through Harmonization of Commercial Law* (New Zealand Association for Comparative Law 2015) 345; S Takahashi, 'The Reality of the Japanese Legal System for Cross-Border Insolvency Driven by Fear of Universalism' (2011) 75 <https://www.iiiglobal. org/node/124> (noting that the analysis of the Japanese system reveals a 'very cautious attitude towards the Model Law and its universalism', and that considering its 'history, culture, geography, and language' Japan's cautious attitude can be explained by a ' "fear" of universalism').

[100] Companies Act 2006 (ch 50) Singapore s 377 (3)(c). As noted in Chapter 1, section 1.4.3, Singapore had later decided to start the legislative process to enact the MLCBI, and in 2017 its Parliament passed a bill that overhauled its insolvency legislation by, inter alia, adopting the MLCBI.

[101] It might also be argued that civil law countries have considered this model to be common law-oriented, where, for example, it mandates judicial cooperation and communication that surpasses the traditional judicial role in many civil law jurisdictions and therefore were reluctant to adopt it. In addition, although the majority of countries that have enacted the MLCBI are civil law jurisdictions, the majority of civil law jurisdictions have not enacted the MLCBI (Note by the IBA Insolvency Section Delegation to UNCITRAL Working Group V based on an article by Gregor Baer, Insolvency Section Co-Chair, published in *Business Law International* (January 2016): 'International Insolvency Convention: Issues, Options and Feasibility Considerations' (with the publisher's permission) para 50 <https://www. ibanet.org/LPD/Insolvency_Section/Insolvency_Section/Projects.aspx#uninsolvencyconvention>). However, the discrepancies between civil law and common law attitudes are more likely a result of path dependency and the status quo bias, which are also linked with loss aversion. Indeed, it has been similarly argued that the Japanese law and the MLCBI differ because the MLCBI is based on common law, and therefore the Japanese version of the model is modified according to a civil law regime (K Yamamoto, 'New Japanese Legislation on Cross-Border Insolvency as Compared to the UNCITRAL Model Law' (2002) 11(2) Int Insolv Rev 67). Yet, 'in reality, Japanese law makes substantive departures from the MLCBI that have nothing to do with the civil-versus-common law issue ... These differences are probably less likely to be due to Japan's desire to limit the discretion of judges in its civil-law trad-ition (indeed, Japanese judges appear to have more discretion at the recognition stage than their American counterparts) than to Japan's substantive preference for territoriality' (AM Kipnis, 'Beyond UNCITRAL: Alternatives to Universality in Translational Insolvency' (2008) 36 Denv J Intl L & Poly 155, 162–63).

[102] About two thirds of the enacting states are associated with civil law traditions.

Significant economies in Europe and elsewhere have also so far refrained from taking action by adopting the MLCBI's global framework.[103] It is difficult to ascertain the reasons for the reluctance of countries such as France or the Netherlands to join the MLCBI regime, especially in view of their active participation in the design of the framework (through contribution to deliberations at UNCITRAL). This inaction in relation to the MLCBI by European countries can be at least partly explained by a status quo bias—the tendency to want things to stay relatively the same—and the influence of legal tradition, hence the more constrained development of the law primarily based on domestic mechanisms.[104] As noted above, the status quo bias operates more generally even in the absence of gain/loss framing and may also be a result of fear of commitment to new regimes. It has been observed in this respect that the status quo bias has distinct implications for the development of legal systems, both domestic and international, because actors prefer to keep the law as it is even when the law lags behind changes including commercial developments.[105]

Moreover, common law countries, even where they have been generally internationally oriented and influential in the field of cross-border insolvency, have also presented certain inclinations to adhere to traditional rules notwithstanding the trend of modified universalism. The Supreme Court of the United Kingdom, for example, in *Rubin v Eurofinance* preferred not to allow a departure from the local traditional law and not to extend the recognition and enforcement of foreign judgments where the creditor was not subject to the foreign forum under the general domestic private international law.[106] The Court noted that 'the introduction of judge-made law extending the recognition and enforcement of foreign judgments would be only to the detriment of UK businesses without any corresponding benefit.'[107] The Court reached a similar conclusion based on the legislation enacting the MLCBI.[108] Even though modified universalism has greater expected utility, departure from existing entitlements may be perceived as a loss—in this case, to local businesses, or in other cases local assets may be perceived as endowments—and be given greater weight compared to the long-term gains. There may be more focus on keeping local assets

---

[103] See Chapter 1, section 1.4.5.
[104] In the Netherlands, for example, in the absence of a treaty and where the EU regime does not apply, the assumption has been that foreign proceedings only have a territorial effect. The domestic law through Supreme Court judgments gradually developed the concept of limited territoriality allowing recognition subject to various conditions (see eg *Yukos*, Supreme Court, September 13, 2013, ECLI:NL:HR:2013:BZ5668).
[105] Broude, 'Behavioral International Law' (n 16) 1140; Korobkin, 'The Status Quo Bias and Contract Default Rules' (n 74).
[106] *Rubin and another v Eurofinance SA and others and New Cap Reinsurance Corporation (in Liquidation) and another v AE Grant and others* [2012] UKSC 46.
[107] ibid [130], per Lord Collins.
[108] ibid [133]–[144], per Lord Collins. See also A Walters, 'Modified Universalisms & the Role of Local Legal Culture in the Making of Cross-border Insolvency Law' Am Bankr L J (*forthcoming*) available at SSRN: <https://papers.ssrn.com/sol3/papers.cfm?abstract_id=3084117> (noting that UK judicial mindset and recent decisions concerning cross-border insolvency 'show powerfully how fidelity to pre-existing local law has shaped the UK's reception of the Model Law').

than on acquiring assets that are situated abroad.[109] Furthermore, the ability to impose the country's laws regarding local assets, locally incorporated companies, and local constituencies may also be perceived as an existing entitlement (endowment) of sovereignty and vested rights. Thus, sovereign actors may be disinclined to defer to foreign laws and prefer imposing the country's laws even where the interests of local stakeholders are not at stake.[110]

The combined effects of loss aversion, status quo bias, and endowment effect might have also contributed to the state of affairs of cross-border insolvency of multinational financial institutions (MFIs), where progress on the global level has so far been relatively slow and the current tendency is still towards state-centric solutions.[111] Thus, notwithstanding the devastating effect of the global financial crisis and predictions that it will be transformative in terms of increased global financial governance, it has been observed that the crisis has been in fact 'a strangely conservative event'.[112] International organizations have noted, with respect to the potential development of a cross-border insolvency regime for MFIs, that: '[A]t least in the short term, it is very unlikely that all key jurisdictions will agree to sacrifice the degree of national sovereignty necessary to implement full universality.'[113] Here universalism is linked to and framed as a loss, namely a sacrifice of state sovereignty. The concern about losses and the clinging to the status quo in the way cross-border insolvency of MFIs has been developing thus far may have been further exacerbated by a negative peer effect, whereby leading economies have been adopting

---

[109] The reluctance of offshore jurisdictions—where companies tend to register but often do their business or have their functional headquarters elsewhere—to adopt the MLCBI and specifically to subscribe to the notion of 'the centre of main interests' (COMI) can also at least be partially explained by the effect of loss aversion. The loss of control over locally registered companies in circumstances where the actual centre is in a foreign forum, is likely given significant weight, even though under a territorialist framework these jurisdictions may gain little by retaining control over locally registered companies, if most assets are located abroad and if these jurisdictions cannot get hold of such assets. Such non-participation in a global framework for cross-border insolvency can be contrasted with non-adherence to international standards imposed by the global financial system where offering weak or lax regulation to market participants may be a rational choice as it can attract capital to offshore financial centres or other small, capital poor countries (C Brummer, *Soft Law and the Global Financial System, Rule Making in the 21st Century* (CUP 2015) 138)). It is doubtful that lack of cooperation with a collective global system for cross-border insolvency has a similar effect.

[110] JAE Pottow, 'Greed and Pride in International Bankruptcy: The Problems of and Proposed Solutions to "Local Interests"' (2006) 104 Mich L Rev 1899, 1922–25 (providing an example of deviation from universalism by the Canadian Supreme Court in *Antwerp Bulkcarriers NV v Holt Cargo Systems Inc* ([2001] SCR 951 Can), which demonstrates how sovereign actors have 'pride' and, thus, an inclination, which is separate from the protection of local stakeholders—in this case Canadian stakeholders did not require protection—to enforce local laws as a matter of sovereign rights regarding assets located within the country's territory).

[111] See Chapter 1, section 1.4.5 and Chapter 6, section 6.3.

[112] E Helleiner, *The Status Quo Crisis. Global Financial Governance after the 2008 Financial Meltdown* (OUP 2014) 2 (arguing that this lack of significant progress is explained by the enduring state-centric foundations of the global financial governance and the specific configuration of power and politics among and within influential countries).

[113] International Monetary Fund, 'Resolution of Cross-Border Banks—A Proposed Framework for Enhanced Coordination' (11 June 2010) para 28 <https://www.imf.org/external/np/pp/eng/2010/061110.pdf>.

ring-fencing state-centric approaches.[114] Such approaches have likely generated certain expectations and have influenced the general nationally driven approach.

Countries might also lack the ability to consider the benefits of modified universalism and to act upon such calculations. Choices of modified universalism may be influenced by various factors, specifically by the inequality of systems and problems of institutional capacity. Certain economies experience institutional constraints and do not yet enjoy a fully developed commercial and insolvency system.[115] Countries may have other more pressing issues on decision makers' agendas. Addressing the problem of cross-border insolvency is often of secondary priority to the development of the domestic foundations of the insolvency and the broader commercial law regime.[116] There may also be information asymmetries among countries, and decisions may be influenced by forceful special interest lobbies.[117]

Yet even if we assume well-meaning and well-informed decisions by interested countries, and even where countries find the resources to address cross-border insolvency, the result could still deviate from an approach that would have better served both the global and local interests. In practice, developing regimes that succeed in putting cross-border insolvency reform on their agenda often address (or have addressed) the matter half-way, introducing improved regimes, yet not fully embracing the modified universalist approach in concrete legislation. South Africa, for example, adopted the MLCBI early in 2000, yet introduced conditions into the regime that meant that the provisions of the MLCBI have not been given effect in the jurisdiction.[118] India's insolvency regime went through important renovations in 2016, and in the process it considered joining the MLCBI or otherwise addressing the cross-border aspects of insolvency, yet thus far the adopted provisions have made only modest improvements.[119] Such cautious approach can be explained by lack of

[114] See Chapter 1, section 1.4.2.
[115] The problem of institutional incapacity and its impact on compliance with the cross-border insolvency system is explored in Chapter 5, section 5.3.1.
[116] See Chapter 5, section 5.3.1.
[117] Consider, for example, the difficulties in taking internationally coordinated actions to combat fiscal or corporate misbehaviour in offshore countries. A notable example from the field of insolvency is the immense difficulty that the international community has encountered, as a result of strong pressure by the industry, when it attempted, through deliberations at UNCITRAL, to address the unfairness and inefficiencies created by international standards on the treatment of financial contracts that protect rights of counterparties to derivatives and other financial contracts at the expense of the stakeholders as a whole (RJ Mokal, 'Liquidity, Systemic Risk, and the Bankruptcy Treatment of Financial Contracts' (2015) 10(1) Brook J Corp Fin & Com L 15). See also the problem of rent-seeking by lawyers and other insolvency professionals who may prefer territorialist approaches where they can benefit from localization of proceedings (noted in Chapter 1, n 42).
[118] South Africa included a reciprocity condition requiring it to designate relevant countries that could invoke the MLCBI provisions, yet such designation never took place (South Arica Cross-Border Insolvency Act 42 of 2000 s 2). See also AL Smith and A Boraine, 'Crossing Borders into South African Insolvency Law: From the Roman-Dutch Jurists to the Uncitral Model Law' (2002) ABI L Rev 138.
[119] As noted in Chapter 1, India's regime provides for reciprocal cooperative arrangements to be agreed with foreign institutions. The calls to adopt the MLCBI were not taken on board at this stage. Leading experts (including the Eradi and Irani Committees) have noted the fact that this approach conflicted with the country's best interest; see eg statements by Sumant Batra, chairman of South Asian law firm Kesar Das and a past president of INSOL International: 'In the absence of provisions dealing with cross-border insolvency, courts in India have struggled to deal with the plethora of international insolvency issues arising before them. This has also served as a deterrent for foreign investors in India.

readiness of the system. Countries may legitimately focus first on addressing more basic deficiencies in their legal system supporting trade and creditor–debtor relationship, before they may start dealing with cross-border insolvency. Yet, on top of such system constraints and prioritizations, the reluctance to accept universalist solutions more robustly is more likely a manifestation of bounds on decision-making, specifically loss aversion, the endowment effect, and the clinging to the status quo, than a choice of option that is the most optimal for the jurisdiction. Furthermore, where emerging economies have had lesser chances to interact with peers in cross-border insolvency cases compared to other countries, a more self-regarding and less cooperative approach can be expected, exacerbating the effect of the territorial biases (see section 2.5.3).

Thus, countries in different positions, both developed and developing regimes, and their various implementing institutions, are likely exposed to varying levels of concern about loss of sovereignty or control when facing decisions regarding how to address the problem of cross-border insolvency. They may give excessive weight to perceived losses and measure them against a current state of affairs. Furthermore, countries and implementing institutions may be averse to changing their current position and departing with perceived endowments, although not necessarily in the same way. Choices of different actors that deviate from the normatively desired approach can be explained by the operation of these biases.

2.5.2 Territorialist short-termism

The phenomenon of bounded willpower can further explain asset ring-fencing, limited cooperation, and other nationally driven approaches in cross-border insolvency. On the domestic level, the insolvency common pool problem applies to the debtor's creditors and is usually resolved through enforcement of mandatory mechanisms that stop individual enforcement, address preferential transactions, and provide a breathing space for the business. However, in cross-border insolvency, in the absence of sufficient coordination, each implicated country may attempt to ring-fence assets for the benefit of local stakeholders, driven by short-term concerns. Enforcement on the global level is limited and is largely decentralized: thus, even where coordination frameworks exist, there are many opportunities to take advantage of other parties and act self-servingly to protect local interests and disregard the impact of actions taken locally on interests outside the jurisdiction. Countries and implementing institutions such as regulators, resolution authorities, or courts may focus on short-term rewards. They may be inclined to satisfy the electorate, the local employees, or other stakeholders even if it is at the expense of long-term gains or risks a potential loss of reputation for the country and its institutions.[120]

The absence of adequate provisions to deal with cross-border insolvency can impede India's growth to enhance and enrich its economic status in a drastic manner' (*Global Restructuring Review*, 'Indian Committee Clears New Bankruptcy Law after Overseas Provisions Added' (29 April 2016)).

[120] Like other biases, short-termism may affect different institutions in different ways, also depending on the type of debtor in issue. For example, countries' regulators may be concerned about satisfying the

The prevalence of national interests and neglect of due consideration of implications on foreign interests during the global financial crisis can be explained by such a short-termism weakness. The notorious example of the handling of the failure of Icelandic banks is illustrative.[121] There, the Icelandic government has enacted legislation favouring local stakeholders (the domestic depositors) notwithstanding an EU approach under which supervision and deposit guarantee in relation to all stakeholders, in the home and host jurisdictions, were supposed to be controlled and guaranteed by the home country.[122] By taking such a territorialist approach, Iceland as the home jurisdiction preferred to focus on local interests, notwithstanding the reputational damage this policy choice entailed. As has been observed, the financial crisis was 'full of examples of national interests being preferred'.[123] In the large-scale cross-border insolvency of *Lehman Brothers*, the actions taken by the US authorities in the initial period after the group's collapse seemed predominantly nationally-driven, where bridge support was given to a US subsidiary (Lehman Brothers Inc) but not to the holding company (Lehman Brothers Holding Inc), which meant that its foreign subsidiaries were pushed into insolvency.[124]

It has been observed that these actions by governments were manifestations of pressures on national politicians and regulators who 'may well be willing to take the mild reputational hit of *ex post* international rebuke if its standing with the do-mestic electorate is enhanced by its conduct of the resolution process'.[125] Arguably, it was clear in these cases what was at stake and the approach taken 'was not driven by misunderstandings but by national imperatives'.[126] These so-called na-tional imperatives are, however, likely manifestations of short-term considerations where in the face of a crisis the long-term commitments, which were based on a global approach to multinational default designed to benefit all participants, were abandoned. It is also expected that the short-termism bias is particularly strong in the MFIs context where cases are rarer; thus, the concern about potential losses in future cases is less vivid and protecting local depositors or the taxpayer can generate surer immediate gains.

---

electorate, particularly in financial institutions' crises, while judges presiding over a commercial cross-border insolvency may be inclined to protect the local stakeholders.

[121] Noted earlier in Chapter 1, section 1.4.5.

[122] PL Davies, 'Resolution of Cross-Border Banking Groups', in M Haentjens and B Wessels (eds), *Research Handbook on Crisis Management in the Banking Sector* (Elgar, Research Handbooks in Financial Law Series 2015) 263.

[123] ibid. See also JM Edwards, 'A Model Law Framework for the Resolution of G-SIFIs' (2012) 7 Cap Mkts L J 122, 131–33; I Mevorach, 'Beyond the Search for Certainty: Addressing the Cross-Border Resolution Gap' (2015) 10(1) Brook J Corp Fin & Com L 183, 191.

[124] The entry into insolvency of the holding company meant that the central cash management system operated by the holding company stopped and cash was not transferred to the foreign subsidiaries. The UK subsidiary (Lehman Brothers International Europe) that was otherwise solvent found itself illiquid as a result and entered insolvency proceedings. The value of the subsidiary was reduced, injuring the subsidiary's creditors and benefiting the creditors of the holding company (Davies, 'Resolution of Cross-Border Banking Groups' (n 122) 263–64).

[125] ibid 274. See also S Gleeson, *International Regulation of Banking Capital and Risk Requirements* (2nd edn, OUP 2012) 418.

[126] Davies, 'Resolution of Cross-Border Banking Groups' (n 122) 274.

As noted above, deviations from modified universalist solutions can also be explained by the incompleteness of the system governing international insolvencies, including a system in which not all aspects of the emerging norms of modified universalism are clearly contemplated in international instruments.[127] If the duties of the home country regarding stakeholders in host jurisdictions and the safeguards contemplated by modified universalism are not universally applicable, countries are less likely to trust a system imposing global solutions.[128] It may, nonetheless, be the case that even when instruments based on modified universalism become more complete, there will be attempts to circumvent them and avoid modified universalist approaches. Thus, the ability to complete the system adequately also requires an appreciation of the desirability of modified universalism, wherein short-termism and the other behavioural tendencies might contribute to territorialist inclinations.

2.5.3 Fairness preferences and peer pressure in cross-border insolvency

As we have seen, experiments show that people can be strongly motivated by other-regarding preferences and develop an expectation of fair treatment from others, including when they are more exposed to clear information about the intentions of their peers. People are influenced not only by material gains but also by their understanding and perceptions of others' actions. Such perceptions can foster cooperation including in common pool scenarios, and they can have implications on the international level. These behavioural forces may also play a role in how countries and implementing institutions approach international insolvency problems.

The expansion of international trade and globalization that has naturally generated more instances of regional and global multinational defaults has meant that increasingly international actors have had more experiences and greater exposures to their peers handling international insolvencies in other countries. In particular, the development of international frameworks for cross-border insolvency have not only increased the exposure to modified universalism but also assisted in acclimating countries to its norms.[129]

Additionally, the growth in attempting direct cooperation and communication between judges presiding over cross-border insolvencies in different countries[130] seems to have significantly contributed to a favourable approach to universalism through genuine cooperation with foreign participants. In the important decisions in the *Nortel* case,[131] for example, where the American and Canadian courts

---

[127] See section 2.1.

[128] See also Chapter 5, sections 5.2.5 and 5.3.1–5.3.2 for a discussion of the effect of lack of trust in foreign participants and foreign systems on compliance with a system based on modified universalism.

[129] JAE Pottow, 'Procedural Incrementalism: A Model for International Bankruptcy' (2005) 45 Va J Intl L 935, 988 (noting that the MLCBI provided countries 'the chance to desensitize gradually to other states' bankruptcy systems').

[130] See Chapter 1, sections 1.4.3 and 1.4.4.

[131] *In re Nortel Networks, Inc*, 532 BR 494 (Bankr D Del 2015); *Re Nortel Networks Corp*, 2015 ONSC 2987 (Ont SCJ [Commercial List]). The decisions in the co-trials in the Canadian and US proceedings have been described as 'monumental' (JL Pottow, 'Two Cheers for Universalism: Nortel's

conducted a highly coordinated joint trial, the presiding judges managed to eventually reach a consistent conclusion regarding the complex question of the allocation of the estates among the stakeholders in the different countries involved in the process. This outcome was probably possible largely because of the relationship the judges have developed through their understanding of the different challenges each judge had to face in their respective jurisdiction. Thus, not only had the cooperation allowed them to exchange thoughts and ideas, but importantly the judges have 'grown to respect each other'.[132] At the same time, deviations from such cooperative approach have growingly encountered disappointment, not only by way of academic criticism, for example following the UK Supreme Court decision in *Rubin v Eurofinance*,[133] but also in terms of the reaction in practice. After *Rubin*, for example, the international community had set to address the potential gap in the MLCBI regarding enforcement of insolvency-related judgments.[134]

Further interactions that are also broader in terms of multinational participation have taken place in recent years between judges involved in international insolvencies, including through the work of IOs that have been organizing international colloquia, and between regulators of different countries.[135] These interactions have perhaps contributed to the development of mutual trust and fairness expectations between these actors, thereby increasing the success of modified universalism.[136] Peer effect, too, has probably contributed to the general movement in the direction of modified universalism and thus to its growing dominance. The MLCBI, which generally reflects a modified universalist approach, has initially been adopted by a limited number of jurisdictions. Only a few countries adopted it shortly after it was endorsed by UNCITRAL in 1997 (notably, South Africa, Japan, and Mexico in 2000). Yet, by the mid-2000s it was embraced by a few additional significant economies, including the United States (2005) and the United Kingdom (2006). Once a good number of leading economies had adopted the MLCBI, there was also more leverage when IOs made efforts to introduce the MLCBI into legal systems, especially in developing countries.[137] Consequently, in the decade between 2005 and 2015, more than thirty additional countries enacted legislation based on the MLCBI.[138]

Nifty Novelty' in JP Sarra and Justice B Romaine (eds), *Annual Review of Insolvency Law* (Carswell 2015) 333).

[132] JL Pottow, 'Two Cheers for Universalism: Nortel's Nifty Novelty' (n 131) 353–55. Indeed, the courts have also recognized the highly contested nature of this case with highly litigious parties and thus the need to put an end to years of expensive litigation.

[133] See Chapter 1, n 282.   [134] See Chapter 6, section 6.2.3.

[135] See Chapter 1, n 262 and Chapter 5, n 74 and accompanying text.

[136] It has been argued that in insolvency, the courts play a major role, however judges are not repeat players and they operate in 'one-shot games' (F Tung, 'Is International Bankruptcy Possible?' (2001) 23 Mich J Intl L 31, 82). The experience in international insolvency has shown, however, a considerable degree of effective interaction. See also Chapter 5, section 5.2.5 for a discussion of the role of mutual trust in promoting compliance with a modified universalist system.

[137] See further Chapter 5, section 5.3.1 for a discussion of the role of IOs in promoting compliance with the cross-border insolvency system.

[138] See Chapter 1, section 1.4.4.

Still, certain countries have had less exposure to peers and fewer chances to develop mutual expectations and the level of trust and understanding of the operation of cooperative solutions in cross-border insolvency, which would lead to closer cooperation and more ease in becoming parties to global frameworks based on modified universalism. It was noted above how some countries have adopted the MLCBI, yet included requirements about reciprocity likely concerned with providing access and recognition to other participants without receiving sure and clear benefits. Other important economies, for example China, have not yet embraced the MLCBI or sufficiently renovated their cross-border insolvency regimes in a manner fully compatible with modified universalism.[139] Limited exposure to positive peer pressure and fewer interactions that could lead to fairness preferences provide an additional plausible explanation of such choices.

2.6 Addressing Territorialist Biases

Different tendencies are thus expectedly in operation when dealing with cross-border insolvencies, and not all inclinations of countries and of different institutions within countries may pull in the same direction. It is also difficult to predict in precise terms how certain biases, such as status quo and loss aversion, would operate on and be influenced by other effects such as peer influence and expectations of fairness. It should also be recalled that findings about biases refer to average behaviour, but individual differences in the operation of these biases also exist. This may also be the case between collective actors, who may show such differences. In addition, actors may perceive endowments and the reference point in dissimilar ways. The status quo concerning the level of territoriality or universality is different in different countries where certain countries already had some level of internationalism concerning cross-border insolvency while others have been initially more territorial, and with less experience in terms of cross-jurisdictional interaction in insolvency cases.

However, extant territorialist approaches may be explained by certain robust biases that are manifested in many different settings. Because people are loss averse, overweighting sure losses, calculating losses by reference to perceived endowments and generally tending to stick to the status quo, clinging to territorialist solutions is natural even where it is not the most desirable approach. Such inclinations are likely exacerbated where countries and institutions are faced with possibilities to enjoy short-term benefits. Thus, the behavioural account of territorialism is more plausible as a general explanation of territorialist inclinations than an explanation based on purely economic choices. Territorialist approaches are likely more often based on bounds on decision-making than on objective calculations of utilities (losses and gains over time).

At the same time, the assumption of the expected utility model about self-regarding behaviour is also overstated and over-pessimistic, as people can develop

---

[139] See also X Gong, 'To Recognise or Not to Recognise? Comparative Study of Lehman Brothers Cases in Mainland China and Taiwan' (2013) 10(4) ICR 240.

other-regarding approaches and be influenced by the behaviour of the group. Thus, even on the international level where enforcement is limited, it may be possible to promote cooperation. Consequently, real-world territorialist inclinations do not necessarily imply the desirability of an approach based on territorialism, nor do they suggest that cooperation and modified universalism solutions are impossible. Negative inclinations may be alleviated, and positive biases enhanced. With regard to individuals, there are for example various programmes, including the classical 'nudges' to tackle temptations and overcome bounded willpower.[140] On the international level, we have noted, for example, how the way options are provided in treaties could induce adherence to its provisions.[141]

Thus, the normative implication of the analysis of actors' choices and behaviour in international insolvency is that cross-border insolvency law should not attempt to yield to territorialism. It should not seek to find compromises to take account of what might be considered as actual territorialist preferences hidden by paying lip service to universalism. Yet, the cross-border insolvency system should not expect a smooth, gradual adherence and full application of a universalist regime either. Instead, it should embrace a debiasing role and attempt to overcome and address bounds on decision-making to promote the consistent application of modified universalist solutions.

Biases may have advantages and disadvantages, and it has been observed that sometimes biases can be useful for decision-making processes.[142] Furthermore, as above-mentioned, certain limitations of the expected utility model's assumption, such as fairness preferences, can also explain positive developments in international law. Yet, to the extent that biases impede choices that can lead to desirable outcomes, the cross-border insolvency system should attempt to provide mechanisms that can overcome these biases and lead to more optimal choices.[143]

For a start, awareness of the biases may help. Recognizing that certain biases might prevent us from achieving the fairest and most efficient system for cross-border insolvency may assist in controlling those biases and in allowing us to approach more objectively the issues in hand. Recognition of biases may help build stronger commitments between countries and implementing institutions. In other words, if we accept that choices of territorial solutions may be driven to some extent by behavioural biases and consequently lead to less desirable solutions, it can already be a step in strengthening the cross-border insolvency system.

Additionally, more concrete mechanisms can be contemplated to reinforce the regime based on modified universalism. It would be useful, for instance, to consider

---

[140] RH Thaler and C Sunstein, *Nudge: Improving Decisions about Health, Wealth and Happiness* (Penguin Books 2008).

[141] See also Chapter 4, section 4.5 (on how instrument design can promote adherence to modified universalist solutions) and Chapter 5, section 5.3.3 (on the possibility that delegation to international bodies overcomes short-termism).

[142] van Aaken, 'Behavioral International Law and Economics' (n 9) 423, 449.

[143] See, in the context of international law, ibid 423, 426, 449 (arguing that on the normative level, international law may have an important debiasing role to play, where it may reorient behaviour so that it is more closely aligned with a desired normative model of choice).

how the system design can affect choices of countries and various institutions and whether certain mechanisms can be used so that bounds on decision-making such as loss aversion and other biases may be overcome. Specifically, such matters as the effect of legislative framing, framing of options and of consequences of non-compliance, and the role of default rules would be most relevant, and so are considerations of how to overcome short-termism tendencies in cross-border insolvency. Equally, the system should look for ways to enhance fairness preferences and inclinations that can foster greater cooperation between relevant actors. Such steps that may align choices with optimal solutions and may not entail frequent risks or impose additional considerable burdens on the system can be valuable.[144]

2.7 Conclusion

After the first chapter described the emergence of modified universalism as a dominant and a normatively desired approach to cross-border insolvency, this chapter addressed the following questions: Why do territorialist inclinations still exist? What might have contributed to the partial success of modified universalism? What does this limited success suggest about the debate between territorialism and universalism and the role of cross-border insolvency law? Proponents of territorialism have been focusing on the glass half-empty, often painting the cross-border insolvency regime in darker colours than it is, as modified universalist solutions have been quite prevalent.[145] Universalists have also acknowledged countries' territorial inclinations, and expressed concerns about the feasibility of what they have perceived as optimal solutions for cross-border insolvency.[146]

This chapter further discussed the possible reasons for adopting or rejecting modified universalism solutions. The concern is, on the one hand, that if territorialism is a real choice of countries then perhaps territorialists' arguments about the desirability of territorialism are merited and cross-border insolvency law should take such countries' choices more seriously. As well, if modified universalism represents an approach that countries cannot apply in practice then perhaps it is futile to pursue it. On the other hand, if there are other more plausible explanations for territorialist inclinations, these should be better understood so that cross-border insolvency law may attempt to address any obstacles that may hold modified universalism back from reaching its full and maximum potential.

To understand countries and implementing institutions' attitudes towards modified universalism, this chapter studied cognitive psychology theories and experiments regarding people's choices and decision-making in real-world situations. Particularly, prospect theory shows that people exhibit certain robust biases affecting their decision-making processes. People's preferences in making decisions systemically

---

[144] See tools discussed in subsequent chapters, eg the use of customary international law as a source (discussed in Chapter 3) or the choice of model laws over treaties and the use of default rules in instruments (discussed in Chapter 4).

[145] See Chapter 1, section 1.4.   [146] ibid section 1.4.1.

violate the axioms of expected utility theory, as decision makers frequently deviate in predictable ways from optimal approaches. Furthermore to bounds on decision-making exposed by the prospect theory, this chapter also took account of studies that showed bounds on willpower and on economic models' assumptions about self-regarding motivations. In addition, it drew from the emerging field of behavioural international law, which is shedding new light on the relevance of extant bounds on decision-making in international law.

Drawing on the insights from cognitive psychology and behavioural international law, it can be appreciated that decisions concerning international insolvency law and choices in practice between universalism and territorialism may be influenced by cognitive biases. Specifically, loss aversion, status quo, and related effects as well as short-termism may explain territorialist tendencies. Modified universalism involves a degree of loss of sovereignty that can be overweighted compared to modified universalism's perceived gains, particularly where the reference point regarding which losses and gains are often measured is a regime that had been based on territorialism, and especially where the country has had fewer chances to interact with peers in cross-border insolvency situations. Generally, countries and their various implementing institutions may be averse to change, although not necessarily to the same extent, when the change is perceived to be associated with a loss. Moreover, if the change involves active decision-making, pursuing it may be particularly difficult, even if it is ultimately desirable. Countries and their decision makers might also be preoccupied by short-term goals and, somewhat like individuals in other contexts, find it difficult to consistently fulfil their commitments. Short-termism and self-regarding approaches can be particularly expected in global common pool scenarios that modified universalism aims to resolve.

Therefore, cross-border insolvency law and the system supporting cross-border insolvency should have a debiasing role. It should attempt to overcome and address possible bounds on decision-making to align choices of relevant actors with welfare-increasing solutions. In addition to being more aware of our inclinations, it is possible to contemplate certain specific measures that could address negative predispositions. The biases promoting the widest adoption and application of modified universalism may be exploited, resulting in the continuation and even acceleration of the current trend that generally favours modified universalism. Subsequent chapters will, therefore, have regard to the influence of biases on decisions as it will be attempted to identify tools to strengthen, stabilize, and close gaps in the cross-border insolvency regime.

3

Modified Universalism as Customary International Law

3.1 Introduction

Previous chapters identified modified universalism as the prominent and most desirable approach for cross-border insolvency, yet one which is still not fully stable and universal. Modified universalism is emerging as a set of norms that prescribe efficient levels of centralization of insolvency proceedings, the application of a single law with limited exceptions, the universal effect of the global process, as well as duties imposed on both home and host jurisdictions, and safeguards that also grant countries residual sovereign control in cross-border insolvency cases. It was shown in Chapter 1 that modified universalism has been quite prevalent in practice, including where key written instruments seem to generally follow its approach. Essentially through rules that unify private international law aspects of insolvency, in addition to certain additional measures, safeguards, and duties, frameworks such as the Model Law on Cross-Border Insolvency (MLCBI) and the EU Regulation on Insolvency Proceedings of 2000/Recast EU Regulation of 2015 (EIR/Recast EIR) have attempted to achieve regional or global collectivity in international insolvencies.

There are, however, still gaps in existing cross-border insolvency frameworks even where they seem to embrace modified universalism (at least implicitly), including in terms of the entities covered and the participating countries.[1] Generally, the status of modified universalism is still quite amorphous, and its norms are often perceived as broad principles or aspects of a general trend. Chapter 2 noted bounds on decision-making and other biases affecting choices, and suggested that the cross-border insolvency system has a debiasing role as it should attempt to align choices with the normatively desired approach, namely modified universalism. Against that backdrop, this chapter considers ways in which modified universalism can be strengthened as a binding norm for cross-border insolvency.

Thus, this chapter addresses how modified universalism may be elevated from a broad approach to a recognized, international legal source that can be invoked and applied in a more concrete and consistent manner across legal systems in circumstances of international insolvencies, alongside the application of written

---

[1] See Chapter 1, sections 1.4.4 and 1.4.5 and the assessment of international instruments in Chapter 6.

The Future of Cross-Border Insolvency: Overcoming Biases and Closing Gaps. Irit Mevorach. © Irit Mevorach 2018. Published 2018 by Oxford University Press.

instruments where such instruments exist.[2] The chapter draws from sources of international law and specifically, the concept of customary international law (CIL). It shows that CIL is a key legal source that, notwithstanding important limitations, fills gaps in international treaties, influences treaty regimes, and regulates in areas not covered by treaties or by other instruments, or regarding countries that are not parties to a treaty or to another regime.

CIL is also useful as a debiasing mechanism because its application does not require active action by all participants, such as entry into a treaty or enactment of model laws, and as it operates as a default (opt-out) rule. Legislative framing of modified universalism as CIL can thus overcome certain key and robust biases (status quo, loss aversion, and the endowment effect) and build on positive inclinations (fairness preferences and peer effect) to enhance the system.

The normative implication is a policy push towards the transformation of modified universalism into CIL, so that it can become part of the international insolvency legal order. This chapter thus explores to what extent CIL can be utilized in the field of cross-border insolvency and regarding modified universalism. It considers possible obstacles, where cross-border insolvency might be perceived in the realm of private law (the cross-border insolvency is conceivably a system of procedural private international law), and where private and public international law may be viewed as distinct disciplines. Against this backdrop, actors and participants in international insolvencies might not realize fully their role as creators and guardians of international law. The problem of restraint in forming international laws might be exacerbated where modified universalism is considered an interim approach in the road to pure universalism.[3]

It is argued in this chapter, however, by drawing both on the developments in the theory and in the practice of private and public international law, that in addition to its debiasing role, cross-border insolvency has a prominent international role. The relevance of international law sources should be highlighted more. To be able to maximize its international objectives, cross-border insolvency law should embrace modified universalism as a stand-alone norm. This chapter further proposes, by drawing on specific examples of cases and of country approaches, the steps that can be taken to formalize modified universalism and transform it from a transitory solution to a binding norm. Against the backdrop of the current state of affairs, this chapter also shows how modified universalism in the form of CIL could be used in future cases to better promote outcomes consistent with its approach.

The chapter proceeds as follows. Section 3.2 overviews the notion of CIL, including how it is formed and applied. It also highlights the limitations of CIL, yet its continued significance. This section also considers how CIL is distinguished from 'general principles recognized as law' (which is another recognized source of international law) and suggests why CIL is more akin than general principles to the type of solutions prescribed by modified universalism, and why it is most relevant

---

[2] The question of instrument choice, particularly the choice between a treaty regime and a regime based on a model law for cross-border insolvency, is considered in the next chapter (Chapter 4).
[3] See Chapter 1, section 1.3.1.

as a source for cross-border insolvency. Section 3.3 considers the advantages of CIL from a behavioural perspective, as a debiasing mechanism. Next, section 3.4 explores the obstacles that might be in the way of formalizing modified universalism as CIL in view of possible narrow perceptions of private international law and cross-border insolvency as well as the way modified universalism has been conceptualized as an interim approach. Section 3.5 argues that such perceptions are not merited. Cross-border insolvency law has a significant international role and modified universalism has the characteristics of a stand-alone norm, separate from the originating theory of pure universalism. Section 3.6 suggests steps to transition modified universalism from a general trend to CIL and demonstrates the benefits of such development for future international insolvencies. Section 3.7 provides summary conclusions.

3.2 Customary International Law (CIL) as a Key International Legal Source

International custom is one of the key sources of international law.[4] It is widely acknowledged as a basis for international law and is applied as such in different legal traditions.[5] It has a privileged position in the international law system and forms the backbone of many areas of international law,[6] including international trade and investment law.[7] As such, CIL is an interesting source to consider for the purpose of stabilizing the cross-border insolvency system and, in particular, the strengthening of modified universalism. This section overviews the nature of CIL and how CIL is formed, who may be a party to CIL or excluded from its application, and how it is applied in domestic regimes. Thereafter, this section considers CIL's inherent limitations, as well as its continued significance as a source of international law, and its important relevance for cross-border insolvency.

---

[4] Statute of the International Court of Justice 1945 art 38. Article 38 lists the sources that the International Court of Justice (ICJ) should use, yet it is also understood as delineating the sources of international law in general (I Brownlie, *Principles of International Law* (OUP 2008) 5). See also MN Shaw, *International Law* (CUP 2014) 5 (noting that this article is 'widely recognized as the most authoritative and complete statement as to the sources of international law'). CIL is considered one of the three primary sources of international law, the other two being treaties and general principles of law, and is the primary source of universal law (B Stern, 'Custom at the Heart of International Law' (2011) 11 Duke J Comp & Intl L 89, 89). See also, generally, on the concept of sources of international law, H Thirlway, *The Sources of International Law* (OUP 2014) 1–3, 11.

[5] A Watson, *The Evolution of Law* (John Hopkins 1985) 43–44.

[6] AT Guzman, 'Saving Customary International Law' (2005) 27 Mich J Intl L 115, 116.

[7] SP Subedi, 'International Investment Law' in MD Evans (ed), *International Law* (4th edn, OUP 2014) 740–41 (noting that even though there is a sizable body of treaties most of the law of foreign investment is still based on customary international law 'which has evolved out of diplomatic exchanges, the jurisprudence of international courts and tribunals, bilateral investment treaties, and a host of "soft law" instruments adopted under the auspices of the UN and its specialized agencies'). See also CL Lim, 'The Strange Vitality of Custom in the International Protection of Contracts, Property, and Commerce' in CA Bradley (ed), *Custom's Future, International Law in a Changing World* (CUP 2016) 205–06. See further section 3.2.5.

3.2.1 Establishing CIL

CIL arises from the general and consistent practice of countries, where that practice is based on a belief in the conformity of the practice with international law.[8] This is the classical understanding of CIL consistent with its description in the Statute of the International Court of Justice (ICJ) as 'evidence of a general practice accepted as law'.[9] Thus, CIL encompasses objective and subjective elements, which are complementary and intertwined.[10] The standard position concerning the relationship between the two elements can be found in the ICJ judgment in the *North Sea Continental Shelf* cases:

Not only must the acts concerned amount to a settled practice, but they must also be such, or be carried out in such a way, as to be evidence of a belief that this practice is rendered obligatory by the existence of a rule of law requiring it. The need for such a belief, i.e., the existence of a subjective element, is implicit in the very notion of the *opinio juris sive necessitatis*.[11]

The objective element of CIL requires sufficient evidence of state practice that follows the potential CIL.[12] Such evidence should show consistency and practice by various relevant actors, although not necessarily by all countries.[13] Additionally, the required recurrence of the practice may depend on the frequency of circumstances that necessitate action pursuant to the CIL.[14] The subjective or psychological element is what countries have accepted as law (*opinio juris*). Thus, evidence of state practice should be complemented by evidence that the practice is regarded as an expression of a rule of international law, a conviction that there was an obligation to follow the norm.

The primary and most direct evidence of the existence of CIL would be the actions of countries through the acts of their organs. Thus, when a country acts in a legally significant way or refrains from acting, it contributes to the development of practice accepted as law.[15] Countries' actions may be discerned, for example, from decisions

---

[8] JL Brierly, *The Law of Nations: An Introduction to the International Law of Peace* (6th edn, OUP 1963) 59–60; Thirlway, *The Sources of International Law* (n 4) 53–91; V Lowe, *International Law* (Clarendon Law Series 2007) 38.

[9] Statute of the International Court of Justice 1945 art 38(1)(b).

[10] Thirlway, *The Sources of International Law* (n 4) 62.

[11] *North Sea Continental Shelf, Judgment* [1969] Rep 3, para 7.

[12] H Thirlway, 'The Sources of International Law' in MD Evans (ed), *International Law* (4th edn, OUP 2014) 100–05.

[13] CA Bradley and M Gulati, 'Withdrawing from International Custom' (2011) 120 Yale L J 202, 210. Such consistency was not demonstrated, for example, in the *Asylum* case (*Columbia v Peru* [1950] ICJ Rep 266, 277) as it was concluded that: 'The facts brought to the knowledge of the Court disclose so much uncertainty and contradiction, so much fluctuation and discrepancy ... and the practice has been so much influenced by considerations of political expediency, that it is not possible to discern in all this any constant and uniform usage, accepted as law.' The ICJ explained, however, in the case of *Military and Parliamentary Activities in and against Nicaragua* [1986] ICJ 98, para 186, that it is sufficient that 'the conduct of States should, in general, be consistent with such rules, and that instances of State conduct inconsistent with a given rule should generally have been treated as breaches of that rule, not as indications of recognition of a new rule'.

[14] Thirlway, *The Sources of International Law* (n 4) 65, 67.

[15] See eg the *Scotia* case (14 Wallace 170 (1871)) decided by the US Supreme Court. In this case, the court found that there was CIL requiring an American vessel to follow certain procedures that it failed to follow. The basis of the CIL was British navigational procedures that were enacted in almost identical terms in legislation of other countries (Shaw, *International Law* (n 4) 59).

to adopt certain legislation and from the decisions of national courts.[16] Additionally, treaties and conventions may point to the existence of CIL.[17] As stated in a *dictum* by the ICJ:

It is of course axiomatic that the material of customary international law is to be looked for primarily in the actual practice and *opinio juris* of States, even though multilateral conventions may have an important role to play in recording and defining rules deriving from custom, or indeed in developing them.[18]

Various instruments that may be considered soft law may also provide evidence of an established CIL or contribute to the evolution of new CIL, being determinative of the *opinio juris* or of state practice.[19] Thus, a nonbinding instrument can have a legal effect on customary law. The wording in such an instrument is important because it must be 'of a fundamentally norm-creating character such as could be regarded as forming the basis of a general rule of law'.[20] It would also be important to consider the level of support given to the instrument by countries, and any statements accompanying such instrument that may be relevant to the assessment of countries' belief about the conformity of the practice with international law.[21]

3.2.2 CIL distinguished from 'general principles of law'

'General principles of law recognized by civilized nations' is a source close to CIL.[22] For general principles of law to emerge, there should be recognition on the part of civilized peoples rather than a general practice among countries.[23] Notwithstanding ongoing controversy around the notion that general principles constitute a separate source of law, general principles have a recognized role in the formation of international law.[24] Thus, it is accepted that general principles exist as a source alongside

---

[16] See *Judicial Immunities of the State* [2012] ICJ Rep 122–23, para 55 ('State practice of particular significance is to be found in the judgments of national courts faced with the question whether a foreign State is immune, the legislation of those States which have enacted statutes dealing with immunity, the claims to immunity advanced by States before foreign courts and the statements made by States, first in the course of extensive study of the subject by the International Law Commission and then in the context of the adoption of the United Nations Convention').

[17] Thirlway, *The Sources of International Law* (n 4) 58, 59.

[18] *Continental Shelf (Libya/Malta)*, Judgment, ICJ Rep 1985, 29–30, para 27.

[19] AE Boyle, 'Some Reflections on the Relationship of Treaties and Soft Law' (1999) 48 ICLQ 901, 904.

[20] *North Sea Continental Shelf, Judgment, ICJ Reports 1969*, 3, para 72; AE Boyle, 'Soft Law in International Law Making' in MD Evans (ed), *International Law* (4th edn, OUP 2014) 130–33.

[21] Boyle, 'Soft Law in International Law Making' (n 20) 130–31.

[22] Both sources concern unwritten norms and they both fill gaps in international systems. The categorization of norms as CIL or as general principles is subject to some debate (N Petersen, 'Customary Law Without Custom? Rules, Principles, and the Role of State Practice in International Norm Creation' (2007) 23(2) Am U Int'l L Rev 275).

[23] B Simma and P Alston, 'The Sources of Human Rights Law: Custom, Jus Cogens, and General Principles' (1988) 12 Austl Y B Intl L 82, 104.

[24] O Schachter, *International Law in Theory and Practice* (Martinus Nijhoff Publishers 1991) 49.

CIL and treaties.[25] CIL too may contain established principles, in which case the application of the principles will derive from that source (ie CIL) and will be thus based on the identification of a general practice among countries.[26]

As a separate additional international source, the general principles seem to refer to those minimum, fundamental principles inherent in every legal system, deriving from the consensus of domestic regimes.[27] Thus, this source is seeking to define the fundamentals of substantive justice and procedural fairness.[28] Countries are bound to general principles based on the universal understanding of basic legal concepts by all legal systems.[29] While there is no unanimity regarding the exact nature of general principles, this source seems to be concerned with principles that have 'an air of permanence, of stability, of having been selected for their evident and perpetual rightness'.[30]

In contrast, CIL is of a more adaptable nature and it may 'vary from society to society'.[31] General principles, at least when understood as referring to the very basic and almost self-evident norms, may also be of less practical importance, when compared with CIL. Indeed, there is limited evidence in international practice of relying on general principles to determine rights and obligations of countries.[32] General principles nonetheless can supplement and fill additional gaps left by the primary sources of treaty and custom.[33]

3.2.3 Effect of CIL

Once CIL has become pervasive enough, countries are bound by it regardless of whether they have codified the laws domestically or through treaties.[34] Unanimity

---

[25] The doctrine of sources recognized general principles of law as one of the sources of international law (Statute of the International Court of Justice, art 38(1); see also B Cheng, *General Principles of Law as Applied by International Courts and Tribunals* (CUP 2006) 25–26)).

[26] Thirlway, *The Sources of International Law* (n 4) 94. cf Petersen, 'Customary Law Without Custom?' (n 22) (arguing that principles, being value-related, should be classified as general principles of international law instead of custom and, therefore, should not require the proof of state practice. Petersen contrasts principles with rules that are conduct-related and must thus be determined through the traditional inductive approach of custom).

[27] Schachter, *International Law in Theory and Practice* (n 24) 50 (Schachter identifies five categories of general principles that have been invoked and applied in international law discourse and cases: the principles of municipal law recognized by civilized nations, general principles of law derived from the specific nature of the international community, principles intrinsic to the idea of law and basic to all legal systems, principles valid through all kinds of societies in relationships of hierarchy and coordination, and principles of justice founded on the very nature of man as a rational and social being, noting that each has a different basis for its authority and validity as law).

[28] CT Kotuby Jr, 'General Principles of Law, International Due Process, and the Modern Role of Private International Law' (2013) 23 Duke J of Comp & Intl L 411, 412.

[29] ibid 422.

[30] Thirlway, *The Sources of International Law* (n 4) 97. Examples include the principle that promises given must be kept or that one who harms or wrongs another must make restitution for the harm done.

[31] ibid 102.

[32] ibid 98–99; Shaw, *International Law* (n 4) 26 (explaining that 'most writers are prepared to accept that the general principles do constitute a separate source of law but of fairly limited scope').

[33] Schachter, *International Law in Theory and Practice* (n 24) 52.

[34] CIL may also be created between certain states or within a region, in which case it may not be a general custom but rather a 'special custom'. To determine the existence and content of such CIL, it is

among all countries is not required for it to have a universal effect. Likewise, if an obligation is included in a treaty but also amounts to CIL, it will also bind countries that are not parties to the treaty.[35] Countries in some cases, however, may be exempted from CIL. Under the doctrine of the 'persistent objector',[36] countries can consistently object to CIL (opt out) in its formative stages.[37] The threshold for being regarded a persistent objector is, however, very high. Thus, the objection should be made widely known.[38] Persistent objections should also be made while the rule is still accumulating and before it becomes CIL. Thereafter, in principle, once the CIL is established, it is no longer possible to opt out of the rule except through specific agreements that establish a different rule.[39]

CIL may be invoked in domestic or international tribunals, yet the application of CIL does not depend on establishing international enforcement mechanisms. Application heavily relies on domestic enforcement structures. Thus, all nations seem to accept that CIL forms an integral part of national law,[40] and that courts should take judicial notice of CIL.[41] When ascertaining the existence and nature of an alleged CIL, domestic courts may have recourse to various types of sources and authoritative material, including 'international treaties and conventions, authoritative textbooks, practice and judicial decisions'.[42] In theory, therefore, there is no need to prove the law, though in practice countries and implementing institutions invoking CIL will attempt to prove the existence of the rules on the basis of which the claim is made.[43] The actual implementation of CIL in national laws differs, however, to some extent, among jurisdictions.[44] In civil law jurisdictions, the general rule is that CIL takes precedence over inconsistent ordinary national legislation and directly creates rights and duties within the territory.[45] In common

necessary to ascertain whether there is a general practice among the states concerned that is accepted by them as law.

[35] Thirlway, *The Sources of International Law* (n 4) 35–36.

[36] For an overview see ibid 86–88.

[37] Bradley and Gulati, 'Withdrawing from International Custom' (n 13) 209; Guzman, 'Saving Customary International Law' (n 6) 211–12, 214.

[38] D Kritsiotis, 'On the Possibilities of and for Persistent Objection' (2010) 21 Duke J of Comp & Intl L 121, 129, noting eg the circumstances in the *Fisheries Case* (Fisheries Case (UK v Nor), 1951 ICJ 116, 131 (Dec 18)) where it was ruled that 'the ten-mile rule for the closing lines of bays "would appear to be inapplicable as against Norway inasmuch as she has always opposed any attempt to apply it to the Norwegian coast"'.

[39] Thirlway, *The Sources of International Law* (n 4) 88. See also Kritsiotis, 'On the Possibilities of and for Persistent Objection' (n 38) 127–34.

[40] E Denza, 'The Relationship Between International and National Law' in MD Evans (ed), *International Law* (4th edn, OUP 2014) 426–27.

[41] Shaw, *International Law* (n 4), 99–100.

[42] *The Cristina* [1938] AC 485, 497; 9 AD, 250 (per Lord Macmillan).

[43] Thirlway, *The Sources of International Law* (n 4) 56.

[44] For an overview see Shaw, *International Law* (n 4) 99–127.

[45] See eg The Basic Law of the Federal Republic of Germany art 25 and HP Folz, 'Germany' in D Shelton (ed), *International Law and Domestic Legal Systems* (OUP 2011); The Italian Constitution of 1947 art 10; and G Cataldi, 'Italy' in D Shelton (ed), *International Law and Domestic Legal Systems* (OUP 2011).

law jurisdictions, CIL is recognized as part and parcel of the legal system.[46] There is also a presumption that legislation is to be construed in a manner that would avoid a conflict with international law.[47]

3.2.4 Limitations and critique

CIL tends to be vague and the way it emerges is rather unclear.[48] Furthermore, because CIL is based on an evolving experience, it is evidently problematic to ascertain at what point rules have reached the stage where they can be applied as CIL.[49] There is also a circularity problem. For a rule to qualify as CIL, countries should feel obligated to follow it, but how would countries feel such legal obligation before the rule becomes customary?[50]

This uncertainty, as well as CIL's reliance on domestic enforcement mechanisms, also makes CIL prone to non-observance, especially when it attempts to address difficult cross-border conflicts.[51] There have also been challenges to CIL for lacking a coherent theory and doctrine.[52] It is arguably impossible to observe the potential universe of the practice of countries to ascertain whether references to CIL are made out of obligation or as a matter of justifying actions.[53] It has also been argued that CIL does not actually affect countries' behaviour and has little impact in view of the lack of enforcement mechanisms on the international level.[54]

Another uncertainty revolves around the question of whose practice and opinion should be considered when attempting to identify the existence of CIL, including the extent to which non-state actors' actions should be taken into account, which

---

[46] eg CIL is part of the public policy of the United Kingdom and part of the domestic law. It does not necessitate the interposition of a constitutional ratification procedure (Shaw, *International Law* (n 4) 99–100).

[47] The process followed by English courts has been explained in *Chung Chi Cheung v R*: 'The courts acknowledge the existence of a body of rules which nations accept among themselves. On any judicial issue, they seek to ascertain what the relevant rule is, and having found it they will treat it as incorporated into the domestic law, so far as it is not inconsistent with rules enacted by statutes or finally declared by their tribunals' ([1939] AC 160; 9 AD 264, per Lord Atkin). In the United States, CIL is federal law and its determination by federal courts is binding on the state courts (see also *Schroeder v Bissell* 5 F 2d 838, 842 (1925)).

[48] Shaw, *International Law* (n 4) 102.

[49] Thirlway, *The Sources of International Law* (n 4) 55.

[50] A D'amato, *The Concept of Custom in International Law* (Cornell University Press 1971) 53, 66 ('But if custom creates law, how can a component of custom require that the creative acts be in accordance with some prior right or obligation in international law? … How can custom create law if its psychological component requires action in conscious accordance with law pre-existing the action?').

[51] See BC Matthews, 'Emerging Public International Banking Law? Lessons from the Law of the Sea Experience' (2010) 10 Chi J Intl L 539, 556–57 (providing the example of the development of the law of the sea where by the mid-twentieth-century coastal countries attempted to exert greater rights over their contiguous sea areas, which led the global community to attempt to codify the customary law of the sea in treaties).

[52] Thirlway notes that CIL is one of international law's 'intellectual puzzles' (Thirlway, *The Sources of International Law* (n 4)). See also K Wolfke, *Custom in Present International Law* (2nd edn, Martinus Nijhoff Publishers 1993) xiii; RB Baker, 'Customary International Law: A Reconceptualization' (2016) 2 Brook J of Intl L 439.

[53] Guzman, 'Saving Customary International Law' (n 6) 150–51.

[54] JL Goldsmith and EA Posner, *The Limits of International Law* (OUP 2005) 39.

countries' actions or omissions should be considered, and whether only the actions of countries that are affected or that are capable of taking action regarding a certain matter are relevant.[55] It seems inevitable that more powerful and more affected countries would be more influential and have a greater role than others in the development of CIL, which arguably entails a certain inequity in the process by which CIL is rendered a source of law.[56] There is also a risk that CIL becomes too sticky and not allow for developments to meet changing circumstances and new needs of countries and of the international business and financial community.[57]

3.2.5 CIL's continued significance

Notwithstanding the difficulties that CIL presents, it continues to hold a privileged position in the international legal system.[58] As mentioned above, most countries accept the application of CIL within their jurisdiction. Countries' actual actions provide the most evident indication of CIL, including actions taking place in international fora. CIL and the practice supporting it could also be discerned from judicial decisions of domestic and of international tribunals, and the increasing use of conventions or soft law may also point to the existence of CIL.

Commentators have also proposed fresh and modern views on CIL theory and noted its persisting importance.[59] There has been some shift from reliance only on induction from national practice in identifying CIL to deducing its emergence from broader data sets, including international pronouncements and activities of non-state actors.[60] Some scholars have also theorized CIL in functional terms, suggesting

---

[55] Thirlway, *The Sources of International Law* (n 4) 59–61.

[56] D'amato, *The Concept of Custom in International Law* (n 50) 96–97; Wolfke, *Custom in Present International Law* (n 52) 78.

[57] Thirlway, *The Sources of International Law* (n 4) 68.

[58] It has been argued that the unwritten international law (CIL and general principles of law) not only counts but may even *gain* importance (Petersen, 'Customary Law Without Custom?' (n 22) 309: 'This is so, in particular, if one accepts that international regimes are not self-contained. It plays a considerable role in the discussions on human rights, democracy, and accountability in the context of international financial institutions, as well as in attempts to introduce human rights' and environmental considerations into the scope of world trade law' (footnotes omitted)).

[59] See eg Guzman, 'Saving Customary International Law' (n 6) 115; Bradley and Gulati, 'Withdrawing from International Custom' (n 13); A van Aaken, 'Behavioral International Law and Economics' (2014) 55 Harv Intl L J 421, 450–56 (2014); BD Lepard, *Customary International Law: A New Theory with Practical Applications* (CUP 2010); AE Roberts, 'Traditional and Modern Approaches to Customary International Law: A Reconciliation' (2001) 95 Am J Intl L 757; AT Guzman, 'Reinvigorating Customary International Law' in CA Bradley (ed), *Custom's Future, International Law in a Changing World* (CUP 2016); Lim, 'The Strange Vitality of Custom' (n 7); O Sender and M Wood, 'Custom's Bright Future: The Continuing Importance of Customary International Law' in CA Bradley (ed), *Custom's Future, International Law in a Changing World* (CUP 2016); Baker, 'Customary International Law: A Reconceptualization' (n 52).

[60] See eg Roberts, 'Traditional and Modern Approaches to Customary International Law' (n 59); Baker, 'Customary International Law: A Reconceptualization' (n 52) (emphasizing the significance of norms created through the work of transnational actors). Furthermore, pursuant to modern views of international law-making, various actors, including non-state actors, may be considered actual creators of international law (A Roberts and S Sivakumaran, 'Lawmaking by Non-State Actors: Engaging Armed Group in the Creation of International Humanitarian Law' (2012) 37 Yale J Intl L 107).

that CIL may be effective when countries interact repeatedly over time, and that it may influence country behaviour through reputational and direct sanctions.[61] It has also been considered that although the development of CIL might be a slow process, with technological changes, the rise of international institutions, and other developments, CIL may emerge more quickly than in the past.[62]

The work of the International Law Association Committee (ILA Committee)[63] and the International Law Commission (ILC)[64] on the formation of CIL,[65] provide additional useful guidance. It is suggested that practice can include a wide range of forms and may be proved not only by physical actions, but also verbal acts and in-action may count as state practice.[66] Specifically, it is noted that:

Forms of State practice include, but are not limited to: diplomatic acts and correspondence; conduct in connection with resolutions adopted by an international organization or at an intergovernmental conference; conduct in connection with treaties; executive conduct, including operational conduct 'on the ground'; legislative and administrative acts; and decisions of national courts.[67]

Additional draft conclusions of the ILC focus on *opinio juris,*[68] and provide that '[A] general practice that is accepted as law (*opinio juris*) is to be distinguished from mere usage or habit.' Evidence of it may take various forms, including:

public statements made on behalf of States; official publications; government legal opinions; diplomatic correspondence; decisions of national courts; treaty provisions; and conduct in

---

[61] Guzman, 'Saving Customary International Law' (n 6) 139. See also AT Guzman, 'A Compliance-Based Theory of International Law' (2000) 90 Cal L Rev 1823, 1844–51, 1874–78; G Norman and J Trachtman, 'The Customary International Law Game' (2005) 99 Am J Intl L 541, 568.

[62] See eg Wolfke, *Custom in Present International Law* (n 52) 59; Guzman, 'Saving Customary International Law' (n 61) 157–59 (proposing that CIL may emerge instantly because *opinio juris*, which is arguably what establishes CIL, can develop or change easily). See also B Cheng, 'Custom: The Future of General State Practice in a Divided World' in R MacDonald and DM Johnston (eds), *The Structure and Process of International Law: Essays in Legal Philosophy Doctrine and Theory* (Martinus Nijhoff Publishers 1983) 532; cf GJH van Hoof, *Rethinking the Sources of International Law* (Kluwer Law and Taxation Publishers 1983) 86.

[63] The International Law Association (ILA) does not have an official status, yet as observed by Thirlway, the membership of the Committee gave its work 'the weight of "teaching of the most highly qualified publicist of the various nations" as contemplated by Article 38 of the ICJ Statute' (Thirlway, *The Sources of International Law* (n 4) 58).

[64] The ILC was formed to undertake the mandate of the general assembly to 'initiate studies and make recommendations for the purpose of ... encouraging the progressive development of international law and its codification' (http://legal.un.org/ilc/).

[65] See ILA Committee 'Formation of Customary (General) International Law' (1984–2000). The ILC commenced the work on CIL in 2012. Draft conclusions were produced on 30 May 2016 and the Commission decided to transmit the draft conclusions to Governments for comments and observations to be submitted to the Secretary-General by 1 January 2018. See International Law Commission, *Summaries of the Work of the International Law Commission* <http://legal.un.org/ilc/summaries/1_13.shtml>; International Law Commission, *Identification of Customary International Law, Text of the draft conclusions provisionally adopted by the Drafting Committee*, A/CN.4/L.872, 30 May 2016 <http://legal.un.org/docs/index.asp?symbol=A/CN.4/L.872> (*ILC Draft Conclusions*).

[66] ILA, *London Conference (2000), Committee on Formation of Customary (General) International Law, Final Report of the Committee* 14–15: <https://www.law.umich.edu/facultyhome/drwcasebook/Documents/Documents/ILA%20Report%20on%20Formation%20of%20Customary%20International%20Law.pdf> (*ILA Final Report*); *ILC Draft Conclusions* (n 65), draft conclusion 6.

[67] *ILC Draft Conclusions* (n 65), draft conclusion 6(2).   [68] ibid Part Four.

connection with resolutions adopted by an international organization or at an intergovernmental conference.[69]

Such acceptance of CIL may be negated where it can be shown that participants when acting in a certain way, were motivated by considerations such as courtesy, convenience, or tradition rather than by a conviction that their acts amount to CIL.[70]

It is recognized that CIL is binding on all countries whether they participated in the relevant practice. Any country in theory can affect CIL and the position of countries may be considered even where they could not in fact take or refrain from taking an action.[71] Surely, where countries do possess the capacity to engage and interact with other parties, such countries would be more influential and thus privileged regarding the formation and shaping of CIL. However, the reliance of international law on the practice of the more powerful countries can ensure lesser deviation from and violation of CIL where these are the same countries that have formed the rules. Constraining violation by powerful countries is crucial for the stability of the system, as the impact of breach could be much more pronounced and widespread where committed by such jurisdictions. In addition, because powerful countries are less affected by CIL violations (as they are more resilient to the implications of a breach), they may be less deterred by it, therefore it is another advantage if these countries play an important role in shaping the rules.[72]

Today, treaty law covers many areas of international law. There are also various other ways for countries to cooperate through soft law instruments.[73] However, CIL remains binding on countries even outside the treaty framework. The two sources operate in parallel and the codification of CIL in a treaty does not abrogate the rule as CIL.[74] CIL still plays an important role, 'regulating both within the gaps of treaties as well as the conduct of non-parties to the treaties'[75] because

---

[69] ibid Draft Conclusion 10.

[70] ICJ in *North Sea Continental Shelf case* [1969] ICJ Rep 44, para 77; *ILA Final Report* (n 66) 35. See also J Crawford, *Brownlie's Principles of Public International Law* (8th edn, OUP 2012) 23 (explaining that 'usage is a general practice which does not reflect a legal obligation: examples include ceremonial salutes at sea and the practice of granting certain parking privileges to diplomatic vehicles').

[71] See eg the decision of the ICJ regarding the *Legality of the Threat or Use of Nuclear Weapons*, where the court found that there was no CIL that prohibited the use of such weapons. The court considered international practice and the possible existence of *opinio juris* of countries even though most of them did not possess nuclear weapons ([1996-I] ICJ Rep; Thirlway, *The Sources of International Law* (n 4) 60).

[72] Guzman, 'Saving Customary International Law' (n 6) 151.

[73] K Raustiala, 'Form and Substance in International Agreement' (2005) 99 Am J Intl L 581. See also Chapter 4, section 4.3.2.

[74] See the *Case Concerning Military and Paramilitary Activities in and against Nicaragua*, where the ICJ held that 'even if the customary norm and the treaty norm were to have exactly the same content, this would not be a reason for the Court to hold that the incorporation of the customary norm into treaty law must deprive the customary norm of its applicability as distinct from that of the treaty norm' (*Military and Paramilitary Activities (Nicar v US)* 1986 ICJ 14, 94–95 (27 June 1986)).

[75] Bradley and Gulati, 'Withdrawing from International Custom' (n 13) 209. See also Lepard, *Customary International Law* (n 59) 3–6; SD Murphy, *Principles of International Law* (Thomson/

countries are bound by CIL even if they have not expressed explicit consent. The effect of CIL is also important regarding matters that are not regulated by treaties or by other instruments, and for newly emerging issues not yet covered by a treaty.[76] In addition, CIL can serve to influence treaty regimes and may be important and relevant for treaty interpretation where, for example, the treaty refers to rules of CIL.[77] It is also an important alternative source to treaties, considering limitations to the use of treaties in international law, including the transaction costs involved and the risk of nonparticipation in such regimes (issues discussed further in Chapter 4).

Thus, important areas of international law, including the law of state responsibility, foreign direct investment, diplomatic immunity, human rights, and state immunity,[78] are governed wholly or partially by CIL, where treaties are not universal, or where a treaty is absent, or where the treaty does not cover all issues. CIL is in use, for example, in international investment law where certain aspects of regulating foreign investment have become settled international law,[79] and where CIL remains of fundamental importance despite the proliferation of bilateral investment agreements in this field.[80] This settled customary international investment law includes, inter alia, the requirement of non-discrimination against,[81] and the fair and equitable treatment of, foreign investors; the entitlement of foreign investors to national treatment once admitted into the country; and the requirement regarding non-discriminatory regulatory measures and obligations to respect human rights by multinational companies.[82] These rules may apply in

West 2006) 78–86; T Meron, 'The Continuing Role of Custom in the Formation of International Humanitarian Law' (1996) Am J Intl L 238.

[76] Bradley and Gulati, 'Withdrawing from International Custom' (n 13) 209; Guzman, 'Saving Customary International Law' (n 6) 119. Where both a treaty and CIL regulate the same situation, normally the treaty is the prevailing *lex specialis*, at least regarding rules that existed at the time of the conclusion of the treaty (Thirlway, 'The Sources of International Law' (n 12) 109).

[77] Guzman, 'Saving Customary International Law' (n 6) 120 (noting the example of the United States Model Bilateral Investment Treaty art II, (Apr 1994) that refers to 'treatment less favorable than that required by [customary] international law').

[78] Guzman, 'Saving Customary International Law' (n 6) 115.

[79] Despite an early lack of consensus. Indeed, the question of treatment of foreign investors under CIL has been subject to heated debate to the extent that there did not seem to be a broad international consensus allowing the crystallization of CIL (*Barcelona Traction, Light and Power Co, Ltd (Belgium v Spain)*, 1970 ICJ 4, 46–47 (5 February)). See also P Dumberry, 'Are BITs Representing the "New" Customary International Law in International Investment Law?' (2010) 28(4) Penn St Intl L Rev 675, 676–78.

[80] See eg C Schreuer and R Dolzer, *Principles of International Investment Law* (OUP 2008) 16–17; Dumberry, 'Are BITs Representing the "New" Customary International Law in International Investment Law?' (n 79) 697–700.

[81] Norms of non-discrimination 'form the fabric of international economic law, and they have long been present in both the international trade and investment law fields' (Lim, 'The Strange Vitality of Custom' (n 7) 206–07).

[82] For more detail see Subedi, 'International Investment Law' (n 7) 740–41. See also Dumberry, 'Are BITs Representing the "New" Customary International Law in International Investment Law?' (n 79) 680.

the absence of a bilateral agreement,[83] or where agreements make reference to CIL,[84] or to fill gaps in treaties when treaties are silent on certain issues.[85]

3.2.6 CIL, general principles, and the cross-border insolvency system

The nature and characteristics of CIL make it an important legal source for a cross-border insolvency system based on modified universalism, and as a useful method to shape the international interactions in this subsystem of international law. CIL is responsive to emerging trends in practice. It is based on experience and it can arise whether written instruments are applicable or not. It applies to all countries, whereas treaties or other instruments only apply to signatories or countries that adopted the instruments. Thus, if modified universalism is recognized as CIL, gaps in the cross-border insolvency system can be filled.[86]

It was noted above that 'general principles of law' is a source close to CIL. It too can fill gaps left in an international sub-system, specifically where fundamental standards of reasonableness, fairness, natural justice, and good faith could be recognized as general principles. General principles could, therefore, assist in the process of applying modified universalism, where such fundamental issues of justice and due process arise.[87] However, general principles may not formalize the measures of modified universalism. As explained in Chapter 1, modified universalism provides a set of norms, including the centralization of the forum and the law and deference to main proceedings through recognition and assistance,[88] that solve the problem of cross-border insolvency; as such, they provide concrete guidance to courts and other parties.[89] It is not merely a system of general principles.[90] At the same time, modified

---

[83] Dumberry, 'Are BITs Representing the "New" Customary International Law in International Investment Law?' (n 79) 698 (explaining that 'custom ... applies to all States, including those which have not entered into any BITs. CIL can, therefore, be invoked by any foreign investor irrespective of whether its State of origin has entered into a BIT with the country where it makes its investment').

[84] Various investment treaties refer to CIL (see eg the example in n 77). CIL is also relevant when it is referred to in an official note of interpretation of a treaty provision (Dumberry, 'Are BITs Representing the "New" Customary International Law in International Investment Law?' (n 79) 698–99).

[85] C McLachlan, 'Investment Treaties and General International Law' (2008) 57(2) ICLQ 361, 400. See also Dumberry, 'Are BITs Representing the "New" Customary International Law in International Investment Law?' (n 79) 700, noting examples of tribunals' decisions that were based on CIL to fill gaps, eg *ADC Affiliate Ltd & ADC & ADMC Management Ltd v Hungary*, Award, 481, 483 (2 Oct 2006) (ICSID) where the tribunal concluded that because the BIT did not 'contain any lex specialis rules' governing 'the issue of the standard for assessing damages in the case of an unlawful expropriation,' it was 'required to apply the default standard contained in customary international law in the present case.'

[86] See section 3.6.2.

[87] General principles of law as a source of international law may fill gaps in the law that might be left by the operation of treaty or CIL (Thirlway, *The Sources of International Law* (n 4) 98, referring to R Jennings and A Watts (eds), *Oppenheim's International Law* (9th edn, Longman Harlow 1992) i. 40). See also Kotuby Jr, 'General Principles of Law' (n 28) 412 (arguing that general principles of law concerning justice and due process should be applied and inform domestic courts dealing with private international law matters such as the determination of the proper choice of law).

[88] See Chapter 1, section 1.3.2.

[89] cf the concept of international comity that notwithstanding its prominent status is considered too vague and uncertain and is understood differently in different systems, therefore may not be recognized as CIL (see section 3.4.1).

[90] On the distinction between rules and principles in the context of international law see G Fitzmaurice, 'The General Principles of International Law Considered from the Standpoint of the Rule of Law' (1957) 92 *Recueil de cours* 7.

universalism is sufficiently flexible, again akin to CIL, which as a legal source tends to be supple and adaptable. The emerging norms of modified universalism accommodate different types of business structures and different degrees of global or regional integration, and they can also adapt to changing conditions.[91]

CIL is also not utterly rigid as a legal source, notwithstanding its universal application through general experience. It can develop gradually over time, and it is possible to change or create new CIL to meet the developing needs of nations.[92] Thus, conduct inconsistent with CIL may in relevant circumstances be a way to create new rules.[93] At the same time, where CIL represents an emerging widespread and normatively desirable practice, its tendency to stick is an important advantage.[94] As noted above, general principles of law are also of a somewhat lesser practical significance where their scope may be limited, and as they are applied quite rarely on the international level. CIL, on the other hand, is a primary international legal source and where modified universalism is established as CIL it can result in greater universality and applicability of its norms.[95] Thus, though general principles can assist in closing residual gaps concerning fundamental issues of justice (thus also contributing to a level of harmonization of substantive laws, as discussed in Chapter 5[96]), CIL is of fundamental importance for the system based on modified universalism.

3.3 The Behavioural Force of CIL

In addition to CIL being a key source for international law that as such can fill gaps in the international system, CIL can also support the debiasing role of cross-border insolvency discussed in Chapter 2. It was noted how people, including actors making choices regarding issues of international law, tend to avoid changes, especially where choices of certain options are perceived as resulting in a loss or in a departure with

---

[91] See Chapter 1, section 1.3.2.

[92] Thirlway, *The Sources of International Law* (n 4) 69. cf the permanent nature of general principles of law (102).

[93] The ICJ explained in this regard that: 'Reliance by a State on a novel right or an unprecedented exception to the principle might, if shared in principle by other States, tend toward a modification of customary international law' (*Military and Parliamentary Activities in and against Nicaragua* [1986] ICJ 98, para 207).

[94] R Brewster, 'Withdrawing from Custom: Choosing Between Default Rules' (2010) 21 Duke J Comp & Intl L 47, 55 (arguing that if customary international law incorporates rules that are net welfare increasing for the international community, then a shift towards the provision of more opt-out rights, including after formation, may be welfare decreasing). cf Bradley and Gulati, 'Withdrawing from International Custom' (n 13) 202 (proposing, based on historical analysis and in view of the modern role and understanding of CIL, that an ability to opt out of CIL after it has become a rule prevents stickiness and hold-out problems and ensures formation quality and adaptability to changing conditions). See also Guzman, 'Saving Customary International Law' (n 6) 169–71 (suggesting expanding the opt-out option from CIL to after the formation stage, but in a more limited fashion).

[95] cf R Bork, *Principles of Cross-Border Insolvency Law* (Intersentia 2017) 2 (suggesting, as well, a principled approach when addressing cross-border insolvency issues. Bork refers, however, to certain commonalities between insolvency foundational principles across legal systems, while the principles considered here refer to the foundations of modified universalism. Specifically, what is proposed in this chapter is that the norms of modified universalism ought to be legalized and become CIL to strengthen the cross-border insolvency system).

[96] See Chapter 5, section 5.3.2.4.

an endowment, and more so if the choice requires active action. Additionally, the way options are framed affects people's choices.[97] Because such tendencies may be in operation in cross-border insolvency, it is important to take them into account in the design of the system and choice of sources and instruments.[98] CIL's behavioural advantages should therefore be considered, where it may promote the adoption of options in line with what is normatively desirable (namely, in line with modified universalism). This section focuses specifically on the framing effect and the preference of default rules, to demonstrate why CIL, as a default system, may increase universal adherence to its norms, in view of extant biases. As such it can also change the reference point and promote the adoption of other instruments. The development of fairness preferences can also explain CIL's evolution and why it can address complex coordination problems and facilitate cooperation.

3.3.1 CIL as a debiasing mechanism

Cognitive psychology studies have shown the effect of legislative framing and the use of default options on choices between alternative options.[99] The importance of default rules has been evidenced in a range of contexts. It has been shown, for example, that people favour agreements that are consistent with legal default rules, or terms of trade that are conventional for the type of bargain at issue.[100] Default rules may even save lives. Thus, it has been shown that many people avoid making an *active* decision about organ donation. This may be due to the stress or physical effort involved, but it is also likely because defaults tend to be perceived as representing the existing state or status quo and change usually involves a trade-off. Adherence to a default option may also be due to perceiving the default rule as representing the recommended, endorsed, option (as well as owing to people's tendency to postpone decisions).[101] Furthermore, switching from a default option may be perceived as a risk and a loss, thus it may be weighed more heavily than the possible gains, because of loss aversion.[102] Such a change may seem a loss, and a loss looms larger than a gain. Thus, a change in the default may result in a change of choice. It was shown, for example, that when donation is made the default, there is significant increase in organ donations.[103]

---

[97] See Chapter 2, sections 2.3.1 and 2.4.3.
[98] The way in which these insights may inform instrument choice and design will be discussed in Chapter 4.
[99] See D Kahneman, JL Knetch, and RH Thaler, 'Anomalies: The Endowment Effect, Loss Aversion and Status Quo Bias' (1991) 5(1) Journal of Economic Perspectives 193, 199 (pointing to studies showing the effect of framing manipulation on a choice between alternative automobile insurance policies).
[100] See eg D Kahneman et al, 'Experimental Tests of the Endowment Effect and the Coase Theorem' (1990) 98 J Pol Econ 1325; R Korobkin, 'The Status Quo Bias and Contract Default Rules' (1998) 83 Cornell L Rev 608.
[101] See eg J Beshears et al, 'The Importance of Default Options for Retirement Saving Outcomes. Evidence from the United States' in J Brown et al (eds), *Social Security Policy in a Changing Environment* (University of Chicago Press 2009) 184–87.
[102] EJ Johnson and D Goldstein, 'Do Defaults Save Lives' (2003) 302 Sci 1338–39.
[103] ibid.

It was also noted earlier how empirical research concerning adherence to options in treaties showed the significant impact of default rules.[104] More generally, behavioural international law studies have stressed the potential importance of default rules in choice architecture in international law.[105] Thus, a rule can be set up as an opt-out rule or an opt-in rule. An opt-in rule means that the default is nonadherence to the rule. In an opt-out scheme, the default is adherence. If people tend not to deviate from default rules, there is an advantage in setting up opt-out rules, especially where universality of the application of the rule is critical. Thus, if sources of international law that provide an opt-out system are used, higher participation may be expected in comparison to opt-in systems.

CIL can be particularly advantageous as a debiasing mechanism of international law. As explained above,[106] CIL is an opt-out system. Countries are bound by customary laws that have developed through the general practice of nations. Although CIL emerges from the consistent practice of countries, it is not a consensual mechanism. It does not require that countries agree to or enact the rule and as such does not represent a deviation from the status quo. The existence of CIL is based on an understanding that it is a norm of the international community. This does not necessarily mean, though, that a given country consents to the norm. Rather, the acceptance of the binding rule must be felt by countries generally.[107] Critically, to not be bound by the rule, a country needs to actively object to it.[108]

Thus, CIL is a mechanism of international cooperation that can promote universal application of the norm because opt-out rules are expected to increase participation, particularly on the global level, in the absence of mechanisms to impose regulation directly on countries' legal systems. It might be harder to ensure universal application through, for example, treaties, as treaties require an active opt-in.[109] The fact that CIL requires adherence (or objection) to the rule in its entirety also promotes integrity of its application.[110] Thus, with no room for cherry picking, it is more likely that the norm will remain uniform and coherent.

It shall be recalled that general principles may close residual gaps in the system and they too operate as a default system; they do not require that all countries subscribe to the principles. The principles become effective through general recognition

---

[104] See Chapter 2, section 2.4.3.

[105] J Galbraith, 'Treaty Options: Towards a Behavioral Understanding of Treaty Design' (2013) 53 Va J Intl L 309; van Aaken, 'Behavioral International Law and Economics' (n 59) 450–52; T Broude, 'Behavioral International Law' (2015) 163 U Pa L Rev 1099, 1140. Choice architecture is the study of how the ways in which options are presented affect decision making (RH Thaler and C Sunstein, *Nudge* (2008) 3).

[106] See section 3.2.1.

[107] AT Guzman, 'Against Consent' (2012) 52 Va J Intl L 747, 776.

[108] It has been noted that the emergence of the 'persistent objector' doctrine (n 36) has been part of an effort to make international law less consensual (see Bradley and Gulati, 'Withdrawing from International Custom' (n 13) 240).

[109] See Chapter 4, section 4.3.4.

[110] van Aaken, 'Behavioral International Law and Economics' (n 59) 452.

or acceptance by countries; thus, what matters is their recognition, not their consent or enactment of measures.[111]

3.3.2 CIL shifting the reference point

As explained in Chapter 2, outcomes are perceived as gains or losses usually relative to a reference point that people denote in the editing phase during the choice process, rather than as final states of wealth or welfare. The reference point usually corresponds to the current position whereby gains/losses are deviations from the reference point. Because of these biases, a negative perception of modified universalism outcomes is expected particularly where the country's reference point is a regime generally based on territorialism, namely, if the country does not have an established internationalist approach in its domestic methods for addressing cross-border insolvency.

Against this backdrop, it can be appreciated that a modified universalist CIL can, in addition to applying directly in areas not covered by treaties or other instruments, also indirectly promote the adoption of instruments (such as the MLCBI) where these instruments reflect modified universalism. A strong leading norm, elevated from a trend to CIL, may gradually affect the reference points of countries and implementing institutions, and level the playing field. When recognized as CIL, countries may feel more obliged to follow modified universalism and, over time, assimilate it into the legal system. Thus, adherence to instruments that are premised on modified universalism would less likely be perceived as a change and as a loss.

3.3.3 CIL inducing multinational cooperation

CIL evolution can also be influenced by positive inclinations where participants, such as regulators, judges, and other authorities, may develop other-regarding preferences and cooperate through CIL. Thus, CIL has a behavioural force as means for multinational cooperation, including in complex circumstances.[112]

A more sceptical approach to CIL concerning its behavioural force has been put forward by rational choice theorists. CIL arguably reflects self-interested behaviour and is created through coincidence or convergence of self-interested policies, or through coercion by one or more countries imposing their self-interest on others. This argument is based on a simple (one-shot) game theory, whereby countries interact in a single game and therefore CIL cannot influence the behaviour where the relevant countries have no reason to cooperate.[113] Because of lack of information and monitoring mechanisms on the international level, so the argument goes, CIL cannot create multistate cooperation. Thus, the emergence of a universal CIL is unlikely and CIL can work only among smaller groups of countries; and even that type

---

[111] S Hall, 'The Persistent Spectre: Natural Law, International Order and the Limits of Legal Positivism' (2001) 12 Eur J Intl L 269, 292.

[112] van Aaken, 'Behavioral International Law and Economics' (n 59) 453–56.

[113] cf Guzman, 'Saving Customary International Law' (n 6).

of cooperation can be explained as self-interested behaviour, not as an obligation under the CIL.[114]

However, a realistic understanding of the development of CIL considers CIL's emergence and evolution through interaction between actors and convergence of expectations.[115] Experimental studies with public-goods games have shown that normative expectations influence people's behaviour. Context and type of participants play a role, but participants do contribute more than expected by rational choice theory as they react to experience they have had in previous interactions with the other actors.[116] CIL does govern and affect behaviour because it emerges from what is considered normal and believed to be the normative expectation. It is a continuous process of compliance or violation.[117]

Variations on the rational choice theory[118] have also explained CIL's formation in more functional terms, namely as rules that emerge through repeated interactions affecting expectations. Thus, CIL can rationally be explained as a norm that countries see as legal rules. Applying standard assumptions about rationality but taking account of repeated interactions, countries can be incentivized to comply with CIL and to cooperate, in particular because of reputational sanctions. Because violation of CIL affects a country's reputation for compliance, CIL can alter behaviour. The presence of CIL generates an incentive to comply because a reputation for compliance with CIL offers benefits to countries, and therefore countries may be willing to forgo a short-term benefit to enjoy the future benefits of establishing or preserving a good reputation.[119]

3.4 Conceptual Impediments

Notwithstanding the rather widespread adherence to modified universalism, it has not been invoked or applied as CIL. As noted earlier in Chapter 1, modified universalism is not explicitly embraced in the global instruments for cross-border insolvency. Courts in common law jurisdictions often apply common law notions akin to a universalist/cooperative approach, noting that modified universalism is recognized as a broad principle under common law, or applying the notion of comity. Yet, comity entails different interpretations and is not universal.[120] Modified

---

[114] Goldsmith and Posner, *The Limits of International Law* (n 54) 87; van Aaken, 'Behavioral International Law and Economics' (n 59) 453–54.

[115] C Engel, 'The Emergence of a New Rule of Customary Law: An Experimental Contribution' (2011) 7 Rev L Econ 767, 769; C Engel and M Kurschiligen, 'The Coevolution of Behavior and Normative Expectations: An Experiment' (2013) 15 Am L Econ Rev 578, 582.

[116] A Chaudhuri, 'Sustaining Cooperation in Laboratory Public Goods Experiments: A Selective Survey of the Literature' (2011) 14 Experimental Econ 47, 47.

[117] Section 3.2.1. [118] See Chapter 2, section 2.2.

[119] See Guzman, 'Saving Customary International Law' (n 6) 133–37. See also Chapter 5 for a discussion of compliance incentives.

[120] The meaning of international comity is rather unspecified. As mentioned in Chapter 1, n 199, comity generally refers to the tradition among judges within the common law camp to cooperate and assist foreign jurisdictions.

universalism that could be applied as a universal and uniform norm has usually been considered a broad concept within the constraints of domestic private international law, to the extent that if we were to try identifying it now as CIL it would be difficult to show consistent practice that is based on belief in the conformity of the practice with international law, and CIL might be disproved.[121]

Reluctance to practise modified universalism even more widely than it has been practised thus far can be explained by the existence of biases affecting decisions and choices, as discussed earlier in Chapter 2. Yet, biases influence actors in different ways, depending, among other things, on how actors perceive the reference point against which they measure gains and losses that may result from taking a certain action. Thus, notwithstanding loss aversion, status quo bias, and related effects, modified universalism has emerged as the dominant approach. However, modified universalism is still often used just as a broad principle rather than as a binding international norm,[122] and therefore the question is whether there is an additional constraint that might be impeding the use of modified universalism as CIL.

It is argued below that the problem could lie in a narrow perception of cross-border insolvency law as a legal field addressing procedures and technicalities. Because cross-border insolvency law primarily regulates the private international law of insolvency, it can be understood as a field disconnected from public international law and public international law sources. As such, cross-border insolvency law might not be sufficiently influenced by international law and might not engage in creating CIL. This problem intensifies where modified universalism is perceived as an interim solution on the path to pure universalism, which holds it in the limbo between a tentative (albeit important) approach and a fundamental norm.

3.4.1 Public and private international law as distinct disciplines

The relation between private and public international law has been a subject of much debate and considerable theoretical development.[123] While in the early nineteenth century private international law was perceived as a category and an integral part of public international law pursuant to the idea of a unitary international law, based on the traditions of *Romanjus gentium*, the *Statutists* and the natural law, in

---

[121] As further discussed in section 3.6.1.

[122] Including by its proponents; see eg Lord Hoffmann's statements in the *HiH* case (n 222 and accompanying text).

[123] See eg JR Stevenson, 'The Relationship of Private International Law to Public International Law' (1952) 52(5) Colum L Rev 561, 564–67; K Lipstein, *Principles of the Conflict of Laws: National and International Perspectives* (Martinus Nijhoff Publishers 1981) 63–64; N Hatzimihail, 'On Mapping the Conceptual Battlefield of Private International Law'(2000) 13 Hague Y B Intl L 57; O Spiermann, 'Twentieth Century Internationalism in Law' (2007) 18(5) Eur J Int L 785; R Michaels, 'Private and Public International Law: German View on Global Issues' (2008) 4(1) J Priv Intl L 121; A Mills, *The Confluence of Public and Private International Law, Justice, Pluralism and Subsidiarity in the International Constitutional Ordering of Private Law* (CUP 2009); Kotuby Jr, 'General Principles of Law' (n 28).

the latter half of that century it evolved and crystallized as a separate field with a distinct role.[124]

Pursuant to this (modern) traditional separation of roles, public international law governs the relations between nations, provides a legal framework for organized international relations, and addresses the rights and obligations of countries with respect to other countries or individuals. Private international law, on the other hand, deals with the domestic laws of countries that govern conflicts between private persons. In this regard, private international law addresses the question of the jurisdictional authority to hear legal disputes where foreign elements are involved, to decide the applicable law, and to recognize and enforce foreign judgments.

Against this backdrop, it has been doubted that rules which are fundamental to private international law could and have generated customary (public) international law. It has been debated, for example, whether concepts related to jurisdiction and choice of law have become CIL. The old internationalist school of private international law, which had viewed it as inseparable from public international law, has pointed to certain private international law rules as CIL. These included the rule that rights *in rem* in immovable and movable property are governed by the *lex situs*, that form is governed by the *lex loci actus*, that procedure is governed by the *lex fori,* and that free choice of applicable law is allowed regarding conflict of laws of obligations. The prevailing view, however, has been that these concepts are in fact private international law rules and not international norms, coinciding with the arguments against the old merging of private international law into public international law.[125]

It has also been argued that the concept of international comity has perhaps amounted to CIL (or else to a general principle of law[126]) in private international law, as through the concept of comity, private international law has pursued internationalist goals, specifically where comity provided prominent ground for the obligation to apply foreign laws.[127] Yet, the force of comity as an international norm has been seriously doubted. It has been argued that comity has been exercised by a rather limited number of countries and has not been widely practised.[128] It is applied in different ways in different jurisdictions pursuant to local understandings of the notion, and it is more prevalent in countries with a common law tradition.[129]

---

[124] A comprehensive assessment of the nature of the relation between private and public international law is beyond the scope of this study. See generally Stevenson, 'The Relationship of Private International Law to Public International Law' (n 123).

[125] P Kalensky, *Trends of Private International Law* (Martinus Nijhoff Publishers 1971) 17; Lipstein, *Principles of the Conflict of Laws* (n 123) 64.

[126] JR Paul, 'Comity in International Law' (1991) 32 Harv Intl L J 1, 1, 7, 8, 27, 44.

[127] See eg R Way, 'Transnational Liftoff and Juridical Touchdown: The Regulatory Function of Private International Law in an Era of Globalization' (2002) 40 Columbia Journal of Transnational Law 209, 242; H Yntema, 'The Comity Doctrine' (1966) 65 Mich L Rev 9.

[128] Paul, 'Comity in International Law' (n 126) 1, 27–44.

[129] In the context of cross-border insolvency as well, comity has been noted mainly regarding assistance by countries that follow the common law legal tradition (see IF Fletcher, *Insolvency in Private International Law* (OUP 2005) 17; A Godwin, T Howse, and I Ramsay, 'The Inherent Power of Common Law Courts to Provide Assistance in Cross-Border Insolvencies: From Comity to Complexity' (2017) 26 Intl Insolv Rev 5, 7 ff).

Thus, for example, comity plays an important role in American jurisprudence and is considered a foundation of American private international law.[130] It also has a role in English private international law, albeit a more limited one.[131] Yet, in other jurisdictions (eg Germany), a public concept of comity plays hardly any role.[132] Comity might not, therefore, be justified on the basis of international legal obligation.[133] It has also been argued that the meaning of comity is ambiguous:[134] it is too vague and therefore cannot generate private international law rules.[135] The international community was not able to form a general concept of comity that can amount to CIL. Even in jurisdictions where it is frequently applied, including in the context of cross-border insolvency, the application of comity is not considered a matter of absolute obligation.[136] It is rather an 'elastic' notion that advances friendly intercourse with other nations and it allows courts in each case to provide the content of the norm.[137] The extension of comity to another country 'is viewed as a unilateral decision of the forum, not as an act required by a rule of the pubic international system'.[138]

Generally, the traditional division between private and public international law and the evolution of private international law as a domestic legal order regulating in the domain of private interests, contributed to the gradual isolation of private international law from international law, and the general exclusion of a role for international sources.[139] This model has resulted in a private international law system that does not contribute much to the ordering of international private relations, but instead often adds to the complexity of international transactions, as private international laws of different system often conflict or operate with broad exceptions creating uncertainty and costs.[140] This division of roles between private and public

---

[130] Paul, 'Comity in International Law' (n 126) 1, 78.

[131] L Collins, 'Comity in Modern Private International Law', in J Fawcett (ed), *Reform and Development of Private International Law: Essays in Honour of Sir Peter North* (OUP 2002).

[132] Michaels, 'Private and Public International Law (n 123)126.

[133] Paul, 'Comity in International Law' (n 126) 1, 79.

[134] ibid 1, 78. In the United Kingdom, Dicey has rejected comity as a foundation of private international law on the grounds of uncertainty (AV Dicey, *Digest of the Law of England with Reference to the Conflict of Laws* (Stevens and Sons London 1896) 10). See also A Mills, 'The Private History of International Law' (2006) 55 ICLQ 1, 31; SA Morales and BA Deutsch, 'Bankruptcy Code Section 304 and U.S. Recognition of Foreign Bankruptcies: The Tyranny of Comity' (1984) 39 Bus Lawyer 1573.

[135] Michaels, 'Private and Public International Law' (n 123) 125.

[136] Comity may be described as 'the deference of one nation to the legislative, executive and judicial acts of another—not as an obligation, but as a courtesy serving international duty and convenience' (D Farmer, 'Chapter 15 Ancillary and Other Cross-Border Insolvency Cases' (2015) 19 Hawaii Bar J 14, 16–17).

[137] *Hilton v Guyot* 159 US 113, 164 (1895); *In re Daewoo Motor Am, Inc.*, 495 F 3d 1249, 1259 (11th Cir 2006). See also B Wessels, *International Insolvency Law* (Wolters Kluwer 2015) 34, 43–46. See further section 3.6 noting various applications of comity in cross-border insolvency cases.

[138] US District Court 17 October 2006, LJN AZ6811. See also Crawford, *Brownlie's Principles of Public International Law* 8th edn (n 70) 23–24 (explaining the difference between general practice, which amounts to CIL and mere habit or usage, which does not reflect a legal obligation, noting that 'such practices are carried on out of courtesy (or 'comity') and are neither articulated nor claimed as legal requirements. International comity is a species of accommodation: it involves neighbourliness, mutual respect, and the friendly waiver of technicalities').

[139] Mills, 'The Private History of International Law' (n 134) 45.   [140] ibid 46.

international law also arguably constrains the ability to regulate the important domain of private international interaction in view of the operation of private power in the global economy.[141]

While the relationship between private and public international law continues to develop and the distinction between the two fields has begun to blur (as further discussed in section 3.5), a disciplinary separation between the two fields is still apparent. Different legal regimes take different approaches. Thus, for example, the tendency in the United States has been towards unifying public international law and choice of law, while in the United Kingdom the separation has been more stable.[142] In Germany, public and private international law are still considered discrete and distinct disciplines.[143] However, the general assumption reflected in commentary in the field of private international law across legal systems is that it is essentially domestic in origin and effect, and that principles and rules concerning the conflict of laws are not international.[144]

3.4.2 Cross-border insolvency as a system of procedural private international law

Cross-border insolvency, being a system primarily regulating the private international law aspects of insolvency, is similarly prone to such isolation from international law. As a specialized field of private international law, it can be perceived as a system regulating within the private domain and mainly providing procedural rules to resolve jurisdictional and choice of law conflicts. Where this is the case, international law sources such as CIL might not be considered relevant for the cross-border insolvency regime. CIL, a key source of international law, may seem beyond the realm and the focus of private international law of insolvency. It may be difficult to form modified universalism as CIL where key players in the field, including judges, legislators, and policy makers, might not see themselves as contributing to the creation of international laws when making decisions in international insolvency. Such actors might not engage with modified universalism in the same way they would have had they been conceptualizing their role as international and their actions as influencing and shaping international law.

---

[141] AC Cutler, 'Artifice, Ideology and Paradox: The Public/Private Distinction in International Law' (1997) 4 Review of Intl Political Economy 261, 279; Mills, 'The Private History of International Law' (n 134) 46.

[142] Michaels, 'Private and Public International Law' (n 123) 121.

[143] ibid 123; N Jansen and R Michaels, 'Private Law and the State: Comparative Perceptions and Historical Dimensions' (2007) 71 *RabelsZ* 345.

[144] Mills, 'The Private History of International Law' (n 134) (noting that 'it is the myth that private international law is not actually international, as it is essentially and necessarily a part of the domestic law of States', referring to: L Collins (ed), *Dicey and Morris on The Conflict of Laws* (13th edn, Sweet & Maxwell 2000) 3; Jennings and Watts (eds), *Oppenheim's International Law* (n 87) 6; Second Restatement of the Conflict of Laws (American Law Institute 1969) s 2; JG Castel, *Canadian Conflict of Laws* (3rd edn, Butterworths (Canada) Toronto 1994) 3; J Verzijl, 'International Law in Historical Perspective' (1968) 1 A Sijthoff Leyden 190, and to the Serbian and Brazilian Loans cases, *France v Yugoslavia; France v Brazil PCIJ Ser A*, nos 20–1 (1929)).

That cross-border insolvency is a body of specific and narrow rules concerning insolvency procedures has been a common understanding and description of this area of the law.[145] Often international insolvency does not exist as a 'systematically elaborated legal framework' and domestic private international law applies.[146] Cross-border insolvency has been generally regarded as 'an arcane and rarified area of specialization'.[147] Narrow assumptions concerning the role of cross-border insolvency have been notable in the practice and observed in the 1980s and early 1990s. It has been noted that countries have generally presumed that international insolvency is an aspect of private law. Such views resulted in limited interest of countries in the field of cross-border insolvency where countries have confined their role to the regulation of procedure concerning international insolvency. This peripheral interest of governments has also arguably constrained negotiations on insolvency treaties and could explain the general failure in concluding treaties in this field.[148]

The approach to cross-border insolvency has evolved over time, and importantly there has been growing recognition of the difficulty in controlling cross-border insolvencies efficiently by relying on the domestic private international laws of national systems. It has been acknowledged that domestic private international laws related to insolvency have preserved the problem of diversity and conflicts between national laws.[149] Consequently, hugely influential uniform frameworks have emerged, notably the MLCBI. Yet, as international instruments that attempt to regulate the specialized field of cross-border insolvency, they too can be understood as merely providing certain tools to address private international procedures more efficiently, but not as creating general norms that intend to influence substantive results. Such understanding of the role of the MLCBI was explicitly expressed by a court in Australia:

The Model Law ... was conceived in an environment of respect for difference between jurisdictions and from this it can be assumed that recognition of foreign judgments, a measure that can protect local creditors and a local court's sovereignty, was to be maintained. *It was promoted as having a procedural effect as opposed to a substantive effect* that might have included automatic recognition and enforcement or effects.[150]

The prominent decision in the *Rubin* case as well reflects a restrained approach with respect to the MLCBI's role. The court refrained from reading the MLCBI in a way that takes account of its possible general intentions to serve the international community and reach certain results, and instead read the law narrowly, with the result that enforcement of the foreign judgment was denied even though it was a judgment of the globally collective main proceedings.[151]

---

[145] Wessels, *International Insolvency Law* (n 137) 1.   [146] ibid 4.

[147] Fletcher, *Insolvency in Private International Law* (n 129) 7.

[148] J Honsberger, *The Negotiation of a Bankruptcy Treaty*, reprinted in 1985 Meredith Memorial Lectures (McGill University 1985) 288, 291; TM Gaa, 'Harmonization of International Bankruptcy Law and Practice: Is it Necessary? Is It Possible?' (1993) 27 Intl L 881, 897). See also Chapter 4 for a discussion of instrument choice for cross-border insolvency, including the use of treaties.

[149] Fletcher, *Insolvency in Private International Law* (n 129) 7.

[150] *Bank of Western Australia v Henderson* (No 3) [2011] FMCA 840 Federal Magistrates court, 2 November 2011, para 43 (emphasis added).

[151] See Chapter 1, n 202. See also JL Westbrook, 'Interpretation Internationale' (2015) 87 Temp L Rev 739.

The important framework for cross-border insolvency applicable in Europe (the EIR/EIR Recast) has also evolved as an aspect of the European Community private international law system.[152] It has been observed that the European insolvency framework has not provided a uniform and comprehensive legal framework.[153] In all, the important advance of cross-border insolvency regimes has been tempered by a modest approach concerning the role of cross-border insolvency law and of the frameworks that are being devised to govern cross-border insolvency cases.

3.4.3 Modified universalism as a transitory approach

A tendency to underrate the role of cross-border insolvency is exacerbated where modified universalism is perceived as an interim solution, inextricably linked to the aspiration to achieve pure universalism. At least in the theory, pure universalism (ie complete unity and universality) is often considered the ultimate ideal for regulating cross-border insolvency and modified universalism the best solution pending movement to true universalism.[154] Modified universalism is thought to provide a pragmatic transitory approach whilst country laws still differ, and one which could foster the smoothest transition to true universalism.[155]

It is inevitable, however, that whilst modified universalism remains conceptually transitory, its ability to solidify and become CIL is undermined. CIL must represent settled obligatory practice,[156] therefore a transitory doctrine would be an oxymoron. True, rules or principles of a temporary character may stay in such an interim state for a long time and until a new regime develops. CIL can change and new CIL can emerge when conduct inconsistent with it may in relevant circumstances show the appearance of new rules. CIL does not have to stay still. Yet, for CIL to emerge in the first place, it should be demonstrated that it is followed consistently based on the belief about the conformity of the practice with international law. It may be difficult to form such a type of law, however, where modified universalism is in this midpoint between an interim solution and a fundamental norm and is conceptually linked to another presumably better approach, thus representing a transitory stage in the development of more ideal rules.

3.5 Reconceptualization: The International Role of Cross-Border Insolvency

These conceptual impediments restricting the role of cross-border insolvency and the status of modified universalism could constrain the transformation of modified universalism from a broad approach to CIL. Yet, the narrow conception of private international law and of cross-border insolvency is misconceived. Private

---

[152] Wessels, *International Insolvency Law* (n 137) 6.   [153] ibid 7.
[154] As it is assumed that countries cannot, for now, be persuaded to subscribe to the universality doctrine in its fullest form (see Chapter 1, section 1.3.1).
[155] ibid.   [156] See section 3.2.1.

international law's international role is growing with the increased importance of multinational cooperation and of international trade. The theorizing of the relationship between private and public international law is developing in such a direction. Cross-border insolvency has a strong international character, as can also be seen from the extensive work of transnational actors in this field. In that regard, modified universalism is the only approach that provides concrete, realistic rules that as such can become the leading norm for the system, in the fulfilment of cross-border insolvency's international role. To become CIL, modified universalism should be conceptualized as a stand-alone approach separate from pure universalism.

3.5.1 Internationalization of private international law

Gradually since the twentieth century and more so in recent decades, the division between private and public international law has become uncertain and blurred.[157] The traditional separation of roles of the two fields no longer fits with the current state of globalization or with modern intervention by countries in terms of regulating private market activities, adding a public interest component to private business law.[158] The conceptualization of the relationship between private and public international law and of the role of private international law is in a state of evolution too, because of these changes in world realities. It is becoming clear that private international law of a narrow character cannot properly address modern challenges in an increasingly interconnected world.[159] It has been noted that while international disputes in the past were largely limited to regional relations among close legal systems, the discourse had become truly global in recent decades.[160] Therefore, private international law should not be perceived as a mere system of technical rules regarding the proper forum and law and the facilitation of recognition and enforcement of foreign judgments.[161] Furthermore, private international law should not insulate itself and attempt to regulate private interactions separately from the broader international order, as such isolation obscures the operation of private power in the global political economy.[162]

There are also growing overlaps and intersections of the roles of each field in practice. Thus, public international law shows a rising interest in economic relations, and multinational corporations and individuals are no longer outside its remit.[163] It has

---

[157] Spiermann, 'Twentieth Century Internationalism in Law' (n 123); Michaels, 'Private and Public International Law' (n 123); Mills, *The Confluence of Public and Private International Law, Justice, Pluralism and Subsidiarity* (n 123); Kotuby Jr, 'General Principles of Law' (n 28); J Waldron, 'Foreign Law and the Modern *Ius Gentium*' (2006) 119 Harv L Rev 129, 135.

[158] See eg Michaels, 'Private and Public International Law' (n 123) 122–23.

[159] Kotuby Jr, 'General Principles of Law' (n 28) 411–12.   [160] ibid.

[161] Kotuby argues that private international law should have an interest and a meaningful role to play in identifying and ensuring compliance with general international principles regarding the way transnational disputes are resolved (ibid).

[162] Cutler, 'Artifice, Ideology and Paradox' (n 141) 279.

[163] Shaw, *International Law* (n 4) 143 (explaining that 'one of the distinguished characteristics of contemporary international law has been the wide range of participants. These include states, international organisations, non-governmental organisations, public companies, private companies and individuals. Human rights law, the law relating to armed conflicts and international economic law are especially

also been noted that public international law is becoming domesticated and more technical.[164] Importantly, the result of increasing intersections and overlaps between private and public international law has been a gradual expansion of the role and scope of private international law.[165] Thus, many of the tasks of private international law, for example, its dealing with recent problems of sovereign state insolvency, might have previously been viewed as belonging to public international law.[166]

Movement towards the internationalization of private international law has been apparent for some time with the conclusion of treaties and other international instruments in recent years on matters of jurisdiction, choice of law, and recognition and enforcement of foreign judgments.[167] This trend has coincided with internationalization of national economies and their increased interdependence. Internationalization can also be seen in the rise of international commercial law and its development from the early stages of the Merchant Law to modern legal orders on a transnational scale.[168] International organizations (IOs) have been playing a significant part. For example, UNCITRAL has been charged with the task of coordinating global law reform to support international trade.[169]

Thus, in a way, we are witnessing a gradual reunification of private and public international law in both theory and practice, although in this process, private international law is not swollen by or fully merged with public international law. Rather, its role and scope are augmented.[170] In view of this growing and more internationally oriented mission of private international law, it has been observed that private international law should continue to evolve and in this process draw lessons from

important in generating and reflecting increased participation and personality in international law'). See also A Clapham, *Human Rights Obligations of Non-State Actors* (OUP 2006); R McCorquodale, 'The Individual and the International Legal System' in MD Evans (ed), *International Law* (4th edn, OUP 2014) 291–94; Waldron, 'Foreign Law and the Modern *Ius Gentium*' (n 157) (commenting, inter alia, on the relevance of the international law concept of *ius gentium*—the law of nations—to individuals, companies, and commercial transactions); Roberts and Sivakumaran, 'Lawmaking by Non-state Actors' (n 60) 122 (noting the Convention on the Settlement of Investment Disputes Between States and Nationals of Other States (arts 25, 36, 18 March 1965, 17 UST 1270, 575 UNTS 159) as an example of an international investment treaty that grants investors procedural rights to enforce investment protections); Guzman, 'A Compliance-Based Theory of International Law' (n 61) (arguing that the focus of international law should continue to shift to less traditional matters and focus more on areas such as international economic law where international law is likely to have more impact).

[164] AM Slaughter and W Burke-White, 'The Future of International Law is Domestic (or the European Way of Law)' (2006) 47 Harv Intl L J 327.

[165] Michaels, 'Private and Public International Law' (n 123) 123.

[166] ibid 137, referring to cases before German courts involving Argentina eg on the question whether Argentina could invoke its own moratorium as internationally mandatory rules.

[167] See eg the Brussels Regulations on jurisdiction and the recognition and enforcement of judgments in civil and commercial matters (2012); The Hague Conference on Private International Law <https://www.hcch.net/>; the MLCBI; and the EIR/Recast EIR.

[168] HJ Berman, 'The Law of International Commercial Transactions' (1998) 2 Emory Journal of International Dispute Resolution 235, 243. For a summary of these developments see R Mason, 'Cross-Border Insolvency and Legal Transnationalisation' (2012) 21 Intl Insolv Rev 105, 108–12.

[169] See the United Nations General Assembly Resolution GA Res 2205(XXI), UN Doc A/RES/2205 (17 Dec 1966) 8.

[170] Way, 'Transnational Liftoff and Juridical Touchdown' (n 127) 219–20; Michaels, 'Private and Public International Law' (n 123) 137–38.

public international law.[171] Such internationalization should not obscure, however, the complexity of entities and the multiplicity of legal systems. Nor should it detract from the pursuit of effective remedies through domestic regulation where appropriate, or the benefits that may derive from a plurality of systems.[172]

3.5.2 Substantive and international impact of cross-border insolvency

The increased role of private international law and the relevance of public international law sources to the mission of private international law should be highlighted more in the context of cross-border insolvency. A broad internationalist approach assigned to private international law is particularly justified in the field of cross-border insolvency where private and public interests intersect: insolvency law is considered 'meta' law.[173] Insolvency principles are closely linked to fundamental public policy and social goals, and insolvency outcomes often impact on the economy and the wider public.[174]

Cross-border insolvency law is not merely procedural, but rather, also affects substantive rights, even where it is mainly confined to the harmonization of private international laws pertaining to insolvency.[175] Through a cross-border insolvency framework based on modified universalism, it is possible to enforce a collective insolvency process on the global level including by requiring the transfer of assets to the central proceedings and imposing additional duties and requirements regarding the conduct of such proceedings with the important substantive result of equitable treatment of creditors wherever located.[176] Cross-border insolvency can also do more than connect national legal systems. It can engage in the identification of best practices and in the formulation of international standards, and it can prevent financial collapse.[177]

[171] Michaels, 'Private and Public International Law' (n 123) 137–38 (concluding that 'in the end, this learning experience may present the biggest influence of public on private international law'). See also Waldron, 'Foreign Law and the Modern *Ius Gentium*' (n 157) 135–38 (arguing that there is room for seeking guidance from foreign law through the notion of the law of nations (*ius gentium*)—'the accumulated wisdom of the world on rights and justice'—including the law of the commercial world, in private law cases).

[172] Way, 'Transnational Liftoff and Juridical Touchdown' (n 127) 239.

[173] M Balz, 'The European Union Convention on Insolvency Proceedings' (1996) 70 Am Bankr L J 485, 486; Wessels, *International Insolvency Law* (n 137) 3.

[174] The claim that insolvency law's role is merely procedural and should be confined to the respect of pre-acquired rights through orderly distribution of the estate has been strongly rejected by proponents of the 'traditionalist' approach (E Warren, 'Bankruptcy Policy' (1987) 54 U Chicago L Rev 775. cf TH Jackson, 'Translating Assets and Liabilities to the Bankruptcy Forum' (1985) 14 J Legal Stud 73).

[175] See also Bork, *Principles of Cross-Border Insolvency Law* (n 95) 17–18, 113–14 (explaining, by reference to old authorities as well as examples from international instruments that: 'One might think that ... [cross-border insolvency law] contains formal conflict of laws rules only, and one might assess the field of conflict of laws as being neutral and anaemic, merely demarcating and impartially allocating national laws to the cross-border issues in question without taking into account the interests of parties involved or at least pursing basic standards. However, it was explained ... decades ago that the rules governing conflict of laws can be based on substantive principles ... and the same holds true for cross-border insolvency law').

[176] See Chapter 1, sections 1.3.2.1–1.3.2.4.

[177] Wessels, *International Insolvency Law* (n 137) 2–3.

Cross-border insolvency is of a true international nature, as many cases of general default involve multinational enterprises with branches and subsidiaries spanning multiple countries.[178] The way a court or authority in one country handles international insolvency cases often has significant implications across borders in numerous jurisdictions, affecting a broad range of stakeholders. The administration of cross-border insolvencies can also have impact on the public and the economy at large.[179] International insolvencies and, to an even larger extent, multinational defaults of multinational financial institutions (MFIs) often not only have an impact on the private business community, but might affect wider public interests, and even threaten the economic and political stability of nation states.[180] The collapse of Lehman Brothers and of other institutions during the global financial crisis are most notable examples.[181] The insolvency of Hanjin Shipping in 2016 is as well an example of how the filing of bankruptcy in one jurisdiction (The Republic of Korea in this case) presented paramount global challenges, where it was a matter of public interest that the Korean proceedings would be swiftly recognized in the multiple shipping destination so that cargo worth millions of dollars could resume moving to its various destinations.[182]

The international insolvency regime is a critical component of the international economic framework. The effective resolution of cross-border insolvency contributes to international trade and investment, as the United Nations General Assembly acknowledged when initiating the work in this field.[183] Cross-border insolvency and its resolution regarding banks and other financial institutions is also an integral

---

[178] See eg the multinational default of *Lehman Brothers* in 2008 (n 181). Many cases are of a smaller scale, but still several jurisdictions may be involved and not necessarily from the same region.

[179] It was commented in the 1990s that: 'Bankruptcy law has become so important to the national economy that reform no longer can be left to a few academics and insolvency practitioners' (DG Boshkoff, 'Some Gloomy Thoughts Concerning Cross-Border Insolvencies' (1994) 72 Wash U L Q 931, 935).

[180] See also Gaa, 'Harmonization of International Bankruptcy Law and Practice' (n 148) 909.

[181] The collapse of Lehman Brothers nearly brought down the world's financial system when it collapsed in 2008 (I Mevorach, 'Beyond the Search for Certainty: Addressing the Cross-Border Resolution Gap' (2015) 10(1) Brook J Corp Fin & Com L 194).

[182] See eg the decision of the US court to provide provisional relief to Hanjin in order 'to continue operating in the ordinary course, to enter U.S. territory without the fear of arrest or seizure, and to bring containers and cargo to land that otherwise would be stuck at sea' (*In re Hanjin Shipping Co Ltd*, 16-3652 (3d Cir September 22 2016). The former General Counsel for Hanjin Shipping America noted that: 'when Hanjin Shipping, once the 7th largest container carrier in the world and the 4th largest container carriers in the transpacific (Asia—US & Canada) trade, filed for bankruptcy, few believed that a "too big to fail" organization like Hanjin would not be given a government bail-out. So, naturally, no one really appreciated the kind of disruption and losses that would subsequently affect the global supply chain' (W Chung, 'Hanjin Shipping: From the Eye of the Storm and Back' (2017) <http://www.marinelog.com/index.php?option=com_k2&view=item&id=25323:hanjin-shipping-from-the-eye-of-the-storm-and-back&Itemid=230>).

[183] General Assembly resolution 52/158 of 15 December 1997 ('convinced that fair and internationally harmonized legislation on cross-border insolvency that respects the national procedural and judicial systems and is acceptable to States with different legal, social and economic systems would contribute to the development of international trade and investment … ').

aspect of the global financial system and the architecture of international financial law.[184]

Already, and for several decades now, transnational actors have been engaged in the creation of standards in insolvency and the development of a framework for cross-border insolvency. The mission of standardization of insolvency laws has been primarily targeted at development of legal systems, importantly in economies in transition (as discussed later in Chapter 5). The work of UNCITRAL on the development of the MLCBI has focused on the international aspects of insolvency and was sought to contribute to international trade and investment. It is a most paramount endeavour in the process of endorsing the international role of cross-border insolvency.[185] Against the backdrop of the general evolution of private international law, such work on international frameworks for insolvency should continue to develop within their broader international context.

3.5.3 Separation of modified universalism from the pure theory of universalism

Creating international binding CIL in cross-border insolvency depends on demonstrating the existence of a certain practice in this field that is understood as law. To the extent that, on the one hand, modified universalism is viewed as a transitory approach, and on the other hand, pure universalism is considered aspirational, there could be a conceptual impediment to the transformation of modified universalism to CIL. If it is understood as an approach which exists only for the interim, modified universalism cannot proceed to a more formalized established norm. As a permanent but merely aspirational concept (at least in the foreseeable future), pure universalism cannot become settled law either. Thus, for universalism to become an established binding CIL and emerge from its constant frail status, it must be based on modified universalism and be reconceptualized from a transitory doctrine linked to pure universalism to a stand-alone norm. The table below (Table 3.1) illustrates this conceptual shift and the way it is akin to the development of a viable international law source:

Table 3.1 The reconceptualization of modified universalism

Emerging CIL	Modified universalism as a transitory approach linked to pure universalism
Established CIL	Reconceptualization: modified universalism as a norm separate from pure universalism

---

[184] C Brummer, *Soft Law and the Global Financial System, Rule Making in the 21st Century* (CUP 2015) 233–34, 319–24.
[185] See also Chapter 6, section 6.2.2 for an assessment of the MLCBI.

The idea that modified universalism should incrementally pursue pure universalism also lacks justificatory grounds. Even though modified universalism originated from pure universalism, it is only modified universalism that provides concrete rules fitting with business and legal realities, thus guiding parties in actual cases. Pure universalism offers the most viable theoretical model for cross-border insolvency, yet it is only modified universalism that translates the model to a practical approach.[186]

Therefore, while the system may strive to increase the universal scope of modified universalism, the aspiration to change modified universalism's nature into a purer form is not practical; in fact, it is conceptually incorrect. Pure universalism is the theoretical foundation of the emerging norms of modified universalism, and both the model and the norms derive from the principles of unity and universality, but pure universalism should not be the final objective of the system. The idea of pure unity through, for example, the application of supranational law applied by a supranational court, or the full convergence of laws, or the centralization of any enterprise in default in a single forum, obscures the complexity of entities and the multiplicity of legal systems.[187] As noted earlier, the internationalization of private international law does not necessitate and may not ignore such complexities and the system could benefit from some degree of legal plurality.[188] Instead, modified universalism can retain its flexible character to accommodate changing conditions and global business needs. Such pliability would also fit with the nature of CIL.

An important argument against a reconceptualization of modified universalism as a stand-alone approach, however, is that this would risk its further development into a more widespread and consistent regime. Formalizing modified universalism might make participants more reluctant to follow it. Arguably, it is this humility and modesty attached to modified universalism that allowed it to grow, through 'incrementalism'.[189] It may be conceived, for example, that, rather than making explicit proclamations about the intentions of frameworks and pointing to concrete international laws, it is better to provide tools that achieve the same intentions without 'scaring off' countries from participating in the regime.

Yet, if modified universalism is eventually transformed to CIL, it can benefit from the additional advantage that it can operate as a debiasing mechanism: namely, it can to some extent address countries' aversions and reluctance to adhere to modified universalist instruments.[190] Furthermore, by concealing the justificatory basis (the

---

[186] See Chapter 1, section 1.3.1.

[187] See also Chapter 5, section 5.3, for a discussion of the limitations of harmonization and delegation.

[188] See n 172 and accompanying text.

[189] JAE Pottow, 'Procedural Incrementalism: A Model for International Bankruptcy' (2005) 45 Virginia J Intl L 935, 939; JAE Pottow, 'Beyond Carve-Outs and Toward Reliance: A Normative Framework for Cross-Border Insolvency Choice of Law' (2014) 9(1) Brook J Corp Fin & Com L 197, 198 ('modified universalism is more specifically an instance of procedural incrementalism, a form of incrementalism that moves for gradually increasing subjugation of sovereignty on seemingly less threatening, procedural matters as a form of acclimation to the imposition of foreign law upon (or at least foreign court control over) domestic insolvency proceedings'). Pottow does suggest, however, an independent normative theory for choice of law based on modified universalism. See also generally S Block-Lieb and TC Halliday, 'Incrementalism in Global Lawmaking' (2007) 32 Brook J Intl L 851.

[190] See section 3.3.1.

source) of certain solutions and focusing on technical results, there is a risk that both the frameworks' design and the application of the rules they prescribe in practice, would be inconsistent. It is also more difficult to fill in gaps in the system in the absence of a general, settled norm. Finally, it was perhaps the case in the earlier stages of development of the cross-border insolvency system that some obscurity regarding its norms was merited, so that frameworks could gain initial traction and expand. Yet, as shown in Chapter 1, the cross-border insolvency system has gone through significant development, and the main cross-border insolvency instrument (the MLCBI) has been adopted by many. It is now, therefore, time to stabilize the system further, including through greater clarity about its underlying norms and about their legal status.

A related argument against the separation of modified universalism from pure universalism could be that retaining the more ideal aspiration of achieving complete unity and universality can push countries towards greater universalism at least up to a certain point. Arguably that aspiration is not harmful. However, it is exactly that sort of connection to pure universalism that leaves modified universalism in a susceptible position and limits its ability to develop into a settled norm that can be followed consistently and be utilized to fill gaps in the system. The conceptual separation of modified universalism from the originating theory does matter and is timely. Such separation and the use of CIL as a source for cross-border insolvency, while requiring that modified universalism is understood and used as a stand-alone norm, should not cause concern to proponents of incremental developments in this field. The use of CIL does not preclude developments because it is a source that is flexible and changeable. As aforementioned, CIL can evolve over time, and it is possible to change or create new CIL to meet the developing needs of nations.[191]

3.6 Transformation: Modified Universalism Becoming CIL

The full realization of the internationalist role of cross-border insolvency and the adoption of modified universalism as the leading approach, not only in the interim, can pave the way towards its attainment of greater and more straightforward usages, which in turn can result in the transformation of modified universalism from a broad approach to CIL. As explained above, CIL is not a tidy notion and the identification of the exact stage of its formation is elusive. Generally, there are myriad problems associated with CIL's theory and practice. Yet, the existence of CIL can be evidenced from a range of actions (and inactions) and if identified and proved, it can provide important advantages for the cross-border insolvency system. Thus, this section attempts to highlight what might still be missing in the way in which modified universalism is practiced and to suggest certain steps that could be taken to achieve the transformation of modified universalism to CIL. This section also demonstrates how modified universalism in the form of CIL could be used in the future to better promote consistent adherence to its norms.

---

[191] See section 3.2.6.

3.6.1 Evidence of a general practice accepted as law

Modified universalist approaches are already widespread in the practice. Modified universalism seems to have generally guided the key existing frameworks for cross-border insolvency. These frameworks, in particular the MLCBI, have been applied quite successfully by participating countries.[192] This practice is also not confined to a few specific jurisdictions, although it is undoubtedly more paramount in certain countries and regions.[193] It is also not limited to specific entities, though a modified universalist practice is less established with regard to multinational enterprise groups and MFIs.[194] The growing usage of cross-border insolvency protocols and the increased cooperation between courts and between insolvency representatives in cross-border insolvencies are also demonstrations of a modified universalist practice.[195] Thus, important indications that can point to an emerging CIL in cross-border insolvency do exist, and as mentioned above, to establish CIL it is not required that all countries subscribe to the norm. Furthermore, where there are deviations from modified universalism in practice, these seem to result from difficulties in acting decisively, for example adopting the MLCBI, or accepting certain elements of the global framework. Such deviations probably result from some degree of loss aversion, a status quo bias, or a lack of system readiness, as well as difficulties in maintaining universalist commitments because of short-termism,[196] rather than from persistent objection and opposition to modified universalism.[197]

Yet, for modified universalism to finally transform from an emerging to an established CIL, it is crucial that its application by relevant actors is generally pervasive and consistent. Hesitancy, uncertainty, contradiction, fluctuation, and discrepancy in invoking and applying the norm can undermine and ultimately negate the identification of CIL. Furthermore, the norm should be accepted as law. Thus, CIL might be disproved where it can be shown that participants were not motivated by a legal duty and acted in the belief that their acts did not amount to customary law. It has been argued, for example, regarding the concept of international comity that '[A]t best, it is only incidental

---

[192] See Chapter 1, section 1.4.4.　　　[193] ibid, sections 1.4.4–1.4.5.

[194] ibid, section 1.3.2.1. See also BC Matthews, 'Prospects for Coordination and Competition in Global Finance' (2010) Proceedings of the Annual Meeting (American Society of International Law), Vol 104, International Law in a Time of Change (2010) 289, 291–95 (identifying some convergence of key rules pertaining to the resolution of banks that may amount to CIL, but also noting the gap in the cross-border resolution system).

[195] It was already suggested in the 1990s that a cross-border insolvency Concordat and cross-border insolvency agreements, which aim to create close cooperation, and in the case of the Concordat, the centralization of the process in a lead forum, are likely to become evidence of an international customary norm (Gaa, 'Harmonization of International Bankruptcy Law and Practice' (n 148) 882; DH Culmer, 'The Cross-Border Insolvency Concordat and Customary International Law: Is it Ripe Yet' (1999) 14 Connecticut J Intl L 563). See also Mason, 'Cross-Border Insolvency and Legal Transnationalisation' (n 168) 126 (suggesting that cross-border agreements may reflect modern merchant law or even international customary law, referring also to a lecture by Professor Bob Wessels where he expresses similar views regarding the use of cross-border agreements).

[196] See Chapter 2, sections 2.5.1 and 2.5.2.

[197] As noted in section 3.2.3, the threshold for qualifying as a persistent objector is very high.

that some civil-law systems arrive at results comparable to the decisions of US courts.'[198]

Regarding cross-border insolvency, it can be argued that because decisions or actions taken in this field are often either not explicitly based on modified universalism, or are based on modified universalism as a broad approach linked to independent domestic common law developments,[199] its usage is in fact a demonstration of a tradition but not of CIL.

To establish modified universalism as autonomous CIL and make the identification of CIL more plausible, clear pronouncements are needed that can show a consistent acceptance of modified universalism and the application of the norm in accordance with international law. Of primary importance is how countries address cross-border insolvency, especially influential countries (significant economies such as the United States and the United Kingdom, as well as new emerging cross-border insolvency 'hubs'[200]) that are more often affected by the norm and have the chance to interact with other state actors and shape the norm in the process.

State actors' actions matter also when they proclaim intentions and act in international fora, including when deliberating on international instruments or other mechanisms in the form of hard or soft law, as such actions can demonstrate a crystallization of CIL. As noted above, evidence of CIL is increasingly deduced from international pronouncements, and from what countries do through IOs.[201] The work of transnational actors has become central to the creation of standards and norms, and pronouncedly in the field of insolvency. Much of the developments in international insolvency take place under the auspices of UNCITRAL, in coordination with the World Bank. Extensive work is also done by regional institutions such as the EU Commission. The development of cross-border solutions for MFIs have thus far been mainly within the purview of the International Monetary Fund (IMF) and the Financial Stability Board (FSB).[202] These institutions and the countries' representatives who provide input in international deliberations can in their work on the design, reform and renovation of international frameworks have regard to international law sources and engage in the development of international laws. Existing international frameworks for cross-border insolvency have been somewhat obscure regarding the approach they are following,[203] and thus there is room for

---

[198] Paul, 'Comity in International Law' (n 126) 1, 35.

[199] See eg the proclamations of the meaning of modified universalism by the UK Supreme Court in *Rubin and another v Eurofinance SA and others and New Cap Reinsurance Corporation (in Liquidation) and another v AE Grant and others* [2012] UKSC 46 para 16 ('there has been a trend, but only a trend, to what is called universalism …'), or the narrow interpretation of modified universalism and thus the refusal to defer to the insolvency process in India by the Scottish court in *Hooley* (Chapter 1, n 283 and accompanying text).

[200] See eg the emergence of Singapore as a cross-border insolvency hub (R Kannan, Supreme Court of Singapore, 'The cross-border project—a "dual-track" approach', INSOL International Group of 36 Meeting in Singapore on 30 November 2015 <http://www.supremecourt.gov.sg/Data/Editor/Documents/Insol%2036_Speech_khb_upload%20version.pdf>).

[201] See sections 3.2.1 and 3.2.5.   [202] See Chapter 6, section 6.3.

[203] ibid sections 6.2 and 6.3.

clearer pronouncements of the universal application of modified universalism, intended for general adherence.

How the key players of cross-border insolvency, namely bankruptcy courts and other implementing institutions, especially in countries most influential in this field, refer to and apply norms of modified universalism is also crucial and could matter beyond the creation of precedence within the jurisdiction, as it can influence and form CIL. Such actors when reaching decisions in line with modified universalism could proclaim the intention of following its prescribed solutions more explicitly and as a matter of obligation. Especially where provisions in instruments are insufficient to address all aspects of a given issue or where the country is not a party to an international framework, modified universalism norms become most relevant. In such cases, instead of, for example, solely relying on inherent discretionary powers in the legal system to assist foreign courts, or grounding decisions on notions such as comity that are often vague and confined to specific countries,[204] courts could explicitly refer to modified universalism as the guiding international law and, in the process, establish the acceptance of modified universalism as CIL.

The case of *Nortel*, for example, demonstrates a modified universalist approach followed by both the American and Canadian courts who acted in concert in many ways to achieve a cooperative, consistent solution and who have designed a resolution for the enterprise that fitted with its unique structure within the ambit of a global approach to multinational default, in line with the flexibility enshrined in modified universalism.[205] Nonetheless, the courts refrained from articulating their decisions in this way. The American judge specifically noted that: 'To be clear, the Court's pro rata allocation *is not the "new order" which the pro rata proponents urge with terms such as "universalism"* ... .'[206] The court avoided an attempt to shape a more general norm for addressing a complex case involving a multinational group, pursuant to modified universalism, and instead confined the solution to the facts of the case. However, a clear reference to global norms of modified universalism in future cases of similar circumstances instead of to modified universalism as (for example) a 'term', can provide evidence of its acceptance as CIL.

---

[204] See also JJ Chung, 'In Re Qimonda AG: The Conflict Between Comity and the Public Policy Exception in Chapter 15 of the Bankruptcy Code' (2014) 32 Boston U Intl L J 89, 96, 104 (noting that comity is ambiguous and ill-defined); KJ Beckering, 'United States Cross-Border Corporate Insolvency: The Impact of Chapter 15 on Comity and the New Legal Environment' (2008) 14 L & Bus Rev of the Americas 281 (noting that: 'The major historical impediment to achieving sustainable unification in cross-border corporate insolvency administration is comity based theoretical analysis in bankruptcy reorganization for dissolution cases' and that: 'By maintaining comity as the focal point in the ... United States judiciary, which is still possible under the construct of Chapter 15, forward-looking reform of antiquated bankruptcy law in foreign countries will be negligible, at best'). Indeed, 'particular rules of comity, maintained consistently without reservation, may develop into rules of customary law' (Crawford, *Brownlie's Principles of Public International Law*, 8th edn (n 70) 24, giving the example of some diplomatic tax exemptions that were originally granted as a matter of comity but are now consolidated as legal requirements in Art 36 of the Vienna Convention on Diplomatic Relations, 18 April 1961, 500 UNTS 95).

[205] See Chapter 1, section 1.3.2. See also JAE Pottow, 'Two Cheers for Universalism: Nortel's Nifty Novelty' in JP Sarra and Justice B Romaine (eds), *Annual Review of Insolvency Law* (Carswell 2015).

[206] *In re Nortel Networks, Inc*, 532 BR 494 (Bankr D Del 2015) 111 (emphasis added).

In other cases, American courts reached universalist decisions based primarily on the MLCBI, but also the principle of international comity enshrined in Chapter 15 of the Bankruptcy Code (the American version of the MLCBI). In the case of *In re Daebo*,[207] for example, the bankruptcy judge, referring also to *In re Atlas Shipping*[208] noted that: 'Chapter 15 "contemplates that the court should be guided by principles of comity and cooperation with foreign courts in deciding whether to grant the foreign representative additional post recognition relief".'[209] Relying on the principle of comity the court then granted certain relief to the foreign Korean rehabilitation proceedings and vacated attachments pursuant to the Korean stay of actions concerning the company's assets. This decision was in line with modified universalism norms regarding recognition, cooperation, and relief,[210] yet modified universalism was not mentioned explicitly.

In future cases of this kind, judges could, in addition to applying domestic concepts of international comity, and especially where technical rules in statute require reinforcement or a separate justificatory force, refer explicitly to modified universalist norms that require uniform adherence, thus contributing to the transformation of them into CIL. The fact that powerful nations such as the United States have adopted international instruments, especially the MLCBI, should not be a factor working against modified universalism becoming CIL; rather, this development should be a catalyst for making the norms that such instruments pursue more widespread. The inclination could be to just rely on provisions of instruments as adopted locally and refrain from considering norms beyond the instruments,[211] thus impeding the use of modified universalism as an international norm. Yet, appreciating the role of key actors as creators of international law and the potential of modified universalism to become universal, international law that transcends local differences can help overcome such tendencies.

Taking such an approach and basing decisions more directly on modified universalism, thus providing harder evidence about its prevalence, can be seen in cases such as *re Maxwell* where the US court announced that: 'the United States in ancillary bankruptcy cases has embraced an approach to international insolvency which is a

---

[207] *In re Daebo International Shipping Co*, Ltd, 543 BR 47 (2015), para 2.
[208] *In re Atlas Shipping A/S*, 404 BR 726, 739 (Bankr SDNY 2009).
[209] Chapter 15 of the US Bankruptcy Code refers to the principle of comity in articles 1507 and 1509.
[210] See Chapter 1, section 1.3.2.3.
[211] See eg the position expressed in *Re Bear Stearns High-Grade Structured Credit* 374 BR 122 (Bankr SDNY 2007) aff'd 389 BR 325 (SDNY 2008) where it was held that there is no residual common law discretion under Chapter 15. See also US House of Representatives, 'Bankruptcy Abuse Prevention and Consumer Protection Act of 2005: Report of the Committee on the Judiciary House of Representatives to accompany s 256 together with dissenting, additional dissenting and additional minority views' 109th Congress 1st Session, Report 109–31 Part 1 (8 April 2005) 110 <https://www.congress.gov/congressional-report/109-congress/house-report/31/1> ('Chapter 15 is intended to be the exclusive door to ancillary assistance to foreign proceedings. The goal is to concentrate control of these questions in one court'). Another example is the approach of the Supreme Court of the Bahamas in the case of *In the Matter of Caledonian Bank Limited* (In Official Liquidation under Supervision of The Grand Court of The Cayman Islands) 2015/COM/com/00034 where it was held that statutory provisions on cross-border insolvency restricted the application of common law as a route for granting assistance (thus the foreign liquidators could not get assets owned by the bank that were in the Bahamas).

modified form of universalism accepting the central premise of universalism … ',[212] or in the decision of the UK Supreme Court in the case of *HiH*[213] where Lord Hoffmann stated that:

The primary rule of private international law which seems to me applicable to this case is the principle of (modified) universalism, which has been the golden thread running through English cross-border insolvency law since the 18th century. That principle *requires* that English courts should, so far as is consistent with justice and UK public policy, co-operate with the courts in the country of the principal liquidation to ensure that all the company's assets are distributed to its creditors under a single system of distribution.[214]

Another example of a rather robust usage of universalism by a UK court in the context of MFI cross-border insolvency and regarding the application of the EU Winding-up Directive[215] can be observed in the case of *Kaupthing Bank HF.*[216] The issue in this case was whether Icelandic law (the law of the home member state) had an extraterritorial effect in cross-border insolvency scenarios in the EU even where that law otherwise only had domestic application. Lord Justice Briggs held that:

The very essence of the universalism sought to be achieved by making the insolvency law of the home Member State applicable across the territory of all Member States depends upon that being achieved in relation to every potential home Member State in which a credit institution is regulated and has its head office regardless whether, apart from those instruments, that State's insolvency law would be anything more than domestic in its application. If that were not so, then the creation of a universally applicable law (subject to strict exceptions) for the insolvency of credit institutions, and other entities, would fall at the first hurdle, in relation to any home Member State the insolvency law of which did not already have cross-border effect.[217]

In Canada, the case of *Re MtGox Co Ltd*,[218] is illustrative of the more vigorous approach to the application of modified universalism. In this case, an Ontario Court recognized Japanese bankruptcy proceedings and specifically noted modified universalism as a leading norm in cross-border insolvency:

There is increasingly a move towards what has been called modified universalism. The notion of modified universalism is court recognition of main proceedings in one

---

[212] *In Re Maxwell Communication Corp*, 170 BR 800 (Bankr SDNY 1994).

[213] *In re HIH Casualty and General Insurance Ltd* [2008] UKHL 21 [2008] 1 WLR 852.

[214] ibid para 30 (emphasis added). See also the statements of Lord Clarke in *Rubin*, expressing the minority view in this case, and voicing such obligation to follow modified universalism. Lord Clarke considered that the judgment of the US Bankruptcy Court in issue was 'a judgment in, and for the purposes of, the collective enforcement regime of the insolvency proceedings, and was governed by the sui generis private international law rules relating to insolvency'. Therefore, the US judgment should have been recognized and enforced in the United Kingdom. Lord Clarke disagreed with the majority view that such development would be a 'radical departure from substantially settled law'. He continued to state that such an approach would: 'would in essence be an application of the principle of modified universalism. It seems to me that in these days of global commerce, the step taken by the Court of Appeal was but a small step forward … ' (*Rubin and another v Eurofinance SA and others* and *New Cap Reinsurance Corporation (in Liquidation) and another v AE Grant and others* [2012] UKSC 46 paras 202 and 204, per Lord Clarke).

[215] See Chapter 1, section 1.4.4.

[216] *Tchenguiz & ors v Kaupthing Bank HF* [2017] EWCA Civ 83, CA, 2017 WL 00817001.

[217] ibid para 68.   [218] *MtGox Co., Ltd (Re)*, 2014 ONSC 5811.

jurisdiction and non-main proceedings in other jurisdictions, representing some com-promise of state sovereignty under domestic proceedings to advance international comity and cooperation. It has been advanced by the United Nations Commission on International Trade Law (UNCITRAL) Model Law on Cross Border Insolvency, which Canada largely adopted by 2009 amendments to the CCAA and the BIA.[] Before this amendment, Canada had gone far down the road in acting on comity principles in inter-national insolvency . . . [219]

In new cross-border insolvency hubs such as Singapore it is also possible to detect some straightforward usages of modified universalism/ internationalist rules by the courts, accepting with visionary confidence the reality of global businesses. For example, in a decision from 2016 a Singapore High Court judge noted:

Ultimately, the question of whether a stay of proceedings *elsewhere* ought to be granted to facilitate a restructuring under a scheme of arrangement here is a matter for consider-ation by the Court where those proceedings are being brought. It will depend in such a situation on the domestic laws of that jurisdiction, and principles of comity and *modified universalism.*

. . .

Where businesses entities are interconnected and cross-border in nature, it is only to be expected that restructuring of such business entities is undertaken on a composite, interconnected and inter-related basis. The formulation of such a composite plan is a long, involved and complicated exercise simply by reason of the involvement of multiple jurisdictions with different restructuring regimes and the interweaving of multifarious business and creditor interests. The individual plans for the units that collectively make up the composite plan will therefore take time to formulate and finesse. *The Courts must recognise and not turn a blind eye to this reality.*[220]

Still, the legal status of modified universalism is not always clear. In the *HiH* judgment mentioned above,[221] which is generally viewed as a strong expression of universalist inclinations, Lord Hoffmann considered modified universalism a thread running through English law, an aspiration, a principle rather than a rule.[222] A further stepping up of the usage of modified universalism would be to invoke and apply it as CIL, namely as a binding international norm.

Decisions of international tribunals could contribute to entrenching modi-fied universalism as CIL as well, if they pronounce modified universalism norms more explicitly. Currently, there is no specialized international tribunal for cross-border insolvency and no mechanism for dispute resolution in the existing global

---

[219] ibid para 11.

[220] *Pacific Andes Resources Development Ltd and other matters* [2016] SGHC 210, paras 20 and 72 (some of the emphases added). See also the decision of the Singaporean High Court in *Re Gulf Pacific Shipping Ltd (in creditors' voluntary liquidation) and others* [2016] SGHC 287, para 10: 'the traditional territorial focus on the interests of local creditors no longer has primacy over more internationalist concerns.'

[221] See n 213.

[222] Indeed, a 'potent' principle (*In re HIH Casualty and General Insurance Ltd* [2008] UKHL 21, [2008] 1 WLR 852 para 7).

framework for insolvency;[223] however, the Court of Justice of the European Union (CJEU) is highly influential in this field beyond the EU region. Not only does it have the authority to resolve uncertainties regarding the cross-border insolvency framework applicable within the EU, its decisions have influenced developments globally, especially as the existing EU frameworks and the MLCBI have many overlapping concepts.[224] Important issues arising during cross-border insolvencies taking place in member states which are party to the framework are referred to the CJEU. In this regard, the CJEU is often guided by and refers to the notion of 'mutual trust' in resolving private international law matters pertaining to insolvency.[225]

For example, in *MG Probud*,[226] it was not clear whether the German authorities where a Polish company had a branch could order enforcement measures regarding assets of the company situated in Germany, in circumstances where the main proceedings were taking place in Poland. The CJEU concluded that the German authorities erred in their attempt to impose such local enforcement measures. The court noted the universality of the main Polish proceedings based on the provisions of the EIR. It further stated, also citing *Eurofood*,[227] that, pursuant to the EIR provisions and recitals, proceedings opened in a member state must be recognized and be given effect in all other member states. This rule, the court explained, 'is based on the principle of mutual trust'.[228]

Mutual trust is certainly a core notion that facilitated the establishment of the compulsory cross-border insolvency system within the EU.[229] The premise of mutual trust in the administration of justice in the EU requires giving full faith and credit to courts of other member states. It has been referred to as 'the central buzzword of the EU'.[230] Like comity, however, mutual trust is a vague concept,[231] and its justificatory force is limited.[232] It is also confined in the EIR/Recast EIR context to the relationship between states within the region.[233] Conversely, a reference to modified universalism could both provide concrete justification for the decision to

---

[223] See Chapter 5, section 5.3.3.　　[224] See Chapter 6, section 6.2.

[225] See also Chapter 5, section 5.2.5.

[226] *MG Probud Gdynia sp* Case C-444/07 (2010) ECR I-00417.　　[227] ibid para 27.

[228] ibid para 27.

[229] Mutual trust is noted in recital 65 of the Recast EIR (replacing recital 22 of the EIR) as the basis for recognition and the limited grounds for non-recognition. The importance of mutual trust was emphasized by the CJEU in the *Eurofood* case (*Eurofood IFSC Ltd, Re* (C-341/04) 2006 para 39. See also *MG Probud Gdynia sp* Case C-444/07 (2010) ECR I-00417 para 28. It has been noted that 'the political will of mutual trust' is the basis of the EU cross-border insolvency regime (CG Paulus, 'The ECJ's Understanding of the Universality Principle' (2014) 27(5) Insolv Int 70, 71).

[230] M Weller, 'Mutual Trust: In Search of the Future of European Union Private International Law' (2015) 11(1) Journal of Private International Law 64, 68.

[231] Wessels, *International Insolvency Law* (n 137) 46 (noting the shared legal heritage between comity and the principle of mutual trust underlying the EU cross-border insolvency regime).

[232] Weller, 'Mutual Trust' (n 230) 101 (noting that 'the justificatory force of mutual trust is limited. Using mutual trust as legal fiction does not work, at least not beyond the point reached in the system'). See also I Tirado, 'An Evolution of COMI in the European Insolvency Regulation: From "Insolvenzimperialismus" to the Recast' in JP Sarra and Justice B Romaine (eds), Annual Review of Insolvency Law (Carswell 2015) 819, 827 (noting that the notion of mutual trust has often been ignored).

[233] See also Paulus, 'The ECJ's Understanding of the Universality Principle' (n 229) 71.

require that full effect be given to the foreign main proceedings, and contribute to the evolution of modified universalism from a broad approach to CIL.

The transformation of modified universalism to CIL may not take a very long period of time in view of the already existing widespread universalist practice and generally the extensive traction that modified universalism has gained in recent years. What is required is not taking a big leap to pure universalism, but settling on the norms of modified universalism. Indeed, certain aspects of modified universalism may become CIL more quickly than others if they are more advanced and solid.[234] Certainly, to develop the norms into CIL requires that countries and implementing institutions have opportunities to interact. Yet, cross-border insolvency cases are not a rare phenomenon, and as the effect of the global financial crisis is still likely to be felt in years to come, it is expected that the practice will continue with significant intensity.[235] Changes in political powers and shifts of economic centres also mean that country interaction is likely to spread more, creating a critical mass and concentration of activity conducive to CIL.

It is important to note, however, the evolutionary nature of CIL and hence the fact that the work on modified universalism's transformation and further development is a process: '[T]he customary process is in fact a continuous one, which does not stop when the rule has emerged ... Even after the rule has 'emerged', every act of compliance will strengthen it, and every violation, if acquiesced in, will help undermine it.'[236] CIL is a work in progress.[237] It will therefore, be, vital to continuously work on creating and guarding modified universalism as a customary norm, so that it is spoken of as law, compelled by international law, supplementing and supplanting other conflict of laws rules, and providing the needed justification for a global approach to multinational default.

The limitations of CIL should also be recalled, including in terms of its level of generality and difficulties of identification. Thus, the notion of elevating modified universalism to the status of CIL should not be understood as a replacement of international negotiations and deliberations that attempt to close gaps in the system.[238] To the contrary, creating and guarding modified universalism as an international custom should facilitate negotiations based on modified universalism, including because of the behavioural force of CIL and its ability to shift the reference point of actors regarding universalism. Vice versa, the development of regional and international frameworks can further define and develop the CIL rules.

---

[234] eg the norm concerning choice of law is less settled than the one on choice of forum (see Chapter 1, section 1.3.2.2).

[235] It has been observed that international law tends to develop after crises; see H Charlesworth, 'International Law: A Discipline of Crisis' (2002) 65(3) MLR 377.

[236] MH Mendelson, 'The Formation of Customary International Law' (1998) 272 Recueil Des Cours 155, 175.

[237] P Malanczuk, *Akehurst's Modern Introduction to International Law* (7th edn, Routledge 1997) 45.

[238] The next chapter considers which type of instrument may be most effective for this purpose, such as a treaty or model law.

3.6.2 Use of CIL in future cross-border insolvencies

Modified universalism established as CIL can promote a wider coverage and a more consistent application of the norms. As described in Chapter 1, cross-border insolvency is not an area fully addressed by treaties; current frameworks of cross-border insolvency, in particular the MLCBI framework for global insolvency has been adopted by many but not all countries; generally, not all countries' legal systems contain regimes akin to modified universalism; not all regions have introduced regional cross-border insolvency frameworks (and the composition of integrated markets where regional frameworks for cross-border insolvency apply is not static either; see eg events such as Brexit); the MLCBI may not apply to all entities; there are gaps in the rules contained in existing frameworks;[239] and various issues arising under the frameworks require interpretation.[240]

Modified universalism, standing on its own two feet, emerging as CIL, can assist in closing gaps in the complex international system.[241] The pervasiveness of CIL as an international legal source is of important advantage where modified universalism requires universality and full coverage of the market (market symmetry[242]). Once CIL has become prevalent, countries are bound by it regardless of whether they have codified the laws domestically or through treaties unless they have actively objected to it. As such, CIL is also a debiasing mechanism because it operates as a default norm. Thus, while more action through the recognition of the international role of cross-border insolvency is important, it is enough that modified universalism is practiced generally and especially by influential economies and transnational actors. Parties that are more averse to change will still become party to the norms of modified universalism.

In practical terms, this means that in future cases involving countries that have not taken action to adopt the MLCBI, ensure that it becomes effective,[243] become a party to any other international framework, or enact rules that facilitate global collective insolvencies, it will still be expected that such countries (and their implementing institutions) follow modified universalism. It will also be possible to rely on uniform norms of cross-border insolvency rather than invoke domestic mechanisms when,

---

[239] See the assessment of international instruments in Chapter 6.

[240] It has been argued that the MLCBI was intentionally vague in various areas and it is the role of the courts to address the gaps (S Gopalan and M Guihot, 'Recognition and Enforcement in Cross-Border Insolvency Law: A Proposal for Judicial Gap-Filling' (2015) 48 Vanderbilt J Transnat L 1225). It is argued in this chapter that modified universalism based on CIL can assist in closing the existing gaps and promote the consistent application of provisions in the international instruments.

[241] cf regarding foreign investments when, even though bilateral treaties dominate the legal regime, many investments are not covered by the treaties, yet the legal rules included in the treaties seem to have become CIL and, therefore, are generally more universally binding (ADZ Guanawardana, 'The Inception and Growth of Bilateral Investment Promotion and Protection Treaties' (1992) 86 Proc Am Soc'y Intl L 544, 550; B Kishoiyan, 'The Utility of Bilateral Investment Treaties in the Formulation of Customary International Law' (1994) 14 Nw J Intl L & Bus 327, 329. See also Guzman, 'Saving Customary International Law' (n 6) 119).

[242] See Chapter 1, section 1.2.3.1.

[243] See eg the adoption of the MLCBI by South Africa in 2000 with conditions that meant that thus far it still has not entered into force (see text accompanying n 246).

for example, recognition, relief, or assistance is sought in a foreign jurisdiction. Such norms may be invoked by foreign actors[244] in the court or other body presiding over the process. If such rules are rejected by the relevant institution, the rejection may be regarded a breach of international law.[245] Provisions in international instruments too would apply to countries not party to the framework to the extent that the framework reflects the rules of CIL. Thus, even where a framework does not bind certain countries, its provisions may form part of the global legal order of insolvency.

An example of this future effect of modified universalism when formed as CIL is when actions are sought in a country such as South Africa, which, although it is a signatory to the MLCBI, has not given effect to the provisions of the MLCBI in its jurisdiction. Specifically, the problem has been that South Africa included a reciprocity requirement in their version of the MLCBI requiring that countries will be designated for the purposes of the application of that law; however, no country has yet been designated.[246] Therefore, when, for example, foreign insolvency representatives need to obtain recognition and relief in the jurisdiction, they may seek it on the basis of domestic private international rules including the principles of comity, convenience, and equity, as understood under local law based on the writings of the Roman-Dutch authorities.[247] Recognition of the foreign proceedings may not generate the type of relief that would ensure a global approach to multinational default, as recognition under domestic South African law does not necessarily stops all actions against the debtor and it may still be possible to pursue the debtor locally including seeking the opening of local sequestration proceedings.[248] In that regard, the approach of implementing institutions to cross-border insolvency under the South African regime has been considered a modified version of territoriality where significant importance is attached to the protection of interests of local creditors.[249] The turnover of assets to the foreign collective process may be circumscribed by ring-fencing in favour of local creditors.[250] Even once South Africa designates countries, thus bringing (its version of) the MLCBI into force in the jurisdiction, the result would be the existence of two parallel regimes, whereby insolvency representatives, courts, and other relevant actors from non-designated

---

[244] State as well as non-state actors, as relevant in the circumstances. As noted above (n 163 and accompanying text) both states and non-state actors may be subjects of rights and obligations under international law as the scope of international law has been expanded, alongside the internationalization of private international law.

[245] Still, compliance and enforcement are significant challenges in the international realm, as discussed in Chapter 5.

[246] See Chapter 2, n 118.

[247] A Smith, 'Some Aspects of Comity and the Protection of Local Creditors in Cross-Border Insolvency Law: South Africa and the United States Compared' (2002) 14 S Afr Mercantile L J 17, 18, 28; A Smith and A Boraine, 'Crossing Borders into South African Insolvency Law: From the Roman-Dutch Jurists to the Uncitral Model Law' (2002) 10 135, 138. See the application of domestic law in recognition proceedings from concerning a foreign bankrupt in *Lehane No v Lagoon Beach Hotel (PTY) Ltd And Others* 2015 (4) SA 72 (WCC) and in *Lagoon Beach Hotel (PTY) Ltd v Lehane No And Others* 2016 (3) SA 143 (SCA).

[248] Smith, 'Some Aspects of Comity and the Protection of Local Creditors' (n 247) 34.

[249] ibid 32, 34.

[250] ibid 58 referring eg to the order in *Ex parte Getliffe & another: In re Dominion Reefs Ltd* 1965 (4) SA 75 (T).

countries may be in a disadvantageous position.[251] Or it might be that implementing institutions would interpret provisions in line with the domestic approach, under-mining universalism under both the international and the domestic routes. Where modified universalism is understood as the CIL, however, it can overcome outdated notions of comity and reciprocity,[252] and equalize the treatment of foreign proceed-ings and the approach to foreign requests. It can provide a coherent legal basis, for example, for a swift recognition of the foreign proceedings and the granting of relief to allow the process to take place on a global collective basis.

CIL can also assist when taking actions in cross-border insolvencies in countries such as China, which has not adopted the MLCBI. Recognition and enforcement in China of foreign insolvency proceedings are conditioned on the existence of a relevant international treaty, in addition to other requirements, such as that the insolvency proceeding shall not jeopardize the sovereignty and security of the state or public interests.[253] This specific domestic cross-border insolvency regime that was introduced in China in 2006 still put obstacles to smooth administration of cross-border insolvencies. For example, in litigation in the context of the *Lehman Brothers* cross-border insolvency, a Chinese court considered that the UK insolv-ency representatives should be denied recognition of the effects of the proceedings opened in the United Kingdom in China (with regard to property situated in China) because of lack of reciprocity, as China did not have a relevant arrangement with the United Kingdom even though the United Kingdom has adopted the MLCBI. It was also noted in this regard that:

> there was no precedent judgment that the United Kingdom courts recognized and enforced the insolvency rulings rendered by Chinese courts. Therefore, our court can protect the le-gitimate rights and interests of the domestic creditors in priority in the way of accepting the lawsuit and ordering attachment on the assets.[254]

Going forward, where modified universalism is applied as CIL, foreign insolvency representatives should be able to invoke it and attempt recognition and enforcement to promote a collective global approach in the foreign main forum, including in such circumstances where the relevant country is not a party to uniform frameworks and so long as it is not a persistent objector to the CIL regime.

---

[251] It has been observed in this regard that 'when comparing the two structures, it is clear that foreign representatives and foreign creditors from designated countries, in other words those who will enjoy the benefit of the provisions of the Cross-Border Insolvency Act 42 of 2000, will be in a much better pos-ition than those coming from non-designated countries' (A Boraine, 'Elements of Bankruptcy law and Business Rescue in South Africa', unpublished note (2015) (on file with author); Smith and Boraine, 'Crossing Borders into South African Insolvency Law' (n 247) 138).

[252] RH Zulman, 'Cross-Border Insolvency in South African Law' (2009) 21 S Afr Mercantile L J 804, 816–17 (noting that comity and reciprocity enshrined in the South African version of the MLCBI are outmoded and not in conformity with modern thinking on the subject).

[253] Article 5 of China's Enterprise Bankruptcy Law 2007. See also the regime in India, where, as noted in Chapter 1, section 1.4.3, provisions on cooperation in cross-border insolvency are currently based on entering into reciprocal arrangements.

[254] X Gong, 'To Recognise or Not to Recognise? Comparative Study of Lehman Brothers Cases in Mainland China and Taiwan' (2013) 10(4) ICR 240.

As mentioned earlier, CIL also plays a role regulating within the gaps of treaties or other instruments. For example, based on modified universalism's norm of cooperation,[255] courts and other authorities would have the authority and the duty to cooperate and communicate, including where the debtor is an entity that is not explicitly covered under existing instruments. The case of *Lehman Brothers* is illustrative.[256] Cooperation was achieved in this case because of participants' initiative and voluntary will, yet cooperation was significantly constrained.[257] The enterprise type and structure (ie the fact that Lehman Brothers was an MFI/enterprise group) resulted in aspects of the case falling outside the scope of existing instruments.[258] Where modified universalism is recognized as CIL, cooperation would become a universal legal requirement, including for the purpose of reaching efficient centralized solutions for more complicated enterprise structures. Thus, for example, the seeking of a more coordinated and centralized approach in circumstances such as those in Lehman Brothers, including the flow of information into the central proceedings, could be based, in the absence of applicable rules, on modified universalism's norms.[259]

As modified universalism established as CIL is flexible enough to accommodate changing conditions, it can also be invoked regarding newer types of processes and procedures that may not be covered in written instruments. The shift in the focus of insolvency procedures from formal liquidations to rescue-oriented and other informal processes, including in the time approaching insolvency where there is likelihood of insolvency or financial difficulties, is an example of such changes in the practice of insolvency that instruments may be slow to capture.[260] However, modified universalism norms can be invoked regarding interim, out-of-court, or pre-insolvency procedures even where they are not covered within the scope of cross-border insolvency domestic laws or international instruments. An example of such an approach is the decision of the Singapore court in the *Gulf Pacific Shipping* case.[261] In this case, the court, based on 'internationalist concerns', decided to recognize the appointment of liquidators over Hong Kong shipping company Gulf Pacific, and grant the requested assistance, despite the debtor being in out-of-court proceedings regarding which the domestic powers of assistance were constrained.

---

[255] See Chapter 1, section 1.3.2.3.

[256] *In the Matter of Lehman Brothers International (Europe) (in administration)* [2011] EWHC 2022 (Ch).

[257] See Chapter 1, section 1.4.5. See also PL Davies, 'Resolution of Cross-Border Banking Groups' in M Haentjens and B Wessels (eds), *Research Handbook on Crisis Management in the Banking Sector* (Research Handbooks in Financial Law Series 2015) 263-4; JM Peck, 'Cross-Border Observations Derived from My Lehman Judicial Experience' (2013) 30 Butterworths J Intl Banking & Fin L 131.

[258] Mevorach, 'Beyond the Search for Certainty' (n 181) 191.

[259] Subject to safeguards (see Chapter 1, section 1.3.2.4). Since the fall of Lehman Brothers, UNCITRAL has been developing model provisions concerning enterprise groups (deliberations are still ongoing). Thus, going forward, CIL may address gaps in the new regime including in terms of its universal application pending wide enactment by countries (see Chapter 6, section 6.2.4).

[260] See Chapter 1, n 66 and accompanying text.

[261] *Re Gulf Pacific Shipping Ltd (in creditors' voluntary liquidation) and others* [2016] SGHC 287.

Furthermore, to the extent that CIL does not contradict special treaty law,[262] it can override conflicting laws in civil law countries and will be considered part and parcel of the public policy in common law jurisdictions where legislation is to be construed in a manner that would avoid a conflict with the international norm. Thus, modified universalism understood as CIL can provide the separate, *sui generis*, basis and justification for the uniform private international laws based on global collectivity. Any ordinary domestic private international laws could sit alongside the cross-border insolvency CIL regime rather than be considered in conflict with it in the given circumstances.

Thus, in future cases with circumstances of the type arising, for example, in *Rubin*,[263] where the existing cross-border insolvency instrument might not provide a clear answer (in that case regarding the question of enforcement of insolvency-related judgements of the main insolvency forum[264]), the foreign insolvency representative would be able to rely on modified universalism as an international norm.[265] Such outcome was unattainable in the *Rubin* case and the request to enforce the judgment of the central foreign court was denied because modified universalism was applied as a general principle of common law subject to the domestic private international law regime.[266]

In other circumstances, courts may be asked, for example, to give full effect to a foreign stay on actions concerning the assets of the enterprise, instead of (as happened in *Pan Ocean*[267]) applying domestic *ipso facto* rules that allow termination of contracts, thus undermining the collectivity of the cross-border insolvency process. Similarly, courts could be asked to recognize transactions already approved by foreign main reorganization proceedings, instead of (as happened eg in *Elpida*[268]) applying the domestic rules concerning assets sales. The application of the domestic rule can undeniably delay the process as well as provide local creditors an unjustified chance to challenge the sale, undermining the norm of a global, non-discriminatory approach, prescribed by modified universalism.[269]

---

[262] eg it has been persuasively noted that it is not possible to circumvent the provisions of the EIR to achieve universalist 'ambitions', because the concepts enshrined in the EIR have autonomous meaning (G McCormack, 'Universalism in Insolvency Proceedings and the Common Law' (2012) 32(2) OJLS 325, 340–41). Treaties or other instruments may, however, explicitly refer to CIL, or provide a 'saving' language, making specific references to sources other than the instrument provisions. A provision of this type, albeit one that refers to domestic sources, exists in the MLCBI in art 7 ('Nothing in this Law limits the power of a court to provide additional assistance to a foreign representative under other laws of this State.') The MLCBI also requires that its interpretation take account of the instrument's international origin (n 275 and accompanying text).

[263] *Rubin and another v Eurofinance SA and others* and *New Cap Reinsurance Corporation (in Liquidation) and another v AE Grant and others* [2012] UKSC 46.

[264] See also Chapter 6, section 6.2.3.

[265] Since *Rubin*, UNCITRAL has been developing a model law on the enforcement of insolvency-related judgments (deliberations are still ongoing). Thus, going forward, CIL may assist in closing gaps in the new regime including in terms of its universal application pending wide enactment by countries (see Chapter 6, section 6.2.3).

[266] See Chapter 1, section 1.4.5.   [267] See *Pan Ocean* [2014] EWHC 2124 (Ch).

[268] See *In re Elpida Memory, Inc,* No 12-10947 (D Del 16 Nov 2012).

[269] See Chapter 1, section 1.2.3.3.

Modified universalism based on CIL could also serve to influence treaty and other regional or international regimes and can be utilized and be relevant for their interpretation. It could reinforce technical rules enshrined in international instruments where the instrument refers to the rules of CIL. Currently, requirements in cross-border insolvency frameworks, for example: cooperation 'wherever possible'[270] or 'to the maximum extent possible',[271] could be understood in different ways.[272] They could be interpreted in a universalist manner, suggesting obligatory cooperation to achieve universality within the parameters of modified universalism. Yet, they could be also understood as suggesting cooperative territorialism, namely self-serving cooperation that promotes local interests in the case at hand, still allowing, for example, ring-fencing of assets if that appears to be in the interests of national stakeholders.[273] The lack of clear statements concerning the level of universalism that should be followed also renders proclamations of objectives—such as effectiveness, efficiency, or fairness stated as the aims of cross-border insolvency systems[274]—open to interpretation and variation in the cross-border context. Thus, fairness and efficiency may be viewed from the vested rights (territorial) standpoint or from a global (universalist) perspective. Going forward, CIL can be used to ensure a consistent application of objectives and requirements enshrined in frameworks in line with modified universalism. Modified universalism based on CIL can also provide specific substance to requirements to interpret instruments by having regard to their 'international origin'.[275]

As noted above, the formation of CIL does not negate deliberations on international instruments. Modified universalism becoming CIL should induce such work and, vice versa, can be influenced by the development of frameworks. The more such specific regimes emerge and become comprehensive, reliance on CIL is reduced. However, treaty and other regimes do not abrogate CIL. In addition to addressing newly emerging issues not yet fully covered by frameworks, and providing a foundation for the design of new frameworks, CIL remains applicable even where issues are addressed in instruments. It can provide a fallback parallel system in circumstances of current or future gaps as well as influence the frameworks and their consistent application.

---

[270] See Key Attributes s 7.1 ('The statutory mandate of a resolution authority should empower and strongly encourage the authority wherever possible to act to achieve a cooperative solution with foreign resolution authorities'.)

[271] See MLCBI art 25(1).   [272] See also Chapter 6, sections 6.2.2, 6.2.5, 6.3.1, and 6.3.3.

[273] cf Principle 7.3 of the Key Attributes that requires having regard to impact on financial stability in other jurisdictions when resolution authorities take discretionary national action. See also the discussion in Chapter 6, section 6.3.1.

[274] See the delineation of objectives in the preamble of the MLCBI, further discussed in Chapter 6, section 6.2.2.

[275] See eg MLCBI art 8. See also Westbrook, 'Interpretation Internationale' (n 151) (arguing that 'system' texts that establish an international framework require an international rather than an insular interpretation).

3.7 Conclusion

Lessons from international law as well as insights from cognitive psychology of decision-making highlight the advantages that can be gained from modified universalism conceptualized and formed as CIL. Modified universalism recognized as CIL could fill gaps and promote consistency in the application of regional and international frameworks. Furthermore, a modified universalist CIL can assist in the areas where biases impede movement to more optimal solutions. CIL applies regardless of whether rules have been codified domestically or through treaties, and non-objection is considered a consent to CIL. If the rules of modified universalism are generally understood and believed to be binding, modified universalism will be the default universal rule, embraced as an opt-out regime, and adherence to it would not require positive action. Such use of legislative framing can affect the consequences of inaction and can result in higher participation, with greater universality and integrity, in the application of modified universalism. The emergence of modified universalism as CIL can also contribute to the shifting of the reference point itself, and of the status quo, against which gains and losses are often considered. If modified universalism is understood as the foundational norm, adherence to instruments reflecting modified universalism is less likely to be perceived as a change and as a loss.

The association of cross-border insolvency with private international law, supposedly a field separated from international law sources, could impede, however, such transformation of modified universalism to CIL. A perception of cross-border insolvency as limited to the design of technical private international law rules might inhibit engagement in the formation of laws that would promote global welfare and address shared concerns of the international community. This problem of excessive modesty in relation to the role of cross-border insolvency intensifies where modified universalism itself is still considered attached to pure universalism, not only in terms of its theoretical foundations but also as the final objective. This chapter showed, however, that the role of cross-border insolvency can be reinforced. As a private international law system, it has international objectives to pursue. Private international law generally is increasingly being reunited with the international law system and its role is augmenting. The international nature of cross-border insolvency and the fact that insolvency addresses both private and public interests further justify the solidification of its international role. Thus, cross-border insolvency law should engage in international norm creation and in that regard, could rely on modified universalism where it provides concrete and practical rules that can be followed consistently. Key actors, importantly courts and other authorities presiding over cross-border insolvency cases, as well as regulators, policy makers, and IOs engaged in international insolvency law making, should be less context-dependent and perceive their roles more broadly, considering public, international law sources, and mechanisms for creating and enhancing international obligations.

Such conceptualization of cross-border insolvency law and of the role of key actors in cross-border insolvency cases could promote the transformation of modified universalism to CIL. This chapter also proposed specific steps that could be taken to enhance and stabilize modified universalism and transform it to CIL, by creating evidence of general practice accepted as law. Modified universalism is already a dominant approach, yet more concrete and explicit proclamations of its rules, also emphasizing their universal application, would reinforce, legalize, and formalize its position. CIL formation is a process and not a straightforward one, yet when it is recognized it can be useful in various ways and can strengthen the cross-border insolvency system going forward.

Still, CIL has important limitations. Not only might it be difficult to identify its existence, it also tends to be imprecise; and it may be ignored or viewed as contradicting national rules, especially in view of the short-termism tendencies noted earlier. Modified universalism rules do require further specification and backing up by written international instruments and the consideration of additional measures to ensure compliance. Thus, while international agreements are not required for the emergence of CIL, certain concrete international instruments are vital for the full operationalization of the cross-border insolvency regime. The question whether such operationalization requires a formal treaty or other types of instrument will be discussed next.

4

Instrument Choice and Design

4.1 Introduction

It was argued in the previous chapter that modified universalism should be conceptualized as a stand-alone approach, separate from pure universalism, and that its emerging norms may transform to CIL. However, the limitations of CIL were also recognized. Even where modified universalism has the capacity to become CIL, identifying general practices accepted as law can be a difficult task. Furthermore, cross-border insolvency law necessitates technical, detailed provisions covering the range of private international law matters pertaining to insolvency.[1] The enforcement of CIL could also be undermined by its imprecision and by the way the rules are understood and applied by local institutions. If the system is entrenched in an instrument, identification and compliance can be enhanced. Treaties or other instruments, including soft laws, that are consistent with modified universalism, and that demonstrate universal application can also contribute to the formation and continued force as CIL. The codification of modified universalism emerging norms in instruments can therefore increase universality, both through the application of such instruments and through the establishment of the rules as CIL where the instruments would provide evidence of the practice understood as law.

The question is what type of instrument would be most appropriate for the cross-border insolvency system based on modified universalism. A global framework in the form of a model law already exists (the United Nations Commission on International Trade Law (UNCITRAL) Model Law on Cross-Border Insolvency (MLCBI)), in addition to other frameworks and mechanisms within regions or among groupings of countries or for specific types of entities. The MLCBI is becoming the dominant instrument for the cross-border insolvency of commercial entities. However, it exists without clear justificatory grounds for choosing it as the lead instrument for the system. The importance of the MLCBI has been noted in quite restrained terms thus far. It has been generally perceived as a compromised form

---

[1] In addition to the delineation of obligations concerning assistance and cooperation, the exposition of the duties of home and host country institutions, and the specific safeguards that apply within the framework. cf the considerable action taken in the 1990s to conclude bilateral treaties in the field of international investment because, as noted by scholars, the CIL was considered quite amorphous in this area and as such not providing sufficient guidance and protection (R Dolzer and A von Walter, 'Fair and Equitable Treatment-Lines of Jurisprudence on Customary Law', in F Ortino (ed), *Investment Treaty Law: Current Issues II* (British Institute of International and Comparative Law 2007) 99).

The Future of Cross-Border Insolvency: Overcoming Biases and Closing Gaps. Irit Mevorach.
© Irit Mevorach 2018. Published 2018 by Oxford University Press.

of international commitment; a modest type of instrument that, as such, provides limited mechanisms; and as the step before a better regime can emerge, ideally in the form of a treaty. The MLCBI has also been viewed as soft law representing non-binding obligations, at least when compared to a treaty.[2]

Against this backdrop, it is not clear to what extent further developments, in terms of areas that the MLCBI and related instruments may cover or the types of entities they may address beyond the commercial entities, are desired and justified. Generally, it is not clear whether, going forward, efforts should focus on improving the MLCBI regime or whether other types of instruments are ultimately preferable. To date, important aspects of the cross-border insolvency regime—specifically, the cross-border insolvency of multinational financial institutions (MFIs)—are not covered fully by the MLCBI. Instead, instruments such as principles, key attributes, or contractual commitments by counterparties to certain contracts are utilized.[3] Additionally, at various times, proposals are made for pursuing a treaty or a convention regime[4] in lieu of a model law. Whilst the quest for treaties in this field is generally a story of failure, calls for deliberations on treaties seem to endure where the MLCBI, like modified universalism, is considered a placeholder until more ideal solutions can be pursued.

This chapter seeks to identify the best type of instrument for the global cross-border insolvency system,[5] with the longer term in mind. It questions the predisposition in favour of a treaty as the ultimate solution. It shows that, thus far, the key justification for a global treaty has been the idea that a treaty is required for the pursuit of pure universalism because it is hard law and thus binding. However, this assumption requires a reconsideration. The previous chapter exposed the problem of modified universalism's continued attachment to the purer theory. Thus, an instrument for the system should provide a framework for a *modified* universalist regime. This chapter argues that an instrument for a modified universalist system should have the characteristics of hard law in the sense that the instrument is more likely to promote high levels of precision and obligation. However, it also shows that the assumption that treaties are hard law and thus ideal international instruments is simplistic, as revealed through a broader analysis of the use of treaty and non-treaty law in international law, and in view of economic as well as behavioural perspectives.

Based on this analysis, this chapter argues that while the treaty has potential advantages over non-treaty instruments, it also involves important drawbacks that are likely highly relevant for cross-border insolvency, in terms of extant transactional and behavioural costs that can undermine its ability to achieve the level of precision and obligation required for the system. In contrast, so-called soft law instruments that are utilized in various international law subsystems are important

---

[2] See eg R Bork, *Principles of Cross-Border Insolvency Law* (Intersentia 2017) 10.

[3] These tools and instruments are assessed in more detail in Chapter 6, section 6.3.

[4] Including proposals led by the International Bar Association (IBA) and the Union Internationale des Avocats (UIA) discussed in section 4.2.2. The terms 'treaty' and 'convention' are used interchangeably.

[5] Namely, the instrument for the cross-border aspects of insolvency. The question of harmonization of insolvency laws and the instruments that may be used for this purpose is discussed in Chapter 5, section 5.3.2.

for cross-border insolvency and, in that context, may in fact be 'harder' than a treaty. Specifically, a model law approach can possess the characteristics of hard law, while retaining flexible features that induce participation. As such, it is a type of instrument that can close gaps in the cross-border insolvency system and address biases in the most effective way as compared with other options, including instruments in the form of guides or principles. The chapter also considers how the design of the chosen instrument, be it a model law, a treaty, or another form of instrument, can provide additional debiasing tools through the exploitation of the framing effect and the use of default rules within the instrument. It also considers the effect of the 'salience bias' and how it can be utilized in instrument design to align choices with desired solutions.

The policy implications are the concentration of efforts in improving the coverage, reach, and design of the existing framework based on a model law as a tool that is appropriate in the long term, not only for the transition to other instrument forms.[6] That framework, which is based on model law instruments, should be of the type that provides a complete regime intended for uniform application and enforcement by domestic systems. More tailored solutions, including regulations or, indeed, treaties, can be effective among groupings of countries or certain regions where the economic and behavioural costs of agreeing on formal methods may be less acute.

The chapter proceeds as follows. Section 4.2 overviews the pursuit of treaties and reveals the assumption of treaties as binding hard law that is presumptively most ideal for cross-border insolvency. Section 4.3 considers the hard versus soft law dichotomy traditionally linked to treaties versus other less formal instruments. It investigates the role of treaties in international law and the features that make instruments hard or soft. It further draws insight from behavioural and economic analyses applied to international law regarding the costs of treaties and the probable implications of instrument choice on the level of participation in the framework. Against this backdrop, section 4.4 asks what type of international instrument is likely to provide the levels of precision and obligation required for a system based on modified universalism. In the process, this section offers the grounds for a hard, model law approach to global cross-border insolvency. Section 4.5 addresses issues of instrument design. It makes the argument for exploiting legislative framing to align decisions concerning the enactment and implementation of instruments with the optimal solutions. Section 4.6 provides summary conclusions.

4.2 Treaties and Ideal Universalism

Notwithstanding the challenges of achieving international cooperation regarding the administration of cross-border insolvencies, over the years there have been attempts to conclude treaties in this field, bilaterally between countries and on a global level. This section overviews the pursuit of treaties and shows that success has thus far been

---

[6] The MLCBI and related instruments are assessed in Chapter 6.

limited. Nonetheless, the quest for a treaty regime seems to endure. The assumption is that a treaty, being binding, is ultimately the necessary international instrument to achieve purer forms of universalism. However, this assumption is misconceived where it is modified universalism that should govern international insolvencies, and as treaties may be less hard and binding compared with non-treaty texts.

4.2.1 The pursuit of treaties: a story of failure and hope

Since the end of the seventeenth century and into the twentieth century, countries have negotiated and concluded several bilateral treaties on cross-border insolvency. These treaties addressed basic cross-border insolvency issues and typically involved neighbouring countries or countries with close trading relationships.[7] Additional bilateral treaties have been signed concerning the private international law aspects of civil and commercial law and, in some of these treaties, insolvency has not been excluded from their scope.[8]

It has been more difficult to execute effective cross-border insolvency treaties between multiple parties.[9] There have, nonetheless, been various such attempts to negotiate treaties on a regional level, although these efforts have often failed and resulted in conventions that have not entered into force or that have not been ratified by all parties to the negotiations. For example, a series of private international law and commerce treaties with chapters on bankruptcy were concluded in Latin America between different groupings of countries. The 'Montevideo treaties', which were concluded in 1889 and 1940, contain provisions concerning international

---

[7] For a detailed account see K Lipstein, ch 14 in IF Fletcher (ed), *Cross-Border Insolvency: Comparative Dimensions: the Aberystwyth Insolvency Papers* (United Kingdom National Committee of Comparative Law 1990); K Nadelmann, 'Bankruptcy Treaties' (1944) 93 U Pa L Rev 58; IF Fletcher, *Insolvency in Private International Law* (OUP 2005) 273–75. See also the attempt to agree on a bilateral treaty in the 1970s between the United States and Canada, which ultimately failed (C Felsenfeld, *International Insolvency: A Treatise on the Law of International Insolvency* 1, 3–8 (Juris Publishing 2000)).

[8] See eg the treaties which China has concluded since the late 1980s with various countries on civil and commercial judicial assistance (treaties were signed with France, Poland, Belgium, Mongolia, Romania, Italy, Spain, Russia, Turkey, Ukraine, Cuba, Belarus, Kazakhstan, Bulgaria, Thailand, Egypt, Greece, Cyprus, Hungary, Morocco, Kirghizstan, Tajikistan, Singapore, Uzbekistan, Viet Nam, Laos, Tunisia, Lithuania, Argentina, Republic of Korea, Democratic People's Republic of Korea, United Arab Emirates, Kuwait, Peru, Brazil, Algeria). A treaty on the Mutual Promotion and Protection of the Investment Agreement was also signed with Australia in 1988 which also includes civil and commercial judicial assistance (X Gong, 'To Recognise or Not to Recognise? Comparative Study of Lehman Brothers Cases in Mainland China and Taiwan' (2013) 10(4) ICR 240).

[9] The difficulty of concluding treaties in international insolvency has been noted by many commentators, see eg RA Gitlin and ED Flaschen, 'The International Void in the Law of Multinational Bankruptcies' (1987) 42 Business Lawyer 307, 311–13; DG Boshkoff, 'Some Gloomy Thought Concerning Cross-Border Insolvencies' (1994) 72 Wash U L Rev 931, 935; T Armstrong Panuska, 'The Chaos of International Insolvency—Achieving Reciprocal Universality under Section 304 or MIICA' (1993) 6 Transnatl L 373, 396–97; DC Cook, 'Prospects for a North American Bankruptcy Agreement; Les Prospects Pour une Convention de la Faillite en Amerique du Nord; Los Prospectos Para un Convenio de Quiebra de Norte America' (1995) 2 Sw J L & Trade in the Americas 81, 85–97; J Clift, 'The UNCITRAL Model Law on Cross-Border Insolvency—A Legislative Framework to Facilitate Coordination and Cooperation in Cross-Border Insolvency' (2004) 12 Tul J Intl & Comp L 307, 312; LM LoPucki, 'Global and Out of Control?' (2005) 79 Am Bankr L J 79, 82.

bankruptcies that harmonize private international law rules for insolvency proceedings that span several countries (that are parties to the treaty).[10] These treaties, however, have been of limited appeal, even within countries that were supposed to become parties to the agreements.[11] A more comprehensive convention on private international law was concluded in 1928 at the Sixth Pan-American Conference (the Convention on Private International Law, Havana 1928; also known as the 'Bustamante Code') and contained a chapter on bankruptcy.[12] However, only fifteen of the twenty-one negotiating countries ratified the convention.[13]

A European Convention on Certain International Aspects of Bankruptcy (known as the Istanbul Convention) was drafted under the auspices of the Council of Europe and was opened to ratification in 1990.[14] The convention never entered into force. It required a minimum of three ratifications, but only received one.[15] The European Union (EU) also made an attempt to conclude a convention to regulate insolvency proceedings within the EU.[16] The initiative and negotiations lasted more than thirty years (from 1960 to 1996) and eventually failed to materialize as a convention.[17] A successful treaty was actually concluded between the five Scandinavian countries early in 1933 (the Nordic Bankruptcy Convention; amended in 1977 and in 1982) addressing various private international aspects of insolvency, including the liquidation of banks.[18] On an international level, The Hague Conference on Private International Law first began work on a bankruptcy convention in 1894.[19] This

---

[10] For the 1889 text see E Restelli (ed), *Actas y Tratados del Congreso Sud-americano de Derecho Internacional Privado* (Montevideo 1888–89). See also Fletcher, *Insolvency in Private International Law* (n 7) 595–96, for an unofficial English translation of Title X on bankruptcy. For the 1940 text see *Segundo Congreso Sudamericano de Derecho Internacional Privado, Acta Final, Segunda Edicion* (Montevideo 1940) 61–72. See also Fletcher *Insolvency in Private International Law* (n 7) 597–99, for a reproduction of English translation of the text.

[11] The 1889 Treaty, which contained a chapter on bankruptcy, was ratified by five countries, with another acceding to it in 1933. The 1940 revised treaty was ratified by only three countries.

[12] For the text (in English) of the Havana Convention see 86 LNTS No 1950 (1929) 246–381, reproduced in Fletcher, *Insolvency in Private International Law* (n 7) 600.

[13] TM Gaa, 'Harmonization of International Bankruptcy Law and Practice: Is it Necessary? Is It Possible?' (1993) 27 Intl L 881, 883.

[14] For the text see ETS, No 136, reproduced in Fletcher *Insolvency in Private International Law* (n 7) Appendix III.

[15] Eight countries have signed the treaty. Only Cyprus has ratified it. See Fletcher, *Insolvency in Private International Law* (n 7) 315.

[16] See on the EU Insolvency Convention, M Balz, 'The European Union Convention on Insolvency Proceedings' (1996) 70 Am Bankr L J 485. See also LA Burton, 'Toward an International Bankruptcy Policy in Europe: Four Decades in Search of a Treaty' (1999) 5 Annual Survey of International and Comparative Law 205; PJ Omar, 'The European Insolvency Regulation 2000: A Paradigm of International Insolvency Cooperation' (2003) 15 Bond Law Review 215.

[17] The Convention has been signed by fourteen of the fifteen member states, yet it could not come into effect, as the fifteenth member state, the United Kingdom, refused to sign it.

[18] For the text in English see No 3574, (1935) 155 LNTS 133–39, reproduced in Fletcher, *Insolvency in Private International Law* (n 7) 603. On the Nordic Convention see M Bodgan, Chapter 31, in JS Ziegel (ed), *Current Developments in International and Comparative Corporate Insolvency Law* (OUP 1994) 701–08.

[19] The Second Conference of Private International Law, The Hague, 1894. See Nadelmann, 'Bankruptcy Treaties' (n 7) 66.

work never fully materialized but was later transformed into a model for bilateral treaties that has had some limited influence, for example, on the development of the Nordic Convention.[20]

This limited success of cross-border insolvency treaties[21] led over the years to the development of mechanisms and instruments that do not have treaty status, but address problems of cross-border insolvency and diversity in insolvency laws. Instruments to enhance cooperation and to harmonize aspects of private international insolvency law have been introduced in the form of recommendations, key attributes, and, notably, a model law for global insolvency (as described in Chapter 1). In Europe, the failed attempt to conclude a convention eventually led to the conversion of the draft treaty into a regulation on cross-border insolvency.[22] Directives were also developed for the cross-border winding up and the resolution of credit institutions in Europe.[23] Additional initiatives toward greater harmonization of insolvency laws have been taken on in Europe and in other regions,[24] and globally, there have been efforts to standardize insolvency laws and resolution measures.[25]

4.2.2 The continued quest for a global treaty

Recent decades showed renewed enthusiasm for global treaties addressing cross-border insolvency. Thus, some commentators suggested in the early 2000s that it was time for a multinational treaty on cross-border insolvency. It has been argued that 'national governments must act swiftly to bring their bankruptcy laws back in symmetry with the bankruptcy market' and that 'the most effective way to do this is through the development of a comprehensive international insolvency treaty'.[26] Relatedly, regarding international instruments for cross-border insolvency, including the MLCBI, it was noted that 'while they are a good starting point, national governments need to move beyond them'.[27]

Proponents of treaties have pointed to various weaknesses in the extant cross-border insolvency regime, including the limited adoption of the MLCBI,[28] and linked these perceived weaknesses to the absence of a treaty, noting that:

The fact that so many civil law jurisdictions, including states with an important international trade role, have not adopted the Model Law (but have, in the EU context, become parties

---

[20] Actes de La 5E Conference De Droit International Privé (1925) 341, Journal De Droit International, 1926, 822. See Nadelmann, 'Bankruptcy Treaties' (n 7) 67–68.

[21] 'Success' means here the ability to agree and to ratify a comprehensive treaty on international insolvency between multiple participants.

[22] See Chapter 1, section 1.4.4.　　　[23] ibid.　　　[24] ibid.　　　[25] ibid.

[26] PJ Murphy, 'Why Won't the Leaders Lead? The Need for National Governments to Replace Academics and Practitioners in the Effort to Reform the Muddled World of International Insolvency' (2002) 34 U Miami Interam L Rev 121, 123.

[27] ibid 125.

[28] See eg S Chandra Mohan, 'Cross-Border Insolvency Problems: Is the UNCITRAL Model Law the Answer?' (2012) 21 Intl Insolv Rev 199.

to a binding regulation) directs focus to a binding global regime, such as an international insolvency convention ... [29]

Regarding the cross-border challenges of addressing MFIs in distress, it has also been argued that there is no real substitution for 'formal, binding, enforceable international agreements, if not actual treaties'.[30] Indeed, the weaknesses of the regime for MFI cross-border insolvency were apparent during the global financial crisis.[31] It has also been observed that solutions such as 'living wills'[32] might not be able to address local attempts to ring-fence assets, and that standards or principles developed by international organizations (IOs) have limited effects.[33] Again, the assumption has been that the ultimate solution must be in the form of binding agreements as any informal agreement, the argument goes, will create confusion and chaos.[34]

The idea of developing a convention on the cross-border insolvency of commercial entities has also been considered by international policymakers. UNCITRAL Working Group V, the primary body that addresses issues related to insolvency on an international level, has expressed some support for the idea since 2009.[35] Specifically, in 2014, UNCITRAL took on the task of informally studying the feasibility of a convention by setting up an ad hoc study group.[36] This project was largely driven by certain non-governmental organizations (NGOs) to develop an instrument that represents hard law.[37] The convention project has been discussed in informal

---

[29] Note by the IBA Insolvency Section Delegation to UNCITRAL Working Group V based on an article by Gregor Baer, Insolvency Section Co-Chair, published in Business Law International (January 2016): 'International Insolvency Convention: Issues, Options and Feasibility Considerations' (with the publisher's permission) <https://www.ibanet.org/LPD/Insolvency_Section/Insolvency_Section/Projects.aspx#uninsolvencyconvention> para 16.

[30] BC Matthews, 'Prospects for Coordination and Competition in Global Finance' (2010) 104 Proceedings of the Annual Meeting (American Society of International Law) 104, *International Law in a Time of Change* 289, 292.

[31] See Chapter 1, section 1.4.5.   [32] See Chapter 1, n 230.

[33] Matthews, 'Prospects for Coordination and Competition in Global Finance' (n 30) 292. See also Chapter 6, section 6.3 for a detailed discussion of post-crisis international standards, principles, and certain contractual solutions developed by international organizations (IOs) for MFI resolution.

[34] Matthews, 'Prospects for Coordination and Competition in Global Finance' (n 30) 293. See also the proposal for a treaty-based World Financial Organization (B Eichengreen, 'Not a New Bretton Woods but a New Bretton Woods Process' (6 November 2008) <https://eml.berkeley.edu/~eichengr/not_new_bretton_woods.pdf>, and the proposal of the Institute of International Finance for a treaty on the resolution of financial institutions (Institute of International Finance, 'Making Resolution Robust—Completing the Legal And Institutional Frameworks For Effective Cross-Border Resolution of Financial Institutions' (June 2012) <https://www.iif.com/system/files/Making_Resolution_Robust_20120607.pdf>).

[35] UNCITRAL, A/CN.9/686, Report of Working Group V (Insolvency Law) on the work of its thirty-seventh session (Vienna, 9–13 November 2009) paras 127–28; UNCITRAL, A/CN.9/691, Report of Working Group V (Insolvency Law) on the work of its thirty-eighth session (New York, 19–23 April 2010) para 101 <http://www.uncitral.org/uncitral/en/commission/working_groups/5Insolvency.html>.

[36] UNCITRAL, A/CN.9/798, Report of Working Group V (Insolvency Law) on the work of its forty-fourth session (Vienna, 16–20 December 2013) paras 18–19 <http://www.uncitral.org/uncitral/en/commission/working_groups/5Insolvency.html>.

[37] The IBA and the UIA in particular (UNCITRAL, Proposal for Future Work for Working Group V by the Union Internationale des Avocats (UIA) UNCITRAL Working Group V 37th Session (November 2009) UN Doc A/CN.9/WG.V/XXXVII/ CRP.3; UNCITRAL, 'Comments by the International Bar Association respecting proposals to consider an international convention and/or model law on

meetings in conjunction with UNCITRAL sessions from 2014–16. However, not-withstanding surveys conducted by NGOs showing support for the project and other materials and arguments that have been presented,[38] many delegates partici-pating in the informal discussions expressed doubt about the feasibility and desir-ability of the project, particularly the likelihood that such a treaty will ever enter into force in view of the prior treaty attempts in this field.[39]

4.2.3 Treaty assumptions: hard law for pure universalism

The general aspiration to conclude a global treaty addressing cross-border insolv-ency has been largely based on the assumption that a treaty is a binding instrument and, as such, that it is instrumental for the pursuit of purer forms of universalism. This understanding of the role of treaties has thus been, at least to some extent, linked to the perception of pure universalism as the ultimate solution for cross-border insolvency. As discussed in earlier chapters, although it is modified univer-salism that emerged as the dominant approach, modified universalism has thus far not been conceptualized as a binding norm; rather, it is an interim (or incremental) approach.[40] Relatedly, there has not been a clear idea of what type of instrument would fit modified universalism in the long-term. It is only by considering the pure version of universalism that the form of a treaty has been consistently considered the appropriate international instrument. Thus, early in the 1940s, it was noted that the unresolved problems regarding international insolvency were a continual threat to the development of international commercial relations and that the solu-tion to this problem was the conclusion of bankruptcy treaties that would provide extraterritorial effect to a bankruptcy declared by a court with jurisdiction under the treaty.[41] Still, in more recent years, the idea has been that as soon as it is achiev-able, a single legal regime to govern multinational defaults will be contemplated

---

cross-border enterprise group insolvency' UNCITRAL Working Group V, 38th Session (New York, April 2010) UN Doc A/CN.9/WG.V/WP.93/Add.6 <http://www.uncitral.org/uncitral/en/commis-sion/working_groups/5Insolvency.html>. See also P Rona, Section Subcommittee Update, Legislation and Policy Subcommittee Update, 'The Next Law Reform Frontier—a UN Insolvency Convention' (2015) 9(2) Insolvency and Restructuring International 42 <https://www.ibanet.org/LPD/Insolvency_Section/Insolvency_Section/Projects.aspx>.

[38] See <https://www.ibanet.org/LPD/Insolvency_Section/Insolvency_Section/Projects.aspx> in-cluding Executive Summary and Working Papers for International Insolvency Convention Discussion, December 2015.

[39] For the time being this treaty project seems to have discontinued. The Commission noted in its re-port from 2016 (United Nations, A/71/17, Report of the United Nations Commission on International Trade Law, Forty-ninth session (27 June–15 July 2016) para 247 <http://www.uncitral.org/uncitral/en/commission/sessions/49th.html>) that 'the feasibility of developing a convention on international insolvency issues might continue to be studied informally by an ad hoc, open-ended group of interested participants on the basis of a list of issues prepared and distributed by the Secretariat. However, noting that the agenda of Working Group V was already rather full and that the Secretariat might have little time and few resources with which to conduct this informal work, the Commission agreed that that work should only be undertaken as and when the Secretariat was able to do so'.

[40] See Chapter 1, section 1.3.1 and the proposal in Chapter 3 to transform modified universalism norms to binding CIL.

[41] Nadelmann, 'Bankruptcy Treaties' (n 7) 60–61.

through agreement on an international convention.[42] An international convention has been viewed as the ideal or even the only platform to fully achieve the benefits of universalism.[43]

The modified universalism that is arguably enshrined in certain international instruments has been considered as a mere transitory solution in the absence of a treaty or until a treaty can be concluded.[44] Along such lines, Lord Hoffmann, in the *HiH* case, described modified universalism as a pragmatic approach awaiting the achievement of pure universalism, through the conclusion of an international treaty. Noting that English judges have for many years considered that bankruptcy should be unitary and universal, Lord Hoffmann stated that 'this was very much a principle rather than a rule. It is heavily qualified by exceptions on pragmatic grounds' and 'full universalism can be attained only by international treaty'.[45]

Generally, the so-called middle-ground (modified) approaches to cross-border insolvency have been understood as solutions pending an agreement on a treaty and as desirable in the absence of specific treaty relationships.[46] Proponents of modified universalism have often viewed modified universalism solutions as responses to problems where universalism in its pure form was not achievable without an international convention. As such, solutions have been developed to achieve some of the benefits of universalism without the need to agree on a convention.[47] These non-treaty instruments have been viewed as steps towards universality.[48] Specifically, the MLCBI has been considered 'a more modest first step, avoiding the risk that a treaty might languish for many years, admired but unadopted'.[49] Alternative instruments

---

[42] JL Westbrook, 'A Global Solution to Multinational Default' (2000) 98 Mich L Rev 2276, 2287, 2292.

[43] See eg LA Bebchuk and AT Guzman, 'An Economic Analysis of Transnational Bankruptcies' (1999) 42 J L & Econ 775, 789 ('a treaty clearly would be the best solution to the problem discussed in the paper, but for various reasons, attempts at establishing multilateral treaties on the subject have not fared well ...'); TM Gaa, 'Harmonization of International Bankruptcy Law and Practice' (n 13) 909 ('codifying in bankruptcy treaties the "international common law of bankruptcy" being generated on an ad hoc basis represents the most efficient means to satisfy the common concerns of all participants in any insolvency or bankruptcy matter: predictability in results, efficiency and equity in distribution of the estate's assets, and finality'); J Greene, 'Bankruptcy Beyond Borders: Recognizing Foreign Proceedings in Cross-Border Insolvencies' (2005) 30 Brook J Intl L 685, 726 ('The most obvious way to effect international insolvency cooperation is though treaty or convention.' Though, then also noting that: 'from a practical standpoint, multinational treaties and conventions have proved nearly impossible to enact'); S Gopalan and M Guihot, 'Cross-Border Insolvency and Multinational Enterprise Groups: Judicial Innovation as an International Solution' (2016) 48 Geo Wash Intl L Rev 549, 612 ('until a binding convention is adopted, judicial innovation and pragmatism are the only possible solutions').

[44] See Chapter 1, section 1.3.1.

[45] *In re HIH Casualty and General Insurance Ltd* [2008] UKHL 21, [2008] 1 WLR 852, paras 6–7.

[46] Fletcher, *Insolvency in Private International Law* (n 7) 12.

[47] K Anderson, 'The Cross-Border Insolvency Paradigm: A Defense of the Modified Universal Approach Considering the Japanese Experience' (2000) 21 U Pa J Intl Econ L 681, 682 ('The problem that remained, however, was that universalism in its pure form was not feasible without an international convention, because states were generally unwilling to allow, or give effect to, a foreign court's unfettered extraterritorial actions').

[48] J Smith, 'Approaching Universality: The Role of Comity in International Bankruptcy Proceedings Litigated in America' (1999) 17 B U Intl L J 396, 370.

[49] JL Westbrook, 'Interpretation Internationale' (2015) 87 Temp L Rev 739, 753. See also Greene, 'Bankruptcy Beyond Borders' (n 43) 713–14 (noting that 'unlike a treaty or convention, the Model Law does not mandate a change in the substantive rules in any country's bankruptcy law. Instead, it has

have been generally perceived as the 'art of the possible',[50] implying that a 'state of the art' solution is yet to emerge. Drafters and promulgators of frameworks such as the MLCBI seem to consider the frameworks as first steps and as practical solutions in view of the difficulties of reaching an agreement on a treaty. The premise of the ALI Transnational Insolvency Project, for example, which formulated cooperation principles for the NAFTA region,[51] has been that 'neither harmonization of the insolvency laws of [Mexico, Canada, and the US] nor adoption of a comprehensive treaty concerning insolvency is likely to be achievable in the near future'.[52] Regarding the MLCBI, the following has been noted:

Some who were present when the Model Law CBI was first pursued explained that a soft law solution was pursued at the time as the most expedient alternative, especially in view of the state of law and practice at the time, but that a convention was never ruled out and was considered by some as a desirable long-term solution.[53]

The convention study that was instigated by NGOs in 2014 followed the assumption that instruments developed thus far for global cross-border insolvency are interim solutions—steps towards the more ideal regime that will eventually be based on a convention. Thus, proponents of the convention project have claimed that:

the Model Law CBI was intended to be the first, but not the final, word on encouraging cross-border cooperation in insolvency matters. The Model Law CBI was pursued as the most practical step forward then realistically achievable, given disharmony among national and regional insolvency systems and the ad hoc nature of cross-border judicial and administrative cooperation and communication at the time.[54]

Specifically, the concern has been about the non-bindingness of soft law measures that fall short of treaties. Thus, it has been argued that only a treaty would address the real challenges of cross-border insolvency as it will reflect 'consensus based principles consistent with international law precepts such as state sovereignty'.[55] It will create a regime that is designed to ensure comity and reciprocity, 'which have historically

---

been offered as a model for participating countries to enact, with the hope that its adoption will set into motion cooperation among countries in regard to multinational bankruptcies. As such, Chapter 15 represents only a cautious step towards a universalist approach to international insolvencies').

[50]   Fletcher, *Insolvency in Private International Law* (n 7) 497.   [51]   See Chapter 1, n 261.

[52]   HS Burman, 'Harmonisation of International Bankruptcy Law: United States Perspective' (1996) 64 Fordham L Rev 2543, 2577.

[53]   Note by the IBA Insolvency Section Delegation to UNCITRAL Working Group V (n 29) fn 19.

[54]   ibid para 14 (footnote omitted). See also UNCITRAL Yearbook, Volume XXVIII: 1997, Summary Records of The United Nations Commission on International Trade Law for Meetings Devoted to the Preparation of the Draft UNCITRAL Model Law on Cross-Border Insolvency (12 May 1997), 339 <http://www.uncitral.org/uncitral/en/publications/yearbook.html> (which notes in para 5 that the prevailing view of the Working Group had been that model provisions are preferable over a treaty form. It also noted that: 'Nevertheless, some had expressed the view that certain aspects of the subject would be more appropriately dealt with in an international treaty. If, after adopting model legislation, the Commission felt there was a need for an international treaty, that could be discussed and decided at a later stage').

[55]   Note by the IBA Insolvency Section Delegation to UNCITRAL Working Group V (n 29) para 18.

been important elements of cooperation between states.'[56] Treaties, so it has been argued, 'accomplish cross-border cooperation as a matter of state contract; they are, by their nature, multilateral instruments with binding effect'.[57] It was also thought that the need to address various gaps and conflicts in the current system, especially regarding enterprise groups, requires a stronger, more binding instrument, namely, a treaty.[58]

The previous chapters showed, however, that pure universalism is the theoretical paradigm against which modified universalism has developed, and yet it is modified universalism that translated the pure model into a practicable regime that fits world realities and business structures. What should be asked, therefore, is which instrument can best serve a system based on modified universalism. In fact, a convention may or may not reflect *any* form of universalism. The few attempted and concluded treaties and conventions regarding cross-border insolvency have been inspired by universalism, yet these treaties did not reflect pure versions and most of them included significant concessions toward local interests.[59] Cross-border insolvency treaties (negotiated or concluded) have often tolerated a plurality of proceedings in various circumstances.[60] In most cases, treaties have made only a modest attempt to impose a unified, regional approach.[61] Indeed, treaties may be more—or less—comprehensive and may not even succeed in addressing all of the private international law aspects of insolvency.[62] A treaty could also theoretically reflect a version of territorialism. Under the cooperative territorialism paradigm, for example, countries may sign treaties or conventions to encourage mutually beneficial cooperation among the representatives in relevant cases.[63]

Thus, in practice, there is no inevitable link between a cross-border insolvency regime founded on the ideals of universalism and a convention. In any event, the important question is whether a convention might be a desirable instrument to

---

[56] ibid para 43. See also Greene, 'Bankruptcy Beyond Borders' (n 43) 724 (noting that 'the United States must ... enact reciprocal legislation with as many other nations as possible, regardless of their respective insolvency regimes').

[57] Note by the IBA Insolvency Section Delegation to UNCITRAL Working Group V para 43.

[58] ibid para 16 ('many practitioners and some judges believe that the Model Law should be supplemented by "hard law" (a) to require crossborder insolvency coordination in a world of increasingly globalized commercial enterprise groups, or (b) to resolve intractable disputes or conflicting court orders in cross-border insolvency cases ... ').

[59] Article 48 of the 1940 Montevideo Treaty (n 10), for example, discriminates against local creditors who are preferred over foreign creditors in the distribution of assets located in the country where the proceedings take place.

[60] The Havana Convention and the Montevideo Treaties of 1940 allow the opening of multiple proceedings where the debtor has multiple establishments. The Nordic Convention allows the continuation of non-domiciliary proceedings that commenced before the opening of bankruptcy proceeding, though such proceedings may be stayed and consolidated with the insolvency process.

[61] Fletcher, *Insolvency in Private International Law* (n 7) 285.

[62] The Istanbul Convention, for example, merely provided rules for recognition and effect of opening proceedings but did not lay down rules for direct international jurisdiction.

[63] LM LoPucki, 'Cooperation in International Bankruptcy: A Post-Universalist Approach' (1999) 84 Cornell L Rev 696, 742–43; AM Kipnis, 'Beyond UNCITRAL: Alternatives to Universality in Translational Insolvency' (2008) 36 Denv J Intl L & Poly 155,184 (proposing several modifications to cooperative territorialism that may be adopted by way of a treaty). See also Chapter 1, n 27.

implement modified universalism or whether other instruments are preferable, including the type of frameworks that are currently in use (the so-called soft law instruments, importantly, the MLCBI). A convention is not an inherent element of modified universalism unless and until it is possible to show that it is the best or the only type of instrument that can promote a modified universalist system. To the extent that modified universalism requires a hard instrument, a treaty regime may be the appropriate choice. However, the assumption that a treaty is hard law and the perception that it is the ideal international instrument requires reconsideration.

4.3 Hard or Soft Instruments in International Law

Although treaties are key international instruments, the use of what is called soft law has proliferated and there is in fact no such strict distinction between the two categories of instrument. Furthermore, although treaties have the potential to possess the key features of hard law—precision and obligation—in practice, so-called soft law could exhibit greater hardness than treaties in important respects. These advantages of non-treaty compared with treaty law are considered in this section against the backdrop of economic and behavioural analyses of the utility of international instruments.

4.3.1 The significance of treaties in international law

The treaty is traditionally considered the ideal international agreement.[64] It is a core feature of international law and international relations, recognized as an international law source in the Statute of the International Court of Justice which refers to 'international conventions, whether general or particular, establishing rules expressly recognized by the contesting states'.[65] Furthermore, the binding force of treaties is recognized by the 1969 Vienna Convention on the Law of Treaties, which states that 'a treaty is one of the most evident ways in which rules binding on two or more States may come into existence, and thus an evident formal source of law'.[66]

The predominance of the treaty as a key international law source follows the fundamental international law principle that international obligations should be based on consent: 'the principles of free consent and of good faith and the *pacta sunt servanda* are universally recognized'.[67] It is generally accepted that state sovereignty forbids an automatic effect of obligations and countries may relinquish sovereignty and commit to obligations voluntarily.[68] Thus, consent via an international

---

[64] M Goldmann, 'We Need to Cut Off the Head of the King: Past, Present, and Future Approaches to International Soft Law' (2012) 25(2) Leiden Journal of International Law 335, 342–43 (referring to J Klabbers, *The Concept of Treaty in International Law* (Kluwer Law International 1996) 70, and noting that some maintain this view even though they recognize the difficulties in establishing binding norms).

[65] Statute of the International Court of Justice 1945, art 38(1)(a). See also H Thirlway, *The Sources of International Law* (OUP 2014) 7, 31–52.

[66] Vienna Convention on the Law of Treaties 1969, Article 26.   [67] ibid.

[68] GM Danilenko, *Law-making in the International Community* (Martinus Nijhoff 1993) 58; TF McInerney III, 'Note: Towards the Next Phase in International Banking Regulation' (1994) 7 DePaul

agreement is necessary to override the state sovereignty standard.[69] Furthermore, concrete agreements among countries could provide complete and comprehensive rules with detailed terms that can be uniformly followed by all participants.[70] Thus, treaties can be precise and wide-ranging. The precision of treaties is also considered another element of their legitimacy, as they can reduce doubt and uncertainty,[71] leading to a 'compliance pull'.[72]

As they may contain hard consensual rules, treaties are potentially the most practicable international instruments.[73] They reflect concrete obligations, and therefore may address the 'bindingness' problem. The lack of coercive enforcement and the challenge of ensuring compliance with international norms are key concerns of international law.[74] In this regard, consent embedded in hard law is considered crucial for ensuring compliance. Such consent prompts discipline and it is what makes treaties binding, as countries are expected to respect what they have agreed upon.[75] Without consent, the risk is that countries will ignore the international rules.[76] Hard law based on consent, especially treaties, creates pressure to comply because non-compliance has consequences in terms of harm to reputation.[77] Non-compliance with formal agreements can also result in retaliation measures, such as taking economic action, curtailing assistance, or reducing cooperation in other areas.[78] In this respect, the reciprocity enshrined in treaties is another recognized force that could induce compliance.[79] Thus, when agreeing to treaties, countries are supposed to

---

Bus L J 143, 168–69 (arguing in favour of an international convention to govern international banking regulation, noting that 'the overriding primary rule of international law is the sovereignty and equality of the state', yet, that 'states may, by treaty, commit to certain obligations and commit to implement certain regulations or standards within their own jurisdiction'). See also AT Guzman, 'Against Consent', (2012) 52 Va J Intl L 747, 748 (noting that 'the importance of consent is built into the DNA of international law scholars').

[69] In rare circumstances, sovereignty is overridden by *jus cogens*, which is a type of general customary law having universal application as it is impossible to contract out of these norms by agreement (Thirlway, *The Sources of International* Law (n 65) 154–63). See also obligations based on CIL arising from the general practice of countries followed out of a sense of legal obligation, subject to opting out through persistent objection (Chapter 3, section 3.2.1).

[70] AE Boyle, 'Some Reflections on the Relationship of Treaties and Soft Law' (1999) 48 ICLQ 901, 902–04.

[71] O Schachter, *International Law in Theory and Practice* (Martinus Nijhoff Publishers 1991) 66.

[72] KW Abbott and D Snidal, 'Hard and Soft Law in International Governance' (2000) 54 Intl Org 421, 428–29 (referring to TM Franck, *The Power of Legitimacy Among Nations* (OUP 1990)).

[73] Thirlway, *The Sources of International* Law (n 65) 31.

[74] See Chapter 5 for a discussion of measures to promote compliance (in addition to the use of hard or soft international instruments).

[75] Thirlway, *The Sources of International* Law (n 65) 7.

[76] See AT Guzman, *How International Law Works: A Rational Choice Theory* (OUP 2008) 172–73; AT Guzman 'Against Consent' (2012) 52 Va J Intl L 747, 752.

[77] Guzman, *How International Law Works* (n 76) 34 (noting that: 'A state that is known to honour its commitments will find more partners when it seeks to enter into future cooperative arrangements, will be able to extract more generous concessions in exchange for its promises, and will be able to solve more problems of cooperation than will a state that has a less favourable reputation').

[78] ibid 47.

[79] See also the concept of mutual trust that has been used in the EU to oblige reciprocity and automatic recognition in cross-border insolvencies (see Chapter 3, section 3.6.1, and Chapter 5, section 5.2.5).

comply with the rules, expecting that other parties will also comply; hence, all parties are motivated to honour their commitments.[80] Obligation and compliance can be further enhanced in hard law mechanisms, especially treaties, as they can create new IOs and include dispute settlement provisions.[81]

This notion that countries are bound only through consent is, arguably, what legitimizes international agreements, notably, treaties. Rules contained in such agreements are viewed as products of an international law-making process that is inclusive, where all countries can take part in the proceedings and have significant input in the negotiations, including voicing concerns or objections.[82] If the rules are considered illegitimate because they were not based on unanimous consent, they are arguably also less desirable because countries cannot be sure that the rules will serve their interests. The consent of countries provides the best evidence that the rules will increase global welfare.[83] In this respect, some critical international legal studies have claimed that soft law that is not based on consent is wholly illegitimate where it does not require domestic ratification, because it provides more room for the structural bias of international law and for powerful countries to act in their best interests alone.[84]

4.3.2 Soft law instruments can be harder than treaties

While international law-making has been primarily based on two central sources, CIL and treaties, international law scholars have pointed to the relevance and contributions of soft international law and have observed that a dismissal of the significance of soft law is a 'fallacy'.[85] In practice, the use of soft law instruments has proliferated. In some areas, and in certain subsystems of international law, including international financial and commercial regulations, soft law already dominates the international regulatory framework.[86] Generally, it has been acknowledged that the

---

[80] Guzman, *How International Law Works* (n 76) 42–45.

[81] See eg C Brummer, *Soft Law and the Global Financial System, Rule Making in the 21st Century* (CUP 2015) 124; BC Matthews, 'Emerging Public International Banking Law? Lessons from the Law of the Sea Experience' (2010) 10 Chi J Intl L 539, 556–57. See also Chapter 5, section 5.3.3.

[82] Schachter, *International law in Theory and Practice* (n 71) 66; AE Boyle, 'Soft Law in International Law Making' in MD Evans (ed) *International Law* (OUP 2014) 121; Franck, *Fairness in International Law and Institutions* (n 73) 25ff; TM Franck, 'Legitimacy in the International System' (1988) 82 Am J Intl L 705, 705–11; Franck, *The Power of Legitimacy Among Nations* (n 72) 27–40.

[83] Guzman, 'Against Consent' (n 68) 754–55.

[84] M Goldmann, 'We Need to Cut Off the Head of the King' (n 64) 356–57 (referring to M Koskenniemi, 'Formalism, Fragmentation, Freedom: Kantian Themes in Today's International Law' (2007) 4 No Foundations: Journal of Extreme Legal Positivism 7, 11, and M Koskenniemi, 'Global Governance and Public International Law' (2004) 37 Kritische Justiz 241, 243).

[85] Boyle, 'Soft Law in International Law Making' (n 82) 118. See also Goldmann, 'We Need to Cut Off the Head of the King' (n 64) 343 ('The call for the elimination of soft law reminds one of Don Quixote's fight against windmills').

[86] See eg CM Bruner, 'States, Markets and Gatekeepers: Private-Public Regulatory Regimes in an Era of Economic Globalisation' (2009) 30 Mich J Intl L 125, 172 (noting the standards promulgated by the Organisation for Economic Co-operation and Development (OECD) and the Basel Committee on Banking Supervision); Brummer, *Soft Law and the Global Financial System* (n 81) 120 (noting that in international financial law, commitments are not made by treaty but rather largely through soft law instruments that do not impose formal legal obligations).

generic term soft law is a misleading simplification in view of the wide diversity in the so-called soft law instruments.[87]

Soft law in international law traditionally refers to a variety of quasi-legal, non-binding rules and instruments used in international relations by countries and IOs. As such, soft law is contrasted with hard law, which is, under this divide, always binding.[88] This so-called soft law may include instruments such as guidelines, codes of conduct, recommendations, or core principles promulgated by IOs, such as General Assembly instruments.[89] Thus, conventionally, soft law has been considered a derogation from the ideal international commitment, a weakened version of hard law. Arguably, what makes the law soft is deviation by the parties from a high degree of obligation and a high level of precision of the rules.

However, such softening of international arrangements can occur in varying degrees and in different combinations, suggesting that the distinction between hard and soft law is not a binary distinction.[90] The rigid divide between hard and soft law and between treaties and other less formal instruments ignores the variety of treaties, on the one hand, and the relevance of soft law to law-making, on the other.[91]

As mentioned above, treaties are considered hard because of the assumed precision of the rules they contemplate. On the other hand, soft law is understood as being based on open-textured principles as opposed to the concrete rules embodied in hard law. Pursuant to this distinction, however, some treaties or provisions within treaties can be characterized, de facto, as soft (even though formally binding) because of their vagueness, indeterminacy, or generality[92] while many soft laws operate as the functional equivalent of binding international law.[93]

Soft law instruments, like treaties, are varied, where some may be concluded at a high level of abstractions while other so-called soft law instruments have a high degree of specificity. Thus, non-treaty instruments may be drafted as binding law and can be more precise and practical than provisions in treaties that may be general and vague.[94] Indeed, IOs increasingly use rules that are

---

[87] CM Chinkin, 'The Challenge of Soft Law: Development and Change in International Law' (1989) 38 ICLQ 850.

[88] See eg Boyle, 'Soft Law in International Law Making' (n 82) 119–20. See also D Shelton, 'Soft Law' in D Armstrong (ed), *Handbook of International Law* (Routledge Press 2008); AT Guzman and TL Meyer, 'International Soft Law' (2010) 2 J Leg Analysis 171, 172.

[89] Boyle, 'Soft Law in International Law Making' (n 82) 120. See also, in the context of international financial regulation, Brummer, *Soft Law and the Global Financial System* (n 81) 120–23.

[90] Abbott and Snidal, 'Hard and Soft Law in International Governance' (n 72) 422.

[91] Boyle, 'Soft Law in International Law Making' (n 82) 133; Chinkin, 'The Challenge of Soft Law' (n 87) 851–52. Such hardening of soft law may also include those soft measures (discussed later in Chapter 5) that are aimed at cooperation and the promotion of compliance with the system, which can be proceduralized and incorporated in regulation or in judicial codes of practice (see eg the network of insolvency judges that has been adopted and formalized by various courts, noted in Chapter 1, n 262 and Chapter 5, n 74).

[92] A treaty with vague or weak requirements may be characterized as 'legal soft law' (Chinkin, 'The Challenge of Soft Law' (n 87) 851). See also DP O'Connell, *International Law* Vol 1 (Stevens 1970) 246; Goldmann, 'We Need to Cut Off the Head of the King' (n 64) 336.

[93] Goldmann, 'We Need to Cut Off the Head of the King' (n 64) 337, 344.

[94] Chinkin, 'The Challenge of Soft Law' (n 87) 852.

not formally binding but that entail the characteristics of binding treaties or resolutions.[95]

Furthermore, the use of a treaty form does not ensure a hard obligation.[96] The binding nature of treaty provisions is sometimes merely theoretical, and the enforcement of hard international law may not be readily available. The fact is that consent may not ensure compliance with the obligations, and in practice, treaties are often ignored by countries.[97] Vagueness in treaty provisions may also undermine their enforceability.[98]

At the same time, what may be perceived as soft law can in fact generate a strong compliance pull.[99] Similar economic forces that induce compliance with hard law may operate in the context of soft law norms.[100] In certain circumstances, soft law may be even more effective than traditional hard law, including because of various market or institutional disciplines that may induce compliance, to the extent that the label soft law, which may be given to certain agreements, rules, or standards that are non-binding, may not reveal their actual coercive nature.[101] It has been observed, for example, with respect to international financial law that 'it is at times "harder" than many conventional hard law instruments. UN conventions, for example, are regularly ignored by despots; and when they are, few disciplines can get them to change behaviour.'[102]

Soft law may also interact with traditional hard law and in that process, be transformed into a binding form or lose some or all its non-binding character.[103] As discussed in Chapter 3, soft law may have legal effects on CIL. It may provide evidence for existing CIL or for a sense of obligation (*opinio juris*) that is required to form new CIL.[104] Treaties can also provide a means for focusing consensus and may

---

[95] Goldmann, 'We Need to Cut Off the Head of the King' (n 64) 335.

[96] Chinkin, 'The Challenge of Soft Law' (n 87) 852.

[97] Guzman, 'Against Consent' (n 68) 752–53 (giving the examples of the prohibition on the use of force, many multilateral environmental agreements, human rights commitments, and investment agreements); Brummer, *Soft Law and the Global Financial System* (n 81) 141.

[98] Chinkin, 'The Challenge of Soft Law' (n 87) 863–64 (giving the example of the decision of the High Court of Australia in the case of *The Commonwealth v Tasmania* ((1983) 46 ALR 625) regarding commitments under the UNESCO Convention for the Protection of the World Cultural and National Heritage. One of the questions before the court was whether the terms of the treaty were sufficiently precise to create any binding obligations on the parties that could be enforced and implemented by legislation. One judge concluded that the treaty's provisions did not impose outright obligations upon Australia because of their vague and discretionary nature (noting words and phrases like 'endeavour', 'in so far as is possible', 'each State will do all it can to this end', and 'as appropriate for each country'). The majority concluded, on the other hand, that the treaty did impose a series of obligations, noting that it includes the obligation to take legal measures expressed in the form of a command).

[99] See Chapter 5, section 5.2.1.

[100] Participants in non-traditional, non-treaty instruments may be compelled to reciprocate, to avoid harm to reputation (Brummer, *Soft Law and the Global Financial System* (n 81) 145–47).

[101] ibid 148–52.   [102] ibid 180–81.

[103] Boyle, 'Soft Law in International Law Making' (n 82) 124; Chinkin, 'The Challenge of Soft Law' (n 87) 856–59.

[104] Boyle, 'Soft Law in International Law Making' (n 82) 130. It was noted in Chapter 3 that eg in the field of international investment law, important aspects of the law are still based on CIL, which has evolved over time, including through a host of soft law instruments (SP Subedi, 'International Investment Law' in MD Evans (ed), *International Law* (OUP 2014) 727, 740–41, and Chapter 3, sections 3.2.1 and 3.2.5).

provide evidence for the existence of CIL, though not necessarily because of their binding form.[105] Thus, soft law plays a law-making role similar to a treaty within the traditional understanding of international law instruments, where binding CIL is one of the two key international law sources.[106] Some types of soft law are also a step within the process that leads to the conclusion of a treaty or to the incorporation of, for example, standards, into domestic law.[107] Other instruments may be authoritative interpretive instruments of a binding treaty.[108] It has been observed, therefore, that 'the non-binding force of soft law can be over-stated'.[109]

Where the development of soft law is not based on consent, it does entail the risk of illegitimacy and it might result in rules that do not necessarily reflect what is desired for all affected participants. If the process of developing soft instruments does not follow certain acceptable democratic notions of decision-making on an international level, compliance can also be undermined.[110]

It has been observed, however, that consent is not a guarantee of legitimacy in view of the excessive power that the consent prerequisite might give to small groups. Thus, unanimity can be exploited, especially in deliberations between a large number of parties where there is a risk of holding out during the process to promote narrow interests.[111] The requirement of consent could, therefore, also prevent the development of welfare-enhancing rules because of difficulties in reaching a consensus. Even where consent is eventually reached, often the result is a faded version of the agreement, which may include ambiguous or hollow provisions that cannot create a sustainable international regime.[112]

Thus, in practice, soft law can benefit from the ability to develop international norms through more relaxed processes that may entail delegation to representatives deliberating in IOs. To the extent that the IO's structure is sufficiently universal and inclusive, and decisions are reached through some form of consensual process, the outcomes of deliberations may be considered credible while the process can, at the same time, overcome the difficulties in achieving full democratic representation on an international level.[113]

4.3.3 Economic perspectives: the costs of treaties

The presumption under economic analyses of international law is that decision makers evaluate risks and make choices based on probability calculations.[114] Specifically concerning participation in treaties, the assumption is that parties will

---

[105] Boyle, 'Soft Law in International Law Making' (n 82) 122.
[106] See Chapter 3, section 3.2.   [107] Chinkin, 'The Challenge of Soft Law' (n 87) 859.
[108] Boyle, 'Soft Law in International Law Making' (n 82) 123–28.
[109] Boyle, 'Some Reflections' (n 70) 906.
[110] Brummer, *Soft Law and the Global Financial System* (n 81) 216.
[111] Guzman, 'Against Consent' (n 68) 754; Brummer, *Soft Law and the Global Financial System* (n 81) 207.
[112] Guzman, 'Against Consent' (n 68) 751.
[113] See also Brummer, *Soft Law and the Global Financial System* (n 81) 195.
[114] See Chapter 2, section 2.2.

enter such formal binding agreements where the gains from cooperating in this way are higher than the transaction and sovereignty costs (the constraints on sovereignty). In that regard, international law scholars have pointed to the efficient nature of soft law compared to hard law/treaties, often leading to deliberate choices in executing soft law instruments.

Thus, it has been observed that the costs of reaching a formal consensual agreement might be too high, especially regarding treaties that are aimed at resolving complex coordination problems between multiple participants.[115] Typically, treaties take a long period to negotiate and additional time to go through domestic approval processes,[116] sometimes resulting in setting aside the project altogether, scaling down treaty objectives, or in concluding treaties that will never enter into force.[117] The process of negotiating a soft law, although it could as well be complex and lengthy, may involve a more flexible negotiation process and a less cumbersome ratification procedure, making the creation of international law less costly and more feasible.[118] Soft law is also likely to be more flexible in terms of reviews and amendments compared with treaties where a renegotiation process is usually slow and complicated.[119]

Hard law might also involve significant sovereignty costs.[120] Agreement on formal treaties may include delegation to international or supranational authorities constraining the ability of countries to address issues independently and make their own economic and other decisions. Countries may be reluctant to relinquish such

---

[115] Guzman, 'Against Consent' (n 68) 764–65. See also Matthews, 'Prospects for Coordination and Competition in Global Finance' (n 30) 292 (noting the value of informal arrangements in the international financial sphere in view of the importance of speed and efficiency and taking account of the cumbersome process of negotiating treaties).

[116] Chinkin, 'The Challenge of Soft Law' (n 87) 860. The process differs between countries; in some countries, treaties are self-executing, while to become enforceable in other countries the treaty requires additional internal legislation. There may also be domestic constitutional technicalities to be satisfied before a treaty can be ratified.

[117] See the discussion above on the attempts to conclude multilateral treaties on cross-border insolvency. There are various other examples in other areas, including the failure of the OECD in the 1990s and of the World Trade Organization (WTO) in the 2000s to conclude a global multilateral treaty on investment (Subedi, 'International Investment Law' (n 104) 727–28). In the field of private international law, The Hague Conference on Private International Law has been working on the creation of an international regime for the recognition and enforcement of judgments that will replace the 1971 Hague Convention on the Recognition and Enforcement of Foreign Judgments in Civil and Commercial Matters, which has been ratified by only three countries. This project was later scaled down to focus on international cases involving choice of court agreements, eventually leading to the conclusion of The Hague Convention on Choice of Court Agreements, 30 June 2005. In 2011, it was decided to resume the work on the Judgment Project, which is, at the time this book went to print, still ongoing (see Hague Conference on Private International Law (HCCE), The Judgments Project <https://www.hcch.net/en/projects/legislative-projects/judgments>). cf a notable success in recent times is the conclusion, in a relatively short period of time, of the Cape Town Convention on International Interests in Mobile Equipment (2001); see also the New York Convention (Convention on the Recognition and Enforcement of Foreign Arbitral Awards (1985)).

[118] Chinkin, 'The Challenge of soft Law' (n 87) 860.

[119] C Lipson, 'Why Are Some Agreements Informal?' (1991) 45 Intl Org 495, 500; Goldmann, 'We Need to Cut Off the Head of the King' (n 64) 343; Boyle, 'Soft Law in International Law Making' (n 82) 121; Thirlway, *The Sources of International Law* (n 65) 9.

[120] Abbott and D Snidal, 'Hard and Soft Law in International Governance' (n 72) 436.

powers to external authorities.[121] Hard law is also considered fixed and binding and deviation is perceived as a breach of a formal obligation. The disciplinary forces—reputation, retaliation, and reciprocity[122]—that may work to compel countries to adhere to obligations expressed in formal (hard) international laws can, at the same time, significantly increase the costs of sovereignty loss.

Less formal instruments, on the other hand, may allow countries to retain some flexibility in terms of the level of adherence to the norms. Parties can also avoid delegating extensive powers or they may create weaker international institutions, thus avoiding sovereignty costs.[123] It may be possible to shape soft law norms in a way that fits domestic interests or to deviate from certain elements of the rules that are more contentious. There may also be room for adherence over time, where parties can learn more about the possible outcomes of the agreement, particularly where new and complex norms are at stake.[124] While there are ways to achieve some degree of flexibility within treaties, through the inclusion of reservations or opt-out provisions, a treaty exit can be complicated and unwieldly.[125] Soft law can also enhance cooperation as using this type of law may make it easier to address areas of controversy and to reach a compromise among differing interests.[126]

Countries arguably take full account of the benefits as well as the pitfalls of soft law and make deliberate choices along the hard/soft law continuum. They may thus reduce the bindingness of the obligation or the degree of its precision (making the norm more vague), and avoid delegating enforcement and interpretation of the obligations. Deviations from hard law may provide important benefits, such as increased flexibility, reduced costs, and enhanced cooperation, which parties exchange for any drawbacks of soft law.[127] Movement towards soft law can also be

---

[121] Abbott and Snidal give the example of the US opposition to various autonomous international institutions and note that 'even in NAFTA, where its political influence is paramount, the United States resisted delegating authority to supranational dispute settlement bodies for interstate disputes; only the Chapter 19 procedure for reviewing antidumping and countervailing duty rulings creates significant delegated authority. Congress also explicitly provided that the agreement would not be self-executing in domestic law, limiting delegation to national courts' (ibid 438). See Chapter 5, section 5.3.3 for a discussion of the possible advantages and disadvantages of delegation to external bodies to promote compliance with the cross-border insolvency system.

[122] See section 4.3.1.

[123] Abbott and Snidal, 'Hard and Soft Law in International Governance' (n 72) 439.

[124] ibid 435, 442–43.

[125] Brummer, *Soft Law and the Global Financial System* (n 81) 132; Abbott and Snidal, 'Hard and Soft Law in International Governance' (n 72) 437; Thirlway, *The Sources of International* Law (n 65) 38–44.

[126] Abbott and Snidal, 'Hard and Soft Law in International Governance' (n 72) 444–50.

[127] ibid 423. Abbot and Snidal give the example of the negotiations on the OECD convention restricting foreign bribery in international business transactions. The United States wished all OECD countries to adopt regulatory limits on foreign corrupt practices similar to those that were already in place under US law. While initially supporting a binding treaty, the United States eventually changed tactic to promoting soft law, as the countries that resisted action on this matter were in favour of a treaty as they hoped that the transaction costs involved would impede progress. This led to a compromise in the form of setting a short deadline to negotiate a treaty and agreeing to adopt recommendations in the alternative (ibid 434–35). See also R Abdelal, *Capital Rules: The Construction of Global Finance* (Harvard University Press 2007), 14–15, 214–15 (noting the general preference of the United States for ad hoc globalization that leaves it unconstrained by binding rules); Bruner, 'States, Markets and Gatekeepers' (n 86) 172. See also S Gopalan and M Guihot, 'Recognition and Enforcement in Cross-Border Insolvency Law: A Proposal for Judicial Gap-Filling' (2015) 48 Vanderbilt Journal of Transnational Law 1225,

predicted where 'the actors are states that are jealous of their autonomy and when the issues at hand challenge state sovereignty'.[128] In such circumstances, soft law and soft arrangements may prove advantageous where they can avoid sovereignty costs, for example, by refraining from establishing centralized adjudication mechanisms or delegating powers to external institutions.[129]

Soft law has drawbacks that decision makers may consider in making choices regarding participation in international frameworks. Thus, soft law may provide more room for non-performance. Enforcement of obligations may be more difficult as the pressure to comply may be weaker. Parties to an informal arrangement might comply only with some of the rules, cherry-picking aspects of the norms instead of adhering to the arrangement in its entirety. Parties who adopt soft rules may thereafter apply them inconsistently and under-enforce the soft norms.[130]

Yet, even if compliance is not perfect,[131] it may be preferable to have a desirable rule than not to have it at all (or have a treaty with diluted provisions), which could be the result if international lawmakers insist on all parties consenting to formal agreements.[132] Generally, in view of the many advantages of soft law, the predominance of multilateral treaties as a means for codifying international law has been questioned by international law scholars. Thus, it has been noted that in many circumstances, soft law may be as useful as treaties and less risky because the process of negotiating a treaty may never yield a satisfactory result and may not be ratified by a sufficient number of parties.[133]

4.3.4 Behavioural disadvantages of treaties

The assumption about pure economic choices when considering participation in different types of instruments (in terms of the instruments' level of hardness/softness) should be qualified, considering that decisions are influenced by cognitive biases.[134] Decision processes are constrained, and biases may also impact choices related to international law.[135] Decisions tend to be affected in predictable ways by loss aversion, which may be linked to an endowment effect. People also tend to consider payoffs not in absolute terms but rather relative to a reference point, and

---

1276 (noting by reference to liberal international relations scholarship that countries make choices between hard treaties and soft law such as model laws by taking account of various factors including the reduction of transaction costs).

[128] Abbott and Snidal, 'Hard and Soft Law in International Governance' (n 72) 423.

[129] ibid 444.   [130] Brummer, *Soft Law and the Global Financial System* (n 81) 139–41.

[131] See Chapter 5, section 5.2.1 for a discussion of the problem of compliance in international law, which is prevalent whether treaty or non-treaty law is utilized.

[132] Guzman, 'Against Consent' (n 68) 752; Chinkin, 'The Challenge of Soft Law' (n 87) 861.

[133] Boyle, 'Some Reflections' (n 70) 902–04 (providing the example of the 1992 Rio Declaration on Environment and Development that both codified existing international law and developed new laws, and observing that: 'it is not obvious that a treaty with the same provisions would carry greater weight or achieve its objectives any more successfully. On the contrary, it is quite possible that such a treaty would, seven years later, still have far from universal participation, whereas the Declaration secured immediate consensus support, with such authority as that implies').

[134] Discussed in Chapter 2, section 2.3.   [135] ibid, section 2.4.

generally, they typically show a strong preference for the current position (they are affected by a status quo bias). It therefore follows that choices can also be driven to some extent by the way options are framed.[136]

Specifically, entry into treaties to resolve international problems can present important difficulties in view of the possible biases in decision-making.[137] First, because a loss looms larger than a gain and departing from existing endowments is disliked,[138] the sovereignty costs of treaties may have a larger effect than expected by the standard paradigm based on the expected utility theory. Consequently, such costs may be given greater weight than the value of the potential gains that could result from participating in the treaty framework.

Second, what is understood as hard law, specifically, the conclusion of treaties, requires significant action by countries through their decision makers. Treaty negotiations are often slow, and the ratification process is cumbersome. Considering the greater sensitivity to potential losses than to gains, as well as experiments that have shown that loss aversion has a specific effect when decision makers can *avoid* an option involving a loss as opposed to choosing an option they had to *actively* approach to accept,[139] avoidance of a treaty process may be expected, especially when parties are in a loss frame and even where an economic utility calculation would suggest otherwise.

Third, because of the status quo bias, even if a treaty framework provides important benefits, it might be difficult for parties to take the initiative to enter into a treaty. Any change from the status quo may be unattractive.[140] It has been observed from legal and economic perspectives that the requirement of consent, inherent in treaties, may result in stagnation and the inability to address the most pressing issues we are facing on an international level.[141] Thus, the need for consent can result in excessive conservatism. Even though consent may, in theory, avoid welfare losses for the country, it might be difficult to promote such approach because of a weighty status quo bias.[142] Countries may also view the existing situation as an endowment to which they are likely to ascribe greater value when compared with potential improvements.[143] Thus, even where a treaty could be in the interest of all parties where no country is worse off or all countries gain from coordination, it may still be difficult to reach a consensus and follow through to ratification. There is a risk that international law will become inefficient and decay if it only relies on consent to treaties.[144]

---

[136] See Chapter 2, section 2.3.

[137] A van Aaken, 'Behavioral International Law and Economics' (2014) 55(2) Harv Intl L J 421, 451.

[138] See Chapter 2, sections 2.3.1 and 2.3.2.   [139] ibid section 2.3.1.

[140] As noted earlier, taking an active decision may also be avoided because of the effort it might entail, (see Chapter 3, section 3.3.1). It was also noted that even the global financial crisis has been a rather conservative event and has not resulted in a significant shift of the status quo (E Helleiner, *The Status Quo Crisis. Global Financial Governance after the 2008 Financial Meltdown* (OUP, 2014) 2. cf Brummer, *Soft Law and the Global Financial System* (n 81) 334 (arguing that crises generate action)).

[141] Guzman, 'Against Consent' 747.   [142] ibid 750, 755.

[143] T Broude, 'Behavioral International Law' (2015) 163 U Pa L Rev 1099, 1140.

[144] Guzman, 'Against Consent' (n 68).

Opting for instruments of a less formal character than treaties may, therefore, have a positive influence on actors' choices. That is, the use of non-treaty texts could be a way to overcome biases (it is a 'debiasing' technique) and align choices with desirable outcomes. Specifically, framing an arrangement as softer than a treaty may be considered less threatening to local control and freedom of decision, reducing concerns about a loss of sovereignty. Participants may generally have more flexibility to make decisions regarding the level of adherence to the arrangement. Parties, therefore, are likely to be less prone to loss aversion in such circumstances.[145]

Instruments that are less formal than treaties can also constitute a non-consensual form of rule-making or at least a means to mitigate the behavioural obstacles created by the consent requirement.[146] IOs play an important role, most notably the United Nations.[147] Even where organizations are wedded to consensual processes, they still facilitate negotiations and foster agreements.[148] Consent is no guarantee of a welfare-enhancing agreement because of the risk of holdouts and the power that unanimity requirements might give to small interest groups. The psychological perspective supports this scepticism about the results of consensual frameworks, while taking into account the range of other systemic failures and shortcuts in making decisions in the context of contractual bargaining.[149]

The effect of default rules is relevant as well. The previous chapter discussed the possible use of default rules regarding the formation of modified universalist rules as CIL. Default rules have a significant effect on people's choices in view of the status quo bias and the tendency for inaction.[150] With regard to international instrument choice, behavioural international law suggests that we consider the type of instrument in terms of how it fits into opt-in or opt-out schemes, rather than merely identifying the instrument as soft or hard law (or its position within the soft law/hard law continuum).[151] An instrument based on an opt-out system, or on universal application with no opt-out provision, provides a default system of participation. In an opt-in system, on the other hand, participation requires action.

Treaties are at the one end of the opt-in/opt-out spectrum because they provide an opt-in scheme whereby participation requires formal consent and additional

---

[145] It has been observed that generally when using non-binding methods, countries may be more willing to commit to more significant changes (K Raustiala, 'Form and Substance in International Agreements' (2005) 99 Am J Intl L 581, 582), and that this observation is reinforced to the extent that countries may also be influenced by biases (J Galbraith, 'Treaty Options: Towards a Behavioral Understanding of Treaty Design' (2013) 53 Va J Intl L 309, 360).

[146] Guzman, 'Against Consent' (n 68) 751, 775 (also noting other ways to circumvent the norm of consent including the use of CIL, *jus cogens* and UN Security Council Regulations under ch VII of the Charter).

[147] ibid 781–84.

[148] ibid (providing the example of the WTO that operates by consensus, yet is highly successful and influential).

[149] These include anchoring, availability, self-serving evaluations, framing, the *status quo* bias, contrast effects, and reactive devaluation (B Korobkin and C Guthrie, 'Heuristics and Biases at the Bargaining Table' (2004) 87(4) Marquette Law Review 795. See also van Aaken, 'Behavioral International Law and Economics' (n 137) 457–58).

[150] See Chapter 2, section 2.4.3.

[151] van Aaken, 'Behavioral International Law and Economics' (n 137) 450.

approval procedures.[152] Treaties bind only the parties to them.[153] It might, therefore, be more difficult to promote the universality of norms through treaties.[154] *Jus cogens* is at the other end of the spectrum, as it is an unconditional norm from which no derogation is permitted. CIL is in the middle as it provides an opt-out system, as discussed earlier. Forms of soft law that are less hard than treaties in terms of the required level of consent have the potential to nonetheless oblige more parties to adhere to the norms as they may apply even where there was no formal opt-in. Such laws may not be binding in the same way as a treaty, yet still apply universally.[155]

Therefore, forms of non-treaty law convey important benefits when considering constraints on decision making, specifically regarding making commitments in international instruments. When negotiating a less formal instrument and mitigating the consent requirement, it is more likely that participants will be able to commit to resultant norms that are less hollow and more precise. The use of such types of instruments may also mean that the norms they advance will be adopted by or apply to more parties (compared to the use of treaties), especially when commitments are required in complex areas, where attempts at agreement will more likely generate aversions to change and to losses, and where multiple parties are involved.[156]

Such deviations from the traditional treaty format in terms of the way instruments are concluded and in the level of their formality should be distinguished, however, from the softness of the rules contained *in* the instruments. Open-textured, imprecise provisions could increase rather than decrease the effects of biases such as status quo and loss aversion, where flexible rules provide room for countries to enact and interpret the rules so that they comply with current positions and thus make little progress towards the desirable global solution. In contrast, a high level of precision can reduce the effect of ambiguous texts on self-serving behaviour, whereby participants might interpret provisions in ways that confirm pre-existing conceptions.[157] Inconsistent and ambiguous presentation of commitments and

---

[152] There may be, however, opt-out mechanisms within the treaty (ibid 451).

[153] Chinkin, 'The Challenge of Soft Law' (n 87) 860.

[154] van Aaken, 'Behavioral International Law and Economics' (n 137) 452.

[155] ibid 450 (giving the example of the Financial Action Task Force Recommendations concerning the fight against illegal financing, which although non-binding, have no opt-out and have extraterritorial effect in enforcement).

[156] Agreements to treaties are likely easier where a small number of parties are involved, or where interests are clearly aligned, or where the parties wish to work together and the instrument simply provides the rules for coordination of that work (Guzman, *How International Law Works* (n 76) 764, giving the example of Switzerland and Bolivia, who have no interest in using force against one another and share an interest in continued peace, or the Warsaw Convention that harmonizes standards in air travel, ranging from safety to the tagging of luggage).

[157] The self-serving bias infects negotiations, as people are prone to making judgments concerning existing facts and future probabilities in ways that confirm their pre-existing belief structures (CG Lord et al, 'Biased Assimilation and Attitude Polarization: The Effects of Prior Theories on Subsequently Considered Evidence' (1979) 37 J Personality & Soc Psychol 2098, 2102; B Korobkin and C Guthrie, 'Heuristics and Biases at the Bargaining Table' (2004) 87(4) Marquette L Rev 795, 800 in the context of contractual bargaining).

entitlements in the instrument might result in differing interpretations of the endowment reference points and the understanding of what is fair.[158]

4.4 Hard Model Law for Cross-Border Insolvency

The preceding section acknowledged the central role of treaties in international law. The pursuit of a treaty for global insolvency seems on its face as the best fit with the international role of cross-border insolvency law.[159] However, it was also shown above that, increasingly, instruments that do not have treaty status, including the so-called soft laws, play a major role in international law and often manifest hard law characteristics. Importantly, the cost of concluding a treaty or other instruments may affect the levels of precision and obligation, and biases in decision-making could also undermine the ability to reach and commit to detailed international agreements. Thus, a treaty is neither the only relevant instrument for the governance of subsystems of international law, nor is it always the most effective mechanism. Therefore, this section abandons the notion that treaties are hard and binding and non-treaty instruments are soft and non-binding. Drawing on the continuum of mechanisms, it is argued that in view of the issues arising in cross-border insolvency and the likely influence of bounds on decision-making, an instrument in the form of a model law has the greatest prospect of creating the levels of precision and obligation prescribed by modified universalism.

4.4.1 Facilitating consent to precise, comprehensive, and uniform rules

An international instrument for cross-border insolvency needs to provide detailed and precise terms regarding the international aspects of insolvency that are intended for uniform and consistent application throughout the global market. Modified universalism prescribes a global approach whereby often one forum leads the process and where that process is recognized and given effect throughout the market.[160] A comprehensive and uniform set of written provisions for the international aspects related to insolvency can support such a system. It would replace the myriad of domestic private international laws and provide a single system capable of resolving jurisdictional conflicts and conflicts of law.[161]

For a modified universalist system to be effective, it will also require the detailed delineation of the steps that must be taken by participants during the proceedings

---

[158] van Aaken, 'Behavioral International Law and Economics' (n 137) 461–63. See also Chapter 5, section 5.3.3 for a discussion of the extent to which these problems may be addressed by delegation to international bodies.

[159] See Chapter 3, sections 3.5.1 and 3.5.2 (on the internationalization of private international law and specifically the international role of cross-border insolvency).

[160] See Chapter 1, section 1.3.2.

[161] Uniformity does not mean that the same rules necessarily apply to all types of entities, though. Rather, a comprehensive scheme based on modified universalism would need to consider different business structures (single entities or enterprise groups) and the unique circumstances of MFIs (ibid).

to be able to administer the global process in a coordinated manner. Such a scheme must be clear, must operate in a transparent and predictable way (transparent not only to local but importantly to foreign users), and must apply in a near identical manner throughout the market.[162] Again, this necessitates a comprehensive instrument with detailed and structured provisions that can be implemented uniformly. The chosen instrument should therefore be one that can promote near complete harmonization of the rules regarding cross-border aspects of insolvency. Domestic laws that can hinder effective cross-border administration are proper candidates for harmonization and 'top-down' regulation, which leaves limited scope for adjustment to local systems.[163]

Thus, modified universalism requires an instrument that is not overly flexible or open-ended. An instrument that leaves significant room for national variation in the manner of application of the rules is inadequate for the system's core scheme. A divergent adoption of rules by legal systems is usually envisaged when, for example, IOs design principles, guidelines, recommendations, or key attributes.[164] These types of instrument include recommendations or principles that are often quite flexible with varying levels of prescriptiveness. The task of these forms of instrument is usually development, benchmarking, and modernization of laws.[165] Such instruments are important for the cross-border insolvency system as well, as they can mitigate the diversity of domestic systems' approaches to cross-border insolvency, and particularly where they promote a standardized understanding of insolvency processes that are considered universally fair.[166] However, the enactment of laws based on international recommendations can expectedly result in differences in implementation where multiple legislators take on the task of reform and where that task involves the integration of new concepts within diverse legal systems.[167]

---

[162] In some systems, even when providing measures in legislation or case law concerning recognition, cooperation or relief to foreign insolvency measures, the results are often unpredictable (B Wessels, 'The Effects in the Netherlands of an Order Issued in Indian Insolvency Proceedings' (*Leiden Law Blog*, 25 July 2016) <http://leidenlawblog.nl/articles/the-effects-in-the-netherlands-of-an-order-issued-in-indian-insolvency-proc>, noting the deficiencies of the Indian and the Dutch cross-border insolvency systems: 'It is clear that India has not embraced the UNCITRAL Model Law ... The present Dutch system is no better. Notwithstanding adequate proposals for improved legislation, its basis is largely case law. The District Court applies this case law and uses the legal term "recognition" ... but in the Yukos case the word recognition has not been used. Case law merely allows for a foreign insolvency measure to have effect ... The applicable law is also not set in stone'. See also the examples provided in Chapter 1, section 1.4.5.

[163] Private international laws generally aim to resolve conflicts between jurisdictions and laws, and such a task is significantly undermined if the conflict of laws themselves differ and conflict (Fletcher, *Insolvency in Private International Law* (n 7) 7). See also in the context of the EU Company law harmonization programme, L Enriques and M Gatti, 'The Uneasy Case for Top-Down Corporate Law Harmonization in the European Union' (2006) 27 U Pa J Intl Econ L 939, 957–58, 969. Uniformity of private international law does not challenge the development of local legal policy related to insolvency, but rather determines in a harmonized manner which laws will apply and by which court (cf the discussion of harmonization of substantive insolvency laws in Chapter 5, section 5.3.2).

[164] See eg the Legislative Guide and the Key Attributes noted in Chapter 1, section 1.4.4.

[165] S Block-Lieb and T Halliday, 'Harmonization and Modernization in UNCITRAL Legislative Guide on Insolvency Law' (2007) 42 Tex Intl L J 475, 507, 511. See further Chapter 5, section 5.3.2.

[166] Thus, they minimize resort to modified universalism safeguards that allow the denial of assistance and cooperation (see Chapter 5, section 5.3.2.4).

[167] See Chapter 5, sections 5.3.2.2 and 5.3.2.3.

Instruments that comprise recommendations or principles as well as specific contractual mechanisms imposed on debtors and counterparties can be partially helpful,
but still insufficient where the system requires the application of a structured, comprehensive framework. These types of instrument may specify aspects of the cross-
border system, provide key concepts on what features the system should include,
or promote cooperation[168] or the recognition of certain insolvency tools through
contracts;[169] yet they cannot provide a uniform, complete scheme for cross-border
insolvency. For example, a recommendation or principle that stresses the need for
legal systems to enact measures for the recognition of foreign insolvency proceedings
but does not specify the manner of the application for recognition and the precise
criteria for recognition to be granted, would fail to ensure that a coherent scheme
is invoked speedily and effectively in future cases. Tracking the implementation of
principles in domestic systems might also be difficult. Because they tend to be relatively general, evidence of adoption of instruments containing recommendations or
principles may be subtle and not readily ascertainable.[170]

The psychological perspective further suggests that instruments prescribing flexible norms and optional implementation methods (eg a choice between different
options) will provide more room for the operation of cognitive biases that may impede optimal choices. Thus, if given an open-ended choice regarding the manner of
enactment, implementing institutions might pick from proposed recommendations
or standards that largely correspond with the existing local system. Participants
might be inclined to stick to the status quo and might be less likely to include
measures that surrender control to foreign jurisdictions or to external authorities in
a reformed regime, thus impeding the evolution of an optimal modified universalist
system.

An instrument that is formal and binding, like a treaty, also risks excessive generality. While a treaty may ensure the identical adoption of its provisions by all
participants through a strong obligation to adhere to the instrument, the risk is
that the treaty provisions themselves will not reach the level of precision required.
The precision of treaties might be undermined precisely because they are formal
and are based on consent. Especially when a treaty is attempted among multiple
parties with different approaches to cross-border insolvency (including different
perceptions of the starting position, and reference point against which changes are
measured),[171] it might be difficult to reach the needed level of precision in the design

---

[168] Such as the UNCITRAL Practice Guide on Cooperation (2009) and other tools noted in
Chapter 5, section 5.2.5.

[169] See eg the contractual approach to support recognition of resolution measures developed by the
FSB and supported by the industry, discussed in Chapter 6, section 6.3.2.

[170] Block-Lieb and Halliday, 'Harmonization and Modernization' (n 165) 511 (noting with regard
to the Legislative Guide that 'to assess the harmonizing effect of the Guide, we will need to wait to judge
the influence of the Guide "on the ground;" we will need to study the legislation it inspires and the
implementation of that legislation by courts, insolvency representatives and insolvency professionals').

[171] See Chapter 2, section 2.3.1. See also F Tung, 'Is International Bankruptcy Possible?' (2001) 23
Michigan Journal of International Law 31, 70 ff (arguing, based on a game theory analysis and its application in international relations, that universalist agreements are bound to result in commitments
expressed in terms of imprecise and fuzzy standards).

of the treaty provisions. Between more homogenous systems, treaties that can create a uniform scheme are more feasible and indeed such cross-border treaties are currently in force.[172]

A model law is, on the other hand, likely able to provide that level of precision and comprehensiveness that cross-border insolvency requires.[173] A 'model law' is again only a label. Thus, for example, if an instrument provides recommended model provisions for legislators offering options, where it is envisioned that countries would decide to adopt the entire regime or only certain aspects of it, the instrument may not provide the required level of precision and completeness.[174] However, where a model law framework is designed in a way that provides a whole scheme for uniform adoption, a high degree of cohesion can be expected.[175]

Being less formal than a treaty in terms of the negotiation process, and in view of extant biases that are likely in operation when making choices related to cross-border insolvency,[176] it is more probable that a model law can facilitate agreement on more precise and complete provisions compared with other types of instrument, and can be designed in a manner intended for concrete implementation. A model law is regarded as a non-binding instrument and is negotiated through a more flexible process compared to a treaty. As such, it can be more effective in overcoming aversion to change and expected concerns about surrender (loss) of sovereignty. At the same time, an instrument in the form of a model law can provide a certain, albeit limited, level of flexibility to allow for procedural modifications at the implementation stage to ensure that the scheme fits within the domestic system and can be operative.

To the extent that certain regions operate as semi-federal systems with pooled sovereignty, the institutional setting may allow for the formulation of rules by regional institutions and the direct applicability of the rules to the domestic system, thus significantly overcoming the consent problem that could otherwise undermine precision and uniformity.[177] Particularly in the context of the EU, directly

---

[172] See section 4.2.1.

[173] cf Gopalan and Guihot, 'Recognition and Enforcement in Cross-Border Insolvency Law' (n 127) (as noted in the previous chapter, Gopalan and Guihot suggest that the MLCBI was intentionally vague and it is the role of the courts to address the gaps; while certain gaps may remain, this chapter argues that a model law can be significantly detailed thus promoting uniformity while still inducing participation, compared to other instruments).

[174] See eg the European Model Company Act (EMCA), a private initiative that is aimed at encouraging harmonization of company laws in Europe but where it is envisaged that: 'The EMCA will be designed as a free-standing general corporation statute that can be enacted substantially in its entirety by the Member States, or they may enact selected provisions of the Model Law … However, at the same time the EMCA allows special local considerations and for experimentation with new or different ideas, as Member States are free to opt out of parts of the Model Law in order to implement national company law innovations' <http://law.au.dk/en/research/projects/european-model-company-act-emca/>.

[175] In the UNCITRAL context, the latter example may be given the title of model law, which can connote a high degree of cohesion and comprehensiveness as a 'law' on a particular topic, as opposed to 'legislative provisions' which may suggest that the instrument is less holistic or comprehensive.

[176] See Chapter 2, section 2.5.

[177] Guzman, 'Against Consent' (n 68) 751 (noting that 'the EU represents perhaps the single greatest example of international cooperation on political, social, and economic issues the world has ever seen. It is also an exception to the normal requirement of consent for state-to-state collaboration. The modern EU was made possible only because political processes were created that allow for non-consensual decisions').

applicable (self-executing) regulations are distinguishable from EU directives that require implementation in the domestic system. Directives or any equivalent type of instrument are, in principle, less optimal as instruments for cross-border insolvency compared with a directly applicable regulation because directives may provide more room for manoeuvring in the implementation process that might result in differences and a lack of sufficient uniformity.[178] In any event, a global scheme based on a model law can attempt to bridge between different instruments to form a uniform global system, especially considering that business operations are often not confined to regions.[179]

4.4.2 Inducing credibility and broad participation

An instrument for cross-border insolvency needs to create credible commitments, both to enact or ratify the instrument in the domestic system and to enforce the obligations. Thus, the instrument should overcome the bindingness problem of international commitments to the maximum extent possible. Furthermore, it should induce a high level of participation as modified universalism is a system based on a market-wide application aimed at resolving global coordination issues and imposing a collective process on the global level.[180] Where the cross-border insolvency framework does not have global reach, it cannot fully achieve its functional purpose.

4.4.2.1 Intending a complete adoption

Broad and credible adherence to a cross-border insolvency framework cannot be expected when the instrument is of a significantly flexible nature in that it provides principles intended as mere recommendations, even if the recommendations are designed by country representatives in international fora. Even less can be expected when instruments are promulgated through private initiatives.[181] Such projects may assist policymakers in the process of reforming domestic laws; however, they do not create an obligation to follow the recommendations. Contractual solutions, as well, can enhance commitments to certain behaviour where parties agree that specific

---

[178] Directives also often provide minimum standards or options rather than specific rules for uniform implementation. See eg the Second Company Law Directive regarding the formation of public limited companies and the maintenance and alteration of their capital (Second Council Directive 77/91/EEC of 13 December 1976) and the complementing directives regarding company accounts, where although the intention has been to provide equivalent safeguards for the protection of public company stakeholders, implementation has resulted in diverse rules in some important respects (see with regard to the distribution rules and the implementation of the balance sheet test, J Rickford, 'Legal Approaches to Restricting Distributions to Shareholders: Balance Sheet Tests and Solvency Tests' (2006) 7 EBOR 135, 155).

[179] See eg the case of *Nortel* where the key entities of the enterprise operated both in North America and in Europe (see Chapter 1, n 92 and 94).

[180] See Chapter 1, sections 1.2.3 and 1.3.2.

[181] See eg the EMCA project mentioned in n 174.

measures will apply in a cross-border insolvency context, but their bindingness might be limited.[182]

Because treaties are based on consent, they may create a more coercive, enforceable regime compared to other instruments or measures that do not require an international agreement and that are quasi-legal. The consent requirement inherent in treaties should, in principle, prompt discipline as well as reciprocity. Treaties can also be designed in a way that minimizes deviation from their provisions, as they may constrain the ability to opt out or enter reservations.[183]

However, treaties are binding to the extent that agreements between countries can be reached in the first place and that such agreements are ratified and become operative. Particularly in cross-border insolvency where an agreement is needed among multiple parties, transaction and sovereignty costs are expectedly high, affecting the ability to reach such agreements.[184] Therefore, it is also more likely that a treaty will include optional measures and thus become less obligatory. For example, in the process of negotiating the Istanbul cross-border insolvency treaty[185] parties were not willing to accept the whole package initially provided, and it was eventually left to the countries to not apply certain chapters. The result has been a confused and complicated situation, and the convention has never entered into force.[186] Indeed, the process of treaty adoption might not materialize, especially in view of the unwieldy nature of ratification processes, and as mentioned above, treaties have often remained inoperative or have never entered into force, certainly in the field of insolvency.

Various robust biases may affect the choice of participation in international frameworks, and these are likely strong in insolvency contexts, including when compared with frameworks for resolving conflict of law matters involving international litigation between solvent parties.[187] Cross-border insolvency cases are

---

[182] See Chapter 6, sections 6.3.2 and 6.3.3 for the discussion of contractual tools designed to enhance the recognition of resolution measures in cross-border insolvencies of MFIs, and their limitations.

[183] See also Chapter 5, section 5.2.2.

[184] See also SL Schwarcz et al, 'Comments on the September 29, 2014 FSB Consultative Document, "Cross-Border Recognition of Resolution Action" ' Ctr for Intl Governance Innovation, CIGI Paper No 51, 3 December 2014, 7 <https://www.cigionline.org/sites/default/files/no.51.pdf> (noting that: 'A statutory approach to a resolution regime could best be accomplished by a treaty ... Treaties, however, typically involve years of negotiation').

[185] See n 14 and accompanying text.

[186] Fletcher, *Insolvency in Private International Law* (n 7) 317. The Convention was also eventually very thin and was not comprehensive. It had a very limited scope where it was confined to liquidations and required recognition in limited circumstances (I Tirado, 'An Evolution of COMI in the European Insolvency Regulation: from "Insolvenzimperialismus" to the Recast' in JP Sarra and Justice B Romaine (eds), *Annual Review of Insolvency Law* (Carswell 2015) 823, 824, noting that the limited scope was because of the difficulty of reaching agreement among multiple countries that had 'enormous socio-economic and political differences', and that it was not likely that the Convention would provide an adequate framework where it 'allowed the signatory states to include reservations concerning the chapters on the liquidator's coordination or on secondary proceedings').

[187] See eg the conclusion of The Hague Convention on Choice of Court Agreements, though even in that context the related negotiations on the judgments project have been long and arduous (see n 117). See also S Block-Lieb and T Halliday, 'Incrementalism in Global Lawmaking' (2007) 32 Brook J Intl L 851, 855–56 (noting that 'experts were (and some remain) skeptical of the likelihood of global reform of insolvency laws, both because insolvency law is thought to be more deeply embedded in national traditions and legal cultures than other areas where successful conventions and model laws have been

inherently complex. Insolvency proceedings may affect multiple stakeholders and have implications beyond the debtor and the creditors as they may influence the community, the environment, or the economy. In cross-border insolvency, such concerns translate to a global scale.[188] Thus, while bringing up issues that are also raised in other private international law contexts, international insolvency entails additional complications; hence, agreements in this field are likely to encounter more resistance.[189]

Against this backdrop, committing to and participating in frameworks perceived as changing the status quo might be a significant step, especially when using instruments such as treaties that require more active and cumbersome processes. It is also generally more difficult to identify powerful industry forces that could pull their weight and induce action in cross-border insolvency. The beneficiaries of effective global insolvency proceedings are of a very diverse nature (financial creditors, unsecured trade creditors, employees, etc), may have conflicting interests, and may not be sufficiently organized.[190]

Mechanisms of a softer nature, compared to formal treaties, could, to some extent, mitigate the sovereignty costs as well as address imperfect decision processes that may be expected in the context of agreements on international instruments as well. While instruments in the form of recommendations or principles are too flexible for the purpose of creating a cross-border insolvency regime, agreements on a model law could exhibit high levels of precision as well as produce relatively credible obligations because they are considered less binding than treaties.

Surely, for a model law framework, like a treaty, to become operative requires action from countries and implementing institutions. A model framework provides a scheme that necessitates adoption and enactment as national legislation, namely, some form of consent. It is also an opt-in regime and is not applicable as a default (again, like a treaty). A model law regime is also typically designed through a consensual process whereby decisions are made within an IO through the participation of countries as well as representatives of international and NGOs and requires agreement on the design of the rules. Thus, a model law is also prone to the operation of biases that impede action in the first place, where there is concern about loss and a need to change the status quo.

---

developed, such as sales and arbitration, and because there is wide substantive and institutional divergence of insolvency regimes across the world's nations').

[188] See Chapter 1, section 1.2.3.1.

[189] See also Fletcher, *Insolvency in Private International Law* (n 7) 6.

[190] cf the process leading to the agreement on the Cape Town Convention on International Interests in Mobile Equipment (2001) (a treaty designed to facilitate asset-based financing and leasing of aviation equipment; see <http://www.unidroit.org/instruments/security-interests/cape-town-convention>) where there was immense support and encouragement of the aviation industry to conclude an agreement. While the International Institute for the Unification of Private Law (UNIDROIT) presided over the process, the industry was committed to the project and strongly supported it. In the cross-border insolvency context, where multiple interests are involved, and stakeholders are not organized, an additional concern is that those who *can* organize may also dictate the shape of the legal framework, resulting in a system that may not adequately address all interests involved.

Still, it is likely that more participants will commit to and participate in a model law on cross-border insolvency compared with a treaty. The fact that the model law is less formal or quasi-legal makes it less threatening to state sovereignty and mitigates loss aversion. A model law is also perceived as an instrument that is more changeable compared to treaties where the instrument may be more regularly reviewed and its implementation in domestic laws is considered more flexible, making it also easier for negotiators to reach agreements.

Once a model law is concluded, it nonetheless also creates a certain status quo and may start producing a peer effect when it is enacted by certain countries.[191] The process required to enact a model law is also less cumbersome and is not dissimilar from the enactment of a domestic law. In addition, the fact that a model law provides a complete framework that can be enacted without much modification reduces legislation costs, facilitating wider adoption. This more seamless participation process of model law as compared with treaty law, is particularly important considering the need for regular regime renovations and updates that are expected in the field of cross-border insolvency.[192]

Certainly, the status quo bias and path dependency in *rule-making* might result in adherence to the way norms have typically been developed in international law, and therefore it might be difficult to deviate from the requirement of consent and the use of treaties.[193] In the field of cross-border insolvency however, forms of soft law, namely, instruments other than treaties negotiated through general consensual processes, have been dominant. The problem might be progressing to a uniform framework, in the form of a model law, in areas that have been governed thus far by other types of soft law instruments, which has been largely the case regarding MFIs cross-border insolvency.[194] However, movement from standards to a model law is probably simpler than conclusion of a treaty. Significantly, the promulgation of model laws by country representatives through deliberations in IOs, particularly under the auspices of UNCITRAL, has been perceived as legitimate.[195] This rule-making process is a mitigated consensual one that permits progress and rises above a low common denominator. At the same time, because the process is robust

---

[191] See Chapter 2, section 2.5.3.

[192] The key cross-border insolvency frameworks have undergone continuous revisions; see, eg, the revisions of the MLCBI's Guide to Enactment and Interpretation (MLCB GEI) and of the Legislative Guide since 2005, discussed in Chapter 6.

[193] Broude, 'Behavioral International Law' (n 143) 1141 (noting that members rarely resort to majority voting provisions allowed under the WTO's institutional provisions and stick instead to the culture of consensus).

[194] See Chapter 6, section 6.3.

[195] The UNCITRAL Working Group that deals with insolvency issues deliberates based on general agreement among the representatives, as understood by the chair-person, through discussions and debate, rather than by a count of votes and a demand of formal unanimity. It has been observed about UNCITRAL that the legitimacy of the work it undertakes is built on representativeness in the deliberations, procedural fairness in that representatives from the variety of nations and organizations are heard in a fair way, and on the effectiveness of its prior accomplishment (Block-Lieb and Halliday, 'Incrementalism in Global Lawmaking' (n 187) 898–903). See also Brummer, *Soft Law and the Global Financial System* (n 81) 344 (describing the organizational practice in working groups of committees of reaching 'general' consensus where supermajorities exist).

and is based on wide participation, it can induce adherence and compliance, including where it encourages interaction and learning from the experiences of peer participants.[196]

4.4.2.2 Broad reciprocity

A model law, unlike a treaty, cannot impose obligations on countries other than the country that may enact the model law, as it is merely an instrument that contains provisions for inclusion in the domestic laws of the enacting country. In that sense, a model law is not reciprocal and a country's agreement to adopt such a model law might be undermined where model law provisions may be invoked by parties from countries who have not themselves enacted the model law. Countries may also be concerned about adhering to an instrument where it may be perceived as only benefiting foreign proceedings (ie where the instrument may mainly facilitate seeking recognition, assistance, or relief in the enacting country).[197] In contrast, a treaty may induce greater agreement and obligation to adhere to the regime, as it is based on reciprocity.

However, a model law can impose duties and responsibilities both on home and host countries that enact it, as well as provide mechanisms in the form of safeguards for the enacting countries, to ensure that a foreign forum adheres to certain standards even if it is not party to the regime.[198] In addition, although the existing global model law (the MLCBI) mainly works as a mechanism for recognition of and relief to foreign proceedings, there is no reason why a model law regime could not also include rules regarding direct jurisdiction.[199]

A model law could also include a reciprocity requirement. It is possible, for example, to require that the model law provisions apply only to countries that have also enacted the model law.[200] However, reciprocity of this kind would deviate from the emerging norms of modified universalism that require that recognition and assistance are not conditioned by the similarities of the laws of the host and home country or other forms of reciprocity.[201] Reciprocity also has implications in terms of coverage and participation in the framework where only specific countries may be able to take advantage of the regime.[202] It might even render the instrument

---

[196] See Chapter 5 for a detailed discussion of compliance issues.
[197] Such concerns have been raised eg in EJ Janger, 'Reciprocity Comity' (2011) 46 Texas International Law Journal 441, 446–47 (noting that modified universalism may generate 'asymmetric comity'). See also Bebchuk and Guzman, 'An Economic Analysis of Transnational Bankruptcies,' (n 43) 804–06 (arguing that reciprocity represents a form of international coordination that may facilitate universalism).
[198] See Chapter 6, section 6.2 for a discussion of the MLCBI regime and related instruments, including the use of safeguards.
[199] See Chapter 6, section 6.2.5.
[200] See eg the way the MLCBI has been enacted in South Africa where the provisions apply in respect of 'any state designated by the Minister by notice in the Gazette' (South Africa Cross-Border Insolvency Act 42 of 2000, s 2).
[201] See Chapter 1, section 1.3.2.3.
[202] See also J Clift, 'UNCITRAL Model Law—Alive and Well in 43 Jurisdictions and Counting!' *Global Turnaround* (May 2016) 10 (noting that the way in which reciprocity is framed can also result in uncertainties and delays when parties attempt to invoke the MLCBI, as it might not be clear in advance how the reciprocity provision will be implemented. Clift also notes that a proposal to include

provisions inoperative, as in South Africa, for example, where no country has been designated as a country that can benefit from the provisions of the cross-border legislation that enacted the MLCBI.[203] Thus, instead of promoting universality, the inclusion of reciprocity can significantly constrain the commitment to follow the instrument.

A reciprocity condition is also disadvantageous considering that certain countries might be less ready to enact the framework, compared with other countries, because of their level of development or because of adherence to the status quo.[204] Allowing stakeholders from any country to enjoy the benefits of a framework that is available in other countries can extend the framework's reach. This will also increase the understanding of the operations and benefits of the regime, resulting in greater adherence. Additionally, because an instrument based on modified universalism would include safeguards that ensure a level of sovereign control when the regime is invoked, there should be less concern about controlling who invokes the framework.[205]

Thus, the chosen instrument for the cross-border insolvency system should ideally be based on a notion of *broad* reciprocity that takes account of different notions of reciprocity, including strong reciprocity that is granted even when the party does not consider that reciprocation will provide immediate material benefits.[206] The aim is the eventual wide adoption of the regime as a complete scheme through the gradual understanding of its benefits as well as through mutual positive influences and the fostering of cooperation, as will be discussed further in Chapter 5.[207] The system should preferably be open rather than restrictive in terms of participation, to be able to exert such positive influences on as many parties as possible. The instrument may also emphasize the fact that it is aimed at universal application and that it is based on modified universalism, contributing to its application as CIL.[208] Still, countries may make decisions regarding the enactment of the international instrument in different stages after other countries lead the way and adopt it, instead of restricting the application of the framework in their legislation. In that regard, the fact that a model law scheme is already widely in use (the MLCBI) and has been enacted in many countries is a significant advantage, mitigating concerns about reciprocity and creating further pressure to adhere to the regime. The greater the number of countries enacting a model law, the less reciprocity becomes an issue.

---

a reciprocity provision was rejected in the deliberations on the MLCBI, yet certain countries have introduced a reciprocity requirement, including South Africa, Romania, Mexico, and Uganda).

[203] See Chapter 2, n 118.   [204] See also Chapter 5, section 5.3.1.

[205] At the same time, the cross-border insolvency system can attempt to level the playing field and ensure that countries meet best practice standards including regarding the fair treatment of stakeholders thus minimizing the use of safeguards (see Chapter 5, section 5.3.2.4).

[206] See Chapter 2, section 2.3.5.

[207] See Chapter 5, section 5.2.5. See also JL Westbrook, 'Theory and Pragmatism in Global Insolvencies: Choice of Law and Choice of Forum' (1991) 65 Am Bankr L J 457, 467, 488 (proposing the concept of 'critical mass reciprocity' which is 'sufficient to convince each cooperating state that enough other states have joined in reciprocal relationships to ensure the obtaining of the benefits expected to flow from a particular sort of cooperation').

[208] See Chapter 3, section 3.6.1.

4.4.2.3 Enforcement through domestic mechanisms

After adoption and implementation in the domestic system, a model law becomes internal, hard law. It is binding and can be enforced through the domestic mechanisms. Considering that consent does not ensure compliance with the rules and enforcement is always limited on an international level, a model law approach cannot be considered less effective than treaties and the incorporation of a model law into domestic law through the established local courts and administrative systems means that it is an instrument that can eventually become enforceable. Such incorporation in the domestic system can also facilitate the use of the system by private actors.[209]

Notwithstanding its enforceability, a consistent application of the provisions of model laws across legal systems is a challenge where enforcement is left to domestic institutions and in view of the short-termism bias, namely, behavioural constraints on sticking to commitments over time.[210] Again, however, that challenge exists regarding hard/treaty law as well,[211] and possibly more so if treaties do not provide mechanisms for enforcement of the obligations they contain or where they include vague provisions.

Certainly, in regions with a degree of pooled sovereignty, such as the EU, where political processes have been created that permit non-consensual decisions and the direct application of uniform frameworks, the institutional framework strengthens member states' commitments. Thus, regulations can directly apply to domestic systems, and the uniform application and interpretation of the rules is overseen by the Court of Justice of the European Union (CJEU) in cooperation with the national judiciary of the member states.[212] In other regions, or between countries that have close economic relations or greater similarities in their legal systems, treaties can achieve a high level of obligation.[213] Between such countries, there may be less concern about sovereignty loss and the process leading to an agreement can be less costly. Moreover, the use of a model law instrument does not preclude entry into additional agreements, for example memoranda of understanding (MOUs) to enhance mutual obligations, or a treaty that may contain certain, more general understandings. Such agreements may endorse a model law that will contain the detailed cross-border regime.

A global regime based on a model law can, in any event, provide an overall umbrella framework that ensures that enforcement is not geographically restricted,

---

[209] Abbott and Snidal, 'Hard and Soft Law in International Governance' (n 72) 428.

[210] See Chapter 2, section 2.3.4.

[211] Both types of instruments may include provisions requiring implementing institutions to consider the instrument's international origin when applying its provisions (see eg art 8 of the MLCBI; art 7 para 1 of the United Nations Convention on Contracts for the International Sale of Goods).

[212] See <https://europa.eu/european-union/about-eu/institutions-bodies/court-justice_en>. See further on delegation to international tribunals, Chapter 5, section 5.3.3.

[213] The notable example is the successful Nordic treaty mentioned above in section 4.2. See also A Nielsen et al, 'The Cross-Border Insolvency Concordat: Principles To Facilitate the Resolution of International Insolvencies' (1996) 70 Am Bankr L J 533, 534 (noting that only a few treaties on international insolvency have been concluded and in these instances the participants have had 'close territorial ties and similar legal, economic, and cultural traditions').

connecting such regions or groupings of countries with other countries and regions, especially as cases may cross regional borders. A global framework also provides a fallback system, which is particularly important considering that the composition of regions and the participation of countries in the more localized frameworks is subject to change (the notable recent example is Brexit). It is the overarching characteristic of modified universalism that it takes into account and can respond to such changes in the real world.

4.5 Instrument Design

While important instruments for cross-border insolvency exist, and have been in use for some time—the MLCBI primarily—the potential effects of instrument design on decisions and choices concerning international insolvency have not been explored. This section makes the argument for using default rules in cross-border insolvency instruments—model laws or other forms of instrument if such are chosen—as well as exploiting the salience bias in instrument design to overcome territorial biases resulting from loss aversion, the endowment effect, and inclinations to prefer the status quo.

4.5.1 Default rules in instruments

The use of opt-in or opt-out international legal sources may impact participation in the modified universalist framework in view of bounds on decision-making, specifically the status quo bias, endowment effect, and loss aversion. The framing of options and, particularly, the use of default rules may have an important effect on choices in view of these extant biases. Therefore, CIL was proposed as a debiasing tool, as it is an opt-out system where participation in the regime does not rely on active consent.[214] Regarding instrument choice, model laws, like treaties, are opt-in frameworks that require action to become party to the framework. Nonetheless, the lesser formality and the flexibility in the negotiation and enactment stages of a model law, compared with treaties, likely mitigates the inclination to avoid changes and, as such, model laws provide important advantages compared to the more rigid opt-in adoption process of treaties.[215] Opt-in or opt-out techniques and default rules may have additional important impacts when utilized *within* the chosen instrument (namely in the design of the instrument) as the use of default rules can further impact choices in the process of its enactment and implementation.

An international instrument, such as a model law or a treaty that is an opt-in mechanism initially,[216] may, subsequently, require some flexibility to be provided as to the form, for example, of options, reservations from commitments in a treaty, or the possibility to withdraw from commitments.[217] Such an approach might be

---

[214] See Chapter 3, section 3.3.1.   [215] See section 4.4.1.
[216] Namely, at the stage of entry into the regime, which requires consent or enactment for being bound.
[217] Sub opt-out or later opt-out (van Aaken, 'Behavioral International Law and Economics' (n 137) 451).

necessary where new concepts are contemplated regarding which it is difficult to reach full consensus. Thus, international instruments may reflect differences between legal systems or the fact that some regimes are less ready to agree to new or emerging approaches at the same time as other systems progress to agreement on new mechanisms. Compromises may result in inclusions of discretionary elements and more safeguards, as well as alternative options that may deviate from the optimal approach.[218] Additionally, instruments may not specify all measures in detail. Such flexibility in instruments as well as compromises may be inevitable and, to some extent, required to accommodate differences between legal systems.

However, the inclusion of alternative approaches can lead to the eventual adoption of different schemes by countries, resulting in a confused and a less effective regime. In private international law, and specifically in cross-border insolvency, conflicting approaches could significantly weaken the effectiveness of the regime. Nonetheless, compromises might be unavoidable, especially in this complex and dynamic field. Then, careful consideration may be given to the way flexibility is incorporated into instruments with a view to promoting consistent implementation and aligning choices with optimal solutions.

Behavioural international law highlights the importance of considering which rule would be provided as the default in the instrument, as it is more likely that the default will be the chosen approach compared with other options.[219] Empirical research in international law has been able to show the potential bias in favour of whatever option is framed as the status quo.[220] It will be recalled that a study that investigated optional clauses in treaties found that ratifying countries have accepted the more optimal measure provided for in the treaties (the jurisdiction of the International Court of Justice (ICJ)) at much higher rates when presented with opt-out (default) than with opt-in clauses.[221] These results could have been explained by the powerful effect of framing and the overwhelming preference of default options.[222]

In the context of cross-border insolvency, the presentation of modified universalist solutions as the default options in the chosen instrument may similarly affect the way these solutions are perceived. As default solutions within a scheme that includes different options, the modified universalist options are likely to be regarded as more accepted, more representative of the current state of affairs and of

---

[218] Negotiated options are frequently used in the context of specialized or regional international organizations such as the International Labour Organization (ILO), the Council of Europe, and The Hague Conference on Private International Law (Galbraith, 'Treaty Options: Towards a Behavioral Understanding' (n 145) 321).

[219] van Aaken, 'Behavioral International Law and Economics' (n 137) 451.

[220] Galbraith, 'Treaty Options: Towards a Behavioral Understanding' (n 145) 313, 349 (see also Chapter 2 section 2.4.3).

[221] As explained in the study, negotiators often use different types of treaty options for quite similar substantive provisions across different treaties (Galbraith, 'Treaty Options: Towards a Behavioral Understanding' (n 145) 313). See also Chapter 2, section 2.4.3.

[222] Galbraith, 'Treaty Options: Towards a Behavioral Understanding' (n 145) 335 (concluding that 'findings suggest that opt-in ICJ jurisdictional clauses result in dramatically lower state participation than ICJ jurisdictional clauses framed as opt-outs or to which states can make traditional reservations. The choice of form matters, and matters enormously').

the recommended practice, and less taxing in the sense that they require less effort and action. In any event, the use of default rules does not impose further costs and is a simple design technique, which cannot do harm as such, but has the potential to advance optimal approaches.[223]

In a model law, where each of the provisions requires active opt-in (although it is the intention, it is not compulsory to enact a model law as a complete framework and each country is free to enact it as it sees fit), the solutions that comply with optimal modified universalism may be presented and specified as part of the coherent, default scheme. Any deviations from this scheme, if introduced, would preferably be provided as alternative options. If a treaty regime is ultimately chosen and compromises are required, the modified universalist solutions would ideally be provided as the default rules, subject to an opt-out option (or to general reservations),[224] rather than the other way around where the optimal solutions are provided as alternatives that may be adopted by participants (opt-in options). Legislators enacting a model law or ratifying a treaty will then need to consider whether to opt out or deviate from the default scheme. Such framing is superior to the presentation of the better option as an opt-in, 'extra-mile', discretionary approach that countries may take on board, not only because such presentation will be conceptually more coherent with the framework's aims, but also in view of behavioural inclinations affecting choices.

The way options are framed within instruments may have additional effect at the stage of usage after the instrument has been enacted or ratified by domestic regimes, and where it is invoked and applied in actual cases. That effect may exist, therefore, not only regarding instruments that require consent, enactment, or ratification but also where the instrument directly applies in domestic systems (such as the directly applicable regulation under the legal system of the EU). Thus, the way provisions are presented can affect decisions of implementing institutions such as resolution authorities or bankruptcy courts.[225]

4.5.2 Exploiting the salience bias

Another acknowledged bias that affects choices and that may have particular relevance to instrument design is the salience bias.[226] This bias refers to the fact that 'colorful, dynamic, or other distinctive stimuli disproportionally engage attention and accordingly disproportionally affect judgments'.[227] Thus, it has been shown in

---

[223] Galbraith, 'Treaty Options: Towards a Behavioral Understanding' (n 145) 356 (noting regarding the framing effect that: 'if framing does not matter, then no harm is done; and if it does in fact matter, then its instrumental use can benefit these actors').

[224] See also section 4.5.2 on the effects of a general reservation option compared with an explicit opt-out option.

[225] A notable example in the context of cross-border insolvency of the possible effect of legislative framing is the inconsistent application of discretionary relief provisions provided in the MLCBI, especially concerning the enforcement of judgments of the main proceedings (see Chapter 6, section 6.2.3).

[226] Galbraith, 'Treaty Options: Towards a Behavioral Understanding' (n 145) 350–51.

[227] SE Taylor, 'The Availability Bias in Social Perception and Interaction' in D Kaahneman et al (eds), *Judgement Under Uncertainty: Heuristics and Biases* (CUP 1982) 190, 192.

various experiments that people on average make greater use of data that is available, salient, and vivid, contrary to the standard assumptions about choices based on expected utility calculus.[228] People tend to focus on information that is prominent and ignore what is less visible (rather similarly, the 'availability' heuristic strongly affects judgments as people tend to put excessive emphasis on what is mentally more readily available).[229] The availability of events or features as well as the way in which they are presented and packaged—their saliency—influence choices.[230]

In the context of international law, the study mentioned earlier that found significant differences in participation in jurisdictional clauses in treaties, including higher participation when reservation was permitted, generally compared with when treaties explicitly allowed to opt out, observed that the difference could be explained not only by the status quo bias and the effect of default rules,[231] but also by reference to the salience bias.[232] Thus, the explicit opt-out rule was a more salient way of presenting the option of non-participation than the ordinary rights of reservation. It served 'as an explicit reminder to states that they can opt out'.[233]

This study also provided data showing that ratifying countries have adopted optional compliance mechanisms (negotiated options in relation to dispute resolution in human rights treaties)[234] at higher rates where these were presented in optional protocols compared to when such clauses were provided as opt-in clauses in the main text concerning the additional commitments.[235] The salience bias could again provide a reasonable explanation for these differences in country participation rates. When provided in a separate document with its own separate name, it seemed that the option was much more prominent than when compared with opt-in clauses 'buried discretely in the main text of treaties',[236] and that ratifying countries were subject to something akin to the salience bias.[237]

Designers of cross-border insolvency instruments can incorporate these behavioural insights by making modified universalist solutions salient and distinct, and presenting deviations or non-participation options within the framework with

---

[228] One experiment, for example, showed that people who completed surveys about overdraft fees were less likely to incur such fees in the following months, as they were affected by the saliency of the information, namely the fact that the issue was brought to their attention (V Stango and J Zinman, 'Limited and Varying Consumer Attention: Evidence from Shocks to the Salience of Bank Overdraft Fees' (2011) Fed Res Bank of Phila Research Dept, Working Paper No 11-17 <https://www.phil.frb.org/-/media/research-and-data/publications/working-papers/2011/wp11-17.pdf>). A known experiment of the availability effect showed that when people were asked to estimate word frequency—how many words in a text are likely to start with the letter R compared to words where R appeared in the third position—they provided much larger estimates regarding the former option (words starting with R) than the latter (words having R in third position), despite the fact that there are more words which satisfy the latter option (A Tversky and D Kahneman, 'Availability: A heuristic for judging frequency and probability', (1973) 5(2) Cognitive Psychology 207).

[229] Tversky and Kahneman, 'Availability' (n 228).

[230] C Jolls et al, 'A Behavioral Approach to Law and Economics' (1998) 50 Stan L Rev 1471, 1519.

[231] See section 4.5.1.

[232] Galbraith, 'Treaty Options: Towards a Behavioral Understanding' (n 145) 353.

[233] ibid.

[234] eg opting in to a system whereby a committee of experts can hear complaints between countries.

[235] Galbraith, 'Treaty Options: Towards a Behavioral Understanding' (n 145) 341.

[236] ibid 353.   [237] ibid.

relatively less prominence.[238] Opt-in clauses concerning the optimal solutions may be avoided. Yet if an opt-in mechanism is inevitable, and required to proceed with the negotiations and ensure participation, it would be preferable if it is presented clearly and noticeably (for example, within a distinct chapter, or a separate protocol or annex, instead of hidden in the text).

Exploiting the salience bias can, in this way, mitigate the effect of loss aversion, the endowment effect, and the status quo bias that otherwise can make participants averse to changes and to acceptance of modified universalist solutions in instruments by making the optimal approach visible and prominent. Yet are the designers themselves affected by biases that prevent them from using the framing of instruments to achieve optimal results?

4.5.3 Are negotiators affected by territorial biases?

Like all individuals, the negotiators (the designers of international instruments), are generally affected by all sorts of cognitive biases that can affect decisions.[239] Therefore, it is questionable whether at the stage of negotiation and design, we can expect the negotiators to take measures to overcome biases that may affect later choices in terms of the adoption and use of the instruments by countries and implementing institutions.

It has been considered, however, in the context of treaty design, that there is often an important difference between treaty negotiators and treaty ratifiers in terms of the type of decision makers involved,[240] which suggests that negotiators may be relatively less affected by biases in the negotiation and instrument formation stage. While negotiators are often diplomats with foreign affairs expertise or experts in the subject matter of the treaty with better understanding of the merits of new concepts and mechanisms, ratifiers typically include people of a wider background, usually from the country legislative bodies.[241] Indeed expertise does not rid one of biases, yet ratifiers may still be more concerned about deviations from the status quo and more averse to change compared with the negotiators. Negotiators are also less influenced by the short-termism bias, which affects choices over time and after the instrument has been concluded.[242] Negotiators may also be more affected by positive group pressure[243] when compared, for example, with ratifiers or even judges, as the negotiators usually formulate instruments through intense negotiations and deliberations with peers. Thus ratifiers, and later other implementing institutions, may be more prone to the impact of territorial inclinations, while negotiators may be in a better place to consider the effect of the instrument design on future adherence to and compliance with the regime.[244]

---

[238] See eg the concern expressed in Chapter 6, section 6.2.4 regarding the lack of sufficient prominence in regional and international instruments of the possibility that a mutual COMI be identified to promote group solutions.

[239] Including the cognitive biases discussed in Chapter 2, section 2.3.

[240] Galbraith, 'Treaty Options: Towards a Behavioral Understanding' (n 145) 313.

[241] ibid.   [242] See Chapter 2, section 2.3.4.   [243] ibid 2.3.5.

[244] Galbraith, 'Treaty Options: Towards a Behavioral Understanding' (n 145) 313.

Experience in working on the existing MLCBI by UNCITRAL is a notable example of the general ability of negotiators in the field of cross-border insolvency to overcome significant challenges and break with a territorial status quo.[245] As a leading body with broad representation engaged in reform in this field on the global level, the insolvency working group of UNCITRAL, in the late 1990s, had already been able to develop quite a detailed and innovative framework notwithstanding significant scepticism that its project would ever succeed.[246]

Nonetheless, as mentioned previously, like everyone else negotiators are subject to biases, including those that can impede optimal choices in line with the emerging norms of modified universalism. Awareness of the existence of biases may assist in making more objective decisions.[247] Negotiators can attempt to counteract biases and consider the possibility that the way they form instruments may have important influences thereafter.[248] If negotiators understand the effect of biases, they may be able to consider how to utilize this potential impact of design on decisions and frame options in a way that may increase the likelihood that implementation of the instrument they design will be more aligned with optimal solutions.

4.6 Conclusion

Even though efforts in recent years in the field of cross-border insolvency have focused mainly on the development of mechanisms in the form of model laws, the quest for treaties has not been abandoned and they still seem to be understood as the best approach for the long term. The question of instrument choice, however, requires revisiting the assumptions about treaties that have been dominant in cross-border insolvency debates.

First, it has been assumed that the treaty is the proper instrument for achieving pure universalism. Any other instrument, arguably, represents an interim solution. However, because modified universalism provides a normatively desirable system for cross-border insolvency that fits the real world, the quest should be for instruments that can enhance adherence to modified universalism not only in the short term.

Another assumption is that because treaties are binding, they will provide full reciprocity and strong commitments and will permit the creation of a universalist regime. Treaties are a key international law source and thus are presumptively the most appropriate to fulfil the internationalist role of cross-border insolvency law.

---

[245] See also Chapter 6, section 6.2.

[246] See JL Westbrook, 'Coordination in International Corporate Insolvencies' in RM Lastra (ed), *Cross-Border Bank Insolvency* (OUP 2011) 186 (noting, based on his own experience as an active participant in the design of the MLCBI, how reformers active in the insolvencies of multinational corporations have had to overcome scepticism and parochialism to achieve international cooperation in this field).

[247] See Chapter 2, section 2.6.

[248] Galbraith, 'Treaty Options: Towards a Behavioral Understanding' (n 145) 360 (noting, as well, that later designers of revised treaties will likely be influenced by the decisions of the original designers of initial, including temporary or ad hoc treaties. Therefore, designers should be aware of the influence their choices may have on later designers. Similarly, later designers should take steps to counteract their *status quo* bias).

However, the division between hard and soft law and between formal treaties and non-treaty instruments is less rigid in the real world. Soft law has become an important international law source. In various respects, soft law is often de facto hard and even harder than treaties. Importantly, using instruments other than treaties can reduce transaction costs and behavioural constraints, can induce greater participation, and can respond more quickly to changing market conditions.

Against this backdrop, this chapter suggested that a model law instrument could provide a proper replacement to formal treaty agreements and would also be a more proper instrument compared to those containing recommendations or principles, or those that promote contractual solutions that are, to some extent, currently in use in the field of cross-border insolvency. Participants who design, develop, and implement a model law for cross-border insolvency can operate in the international realm in much the same way as they would under a treaty regime. Thus, a model-law type of instrument fits well with the internationalist role of cross-border insolvency law. It is also a debiasing tool where it can address biases and better align party choices with desirable outcomes.

A model law can prescribe a comprehensive and detailed regime. It is likely to include more precise provisions than might be expected via a treaty regime considering the sovereignty costs associated with treaties, which are likely given greater weight than the value of potential gains, owing to extant biases. A model law can also induce higher obligation levels compared with other instrument options, where implementation is intended as a complete scheme, and can be enforced once incorporated into the domestic law. It can also apply to a wider base of participants compared with treaties where greater 'action avoidance' is expected, and where treaties may lack enforcement mechanisms. Treaties provide the strongest opt-in mechanism and, as such, risk lesser universality, especially when international commitments are required in a complex area such as cross-border insolvency.

A model law regime for cross-border insolvency is thus superior to a regime based on a treaty in important ways, and more adequate than principle-based instruments. A treaty in this field may remain in draft form or be ratified only by some of the parties; it is likely to be vaguer than a model law; and it may be much more difficult for a treaty regime to accommodate changing market conditions. In view of the challenges faced by cross-border insolvency, including its dynamic nature, the ability of a model law to exhibit high levels of hardness coupled with a degree of informality at the stage of instrument design (and revision), presents specific advantages. Additional measures can be adopted to make the instrument chosen more effective. The instrument itself can be designed in a manner that takes account of the effect of biases on choices. Specifically, if modified universalist solutions are provided as the default rules and they are presented in the instrument in a prominent manner, it is more likely that they will be chosen and applied more consistently.

Ensuring consistent application and interpretation of the provisions of model laws as well as increasing their reach and acceptance is still a challenge even where an optimal instrument is used, and its design is such that may align choices with desired outcomes. As proposed in the previous chapter, the transformation of the modified universalist system to CIL can contribute to steadier application of the norms and the closure of gaps in cross-border insolvency instruments. Written instruments, including model laws, themselves can contribute to the crystallization of CIL. The next chapter will suggest additional mechanisms to enhance compliance with modified universalism. The important policy implication proposed by this chapter, however, is the continued effort to develop a regime based on a model framework in a form that provides a uniform system intended for consistent and broad application. Such a system should be precise and comprehensive in terms of the international aspects it addresses, the entities subject to the regime, and the parties that participate in and benefit from the framework.

5

A Normative Framework
for Promoting Compliance

5.1 Introduction

This chapter completes the proposed normative framework for cross-border insolvency. It considers the problem of compliance with a cross-border insolvency system, and suggests ways in which compliance can be induced.[1] The previous chapters have shown how the choice and use of certain international legal sources—unwritten binding norms (mainly customary international law (CIL)) as well as written international instruments (notably, model laws)—can strengthen the system, close gaps, and address biases that may otherwise impede the choices of optimal solutions. Yet, notwithstanding the pervasiveness and behavioural force of CIL, the observance of the norms is not guaranteed, especially where CIL addresses difficult cross-border conflicts. Not only is the identification of CIL complex, it also tends to be imprecise and it may be ignored or viewed as contradicting national rules.[2] Written instruments, even if precise and comprehensive, and designed effectively, do not assure compliance either. Even where so-called soft law is in fact hard in important ways, countries might still underperform.[3]

Generally, compliance is a key concern in international law.[4] Economic analyses of international law have emphasized reputation concerns as well as other incentives or sanctions that may encourage reciprocal behaviour and promote compliance. Behavioural international law scholarship highlights, however, the need to consider the possible impact of biases and bounds on decision-making that may affect choices and actions, including in the international realm.[5] Specifically, behavioural perspectives reinforce the significance of the compliance problem by highlighting the difficulty of making credible commitments in the context of international law. Participants (countries and implementing institutions) may be inconsistent in the

---

[1] 'Compliance' means, in this chapter, adherence to modified universalism norms by countries and implementing institutions, allowing for the centralization of the process; recognizing, assisting, and cooperating with foreign proceedings; and observing the duties imposed on host and home forums (see Chapter 1, sections 1.3.2.1–1.3.2.4). Compliance includes the adoption and consistent implementation of instruments that generally follow the norms (eg the (UNCITRAL) Model Law on Cross-Border Insolvency (MLCBI)).

[2] See Chapter 3, section 3.2.4.   [3] See Chapter 4, section 4.3.2.
[4] See in detail section 5.2.1.   [5] See Chapter 2, section 2.4.

The Future of Cross-Border Insolvency: Overcoming Biases and Closing Gaps. Irit Mevorach. © Irit Mevorach 2018. Published 2018 by Oxford University Press.

manner in which they apply international law and be tempted to focus on short-term policies.[6] Behavioural insights also highlight the problem of the self-serving interpretations of norms, including provisions in instruments,[7] against the backdrop of perceived endowments (existing entitlements) and in accordance with the inclination to prefer not to change the current position (status quo), which could undermine compliance.

These perspectives seem important for the design of a cross-border insolvency system that requires a long-term commitment to the resolution of insolvency at the global level and relies on a readiness for change in view of the advantages of taking a global perspective of multinational default notwithstanding certain losses (of sovereignty, of control over local assets and stakeholders, etc.).[8] Thus, the extant biases—notably loss aversion, the status quo bias, and the endowment effect, as well as short-termism—are likely to be relevant to the problem of compliance with a cross-border insolvency system based on modified universalism. Compliance may also depend on the operation of positive biases, specifically the effect of group pressure and the development of other-regarding preferences that can induce multilateral cooperation.[9]

This chapter explores the extent to which sanctions or other incentives could be effective in the cross-border insolvency context, whether any of these incentives could be reinforced by debiasing techniques,[10] and whether positive biases can be enhanced to foster compliance. Furthermore, this chapter considers the interrelation between compliance and problems of institutional and regulatory capacity. It asks whether the maximization of compliance requires addressing gaps in the domestic, legal, and institutional landscape and whether the creation of a uniform insolvency system (where insolvency laws are fully harmonized) is beneficial and realistic, considering economic and behavioural concerns. Important debated and recurrent claims concerning cross-border insolvency are revisited, including the argument that forum shopping should be controlled and that the harmonization of substantive laws and establishment of an international bankruptcy court will advance fuller universalism.[11] Through this analysis, the chapter provides the justificatory grounds for the design and usage of certain types of compliance mechanisms. Specifically, it highlights the advantages of adopting tailored tools that can strengthen reputation as a driver of compliance. It also considers the limitations of economic sanctions, especially where they may adversely affect the positive inclination to cooperate voluntarily. Therefore, it is suggested that the cross-border insolvency system should continue to mainly use techniques that foster cooperation directly and enhance mutual trust between participants. The chapter also stresses the relevance of 'capacity building'[12] to

---

[6] A van Aaken, 'Behavioral International Law and Economics' (2014) 55(2) Harv Intl L J 421, 432. See also Chapter 2 section 2.3.5.

[7] See Chapter 4, section 4.3.4.   [8] See Chapter 2, section 2.5.1.

[9] ibid section 2.4.5.

[10] Namely, techniques that may address or reduce the effect of biases to align behaviour with normatively desired choices (Chapter 2, n 9 and accompanying text).

[11] See sections 5.3.1 and 5.3.2.   [12] See section 5.3.1.

compliance, and proposes the contours of the type of targeted harmonization and targeted delegation to external bodies that can support the cross-border insolvency system.

The chapter proceeds as follows. Section 5.2 considers economic perspectives of compliance with international law and the efficacy of various economic incentives and sanctions where these have been used in different international law subsystems. Adding to this, this section considers behavioural international law insights, to further inform the design of compliance tools for cross-border insolvency. It shows the possible limitations of the role of reputation as a driver of compliance but also how this compliance force may be enhanced. It also reveals the limitations of disciplinary and economic incentives, especially where they might undermine altruistic cooperation. Against this backdrop, the section then discusses the role of mutual trust in promoting compliance and considers the types of tools that can develop such trust. Section 5.3 examines the interrelation between capacity issues and compliance. It also examines the question of the harmonization of substantive insolvency laws and suggests a form of targeted harmonization that is justified as a compliance tool. This section also discusses what forms of delegation to external institutions can address negative biases and close gaps without creating significant concerns about sovereignty losses. Section 5.4 provides summary conclusions.

5.2 Incentivizing Compliance

Considering that not all aspects of the cross-border insolvency regime can be specified, and assuming enforcement issues, compliance may be undermined. Reciprocal behaviour and trust in the other party's reciprocity is therefore critical, and the question is what sorts of tools may be most effective to foster such cooperative relations in cross-border insolvency. Disciplinary measures and economic incentives may induce compliance. Specifically, at the international level, compliance may be driven by concerns about reputation. So far, however, the cross-border insolvency system has focused on providing forums for interaction and tools for communication as means to enhance cooperation.[13] Yet, there has not been an attempt to rationalize the problem of compliance with an international insolvency system and the types of measures that are most effective. This section analyses the justification of these cooperation tools. It considers the role of mutual trust at the global level.[14] It also considers whether there is merit in utilizing additional incentives for compliance to encourage greater participation in and consistent implementation of the cross-border insolvency regime.

---

[13] See in detail section 5.2.5.
[14] Mutual trust was noted earlier as a key principle of the EU cross-border insolvency system (see Chapter 3, section 3.6.1).

5.2.1 What drives compliance with international law

Any international system, even one based on solid international sources and a largely comprehensive, precise, and well-designed international instrument, leaves regulatory and enforcement gaps.[15] Thus, the bindingness and enforceability of international agreements, including in the form of treaties, standards, or norms, is a key concern. The reality of international law and international relations is the absence of a body that can be really considered to be the equivalent of a government and a lack of an independent legislator and authority that can compel countries to take actions.[16] Enforcement at the global level is limited and largely decentralized.[17] There is, therefore, much room for non-compliance. Even where international agreements exist, there are many opportunities to take advantage of other parties and act self-servingly to protect local interests and disregard the impact of actions taken locally on interests outside the jurisdiction. It was noted earlier how treaties are often ignored by countries.[18] Compliance might be undermined where countries do not adopt the treaty or non-treaty framework or where its interpretation and application is inconsistent, an outcome that may be expected where adoption and implementation are reliant on multiple domestic enforcement mechanisms. Countries and their implementing institutions may underperform when they perceive that cooperation is against short-term interests or where they lack the confidence that other participants will comply.[19]

Compliance with a cross-border insolvency regime based on modified universalism might be prone to short-termism whereby, in the specific case, non-cooperation can present an advantage to local stakeholders, which the country and implementing institutions may wish to protect. Cooperation with foreign institutions or participation in a global framework may also be undermined by the other biases highlighted earlier, importantly loss aversion, status quo, and the endowment effect.[20] A degree of non-compliance may be expected even if instruments and regulatory sources are in place.

The traditional economic approach emphasizes the importance of incentives for ensuring compliance. If people are sufficiently rewarded for compliance and sanctioned or otherwise harmed by non-compliance, they are less likely to cheat and more likely to abide by the implicit agreement.[21] In the international law context,

---

[15] Namely, gaps in the international regime (cf the problem of deficiencies and gaps in domestic legal systems discussed in section 5.3).

[16] AT Guzman, 'Against Consent' (2012) 52 Va J Intl L 747, 763–64. See generally MN Shaw, *International Law* (CUP 2014) 49–51.

[17] van Aaken, 'Behavioral International Law and Economics' (n 6) 433. cf the degree of pooled sovereignty and centralized institutional setting that exists, for example, in the EU region, allowing for greater control of non-compliance.

[18] See Chapter 4, section 4.3.2.

[19] AT Guzman, *How International Law Works: A Rational Choice Theory* (OUP 2008); C Brummer, *Soft Law and the Global Financial System, Rule Making in the 21st Century* (CUP 2015) 119.

[20] See Chapter 2, section 2.5.1.

[21] See eg JJ Laffont and D Martimort, *The Theory of Incentives* (Princeton University Press 2002).

specifically regarding treaty regimes, reputation is considered to be a paramount compliance force. Parties are presumably incentivized to comply and reciprocate as non-reciprocal behaviour entails consequences in terms of harm to reputation; it can also result in retaliation measures.[22]

The effect of concerns about reputation on compliance is also important in non-treaty, non-traditional public international law contexts, as the participants, subject to such regimes, may also be compelled to reciprocate to avoid harm to reputation. It has been observed, for example, regarding the global financial system, which is largely based on soft law mechanisms, that regulators' record of compliance with international standards in this area can affect their reputation and thus their ability to 'create coalitions and alliances in the future'.[23] Poor reputation for compliance has costs. It might affect regulators' ability to credibly commit in future exchanges as well as diminish their group influence. It may have detrimental effect on leadership position of countries and their institutions.

In the context of cross-border insolvency, the adoption of global instruments, co-operation with foreign courts or authorities, and consistent adherence to promises and agreements could improve the country's reputation. Certain countries have shown increased interest in adherence to modified universalism to achieve a leading position in the field of cross-border insolvency. The notable example from recent times is Singapore, which seems keen to become a leader in international insolvency, even attempting to place itself ahead of the United Kingdom by emphasizing where the latter has not been fully compliant with the emerging norms of modified universalism.[24]

As in the traditional public international law sphere, in such subsystems based on (what is regarded as) soft law, too, the relevant authorities may compare 'the expected payoff from compliance to the expected payoff from violation', and therefore 'states will be tempted to violate a soft law agreement only if the nonreputational payoff from violation is larger than the nonreputational payoff from compliance'.[25] Thus, the disciplinary force of reputation is not reserved to traditional public international law; it could be important for the cross-border insolvency system, even where it may continue to rely mainly on a framework based on model laws rather than a treaty regime.[26]

---

[22] See Chapter 4, section 4.3.1.

[23] Brummer, *Soft Law and the Global Financial System* (n 19) 120.

[24] See the comments of the Singapore court in *Pacific Andes* regarding the UK approach in *Gibbs* (*Pacific Andes Resources Development Ltd and other matters* [2016] SGHC 210, paras 47–52 (citing critics of the *Gibbs* decision, including Look Chan Ho, who makes the point that 'the principle in Gibbs is "philosophically incompatible and practically irreconcilable" with the British MLCBI—the former is predicated on territorialism while the latter is steeped in modified universalism'). It has also been observed that the UK common law rule of Gibbs has 'put the UK at risk of being "overtaken by Singapore"' (*Global Restructuring Review*, 'Is the Common Law Gibbs Rule Outdated?' 3 February 2017, quoting Lexa Hilliard QC).

[25] Brummer, *Soft Law and the Global Financial System* (n 19) 145–46. See also Guzman, *How International Law Works* (n 19) 74–77.

[26] As proposed in Chapter 4.

5.2.2 Strengthening reputation as a driver of compliance

Behavioural international law highlights, however, certain potential constraints on the strength of reputation as a driver of compliance. Specifically, the prediction regarding pure calculations of reputational payoffs may neglect the possible effect of constraints on decision-making. Decisions of individuals are strongly impacted by various biases. These biases are thought to be translated to the international level (supra-individual) as well, so that decision-making of different groups of individuals or specific decision-making units may be bounded and deviate from pure economic models' assumptions.[27] Specifically, because of the potential effect of loss aversion (the tendency to give losses greater weight compared with gains),[28] countries may be more concerned with preventing a decline in reputation than in gaining reputation or credibility, even more so when the loss of reputation is perceived as certain, sure, loss.[29] It has also been stressed that reputation may be strongly affected by how behaviour is perceived by others as a result of fairness preferences.[30] Dissemination of information about the behaviour, including the intentions and reasons for the behaviour, especially if it is made salient enough, may therefore be an important factor impacting the force of reputation as a compliance tool.[31]

These insights can usefully inform the design of incentives for compliance with cross-border insolvency frameworks. It may be possible to adopt mechanisms that make information about compliance more salient as well as emphasize how non-compliance may result in the loss of reputation. The cross-border insolvency system may use for this purpose tools such as those already being used by international organizations (IOs) to rate and rank the performance of countries, such as the World Bank Group Ease of Doing Business Index (World Bank Doing Business Report),[32] which includes an insolvency indicator.[33] The World Bank Doing Business Report currently only assesses the position of domestic entities and, in the insolvency indicator, the adequacy of the system for domestic insolvencies. While it might be unable to provide a complete picture of the strength of insolvency systems,[34] the World Bank Doing Business Report does measure the compliance of regulations

---

[27] See Chapter 2, section 2.4.2.   [28] ibid section 2.3.

[29] ibid sections 2.4.3 and 2.4.4.

[30] Namely, bounds on self-interests and inclinations to consider the impact of behaviour on others (see Chapter 2, section 2.4.5).

[31] van Aaken, 'Behavioral International Law and Economics' (n 6) 475–80; R Brewster, 'Reputation in International Relations and International Law' in JL Dunhoff and MA Pollack (eds), *Interdisciplinary Perspectives on International Law and International Relations: The State of the Art* (CUP 2013).

[32] See <http://www.doingbusiness.org/about-us>.

[33] A description of the methodology of the 'resolving insolvency' indicator is available at <http://www.doingbusiness.org/methodology>.

[34] cf the Insolvency and Creditor-Debtor Regimes (ICR) Report on the Observance of Standards and Codes (ROSC), which is part of the IMF–World Bank ROSC program and which more broadly analyses and identifies the areas for improvement in the country's insolvency and credit systems, including the creditor rights and enforcement system; credit risk management, debt recovery, and informal enterprise work-out practices; the formal insolvency system, including its approach to cross-border insolvency; and the effectiveness of the relevant institutional and regulatory frameworks in implementing laws in this area. See on the objectives and methodology of the ICR ROSC: <http://www.worldbank.org/en/programs/rosc>.

with international standards. Importantly, the effectiveness of the Report in influencing countries' behaviour could be exploited to enhance compliance with cross-border insolvency, if a cross-border insolvency component is explicitly added to the indicator.[35] In a modest way, it may be possible to measure and provide relevant information about countries' adherence to global modified universalist frameworks by noting the adoption or non-adoption of the available instruments (eg the Model Law on Cross-Border Insolvency (MLCBI)), or even analysing the manner of adoption and the extent to which there have been significant deviations from the uniform framework.[36] Where the country did not adopt the available international instrument, it may also be possible to assess the domestic regulation and its compatibility with modified universalism norms, especially where these are recognized as binding CIL.[37]

In that regard, emphasizing—in advance of the assessment and through explanatory descriptions of the methodology—the potential reputation loss (ie decrease in rating) from non-compliance with the global framework may contribute to some shift in countries' focus from sovereignty loss to a reputation loss frame. If reports denote a clear and specified weight to non-compliance with cross-border insolvency norms, the loss of reputation may be relatively certain, increasing the effect.[38] In this way, countries may be more inclined to act to adopt a framework or otherwise act cooperatively in order not to lose reputation in more general investment contexts.[39] Reports may also include specific information about the reasons for defecting from the regime by relevant participants.

---

[35] The World Bank Doing Business Report has been subject to important criticism (see eg 'Performance Indices, Ranking the rankings, International comparisons are popular, influential—and sometimes flawed' *The Economist* (8 November 2014) <https://www.economist.com/news/international/21631039-international-comparisons-are-popular-influentialand-sometimes-flawed-ranking-rankings>; see also a report published by the World Bank in 2008 evaluating the Doing Business Report and noting some of the criticism, available at: <http://web.worldbank.org/WBSITE/EXTERNAL/EXTOED/EXTDOIBUS/0,,contentMDK:21645387~pagePK:64829573~piPK:64829550~theSitePK:4663967,00.html>). Yet, it has been highly impactful as a driver of reform. A powerful example of the influence of the World Bank Doing Business Report is the recent harmonization initiative in Europe which apparently has been at least partly driven by an ambition to improve member states' rating in the Report. An EU Action Plan that announced in 2015 a forthcoming legislative initiative for harmonization of aspects of insolvency laws noted the low scoring of certain member states: 'the 2015 World Bank Doing Business Report ranks countries on the strength of their insolvency frameworks on a scale of 0–16. The EU simple average is 11.6, which is 5% below the OECD average for high income countries (12.2). Some Member States score below 8' (European Commission, Action Plan on Building a Capital Markets Union, COM(2015) 468 final, 30 September 2015, 25 <http://eur-lex.europa.eu/legal-content/EN/TXT/PDF/?uri=CELEX:52015DC0468&from=EN>).

[36] For example, where countries include reciprocity requirements that are not included in the model framework.

[37] See Chapter 3, section 3.6.

[38] van Aaken, 'Behavioral International Law and Economics' (n 6) 477.

[39] As explained earlier, when in a loss frame, people on average are more risk seeking, keen to avoid the loss (see Chapter 2, section 2.3.3). Furthermore, this incentive's effectiveness may also derive from the frequency of the rating exercise. It has been shown, regarding the use of punishments, that these are more effective in reducing a behaviour when they are certain and immediately follow the behaviour (U Gneezy and A Rustichini, 'A Fine is a Price' (2000) 29 J Legal Stud 1, 2).

Thus, rating reports related to insolvency may serve as debiasing compliance tools. Their effectiveness can be further enhanced through mechanisms for monitoring information about compliance and for assisting countries in providing evidence about adherence. The cross-border insolvency system already uses certain such mechanisms where adoption of the MLCBI is noted in lists maintained by the United Nations Commission on International Trade Law (UNCITRAL).[40] Additional tools could include further assistance from an expert group that UNCITRAL, other IOs, or relevant Non-governmental organizations (NGOs) operating in the field of international insolvency may set up.[41] Such support is provided, for example, by an expert group working in the field of international secured transactions specifically in the context of aviation. This Aviation Working Group monitors, assesses, and promotes compliance by countries regarding their undertakings under the Cape Town Convention.[42] The group specifies on a designated website what compliance entails and takes further action to maximize compliance, including through setting up a network of contact groups around the world to closely monitor and obtain data and experience that are thereafter analysed by a legal advisory panel. It also publicizes information in a dedicated database to promote reporting on enforcement activity. It provides periodic reports to interested parties on compliance-related matters to increase transparency and the cost of non-compliance, and engages and interacts with contracting countries seeking compliance, including by providing 'state of the art information and education on Cape Town Convention topics'.[43]

5.2.3 Limitations of economic and disciplinary incentives

Even when compliance tools are sufficiently well designed to enhance concerns about reputation, their effect on compliance may not be absolute. It has been observed that obligations in hard or soft law may be more, or less, specific, with some obligations sufficiently ambiguous to make it difficult to determine whether there has been a violation.[44] Such is certainly the case in cross-border insolvency where various obligations may be understood and applied in different ways, for example, a duty imposed on the courts to cooperate 'to the maximum extent possible'.[45]

---

[40] See <http://www.uncitral.org/uncitral/en/uncitral_texts/insolvency/1997Model_status.html>.

[41] See also F Tung, 'Is International Bankruptcy Possible?' (2001) 23 Mich J Intl L 31, 93 (proposing that international institutions may assist in gathering and disseminating information emphasizing reputational costs of non-cooperation in cross-border insolvency).

[42] Cape Town Convention on International Interests in Mobile Equipment (2001) (see also Chapter 4, n 117, 190).

[43] See a summary of Cape Town Convention requirements regarding de-registration and exports (<http://www.awg.aero/projects/capetownconvention/>). Countries have been seeking assistance from the Aviation Working Group. For example, the Russian airline Transaero has sought assistance in applying insolvency rules in the convention correctly, and provided a statement letter confirming intention to comply with the convention and the Aircraft Protocol during the insolvency proceedings instituted against the airline on 16 December 2015 (a letter that was then posted on the website; see <http://www.awg.ero/assets/docs/letter-from-transaero-to-awg-(eng)-and-russia.pdf>).

[44] Brummer, *Soft Law and the Global Financial System* (n 19) 146–48.

[45] MLCBI, art 25(1). See also Chapter 3, nn 271–72 and accompanying texts; Chapter 6, sections 6.2.2 and 6.2.5.

Furthermore, the value of avoiding reputation losses will not be the same for every country or regulator, including in terms of measuring it against other losses. The bounds on decision-making also likely operate in different ways for different actors, where, for example, losses are measured against different 'reference points' (current states of affairs).[46] In the case of developing and emerging economies, non-compliance, for example non-enactment of an international instrument, is often a matter of a lack of capacity and readiness to deal with the more complex, cross-border aspects of insolvency, which raises the question of whether, in the absence of sufficient external assistance, non-compliance is a breach at all.[47]

Additional incentives and disciplinary measures may be used to heighten reputational consequences and induce compliance. Specifically, in systems such as international financial law, which are not grounded in hard law (in the sense that the operationalization is not through institutional frameworks with legal authority to enforce party compliance), disciplinary measures of various sorts have been utilized and imposed by standard-setting bodies and organizations.[48] For example, the International Monetary Fund (IMF) and World Bank Group may make their financial and economic assistance conditional on compliance (eg the adoption of a certain regulation). Yet, such measures only impact countries that require this type of assistance.[49]

More general disciplinary incentives include 'name and shame' or 'blacklisting', where non-cooperating participants are identified, and the disclosure of their non-compliance is accompanied by some form of criticism and condemnation,[50] as well as membership sanctions, where members may be expelled from organizations in cases of non-compliance.[51] These measures have significant limitations, though; indeed, they are utilized quite sparingly. First, they, too, require the detection of violations, and where obligations are ambiguous, the task of sanctioning may be elusive. Importantly, the isolation of participants or their exclusion from organizations counters the objective of broad participation and the ability to resolve global problems.[52] Under treaty regimes, including those regulating traditional public international law matters, cases of coercive enforcement are rare, and sanctions are costly and difficult to employ.[53]

---

[46] See Chapter 2, section 2.3.1.   [47] See section 5.3.1.

[48] For more detail, see Brummer, *Soft Law and the Global Financial System* (n 19) 152–61. See also Guzman, 'Against Consent' (n 16) 781–84.

[49] Brummer, *Soft Law and the Global Financial System* (n 19) 152–54.

[50] ibid 154–55 (giving the example of the Financial Action Task Force that devised standards to identify countries that were not cooperating with the international community in the attempt to address illegal financing. Such countries were included in a 'blacklist' that was made public and was shared with domestic financial institutions).

[51] See eg proceedings against Zimbabwe initiated in 2003 by the IMF for compulsory withdrawal because of lack of cooperation on economic policies, terminated in 2009 after cooperation improved (Brummer, *Soft Law and the Global Financial System* (n 19) 160).

[52] ibid.

[53] A Chayes and A Handler Chayes, *The New Sovereignty: Compliance with International Regulatory Agreements* (Harvard University Press 1995) (the authors propose an alternative 'managerial' model of treaty compliance that relies on the elaboration and application of treaty norms in a continuing dialogue between international officials and non-governmental organizations).

5.2.4 Why we should worry about undermining cooperation

Behavioural perspectives highlight additional aspects of the effect of economic incentives and sanctions that should be taken into account. Specifically, the concern is that such measures might do more harm than good as they could undermine multilateral cooperation.[54] Developing a strong tendency to cooperate is crucial in the cross-border insolvency context. Here, compliance is not just a matter of following standard regulations but is inherently about cooperation and the consideration of interests beyond the short-term benefits to local stakeholders, and outside the country's borders.[55] Considerations of this kind are often required in actual cases by relevant implementing institutions, where the stakes may be high and where self-serving inclinations can impede effective and fair solutions, especially in view of the problem of short-termism that constrain the ability to adhere to long-term commitments.[56] Various examples of the limited cooperation and insufficient consideration of the cross-border effect of local action in cross-border insolvency cases were noted earlier in the book, such as the enactment of discriminatory legislation when Icelandic banks defaulted during the global financial crisis and the actions taken in the United States immediately after the collapse of Lehman Brothers (where the lack of support to the holding company meant that foreign subsidiaries were pushed into insolvency).[57] Even the non-adoption of the MLCBI by many countries is an example of a more isolated and less cooperative approach to cross-border insolvency. Opposite examples have been noted as well, such as the intense cooperation among the US and Canadian courts in the case of *Nortel*.[58]

Altruism and fairness preferences have generally proven to be important behavioural forces.[59] Contrary to the prediction of standard economic models, individuals may be driven by other-regarding and social preferences, which include the desire to reciprocate and cooperate voluntarily and the wish to avoid social disapproval.[60] People may not just act upon self-interests and economic incentives. Altruistic cooperators may consider the impact of their actions on other parties even when they cannot see a concrete benefit that will ensue from such behaviour. People may sacrifice resources to reward behaviour that is perceived as kind and fair, even if reciprocation is costly and provides no present or future material benefit (a behaviour that has been termed 'strong reciprocity').[61] In international relations as

---

[54] E Fehr and B Rockenbach, 'Detrimental Effect of Sanctions on Human Altruism' (2003) 422 Nature 137, 137.

[55] See the duties assigned to home and host jurisdictions under modified universalism discussed in Chapter 1, section 1.3.2.4.

[56] See Chapter 2, section 2.5.2.   [57] ibid.   [58] ibid section 2.5.3.

[59] RM Dawes, 'Social Dilemmas' (1980) 31(1) Annu Rev Psych 169; E Fehr, G Kirchsteiger, and A Riedl, 'Does Fairness Prevent Market Clearing?' (1993) 108(2) Q J Econ 437; J Berg, J Dickhaut, and K McCabe, 'Trust, Reciprocity and Social History' (1995) 10 Games Econ Behav 122; J Andreoni, 'Cooperation in Public Goods Experiments: Kindness or Confusion' (1995) 85 Am Econ Rev 891; E Ostrom, 'A Behavioral Approach to the Rational Choice Theory of Collective Action' (1998) 92(1) Am Pol Sci Rev 1. See also van Aaken, 'Behavioral International Law and Economics' (n 6) 433.

[60] Experimental evidence has shown that a substantive fraction of people exhibit social preferences (E Fehr and A Falk, 'Psychological Foundations of Incentives' (2002) 46 Eur Econ Rev 687, 688–89).

[61] See eg H Gintis, 'Strong Reciprocity and Human Sociality' (2000) 206(2) J Theor Biol 169.

well, even though a country cannot as such act altruistically, it may develop fairness expectations and care about the impact of its behaviour beyond its borders through its internal mechanisms, or specific institutions within the country may develop such preferences.[62]

These preferences may be affected, however, by sanctions and material incentives.[63] Experiments, including in economic settings, show that when economic incentives and sanctions are perceived as fair, altruistic cooperation is not affected. In contrast, when incentives are perceived as unfair, altruistic cooperation may be undermined.[64] The moral legitimacy of the sanction seems an important factor.[65] The threat of punishment tends to be crucial in social systems; yet, when it is perceived to be unfair, it may impede cooperation. Researchers have pointed to the vast psychological literature showing that certain explicit incentives may be perceived as hostile, thus adversely affecting willingness to put extra efforts and act generously.[66] Similarly, it has also been observed that material incentives might undermine the motive to gain social approval and avoid social disapproval, which according to circumstantial evidence and introspection is another prevalent social force.[67] It has also been hypothesized, based on the results of experiments, that while a concrete threat of punishment is likely to undermine voluntary cooperation where it introduces hostility into the relationship, the implicit and vague possibility of punishing a defector *ex post* can have a positive effect on compliance in repeated interaction conditions.[68] Economic and approval incentives may reinforce each other in certain circumstances, but the relationship between economic and non-pecuniary motives is not always straightforward.[69]

The effect of explicit economic incentives could also be unpredictable. Fairness, and thus the types of sanctions perceived as fair, is an elusive notion, particularly when it might be influenced by those same biases such as status quo and perceived endowments that are compared with different reference points.[70] Experiments in behavioural sciences have also specifically shown that sanctions may have detrimental

---

[62] See Chapter 2, section 2.4.5.
[63] Fehr and Falk, 'Psychological Foundations of Incentives' (n 60) 688–89.
[64] Fehr and Rockenbach, 'Detrimental Effect of Sanctions on Human Altruism' (n 54) 140.
[65] ibid.
[66] Framing incentives in positive terms (eg rewards such as bonuses), as opposed to negative terms (eg imposing fines) may affect voluntary cooperation (Fehr and Falk, 'Psychological Foundations of Incentives' (n 60) 693–95). See regarding the Cape Town Convention (n 42) how compliance can generate concrete rewards such as discounts for credit if a contracting country makes certain declarations and demonstrates compliance (the scheme is delineated on the Organisation for Economic Co-operation and Development (OECD) website: <http://www.oecd.org/tad/xcred/ctc.htm>). cf proposals to use the 'name and shame' tool to support adherence to Memorandums of Understanding (MoUs) regarding cross-border insolvency of MFIs, following the example of the International Organization of Securities Commissions (IOSCO) where different categories of signatories are created, including one for non-compliant countries which 'could leverage "naming and shaming" to place additional pressure on countries to adopt the necessary reforms' (SL Schwarcz et al, Comments on the September 29, 2014 FSB Consultative Document, 'Cross-Border Recognition of Resolution Action' Ctr for Intl Governance Innovation, CIGI Paper No 51, £ December 2014, 6 <https://www.cigionline.org/sites/default/files/no.51.pdf>).
[67] Fehr and Falk, 'Psychological Foundations of Incentives' (n 60) 705.   [68] ibid 703–04.
[69] ibid 707.   [70] See Chapter 2, section 2.4.3.

unexpected effects on cooperation,[71] which could be important in a variety of contexts.[72] It is difficult to forecast whether and what sorts of measures may foster or at least not harm cooperation. The possible effect of economic incentives and sanctions in the international realm is particularly uncertain, especially in view of the complex processes and different types of actors involved in making decisions at that level.[73] As noted above, effectiveness of sanctions on international relations is generally limited. Considering the possible unintended consequences of sanctions on cooperation, there is good reason to utilize such tools with caution.

5.2.5 The role of mutual trust

In view of the risks and limitations of economic incentives and sanctions as a means to ensure compliance, the cross-border insolvency system seems 'right' when it mainly uses techniques to foster cooperation directly and enhance mutual trust between participants. Creating forums for meetings, for example, of bankruptcy judges and regulators from different jurisdictions,[74] can be understood as a measure that aims to strengthen mutual trust as a compliance force.

Mutual trust is considered one of the key principles of the EU cross-border insolvency regime. Thus, the principle of mutual trust has facilitated the establishment of the mandatory cross-border insolvency system within the EU.[75] For example, based on this notion, revisiting the decision of a court to exercise jurisdiction by other member states is prohibited.[76] At the same time, mutual trust as applicable in the EU

---

[71] An experiment involving day-care centres, for example, found that when economic incentives in the form of sanctions (fines) were introduced by the centres to reduce the frequency of parents arriving late to collect their children, the result was an increase in that same behaviour. Although a sufficiently large fine may have eventually reduced the misbehaviour, the finding demonstrates that people who engage in various interactions in real life, in situations that are not completely or precisely defined, bring to such 'games' their perception of the strategic situation they are facing, and the introduction of sanctions may change the perception of the game. The experiment has also shown that the increase in non-compliance has also remained the same after the removal of the sanction (Gneezy and Rustichini, 'A Fine is a Price' (n 39) 15).

[72] Gneezy and A Rustichini, 'A Fine is a Price' (n 39) 15–16 (giving the example of an announcement of a government that tax evasions are going to be more severely pursued, which may be interpreted in different ways and have a different effect than the anticipated increased compliance).

[73] See Chapter 2, section 2.4.2.

[74] See eg the Judicial Insolvency Network (JIN) initiative (Chapter 1, n 262 and accompanying text); the insolvency judges' colloquia held jointly by INSOL International, the World Bank, and UNCITRAL <http://www.uncitral.org/uncitral/en/commission/colloquia_insolvency.html>; or associations such as the International Association of Insolvency Regulators (IAIR) <https://www.insolvencyreg.org/>. See also in the context of cross-border insolvency of MFIs, eg Memorandum of Understanding on Cooperation Between the Financial Supervisory Authorities, Central Banks and Finance Ministries of the European Union on Cross-Border Financial Stability 1 (1 June 2008) <https://www.ecb.europa.eu/pub/pdf/other/mou-financialstability2008en.pdf>, and generally S Cho and CR Kelly, 'Promises and Perils of New Global Governance: A Case of the G20' (2012) 12 Chi J Intl L 491 (describing the role of the G20 following the global financial crisis as coordinator of institutions and networks).

[75] See Chapter 3, section 3.6.1.

[76] *Eurofood IFSC Ltd, Re* (C-341/04) 2006 at [39]. See also in the context of the regulation on jurisdiction, and the recognition and enforcement of judgments in civil and commercial matters (Regulation No 1215/2012) SFG Rammeloo, 'EU Law Reform: Cross-Border Civil and Commercial Procedural Law and Cross-Border Insolvency Law' [2014] DQ 44, 50.

has notable limitations as a justificatory ground for granting rights and imposing binding obligations, even within the EU.[77]

Seemingly, mutual trust 'works' in Europe only because it has been translated into mandatory recognition provisions, and implementing institutions do not promote modified universalism solutions beyond what is specifically required in the regime. However, it can be seen in practice that various provisions in the (EU) Regulation on Insolvency Proceedings of 2000 (EIR) have been applied in less conservative ways and more in line with modified universalism, as member states' courts learned through experience and interaction that global solutions can benefit all stakeholders, and that this may have been the intention of foreign courts, not the grabbing of cases. For example, the centralization of group proceedings was viewed with suspicion when it was first attempted in the United Kingdom,[78] but it was later followed more widely.[79] Courts seem to have developed trust in the intentions of other jurisdictions over time, which has allowed a more effective application of the EU insolvency regime.

Certainly, at the global level, where multiple (indeed all) jurisdictions are potentially involved, and no equivalent infrastructure supporting an integrated market for an exclusive grouping of states exists, it is not possible to simply assume or impose trust. Mutual trust on the global level should be conceptualized, therefore, as another important driver of compliance. It is generally acknowledged that a crucial feature of any exchange is that the parties involved have trust in each other.[80] While in a region such as the EU, countries may agree that all systems are deemed trusted and thus trust is imposed, at the global level (and at least to some extent regionally, too), to ensure the optimal application of rules, trust must be encouraged and nurtured through the actions of participants and key organizations that seek to develop actual trust and respect.[81] This understanding of the role of mutual trust as a compliance force that requires continuous support, fits well with a system of modified universalism that embraces a realistic set of norms, considering world realities, including changes and possible fluctuations in cooperative relationships.[82] A dynamic concept of trust is also responsive to changes within regions, which may be driven by political events (the notable recent example being Brexit), and which may affect inclinations to participate in

---

[77] See Chapter 3, section 3.6.1.   [78] In *Re Daisytek-ISA Ltd* [2003] BCC 562.
[79] See Chapter 1, section 1.4.4.
[80] It has been observed that: 'Virtually every commercial transaction has within itself an element of trust, certainly any transaction conducted over a period of time. It can plausibly be argued that much of the economic backwardness in the world can be explained by the lack of mutual confidence inhibiting cooperation in the production and the exchange of goods and services' (KJ Arrow, 'Gifts and Exchanges' (1972) 1(4) Phil & Publ Affairs 343, 357).
[81] See in the context of MFI cross-border insolvency, RM Lastra, 'International Law Principles Applicable to Cross-Border Bank Insolvency' in RM Lastra (ed), *Cross-Border Bank Insolvency* (OUP 2011) 175 (arguing that international rules concerning recognition in cross-border insolvency 'cannot work in a vacuum' and require an environment of mutual trust).
[82] On the possible modifications of cross-border insolvency rules to accommodate different levels of trust, see JL Westbrook, CD Booth, CG Paulus, and H Rajak, 'A Global View of Business Insolvency System' [2010] The World Bank, Law, Justice, And Development Series 240–41.

frameworks and make cooperation between participants less certain, including in cross-border insolvency.

Social motives may generate powerful incentives themselves.[83] Creating opportunities for repeated interactions can strengthen the ties between key actors and thereby incentivize reciprocal behaviour, resulting in successful cooperation.[84] Consequently, cooperation becomes self-reinforcing. Additionally, to the extent that some parties act reciprocally, other parties are more inclined to mimic that co-operative behaviour.[85] Interaction and information about compliance can enhance the 'positive biases' where actors may develop other-regarding preferences and conform with the behaviour of others in a group (who comply) as a result of the effect of peer pressure.[86] On the international level, peer pressure in international relations has been observed as a probable compliance force in research concerning adherence to treaty provisions.[87] Specifically, a study of treaties noted that the fact that information about the early acceptance of the treaty provisions by certain countries was readily available may have influenced other countries which then took the same approach.[88] A similar effect can be noted in cross-border insolvency where adherence to the global regime by economically significant regimes seems to have positively affected participation by others, explaining the relative success and dominance of modified universalism.[89]

Tools that encourage such influences are therefore important. The more participants understand how and why other participants address and administer cross-border insolvencies in certain ways, the more cooperation is fostered.[90] Thus, initiatives such as the JIN,[91] noted earlier, are mostly important where they allow judges to meet and interact.[92] Additionally, the more salient the information about global approaches taken in cross-border insolvencies, *ex ante* in legislation and *ex post* in administration of cases, the more likely it is that other participants follow the same approach. IOs as well as NGOs play a key role, less in terms of sanctioning behaviour and more as facilitators that provide readily available and salient information about participation and compliance as well as forums for communication among key players.

---

[83] See in the context of labour relations, Fehr and Falk, 'Psychological Foundations of Incentives' (n 60).

[84] It was also noted in Chapter 3 that repeated interactions and the development of fairness preferences, as well as concerns about reputation, can explain CIL's formation in functional terms (see Chapter 3, section 3.3.3).

[85] Fehr and Falk, 'Psychological Foundations of Incentives' (n 60) 704 (observing, in the context of employment relationship, that in the presence of reciprocal subjects, the selfish subjects can gain a credible reputation for being cooperative by behaving like the reciprocal subjects, and can ensure themselves employment and a higher material payoff).

[86] See Chapter 2, section 2.3.5.   [87] ibid section 2.4.5.   [88] ibid.

[89] ibid section 2.5.3.   [90] ibid.   [91] See n 74.

[92] Even where the initiative might not cover all cross-border insolvency aspects and safeguards and thus would require that it is complemented by other instruments or indeed by the norms of modified universalism (see C Watters, 'Guidelines for Cooperation and Communication between Courts on Cross-border Insolvency Matters: Too Far or Not Far Enough?' (2017) 38(6) Comp Law 172, 172, noting that the JIN Guidelines do not provide adequate protection to parties when dealing with less developed legal regimes).

As noted in section 5.2.2, expert groups could monitor and provide concrete information on countries' participation and cooperation in cross-border insolvency to reinforce the role of reputation as a driver of compliance, highlighting the cost of non-compliance as well. Such activities can, at the same time, create the needed social pressure that would further induce cooperation, especially where positive information about leadership behaviour is emphasized. For example, IOs, NGOs, or relevant expert groups may publicize model judgments and exemplary cases, thus emphasizing what is expected in terms of compliance and creating greater predisposition of relevant implementing institutions to conform to these community expectations.[93]

Countries and implementing institutions can also lead by example. It was already proposed in Chapter 3 that key players such as decision makers, legislators, regulatory authorities, and courts are important to the fulfilment of the international role of cross-border insolvency law, particularly those in economically significant jurisdictions and insolvency hubs. These actors can contribute to the creation of modified universalism as CIL, which in turn also has a behavioural force where it can foster further coordination.[94] Additionally, key actors should, as prominently as possible, expose their cooperative approaches to the international community in various ways, including when they interact in colloquia and other forums.

5.3 Addressing Gaps in Domestic Systems

Mutual trust depends, however, not only on trust in participants' intentions to cooperate, but also on trust in foreign insolvency systems and their administration of justice. It is a reality that the legal systems of the world differ, and these differences include divergences in insolvency laws, the processes adopted for liquidation or restructuring, and various other laws related or relevant to insolvency.[95] Legal systems also differ in terms of their level of development and sophistication, including in terms of the expertise, knowledge, education, and experience of the various players and bodies operating the insolvency system (these latter types of differences are together referred to as related to systems' 'institutional capacity').

So far, the cross-border insolvency regime has largely relied on the enforcement and operationalization of its norms by domestic systems. There is currently no international bankruptcy court.[96] Furthermore, international instruments for

---

[93] Building on platforms such as Case Law on UNCITRAL Texts (CLOUT), maintained by the UNCITRAL Secretariat. CLOUT is a system 'for collecting and disseminating information on court decisions and arbitral awards relating to the Conventions and Model Laws that have emanated from the work of the Commission. The purpose of the system is to promote international awareness of the legal texts formulated by the Commission and to facilitate uniform interpretation and application of those texts' (<http://www.uncitral.org/uncitral/en/case_law.html>).

[94] See Chapter 3, section 3.3.3.

[95] Including corporate law, finance law, commercial law, intellectual property law, tax law, and labour law (as noted in R Bork, *Principles of Cross-Border Insolvency* (Intersentia 2017) 256).

[96] See section 5.3.3.

cross-border insolvency mainly unify private international aspects and, to a much lesser extent, attempt to harmonize substantive laws and processes.[97] There have been, however, important efforts in recent decades to standardize insolvency laws, including resolution tools for financial institutions, through principles and recommendations developed by key IOs.[98] Beyond these efforts, the question of the harmonization[99] of insolvency laws is an open and highly debated one.

This section considers the extent to which the problems of the capacity and quality of, and differences between, legal systems may affect compliance with a cross-border insolvency system. It takes account of the extant biases, discussed earlier, to understand how these may interact with capacity problems, as well as with the expected outcomes of harmonization efforts. It also considers whether some degree of delegation to external institutions could be useful for promoting compliance in view of such capacity problems as well as the likely operation of cognitive inclinations that may affect the commitment of local institutions over time.

5.3.1 Capacity building

A cross-border insolvency system based on modified universalism does not rely on the creation of external institutions. Instead, the system's operation and enforcement may be actioned through local mechanisms and the local implementing institutions. These institutions should be able to fulfil this role designated to them by the global system, otherwise compliance is undermined.[100] Yet, in the real world, legal regimes have different levels of institutional capacities, including the functioning of the system that supports debtors in distress.[101] Some regimes exhibit a high level of expertise, where the institutions engaged in insolvency possess the relevant knowledge through education of the professionals and accumulated experience, in addition to having in place a developed, well-functioning, and efficient judicial and administrative system with a strong rule of law and due process mechanisms. Other systems may lag in some, or all, of these fundamental aspects of the system to the extent that they may be unable to properly implement and operate the cross-border insolvency regime, whether it is based on treaty or non-treaty instruments.[102]

---

[97] Although the cross-border frameworks may, nonetheless, pursue substantive principles and have important substantive impact, as discussed in Chapter 3, section 3.5.2.
[98] Significantly by UNCITRAL, the World Bank, the IMF, and the FSB which developed the insolvency and the resolution standards (see Chapter 1, section 1.4.4).
[99] This chapter uses the term 'harmonization' in a broad sense, entailing greater or lesser harmonization, including in the form of standardization. There is a subtle difference between harmonization and standardization, where harmonization seeks to eliminate differences and unify laws, and standardization merely promotes conformity with international standards. Yet, even harmonization may not envisage complete uniformity (see W Menski, *Comparative Law in a Global Context: The Legal Systems of Asia and Africa* (2nd edn, CUP 2006) 39).
[100] See in the context of MFI cross-border insolvency, Lastra, 'International Law Principles Applicable to Cross-Border Bank Insolvency' (n 81) 172.
[101] The effectiveness of the substantive insolvency laws and the question of harmonization will be discussed separately in section 5.3.2.
[102] TF McInerney, 'The Emerging Developmental Approach to Multilateral Treaty Compliance' (2005) 1 <http://treatyeffectiveness.org/wp-content/uploads/2012/05/McInerney_Developmental_

Capacity deficiencies might exist even when the jurisdiction has modern insolvency legislation and the country is party to an existing cross-border insolvency framework. It has been observed, for example, regarding the Greek insolvency system, that even though it has undergone comprehensive reform in line with international standards, it has demonstrated important institutional shortcomings.[103] Even in significant and fully developed economies, certain regions or states within, for example, a federation may have relatively limited capacity and knowledge if most insolvency, especially cross-border insolvency, cases take place elsewhere in the country, thereby constraining the development of the needed expertise.[104]

Is it, however, sufficient that only certain jurisdictions, and states within countries, can cope with cross-border insolvency cases properly? If the cross-border insolvency system could operate through the placement of cases in such forums and insolvency hubs, there may be less concern about the lack of capacity in other places. Because the central, economically significant, and more advanced jurisdictions often host the economic centres of multinational entities (they are the debtors' home country), it may be possible to administer cross-border insolvency cases from these forums, thereby depending less on the development of other legal systems.

Even where the debtor's centre of main interests (COMI)[105] is outside such jurisdictions, it may be possible to move the centre for insolvency purposes, or even just the proceedings, and conduct the insolvency in a regime that is more able to resolve the distress situation. Such case shifts for insolvency and restructuring purposes are quite common in the practice. For example, owing to certain deficiencies in the Greek system supporting insolvencies, some significant debtors have restructured their debt abroad following the global financial crisis. This occurred in circumstances where the economic centre of these entities was in Greece and sometimes where there was no real connection to the foreign jurisdiction, as debtors or their creditors lacked sufficient faith in the local regime.[106]

Approach.pdf> (noting the ineffectiveness and low level of compliance with multilateral treaty regimes among developing countries especially because of lack of capacity).

[103] CG Paulus et al, 'Insolvency Law as a Main Pillar of Market Economy—A Critical Assessment of the Greek Insolvency Law' (2015) 24(1) Int Insolv Rev 1, 12 (noting that the Greek insolvency system has been grossly underused and that most cases have ended in value-destructive piecemeal liquidations). See also C Klissouras, 'Promoting Global Solutions Against Fundamental Inefficiencies of National Laws: A Case for International Harmonization of Civil Procedure Laws' Law, Justice and Development Week, World Bank Group, 20–24 October 2014 <http://siteresources.worldbank.org/EXTGILD/Resources/Klissouras_Insolvency_PanelDiscussionPaper.pdf> (noting fundamental shortcomings of the Greek court system and the general rules of civil process).

[104] See eg in the United States, the predominance of New York and Delaware in the conduct of insolvency cases, which can affect the expertise of institutions in other states. It has also been noted regarding the German system that even though it has cross-border insolvency legislation in place, the problem is in its application in practice as 'it can take judges a very long time to investigate whether the foreign insolvency proceedings are compatible with German public policy . . . there are only a few judges in Germany who are able to handle it with the necessary speed' (*Global Restructuring Review*, 'International Debt Restructuring: Can Other Jurisdictions Compete with London and New York?' (1 March 2017) quoting Ivo-Meinert Willrodt).

[105] See on the jurisdictional norm of modified universalism, Chapter 1, section 1.3.2.1.

[106] Klissouras, 'Promoting Global Solutions Against Fundamental Inefficiencies' (n 103) (mentioning the example of Greece's third largest mobile operator, which was restructured in 2009 by way of a prepack restructuring of holding companies under the UK administration process, even though all

Forum shopping for insolvency purposes is, therefore, a way in which to resolve capacity constraints and thus improve compliance.[107] Where the shift to a different jurisdiction can benefit all stakeholders because the institutions and system supporting the insolvency of the chosen forum can resolve the insolvency situation more effectively and fairly,[108] and the benefit of the shift outweighs the costs of opting for a forum different from the original economic home country, there is little justification in remaining there.[109] From a system design perspective, capacity problems suggest that forum shopping should be allowed and even facilitated, for example, through mechanisms for hearing foreign creditors without the need for them to physically appear in court and, importantly, by requiring that the original forum provide all the assistance needed to effectuate the shift. Forum shopping for such reasons certainly should not be constrained by the global framework and should be distinguished from forum abuse.[110]

It should also be recalled that modified universalistic norms are sufficiently flexible to accommodate a regime that allows shifts in jurisdiction. What modified universalism requires is that the process is centralized in a manner fitting the business structure and insolvency scenario.[111] The most efficient and predictable forum is often the one in the debtor's original home country; however, in some scenarios, a different forum may be more adequate.[112] In circumstances where the original forum is deficient, a forum shift can promote compliance. From compliance and specifically capacity perspectives, therefore, it is important that the jurisdictional test that the system adopts is to some extent 'movable' or changeable,[113] even if the choice is thereafter scrutinized to ensure that there was no abuse.[114]

Forum shopping as a tool for resolving the gaps in systems capacity has important limitations, though. Even when the global framework is mindful to facilitate movements, these may still be too costly,[115] considering the size of the business

---

the aspects of the debtor (assets and economic centre) were located in Greece, and noting that many enterprises relocated their balance sheet to Luxembourg, the United Kingdom, or the United States at that time, apparently to ensure that their borrowing or restructuring initiatives would not be subject in the future to the Greek court process).

[107]   It is also a tool for exploiting legal innovation across borders (see section 5.3.2.2).

[108]   The relevance of differences in substantive insolvency laws and processes to the question of forum choice will be discussed in the next section.

[109]   See also I Mevorach, 'Forum Shopping at Times of Crisis: A Directors' Duties Perspective' (2013) 4 ECFR 524, 538–40 (suggesting that corporate migrations for better insolvency outcomes fit with the international standard concerning the duties of directors at times approaching insolvency).

[110]   See section 5.3.2.2.   [111]   See Chapter 1, sections 1.3.2.1 and 1.3.2.2.

[112]   ibid section 1.3.2.1.

[113]   cf the critics of COMI as a test for jurisdiction in insolvency who argue that it is too fuzzy and thus too prone to manipulation (G McCormack, 'Jurisdictional Competition and Forum Shopping in Insolvency Proceedings' (2009) 68(1) CLJ 169, 196; H Eidenmüller, 'Free Choice in International Company Insolvency Law in Europe' (2005) 6 EBOR 423, 428, 430–31; DA Skeel, 'European Implication of Bankruptcy Venue Shopping in the US' (2007) 54 Buff L Rev 439, 463; WG Ringe, 'Forum Shopping under the EU Insolvency Regulation' (2008) 9(4) EBOR 580, 612; P Torremans, 'Coming to Terms with the COMI Concept in the European Insolvency Regulation' in PJ Omar (ed), *International Insolvency Law Themes and Perspectives* (Aldershot 2008) 181).

[114]   See section 5.3.2.2 for a discussion of abusive forum shopping.

[115]   See also H Eidenmüller and K van Zwieten, 'Restructuring the European Business Enterprise: The EU Commission Recommendation on a New Approach to Business Failure and Insolvency' (2015) 16 EBOR 625, 627.

or the need for it to remain in the native forum for operational purposes (eg when a reorganization is contemplated and the continued operation of the business within the country is envisaged).[116] Excessive and repeated movements out of a jurisdiction would also mean that such countries from which debtors tend to flee when insolvency looms remain largely incapacitated in this area, as they cannot develop expertise and gain important experience in handling cross-border insolvencies.

Furthermore, cross-border cases, even those that take place in a jurisdiction that has the capacity to deal with the case, would usually necessitate the assistance of other countries that host aspects of the enterprise, or of the original home country of the debtor from where they moved. It is a core aspect of modified universalism that jurisdictions hosting the elements of a debtor business play an ancillary role, supporting a global approach to multinational default.[117] Thus, even if the global system would not expect certain countries to supervise insolvency cases with cross-border aspects, it must envisage that countries other than key jurisdictions might also need to address elements of such cases in a way that is conducive to a global collective approach.[118] Host forums may need to handle pieces of the case locally or play some role by providing assistance to the main forum.[119] Yet, where a domestic system struggles to cope with insolvency cases, it will have even greater difficulties when the case contains cross-border elements and is linked to proceedings taking place abroad. Inherently, cross-border insolvency cases are more complicated compared to purely domestic ones as they may require an appreciation of the effects of decisions and actions on the foreign aspects of the process or an understanding of laws and procedures of foreign regimes.

Addressing cross-border elements effectively also requires an appreciation and implementation of universalist concepts, with which certain jurisdictions may be less familiar. As noted earlier, countries and implementing institutions may be affected by some of the robust biases that influence decisions regarding cross-border insolvency.[120] A lack of readiness and the limited capacity of the legal system may exacerbate the bounds on decision-making, such as loss aversion and status quo bias. Some regimes may have less opportunity to develop the needed experience and expertise (eg of regulators and judges) to deal with cross-border insolvency cases as fewer such cases land on their shores. They are, therefore, less exposed to the peer pressure that induces cooperative relations and might be slower at adapting their (so-called) reference point, which may remain more territorialist, impeding further action and change.

The problem of the lack of readiness to adhere to universalist solutions is also self-reinforcing where, because of limited capacity, even when cross-border cases

---

[116] See also Mevorach, 'Forum Shopping at Times of Crisis' (n 109) 538–39; A Walters and A Smith, ' "Bankruptcy tourism" under the EC Regulation on insolvency proceedings: a view from England and Wales' (2010) 19(3) IIR 181.

[117] See Chapter 1, section 1.3.2.3.

[118] As discussed in Chapter 1, section 1.3.2.1, the jurisdiction rule under modified universalism takes account that opening local proceedings may be efficient in certain circumstances.

[119] See the norms concerning recognition and assistance, discussed in Chapter 1, section 1.3.2.3.

[120] See Chapter 2, section 2.5.

take place in the country, the expertise may not develop, or the process may be slow. In circumstances of institutional incapacity, the fact that a case is a cross-border one might be altogether ignored. Moreover, institutions (eg courts) may apply domestic laws without due regard to the international implications, which might be perceived as too complicated.[121] For example, if a company's seat is considered to be located within the jurisdiction, based on the local private international law related to insolvency, local institutions may disregard the jurisdictional tests in global frameworks and consider the case a domestic one, or they may ignore the need to take a group-wide approach in cases where the country hosts subsidiaries of a multinational enterprise. The result might be fragmentation and deviation from the norms of modified universalism as well as continued incapacity, as experience is not developed.

The difficulty of adhering to modified universalism in the face of capacity problems is worsened further when the global framework itself may be adopted in ways not entirely congruent with the original intentions of its designers, including because of the lack of familiarity with the notions of cross-border insolvency enshrined in international instruments. Additional conditions may be added at the stage of the enactment of the framework into the local regime, which may constrain its smooth application thereafter. For example, with regard to the existing MLCBI, the notion of reciprocity (understood as providing assistance only to parties from certain countries who also adopted the same regime or that are designated in the enacting legislation)[122] or expansions of the public policy safeguard[123] may be employed, thus limiting the application of recognition and assistance mechanisms. Such modifications in the enactment of a global framework, and their implementation in practice, can be explained by the bounds on decision-making, as submitted earlier, as well as by the lack of experience in this field.[124]

The shortcomings of systems supporting cross-border insolvency may also affect the level of trust of other countries and their implementing institutions in these systems. It was suggested in the previous section that mutual trust should be embraced as a cornerstone of the global insolvency system and that it should be understood as a driver of compliance. Such 'real trust' that is not imposed but developed also depends on trust in the integrity of foreign institutions. It is perhaps expected that it is easier for countries with some tradition of cooperation and familiarity with each other's institutions to, as a matter of course, recognize the other country's foreign processes and decisions. Yet, even such cooperative relations may be undermined in view of the global gaps in capacity. For example, the UK court decision in *Rubin* to refuse to enforce a US court judgment has been explained by concerns about creating a precedent that would have to be applied in the case of

---

[121] These observations are largely based on conversations with various market participants in developing jurisdictions and emerging markets.

[122] See eg the way the MLCBI was enacted in South Africa (Chapter 1, n 299 and accompanying text).

[123] See eg the way the MLCBI was enacted in Romania (Chapter 1, n 300 and accompanying text).

[124] It was against this background that it was noted in Chapter 2 that the lack of readiness and problems of capacity of domestic systems likely slows adherence to and endorsement of modified universalism (Chapter 2, section 2.5.1).

insolvency judgments issued by courts in other, perhaps less sound, jurisdictions.[125] Furthermore, as long as real trust in legal systems is low, it also reinforces incapacity, where it limits exchanges and cooperation that could increase the knowledge, confidence, and understanding of cross-border insolvency issues.

Therefore, to make it work, the cross-border insolvency system demands that domestic regimes' capacity be constantly improved. Generally, international law has been increasingly relying in recent decades on development and focused on effectiveness by connecting assistance and aid to facilitating treaty implementation. Thus, a developmental approach to compliance has become paramount in response to the growth and expansion of international law, particularly in view of the significant compliance challenges of implementing multilateral treaties with a global scope in developing countries.[126]

To improve the capacity of the system supporting cross-border insolvency, certain measures can be adopted by developing countries and emerging economies to make themselves readier for increased participation in the global system. It has been observed, for example, that emerging economies could take intermediary steps, when they may not be ready to adopt the existing written international instruments, such as the adoption of cross-border protocols, to acclimatize themselves to cross-border insolvency issues.[127]

There has been growing recognition in international law, however, that the ability of countries to comply with international obligations, typically those enshrined in treaties, is integrally linked to external assistance.[128] With regard to cross-border insolvency, as mentioned earlier, the lack of capacity is often self-reinforcing, and thus resolving it without external assistance can be highly challenging. The implementation of international commitments can also be costly and insufficiently high in the priority of systems struggling in multiple areas, restricting actions in the more advanced field of cross-border insolvency.

The cross-border insolvency system, therefore, partially relies on capacity building through external assistance, and it should conceptualize capacity building as another critical compliance tool. Capacity building or 'capacity development' generally refers to promoting the development goals of communities and governments. It aims to enhance the skills and competencies of people as well as the relevant bodies and organizations to overcome the obstacles and causes of underdevelopment.[129]

[125] A Briggs, 'Rubin and New Cap: Foreign Judgements and Insolvency' (2013) Legal Studies Research Paper 7, 11 (suggesting that: 'There is a risk, and probably not a small one, that if the court had been willing to give effect to the US repayment judgment against those who had held office in the Rubin case, it would have been rather difficult to explain why the same would not be done in respect of a judgment from a Russian court, purporting to liquidate a company whose patron-oligarch had managed to get on the wrong side of state power ... Perhaps the rational solution is simply to refuse to give effect to any of these judgments').

[126] McInerney, 'The Emerging Developmental Approach' (n 102) 2.

[127] S Kargman, 'Emerging Economies and Cross-Border Insolvency Regimes: Missing BRICS in the International Insolvency Architecture (Part II)' (2013) 7(1) Insolvency and Restructuring International 8.

[128] McInerney, 'The Emerging Developmental Approach' (n 102) 17.

[129] Capacity-building projects are included in the programs of the various IOs and NGOs that work in development, including the World Bank, the IMF, the UN, and the European Commission. See also

Importantly, poverty reduction, the fundamental goal of leading development organizations,[130] is considered to be dependent on reform efforts to improve economic performance. In that regard, it is acknowledged by key organizations such as the World Bank Group and IMF that countries often lack the capacity to implement the needed reforms.[131] The implementation of economic policies in particular relies on countries' institutional capacity. This includes 'the establishment and operation of appropriate regulatory and/or prudential frameworks for companies and banks [and] the making and enforcement of rules and laws and judicial reforms'.[132] When capacity is weak, the consequence for society can be costly. Therefore, development organizations devote significant funds and effort to capacity building by way of technical assistance and training, recognizing that 'capacity limitations—rather than [the] lack of political will—often impede [the] implementation of economic reforms'.[133]

Thus, capacity building is a fundamental and far-reaching effort to eliminate poverty and increase shared prosperity. Improving the legal system and institutions supporting insolvency is principally aimed at advancing the fundamental objective of poverty reduction, and this should be pursued regardless of whether it is envisaged that a given jurisdiction is likely to need to deal with cross-border insolvency cases. With improved systems supporting insolvency, countries should expect to increase the access to credit of local businesses and the ability of commercial banks to support business, as well as attract more foreign investment, promoting growth and stability in the economy.

Yet, capacity-building efforts also contribute to closing the capacity gaps relevant to the cross-border insolvency system. Thus, the system may piggyback on existing development initiatives,[134] linking the implementation of the cross-border insolvency framework to broader development processes, especially those related to the improvement of commercial systems and insolvency. Technical assistance and training programmes can also be targeted to improve the expertise and knowledge in cross-border insolvency.[135] Projects can further focus on aid in the creation of

---

the World Bank Group Country Policy and Institutional Assessment, which is a tool for 'rating of countries against a set of sixteen criteria grouped in four clusters: economic management, structural policies, policies for social inclusion and equity, and public sector management and institutions' (<https://data.worldbank.org/data-catalog/CPIA>).

[130] See eg the current overarching mission of the World Bank Group which is 'to end extreme poverty and promote shared prosperity.' (<http://siteresources.worldbank.org/DEVCOMMINT/Documentation/23394965/DC2013-0002(E)CommonVision.pdf>). Poverty reduction has been the agreed framework for international development assistance that was initiated by the IMF and the World Bank in 1999 under the auspices of the Comprehensive Development Framework (McInerney, 'The Emerging Developmental Approach' (n 102) 7).

[131] See International Monetary Fund, IMF Staff, 'The Role of Capacity-building in Poverty Reduction', March 2002 <https://www.imf.org/external/np/exr/ib/2002/031402.htm>.

[132] ibid.

[133] ibid. See also The IMF policy statement on technical assistance available at: https://www.imf.org/external/pubs/ft/psta/.

[134] In particular, the assessment and assistance programs of the IMF and World Bank Group in various key pillars of the international financial architecture, including insolvency (see <http://www.worldbank.org/en/topic/financialsector/brief/insolvency-and-debt-resolution>).

[135] Such work may also be undertaken by NGOs specializing in international insolvency, eg the International Insolvency Institute and INSOL, and by regional development organizations, where such

insolvency hubs within regions, where such development requires external assistance.[136] Assistance should tackle the initial phases of the adoption and enactment of cross-border insolvency instruments, ensuring that adoption is uniform and fits with the designers' intentions as well as integrated into the local system.[137] It should also support domestic regimes thereafter to promote the consistent and effective implementation and operation of the adopted frameworks and modified universalistic norms as they continue to develop and emerge as CIL in this field.[138] Capacity building should thus be viewed as an ongoing effort that includes monitoring components that look at effective implementation over time and responsiveness to changing conditions.

Work on effective implementation in regimes identified as having capacity gaps would importantly also promote the understanding of the global framework for cross-border insolvency, specifically highlighting its benefits to all participants and explaining how these gains outweigh concerns about sovereignty loss. In this way, the capacity-building tool is also debiasing, as it takes account of behavioural constraints such as status quo bias and loss aversion and attempts to address them. Capacity building may also tackle procedural gaps affecting due process, for example by designing civil procedure standards and model provisions for adoption in domestic laws as well as aiding in their enactment and implementation.[139]

Finally, while capacity building usually refers to work in developing and emerging markets, developed regimes may also lag behind. Various aspects of the global system at different times may be especially innovative and require general institutional support for all legal systems. In that regard, tools developed by IOs and NGOs that assist in the enactment and implementation of cross-border insolvency frameworks, importantly through forms and model tools for cooperation, should also be understood as aiming to build global cross-border insolvency capacity.[140]

---

organizations may be able to provide technical support to domestic institutions. The problem of lack of specialization may be especially acute in developing regimes, including because often both horizontal and vertical rotation of judges is frequent, resulting in loss of experience at the level of the implementing institutions and impeding the development of expertise.

[136] See eg the recent emergence of Saudi Arabia as a regional arbitration hub following the enactment of a new law in 2012 based on the UNCITRAL Model Law on International Commercial Arbitration (Kingdom of Saudi Arabia, Law of Arbitration, Royal Decree No. M/34, 16/4/2012).

[137] Such efforts are indeed taking place; see eg the work of the World Bank with the member countries of the Organization for the Harmonization of Business Law in Africa (OHADA), resulting in their adoption of the MLCBI in 2015.

[138] See Chapter 3.

[139] Klissouras, 'Promoting Global Solutions Against Fundamental Inefficiencies' (n 103) (arguing in favour of harmonization of civil procedure rules in Europe). See also European Parliament, DG for Research Working Paper, 'The Private Law Systems in the EU: Discrimination on Grounds of Nationality and the Need for a European Civil Code' Legal Affairs Series, JURI 103 EN <http://www.europarl.europa.eu/workingpapers/juri/pdf/103_en.pdf>.

[140] See eg the Key Attributes, I-Annex 2 (Essential Elements of Institution-Specific Cross-border Cooperation Agreements); the EU Cross-Border Insolvency Court-to-Court Cooperation Principles and Guidelines (2014) <http://www.tri-leiden.eu/uploads/files/EU_Cross-Border_Insolvency_Court-to-Court_Cooperation_Principles.pdf>; The American Law Institute (ALI), 'Principles of Cooperation Among the NAFTA Countries Transnational Insolvency' (2003); The American Law Institute (ALI) and the International Insolvency Institute, 'Transnational Insolvency Global Principles for Cooperation in International Insolvency Cases' Report (2012) (IF Fletcher and B Wessels, Joint Reporters)

Capacity-building efforts in developing as well as developed countries may also attempt to circumvent capacity constraints and find alternative solutions that could promote systems' efficiency. Specifically, because the court systems in many countries have limitations in dealing with cross-border insolvency cases, with greater challenges regarding MFIs, alternative ways in which to deal with such cases may be preferred, including the involvement of other bodies instead of the court or the operation of procedures out of court in appropriate circumstances.[141]

5.3.2 Targeted harmonization

Modified universalism does not prescribe convergence or harmonization of all insolvency laws and processes.[142] The question is, however, whether efforts to unify laws are conducive to compliance with the global system. The harmonization of insolvency laws is theoretically a way to ensure full uniformity, which can enhance trust between systems.[143] It has also been argued that harmonized rules may create greater certainty about the compliance of other countries with best practice standards, as well as about the rules that will apply in circumstances where the debtor operates in more than one country, thus also reducing complexities and increasing *ex ante* and

---

<https://www.iiiglobal.org/sites/default/files/alireportmarch_0.pdf>. See also mechanisms to assist in implementation of cooperation tools, eg the *UNCITRAL Practice Guide on Cooperation* (2009) which provides information on practical aspects of cooperation and communication in cross-border insolvency cases <http://www.uncitral.org/uncitral/en/uncitral_texts/insolvency/2009PracticeGuide.html>; *UNCITRAL Model Law on Cross-Border Insolvency: The Judicial Perspective* (2013) (designed to assist judges with questions that may arise in the context of an application for recognition under the MLCBI) <http://www.uncitral.org/uncitral/uncitral_texts/insolvency/2011Judicial_Perspective.html>.

[141] See eg the initiative in Europe to develop a Directive that focuses on out-of-court restructuring measures (n 149 and accompanying text). In the MFI context, regulatory authorities often have the lead role, and especially with respect to systematically important financial institutions (SIFIs) are regarded as best equipped to deal with the complexities of a failure of a global financial firm. cf an opposite approach reflected in the US Financial Institutions Bankruptcy Act 2017 under which the bankruptcy system and courts may be used to resolve MFIs. Doubts have indeed been raised in the United States regarding this development, specifically whether the court is able to act quickly enough to resolve banks and especially major ones, such as Lehman Brothers (see *Global Restructuring Review*, 'Chapter 11 Update Makes Bank Resolution in Court "Credible", but Doubts Linger' (21 April 2017); see also JN Gordon, et al, 'Financial Scholars Oppose Eliminating "Orderly Liquidation Authority" As Crisis-Avoidance Restructuring Backstop' 5 (23 May 2017 letter to Congress) <https://www.law.columbia.edu/sites/default/files/microsites/law-economics-studies/scholars_letter_on_ola_-_final_for_congress.pdf>).

[142] See Chapter 1, section 1.3.2.

[143] Bork, *Principles of Cross-Border Insolvency* (n 95) 242. Standard-setting IOs have also emphasized that deficiencies in legal systems are an obstacle to the effectiveness of cross-border insolvency and resolution. The MLCBI Guide to Enactment and Interpretation (GEI), for example, notes that 'national insolvency laws . . . are often ill-equipped to deal with cases of a cross-border nature. This frequently results in inadequate and inharmonious legal approaches, which hamper the rescue of financially troubled businesses, are not conducive to fair and efficient administration of cross-border insolvencies, impede the protection of assets of the insolvent debtor against dissipation and hinder maximization of value of those assets' (MLCBI GEI, 20–21). The Key Attributes state that 'in order to facilitate the coordinated resolution of firms active in multiple countries, jurisdictions should seek convergence of their resolution regimes through the legislative changes needed to incorporate the tools and powers set out in these Key Attributes into their national regime' (Key Attributes, 4).

ex post efficiency.[144] The harmonization of laws may also reduce, or even eliminate the need to forum shop for better systems; if forum movements continue, such harmonization may ensure that they are not abusive.[145] Harmonization may eventually create a single substantive law that would get closer to pure universalism.[146] However, this packaged argument in favour of harmonization, as it may be linked to the advancement of the cross-border insolvency system, requires unpacking. It encompasses different possible policy motivations, some more realistic than others or entailing lower or higher (economic and behavioural) costs. Indeed, instead of wholesale harmonization, it is suggested in this section that enhancing compliance depends on continuing the targeted efforts at standardization, and the development of tools for complex cross-border insolvency scenarios.

5.3.2.1 Harmonization and pure universalism

Universalism in its pure form envisages a single forum applying a single insolvency law, possibly a supranational legal system. A key critique of pure universalism is that it relies on the convergence of laws, which might be unrealistic. Universalists in turn have argued that convergence in insolvency can be expected over time.[147] One possible way in which to accelerate such a process would be to pursue 'top-down' harmonization actively.[148]

The argument that harmonization should be pursued to purify the global cross-border insolvency regime seems to have influenced harmonization efforts in Europe. In 2016, the European Commission put forward a proposal for a Directive on insolvency and restructuring (EU proposal for a Directive on preventive restructuring),[149]

---

[144] Reducing the cost of credit as well as of insolvency proceedings (Bork, *Principles of Cross-Border Insolvency* (n 95) 238–41). See also in the context of the EU Capital Markets Union Action Plan, the argument that 'convergence of insolvency and restructuring proceedings would facilitate greater legal certainty for cross-border investors and encourage the timely restructuring of viable companies in financial distress' European Commission, Action Plan on Building a Capital Markets Union, COM(2015) 468 final, 30 September 2015, 24 <http://eur-lex.europa.eu/legal-content/EN/TXT/PDF/?uri=CELEX:5 2015DC0468&from=EN>). The MLCBI GEI notes in regard to dealing with cases of a cross-border nature that 'the absence of predictability in the handling of cross-border insolvency can impede capital flow and be a disincentive to cross-border investment … ' (MLCBI GEI, 21).

[145] See eg the arguments in favour of harmonization of insolvency laws in Europe in Eidenmüller and van Zwieten, 'Restructuring the European Business Enterprise' (n 115). See also INSOL Europe (2010), *Harmonisation of insolvency law at EU level*, European Parliament, Directorate General for Internal Policies, Policy Department C: Citizens' Rights and Constitutional Affairs, Legal Affairs, PE 419.633 <http://www.eesc.europa.eu/sites/default/files/resources/docs/ipol-juri_nt2010419633_ en.pdf> (the report identified numerous differences in restructuring laws across the EU which arguably have produced an uneven playing field, incentivized forum shopping, and acted as a barrier to the adoption of restructuring plans in cross-border cases).

[146] JL Westbrook, 'A Global Solution to Multinational Default' (2000) 98 Mich L Rev 2276, 2294. See also Bork, *Principles of Cross-Border Insolvency* (n 95) 242.

[147] Westbrook, 'A Global Solution to Multinational Default' (n 146) 2288 ff. See also Chapter 1, sections 1.2.1 and 1.3.1.

[148] As opposed to spontaneous convergence ('bottom-up' harmonization).

[149] European Commission, 'Proposal for a Directive of the European Parliament and of the Council on preventive restructuring frameworks, second chance and measures to increase the efficiency of restructuring, insolvency and discharge procedures and amending Directive 2012/30/EU' COM(2016)

attempting to harmonize some of the aspects of insolvency law in Europe, focusing mainly on pre-insolvency restructuring. The main proclaimed objective of this initiative was to address barriers to the free flow of capital that result from differences between national laws and procedures on preventive restructuring, insolvency, and second chance.[150] This initiative seemed, however, to be at least partially motivated by frustration about the limited universalism thus far achieved through the insolvency regulation applicable in the EU, including after its revision and recast. Since the EU Convention on cross-border insolvency of 1995, and through the EIR to the Recast EIR, mitigated universality has been the model adopted.[151] During the global crisis—despite the existence of frameworks that generally follow a universalist approach—several large cross-border insolvency cases were in fact handled within territorial borders, often without sufficient cooperation.[152] Countries seem prone to self-interested driven action, it has been noted.[153] Additional anti-cooperation incentives including negative forum shopping, national sovereignty, and different philosophies are also embraced by different countries, specifically those more universally or otherwise more territorially oriented and those more market- or community-oriented. Thus, a harmonization initiative seemed necessary.[154]

Regional harmonization must be distinguished from global harmonization, as there may already be high levels of similarity between laws regionally as well as the existence of a common market, a common currency, and relevant institutions. Still, the pursuance of pure universalism as an objective is problematic generally, within regions and globally.[155] The argument that harmonization should be pursued to make a cross-border insolvency regime fully universalist assumes that modified universalism is an interim approach. However, as argued earlier, the final objective of a cross-border insolvency system should not be pure universalism, but rather promoting a universal and consistent application of a system based on modified universalism. That system fits with the diversity of business structures and the size of the market, which requires more nuanced solutions (in regions as well).[156] Harmonization cannot be justified, therefore, by pointing to pure universalism as the goal. Still, the question is whether harmonization is important for strengthening a system based on *modified* universalism.

---

723 final <http://ec.europa.eu/information_society/newsroom/image/document/2016-48/proposal_40046.pdf>.

[150] ibid Recital 1. See also European Commission, Action Plan on Building a Capital Markets Union, COM(2015) 468 final, 30 September 2015, 25 http://eur-lex.europa.eu/legal-content/EN/TXT/PDF/?uri=CELEX:52015DC0468&from=EN.

[151] O Vondracek, European Commission (DG Justice & Consumers), EU Insolvency Initiative, presentation at the Insolvency Law Association (ILA) Academic Forum and Annual Conference (March 2016) (on file with author). See also Eidenmüller and van Zwieten, 'Restructuring the European Business Enterprise' (n 115) 629 (pointing to the shortcomings of the EIR regime, and noting that, against that backdrop, the European Parliament tasked the European Commission in 2012 with investigating the merits of harmonization of some aspects of member states' insolvency and/or restructuring regimes).

[152] See Chapter 1, section 1.4.5.

[153] Vondracek, presentation at the Insolvency Law Association (ILA) Academic Forum and Annual Conference (n 151).

[154] ibid.   [155] See Chapter 1, section 1.3.1.   [156] ibid section 1.3.2.

5.3.2.2 *Justifications based on efficiency and trust*

In principle, people may place higher trust in a system with which they are familiar (ie if it is like their own).[157] Thus, trust may be enhanced if legal systems are similar, even if they are not as effective. Certainty and consequently predictability and efficiency regarding the applicable law may also be increased by harmonization. It is obviously easier to rely on one than on multiple laws.[158]

However, the possibility of achieving such full convergence that will result in a *de facto* single legal system is likely only to the extent that countries believe that such single law will benefit their legal regimes beyond the benefit that may ensue for the global insolvency system. Otherwise, a country subject to a harmonization process of substantive laws may only minimally comply with it while retaining much of the local contexts, resulting in significant differences remaining between systems. This has even been the experience regionally to some extent, for example with regard to the ambitious EU company law harmonization programme.[159] Regarding the EU insolvency harmonization initiative, it has been noted that at the stage where the EU Commission proposed recommendations on preventive restructurings,[160] some member states did not even react to its initiative, which led to the proposal for a Directive on preventive restructuring.[161] Generally, where harmonization is pursued via flexible instruments, participants may cherry pick and implement recommendations in different ways.[162] To reach the true harmonization of substantive laws, hard law such as directly applicable regulations or, at the global level, model provisions aimed at identical implementation may be needed.[163] The harmonization must also be sufficiently comprehensive.[164]

---

[157] See also Bork, *Principles of Cross-Border Insolvency* (n 95) 242.

[158] In the context of the EU harmonization initiative, the Action Plan noted that 'convergence of insolvency and restructuring proceedings would facilitate greater legal certainty for cross-border investors and encourage the timely restructuring of viable companies in financial distress. Consultation respondents broadly agreed that both the inefficiency and divergence of insolvency laws make it harder for investors to assess credit risk, particularly in cross-border investments' (European Commission, Action Plan on Building a Capital Markets Union, COM(2015) 468 final (30 September 2015) 24 <http://eur-lex.europa.eu/legal-content/EN/TXT/PDF/?uri=CELEX:52015DC0468&from=EN>).

[159] See eg J Rickford, 'Legal approaches to restricting distributions to shareholders: balance sheet tests and solvency tests' (2006) 7(1) EBOR 136, 179 ('perhaps as one who negotiated the Second and Fourth Directives on behalf of the United Kingdom and had a hand in their implementation, I may be allowed to end by reflecting that the history of this topic illustrates the naiveté of ambitious harmonizers (including myself) and the dangers of imposing detailed and rigid solutions which will fail to meet the test of changing times ... ').

[160] European Commission, Recommendation of 12 March 2014 on a new approach to business failure and insolvency, COM(2014) 1500 final <http://ec.europa.eu/justice/civil/files/c_2014_1500_en.pdf>.

[161] Eidenmüller and van Zwieten, 'Restructuring the European Business Enterprise' (n 115) 665 (noting that: 'It appears that the inclination of Member States to accept this invitation has not been strong (to put it mildly)—large Member States such as the UK, France, Germany and Italy[] in particular have not reacted at all to the European Commission's initiative' (footnote omitted)).

[162] See Chapter 4, section 4.4.1.

[163] See in the context of the EU harmonization initiative, H Eidenmüller, 'Contracting For a European Insolvency Regime' University of Oxford and ECGI, Law Working Paper No 341/2017.

[164] ibid. See also Eidenmüller and van Zwieten, 'Restructuring the European Business Enterprise' (n 115) 652 (noting with regard to the EU initiative that 'had the European Commission really aimed

Such hard harmonization is risky, however, where it might affect the ability of countries to develop their systems further, especially where harmonized rules represent compromises. That the harmonization of laws generally entails significant risks has been highlighted by economic analyses of the law. Thus, harmonization might constrain constructive competition that could otherwise lead to improvements in domestic regimes.[165] Top-down harmonization that imposes template solutions or requirements might prevent innovation and result in the stagnation of legal systems, which might become inflexible as a result and unresponsive to changing market conditions.[166] Such stagnation is particularly problematic when it affects all insolvency cases, not only cross-border insolvencies, and where it implicates various laws related to insolvency (not only insolvency laws), depending on the extent of the harmonization project.

Importantly, the development of restructuring and resolution processes is an area of constant evolution.[167] Insolvency and restructuring procedures often develop by adjusting to changing market conditions.[168] In such experimentation and development processes, legal systems may learn from and compete with each other, resulting in a degree of convergence.[169] Yet, when not bound by mandatory harmonization, domestic systems are not locked in a state of uniformity. Thus, countries can continue to develop insolvency solutions, including learning lessons from other countries' experiences.

Reinforcing these economic concerns, behavioural perspectives may also caution about the possible results of hard, comprehensive harmonization projects. Thus, efforts to harmonize insolvency laws might face significant sovereignty costs and concerns, intensified by decision-making bounds, including status quo bias, loss aversion, and the endowment effect.[170] Countries are likely to be averse to losing control over law-making and it may be predicted that they would view the existing

---

to take significant step towards harmonisation, it would have had to regulate on many more of the issues raised by pre-insolvency company restructurings, and in more depth').

[165] See eg RK Winter, 'State Law, Shareholder Protection, and the Theory of the Corporation' (1977) 6 J Legal Stud 251, 291–92; DR Fischel, 'The "Race to the Bottom" Revisited: Reflections on Recent Developments in Delaware's Corporate Law' (1982) 76 Nw U L Rev 913, 922; FH Easterbrook, 'The Race for the Bottom in Corporate Governance' (2009) 95 Va L Rev 685, 688; Eidenmüller, 'Contracting For a European Insolvency Regime' (n 163).

[166] See also in the context of the EU company law harmonization programme, L Enriques and M Gatti, 'The Uneasy Case for Top-Down Corporate Law Harmonization in the European Union' (2006) 27 U Pa J Intl Econ L 939, 973, 976.

[167] See eg the development of a range of restructuring mechanisms in legal systems in recent years, or the various tools developed for the resolution of financial institutions, such as the single point of entry (SPOE) strategy (see Chapter 1, n 103).

[168] See, for example, the effect of developments in the finance market on the evolution of insolvency procedures in the United Kingdom and the United States that have driven these regimes to meet 'somewhere in the middle' (S Paterson, 'Rethinking Corporate Bankruptcy Theory in the Twenty-First Century' (2016) 36(4) OJLS 697, 702, referring to G McCormack, 'Control and Corporate Rescue—An Anglo-American Evaluation' (2007) 56(3) Intl Comp LQ 515, 516; M Harner, 'The Corporate Governance and Public Policy Implications of Activist Distressed Debt Investing' (2008) 77 Fordham L Rev 703, 757–58).

[169] See, in particular, the movement towards reorganization-oriented regimes across legal systems in recent decades (Chapter 1, section 1.2.3.3).

[170] See Chapter 2, sections 2.3.1–2.3.3.

state of their endowment as the reference point.[171] Attempts to reach a uniform approach run the risk of resulting either in low common denominators or in the limited implementation of the uniform rules.[172] Simultaneously, countries may also have rational reasons to prefer certain rules over others to promote differing policies including moral judgments in the shaping of their domestic regimes.[173] Therefore, where a cross-border insolvency framework attempts to harmonize substantive laws comprehensively, it can attract greater resistance and ultimately less compliance with the core cross-border insolvency norms.

As noted earlier, the institutional setting in certain regions may allow for the formulation of rules by the region's institutions and the direct applicability of the rules to the domestic systems, significantly overcoming the consent problem that could otherwise undermine uniformity.[174] Instruments such as directives, however, may provide more room for manoeuvring in the implementation process, which may result in important differences.[175] Even directly applicable regulation requires a negotiation process that may entail substantial compromises. Although negotiators may be less affected by biases compared with ratifiers or implementing institutions,[176] they are still unlikely to be free from bounds on decision-making and from the inclination to stick to a certain current position, especially when negotiating a hard harmonization instrument that will be binding and will provide little room for local deviation.

Relatedly, constraints on innovation might also undermine the use of forum shopping as a compliance tool. It was argued above that forum shifts can address capacity gaps. Forum shopping can also be conceptualized as a measure for exploiting and maximizing innovation across borders. The practice has shown that the stakeholders of distressed debtors often benefit from forum shifts not only by overcoming capacity gaps, but also when another forum has provided a more flexible restructuring regime that could maximize value.[177] However, when development is constrained by harmonization, the (good) forum-shopping tool is undermined, too.

---

[171] T Broude, 'Behavioral International Law' (2015) 163 U Pa L Rev 1099, 1140.

[172] See also in the context of the EU Company law harmonization programme, Enriques and Gatti, 'The Uneasy Case for Top-Down Corporate Law Harmonization' (n 166) 954–55.

[173] See also AM Kipnis, 'Beyond UNCITRAL: Alternatives to Universality in Transnational Insolvency' (2008) 36 Denv J Intl L & Poly 155, 180 (noting the rich diversity of policy choices on the global scale that are likely to prevent any consensus with respect to substantive law).

[174] See Chapter 4, section 4.4.1.   [175] ibid section 4.4.1.   [176] ibid section 4.5.

[177] See, for example, the successful attempt of the electronic company Z-Obee Holding to replace proceedings in Hong Kong with a provisional liquidation process in Bermuda. The appointment in Bermuda was approved on 17 February 2017 (*In re Z-Obee Holdings*). Justice Kawaley of the Supreme Court of Bermuda explained that the purpose of initiating Bermudian proceedings was that Bermuda's provisional liquidation mechanism can be used for restructuring purposes, whereas Hong Kong's is used only for liquidation. Lilla Zuill, who acted for Z-Obee in Bermuda told the magazine *Global Restructuring Review* that the move meant that the company was 'able to avail itself of Bermuda's more flexible restructuring regime to avoid a restructuring being derailed by Hong Kong's lack of modern restructuring law' (*Global Restructuring Review*, 'Electronics Group Swaps Hong Kong for Bermuda's "More Flexible" Regime' (24 February 2017)). There have been many other such cases of forum shifts for the purpose of benefiting from various procedures that can benefit the stakeholders as a whole, eg: *Re Indah Kiat International Finance Company BV* [2016] EWHC 246; *Re Apcoa Parking Holdings GmbH* [2014] EWHC 3849 (Ch); *Re AI Scheme Limited* [2015] EWHC 1233 (Ch); *Re Codere* [2015] EWHC 3778 (Ch); *PIN Group SA* (Amtsgericht Köln, 19 February) (73 IE 1-08); *Gallery Capital SA v In the*

It has been argued that forum shifts for insolvency purposes are in any event unfair because only the larger debtors can attempt a shift, while smaller entities are unlikely to be able to exploit this opportunity.[178] Further, contrary arguments have been put forward, as it has been noted that small firms have also managed to access foreign insolvency and restructuring proceedings either by shifting their economic centre or by making use of foreign procedures that are not within the scope of cross-border insolvency frameworks.[179] Whatever the case may be, even if forum shopping is available for some debtors more than for others, it is still an important tool. Even if it is used in a subset of cases of large debtors, it can benefit many groups of stakeholders affected by such large collapses. Indeed, this tool should be available and accepted when a shift benefits the general body of stakeholders, not the debtor or certain creditors at the expense of others.[180]

In contrast, forum shopping that is abusive should be constrained, including self-serving shifts where the debtor or influential creditors may attempt to move to a forum that is favourable to them at the expense of the general body of creditors. Such forum shopping would breach the norms of modified universalism, which are premised on global collectivism for the benefit of all stakeholders wherever located. A typical example is where a debtor attempts to change the insolvency forum to avoid a directors' liabilities regime and where the new regime is lax (compared with the Insolvency Standard).[181] Competition on directors' liability rules and other measures that aim to protect creditors or certain constituencies thereof (especially the weaker stakeholders), such as avoidance laws, directors' duties, and special priorities, is less akin to constructive competition.[182] These aspects of the insolvency regime also

Matter of Gallery Media Group Ltd (2010) WL 4777509. See also the Singapore High Court's decision in *Pacific Andes Resources Development Ltd* [2016] SGHC 2010 (where Kannan JC noted the benefits of what he called 'good forum shopping'); R Kannan, 'The Gibbs Principle: A Tether on the Feet of Good Forum Shopping' (2017) 29 Singapore Academy of Law Journal 42.

[178] Eidenmüller and van Zwieten, 'Restructuring the European Business Enterprise' (n 115) 633 (referring to the INSOL Europe Report (n 145) that found that disparities between the laws of member states were a source of competitive disadvantage and of forum shopping for those able to engage in forum shifts to overcome this disadvantage).

[179] Eidenmüller, 'Contracting for a European Insolvency Regime' (n 163) 27 (noting in particular the use of the UK Scheme of Arrangement to restructure foreign small and medium enterprises). See also J Payne, 'Cross-border Schemes of Arrangement and Forum Shopping' (2013) 14 EBOR 563, 586–88.

[180] See the comments by Mr Justice Newey in *Codere Finance (UK) Limited* [2015] EWHC 3778 (Ch) para 8: 'Plainly forum shopping can be undesirable. That can potentially be so, for example, where a debtor seeks to move his COMI with a view to taking advantage of a more favourable bankruptcy regime and so escaping his debts. In cases such as the present, however, what is being attempted is to achieve a position where resort can be had to the law of a particular jurisdiction, not in order to evade debts but rather with a view to achieving the best possible outcome for creditors. If in those circumstances it is appropriate to speak of forum shopping at all, it must be on the basis that there can sometimes be good forum shopping'.

[181] Mevorach, 'Forum Shopping at Times of Crisis' (n 109) 531–32. See also Eidenmüller, 'Abuse of Law in the Context of European Insolvency Law' (n 110) 11.

[182] LA Bebchuk, 'The Debate on Contractual Freedom in Corporate Law, Forward to Symposium, Contractual Freedom in Corporate Law' (1989) 89 Colum L Rev 1395, 1405–06; FH Easterbrook and DR Fischel, 'The Corporate Contract' 89 Colum L Rev 1416, 1436–42; Mevorach, 'Forum Shopping at Times of Crisis' (n 109) 548–49. See also Westbrook, 'A Global Solution to Multinational Default' (n 146) 2293–94 (noting the important benefits of similarity in priority and avoidance rules which can

require less innovation and they generally tend to be more stable. Thus, regarding such rules, harmonization is more important and less risky. Yet, even here, caution is merited where the harmonization process may result in rules that are either too rigid or too relaxed, taking account of the difficulties in reaching agreements and changing the status quo in legal systems.[183]

Therefore, while in theory trust, certainty, and efficiency could be enhanced by creating a uniform insolvency law, in reality only a limited degree of uniformity may be achieved, especially at the global level. Attempting a hard, top-down harmonization is also a threat to innovation. It might therefore weaken rather than increase compliance with the cross-border insolvency system.

5.3.2.3 Development of legal systems through standardization

The operationalization of and compliance with modified universalism require that legal systems possess certain processes of sufficient quality and effectiveness where cross-border cases are handled in domestic forums and pursuant to domestic laws. It may be recalled that the modified universalism rule of centralization dictates that the law of the forum that presides over the cross-border case usually applies.[184] That forum should be able to address the cross-border case and, to be able to do this, it should contain certain effective laws and procedures for insolvency cases.

The reality, however, is that legal systems differ in terms of their insolvency laws and the level of their development and effectiveness, which means that some systems are more capable than others to address insolvency cases effectively. Still, the centralization of the law and forum under modified universalism addresses the problem of the possible deficiencies in substantive domestic laws to some extent, where only some jurisdictions, the home forums that preside over the centralized process, may need to have the tools to handle the case. Other systems may only need to play an ancillary role. The home forum would tend to be in key jurisdictions where multinationals base their headquarters, and such jurisdictions are often the more developed in terms of their insolvency systems. Where this is not the case, a different insolvency forum, and laws, may be chosen by the debtor or main creditors through forum shopping.

The ability to select a forum, while important as a compliance tool, entails limitations, in terms of costs and other considerations about the location of the debtor.[185] Furthermore, modified universalism accommodates business structures that may require a more decentralized approach. Thus, more than one set of laws may be applied, for example, in certain circumstances where a decentralized group

---

promote equality among stakeholders and predictability concerning protections across borders), and Bork, *Principles of Cross-Border Insolvency* (n 95) 243 (noting the importance of the principle of equal treatment of creditors).

[183] Furthermore, protective measures too must fit with systems' institution and culture to function effectively. Doubts have also been expressed about the ability of top-down rules, for example through EU harmonization initiatives, to adequately take into account and protect the interests of weak creditors (Enriques and Gatti, 'The Uneasy Case for Top-Down Corporate Law Harmonization' (n 166) 951).

[184] See Chapter 1, section 1.3.2.2.   [185] See section 5.3.1.

faces insolvency.[186] This means that that to prevent destruction of value, jurisdictions other than those that are the home of multinationals need effective laws that can address the aspects of a multinational enterprise affecting stakeholders both within and outside that jurisdiction. Additionally, even when playing an ancillary role, host jurisdictions may need to enforce judgments of the main forum or provide relief that requires taking certain actions locally.[187]

Closing regulatory gaps is, therefore, important for the cross-border insolvency system to function well; yet, this may not depend on harmonization, which aims at uniformity across legal systems. When systems lag behind, as their laws are deficient or as important processes for insolvency are not available, the problem can be resolved by addressing these gaps within the legal system without interfering with the laws and processes of other more developed regimes. Domestic systems may address such issues through their internal mechanisms, thereby learning from and being influenced by developments in other systems,[188] or they may be assisted by the guidance of international standards containing recommendations on best practices.[189] Many countries have undergone reform and modernization in their insolvency systems in recent years.[190] In developing regimes, external assistance in the implementation of best practices is often required (see the discussion about capacity building and assistance by IOs in section 5.3.1). Such developmental efforts are important, and their aims reach beyond cross-border insolvency.[191]

In any event, the development of legal systems requires a focused effort in those countries that need to advance their laws. Development is not dependent on similarities of laws across systems, however. Instead, the development of legal systems is based on conformity with best practice standards (ie standardization). Certainly, such standards themselves are extracted from the experiences of legal systems, often the more developed regimes; yet, they may not be identical to any given legal regime and may not require that laws are implemented in an identical manner. In fact, it is

---

[186] See Chapter 1, section 1.3.2.2.   [187] ibid section 1.3.2.3.

[188] Spontaneous convergence takes place through various levels of imitation where more advanced systems influence other legal systems that require modernization.

[189] As noted earlier, the purpose of instruments providing standards, recommendations, high-level principles or key attributes is usually development and modernization of laws (see Chapter 4, section 4.4.1).

[190] Eidenmüller and van Zwieten, 'Restructuring the European Business Enterprise' (n 115) 627 (noting such developments around the world and explaining that these have been at least partly fuelled by regulatory competition). Specifically, in Europe, countries have developed procedures to compete with the United Kingdom's scheme of arrangement. For example, Germany reformed its restructuring regime in 2012 (Eidenmüller and van Zwieten, 'Restructuring the European Business Enterprise' (n 115) 627); Spain introduced the 'homologated refinancing agreements' in 2015 (I Tirado, 'Out of Courts Debt Restructuring in Spain. A Modernised Framework' (on file with author)); A Dutch draft bill was published on 5 September 2017 which seeks to introduce pre-insolvency proceedings in the Netherlands (see Amendment to the Bankruptcy Act in connection with the introduction of the possibility to confirm a private restructuring plan in order to prevent bankruptcy (Act on the confirmation of a private restructuring plan in order to prevent bankruptcy, unofficial English translation), <http://www.resor.nl/eventbanner/RESOR_Amendment_to_the_Bankruptcy_Act.pdf>).

[191] An important motivation is addressing a financial crisis and specifically high levels of non-performing loans (NPLs). This was indeed another reason for the EU harmonization initiative (see Recital 2 of the EU proposal for a Directive on preventive restructuring).

important that standards on insolvency are implemented in a way that fits the general legal system and that the laws ensuing from the reform are integrated with other related laws and procedures.[192] Such has been the thrust of the work on standardizing, benchmarking, assessing, and implementing standards related to insolvency laws by key IOs. The World Bank Principles, which, together with the Legislative Guide, form the Insolvency Standard,[193] proclaims that:

First, effective systems respond to national needs and problems. As such, these systems must be rooted in the country's broader cultural, economic, legal, and social context … This calls for an integrated approach to reform, taking into account a wide range of laws and policies in the design of creditor/debtor regimes and insolvency systems. …. Adapting international best practices to the realities of countries requires an understanding of the market environments in which these systems operate …The Principles are designed to be flexible in their application and do not offer detailed prescriptions for national systems … [194]

Regarding certain countries, particularly neighbouring states within a region that exhibit similar developmental problems, uniform substantive laws related to insolvency and the commercial system generally are likely to be beneficial. A uniform effort to develop the laws can be more efficient and less costly in such cases, as countries with relatively limited resources and experiences can profit from economies of scale in law-making. Uniformity can also make an entire region more attractive to foreign investors. A typical example of a successful effort of this sort is the harmonization of business law, including insolvency, through the Organization for the Harmonization of Business Law in Africa (OHADA). That organization was created with the aim of fostering economic development in West and Central Africa.[195] By harmonizing commercial laws and systems throughout the region, the organization aims to attract foreign investment and improve the economies of its members.[196]

---

[192] See also M Balz, 'The European Union Convention on Insolvency Proceedings' (1996) 70 Am Bankr L J 485, 486 (noting the character of insolvency as a 'meta-law' which modifies or supersedes practically all other branches of national legal systems and is intertwined with many types of local substantive law such as real estate law, the law of secured credit, tax law, and labour law).

[193] See Chapter 1, section 1.4.4.

[194] World Bank Principles, 1–2. The first general principle on insolvency follows this approach and states that 'though country approaches vary, effective insolvency systems should aim to: (i) Integrate with a country's broader legal and commercial systems'. See also Legislative Guide, 1 (which states that its purpose is 'to assist the establishment of an efficient and effective legal framework to address the financial difficulty of debtors. It is intended to be used as a reference by national authorities and legislative bodies when preparing new laws and regulations or reviewing the adequacy of existing laws and regulations'). In the context of MFIs, see International Monetary Fund, 'Cross-Border Bank Resolution: Recent Developments' (2 June 2014) 21 ('Reforms to enhance resolution regimes should be tailored to the complexity of financial systems in different jurisdictions').

[195] To date it is made up of seventeen African countries.

[196] See eg C Manga Fombad, 'Some Reflections on the Prospects for the Harmonization of International Business Laws in Africa: OHADA and Beyond' (2013) 59 Africa Today 50; B Fagbayibo, 'Towards the Harmonisation of Laws in Africa: Is OHADA the Way to Go?' (2009) 42 Comparative and International Law Journal of Southern Africa 309; A Menezes and W Paterson, 'One Insolvency Law, Seventeen Countries: A Brief Overview of the Revised OHADA Uniform Act on Insolvency' (2016) 1 INSOL World 28. See also on the possible lessons for other regions facing similar challenges, eg the Southern Africa Development Community (SADC), ND Leno, 'Development of a Uniform Insolvency Law in SADC: Lessons from OHADA' (2013) 57 J African L 259.

However, wholesale harmonization that reaches all countries cannot be justified by an alleged need for development.[197]

5.3.2.4 Effect of standardization on the use of safeguards

In addition to the focused development of insolvency laws in specific legal systems, the bridging of gaps to support cross-border insolvency also requires certain standards to apply across all legal systems, particularly such standards that concern the fair treatment of stakeholders. The universal application of such standards is important because they promote a consistent and minimal application of modified universalism's safeguards concerning fairness, non-discrimination, and due process ('public policy' issues) that allow participants to deny assistance and cooperation.[198]

Minimizing the use of safeguards can promote compliance. Yet, again, what it requires is limited harmonization in the form of standardization of stakeholder protections, rather than uniformity of laws. Standardization may be through instruments that include recommendations, principles, or international best practices that help all legal systems when they seek reform and modernization.[199] Using such soft law mechanisms can induce adherence to the standards when instruments do not require a cumbersome adoption process, do not pose a significant threat to state sovereignty, and allow countries to retain significant control over law-making.[200] Still, standards concerning the fair treatment of stakeholders should be based on widely recognized principles concerning equality, justice, and due process. The recognized international law source of the 'general principles of law recognized by civilized nations'[201] can then bridge any remaining gaps in the system,[202] and apply universally without the need for the active adoption of norms.[203]

Such standardization supports the operation of modified universalism norms where courts or other bodies can assess the fairness of foreign systems based on universal standards and high-level principles. Because such standards and principles are broad, they do not pose the risk that countries will easily reject recognition or deny relief to foreign proceedings every time a foreign system does not employ the exact

---

[197] cf the harmonization initiative in Europe which seems to have been at least partly fuelled by development concerns (the Action Plan that announced in 2015 the forthcoming legislative initiative and its rationale noted the low scoring of certain member states in the World Bank Doing Business Report (see n 35)).

[198] See Chapter 1, section 1.3.2.4.

[199] See generally on the use of standards in legislation and law-making, R Tomasic, 'The Sociology of Legislation' in R Tomasic (ed), *Legislation and Society in Australia* (Allen & Unwin, Sydney 1980). See also TC Halliday and BG Carruthers, 'The Recursivity of Law: Global Norm Making and National Lawmaking in the Globalization of Corporate Insolvency Regimes' (2007) 112 AJS 1135.

[200] See Chapter 4, sections 4.3.3 and 4.3.4.   [201] See Chapter 3, sections 3.2.2.

[202] It was suggested earlier that general principles as an international law source can fill gaps left in the international sub-system of cross-border insolvency, specifically where fundamental standards of reasonableness, fairness, natural justice, and good faith can be recognized. Identifying the general practice of countries is not required. See Chapter 3, sections 3.2.2 and 3.2.6. See also Bork, *Principles of Cross-Border Insolvency* (n 95) 19–20 (proposing that harmonization can be enhanced by what he calls a 'principles-based approach').

[203] See Chapter 3, section 3.3.1.

same process.[204] At the same time, applying safeguards by reference to international standards reduces the risk of self-serving interpretation of safeguards based on different reference points and understandings of what is fair. Standard-setting as well as monitoring and assisting in compliance with standards can promote a level playing field in the way in which stakeholders are protected under insolvency regimes. The result can then be that safeguards are applied sparingly in rare cases and coordination in cross-border insolvency increases.

5.3.2.5 *Tools for complex cross-border insolvencies*

Finally, targeted harmonization as a compliance tool can ensure that certain measures are available in domestic systems to support the cross-border insolvency framework; these may not emerge 'bottom-up' in domestic systems or through spontaneous convergence at given points in time. It was already noted in section 5.3.2.3 that for the cross-border insolvency system based on modified universalism to function and for countries and implementing institutions to be able to comply (effectively host main, or ancillary, proceedings), legal systems that have functional insolvency laws and processes are necessary. It was suggested that in order not to curtail innovation and to ensure that laws are integrated with the local system, regulatory gaps should be bridged through targeted standardization in specific countries.

However, regarding certain entity structures, especially those of a significant size, tools may not emerge sufficiently quickly and reach many domestic legal systems where the insolvency of such entities may be less frequent and the case itself may be more spread across systems, slowing the emergence of centralized solutions. The result may perpetually constrain the ability to address the cross-border insolvency of such enterprises effectively and coordinate across borders. Expectedly, domestic systems, and not only those in developing regimes, may lack sufficient tools to address the more complex and sophisticated business structures (known to date or that may emerge in the future) such as enterprise groups, as well as the more complicated insolvency scenarios (eg when it is required to stabilize a distressed MFI).[205] Enabling such enterprises to achieve insolvency objectives requires deliberations at the international level and broader harmonization across all systems, although that is confined to providing minimum uniform tools, thereby allowing domestic systems to continue to develop additional mechanisms.[206]

---

[204] See also Bork, *Principles of Cross-Border Insolvency* (n 95) 41 (noting regarding the principle of mutual trust that it should not refer to 'an ideal that the proceedings will be identical, but must rather concern the idea that such proceedings will be fair and in accordance with the rule of law').

[205] See also E Hüpkes, 'Allocating Costs of Failure Resolution' in RM Lastra (ed), *Cross-Border Bank Insolvency* (OUP 2011) 124 (noting that: 'It is hardly realistic to expect to put in place a supranational regime or achieve a full harmonization of all national bank resolution frameworks. However, convergence in a few critical areas could help enhance predictability and consistency of the treatment of counterparties in a resolution and also the prospects of achieving a coordinated solution across borders': referring to the Basel Committee on Banking Supervision, 'Report and Recommendations of the Cross-Border Bank Resolution Group' (March 2010), Recommendation 1).

[206] See eg the development of tools such as procedural and substantive consolidation for enterprise groups by UNCITRAL at times when such mechanisms were generally absent in legal systems (Legislative Guide, Pt three) and the resolution tools provided in the Key Attributes, s 3. See further on

5.3.3 Delegation to international bodies

Thus far, the existing global framework has been operating without a centralized international authority; however, in certain regions, notably the EU, a degree of institutional supranationalism exists at the regional level.[207] Yet, the question of whether the global framework should aspire to create an international authority for addressing cross-border insolvencies is an open one, to some extent linked to the debate on a treaty for cross-border insolvency and to the general view of the interim nature of modified universalism.[208] Indeed, the establishment of a supranational bankruptcy court has been considered to be an ideal solution for achieving pure universalism.[209] Modified universalism, on the other hand, has attempted a more realistic approach as it is premised on centralizing proceedings within domestic forums as well as encouraging cooperation or coordination among domestic proceedings.[210] It was suggested that insolvency cases often require long-term supervision and the complex implementation of solutions, which may most efficiently take place in the territory in which the business has been active. Moreover, the variety of business structures operating across borders and the different insolvency solutions that may be pursued in different circumstances mean that directing all cross-border insolvency cases to international courts or other bodies might be unnecessary as well as impractical.[211]

From the perspective of compliance, however, delegation to external authorities may have certain important advantages. Compliance is undermined when the international system is largely decentralized and when it relies on domestic enforcement mechanisms. In addition, international actors may be affected by dominant biases that influence decisions and choices, including the tendency to interpret rules against different reference points as well as bounds on willpower and thus difficulties adhering to commitments and applying international agreements consistently. The discussion in the previous sections considered how to, nonetheless, incentivize compliance by reinforcing the effect of concerns about reputation and fostering mutual trust. It was also suggested that trust can be enhanced by bridging capacity gaps and addressing deficiencies in legal systems by capacity-building work and targeted harmonization.

Delegation to international bodies is an additional way in which to deal with institutional capacity gaps. Cross-border insolvency cases frequently raise difficult and complicated issues. Certain legal systems may struggle to deal effectively with insolvency matters, especially restructuring and resolution mechanisms, in addition to international complications. An external body comprising experts in the field of cross-border insolvency that may be given the task of addressing cross-border insolvency cases or issues arising during the proceeding may assist in alleviating capacity

---

the work of UNCITRAL and the FSB regarding cross-border insolvency of enterprise groups and MFIs in Chapter 6, sections 6.2.4 and 6.3.1–6.3.2.

[207] See the role of the Court of Justice of the European Union (CJEU) or the Single Resolution Mechanism (SRM) for the resolution of bank failures in Europe (Chapter 1, n 87 and accompanying text).

[208] See Chapter 4, section 4.2.3.   [209] See Chapter 1, section 1.2.1.

[210] ibid sections 1.3.2.1–1.3.2.4.   [211] ibid section 1.3.2.1.

problems and as a result also the need to forum shop for more efficient systems.[212] Forum shopping, even if it benefits the general body of stakeholders, could create a degree of distrust and hostility that might undermine the system.

The delegation of implementation functions to international bodies may also serve as a debiasing tool. Thus, when the participants of global frameworks agree to delegate authority to external institutions, they reduce the risk that compliance will be undermined by inconsistent interpretations of commitments where each legal system's institutions may adopt their own view of the meaning of the text (even when it is uniform) and its correct application. Assigning the implementation of the global framework to external bodies can make the commitment to the agreed norms more credible and less changeable, as well as reducing the effect of textual ambiguity and reference points that could otherwise lead to competing perceptions of what is fair[213] and to resorting to territorialism.

Delegation is a recognized mechanism for dealing with the problem of short-termism in governance contexts (as opposed to addressing individuals' bounded willpower where the classical technique is nudges to circumvent temptations[214]). One example is delegation to independent central banks to ensure that politicians cannot exploit monetary policy for their political benefit.[215] In the context of international relations, delegation may be to international institutions or tribunals.[216] The delegation of authority to international tribunals can also create a forum for non-consensual rule-making, mitigating the problem of consent that can impede the creation of welfare-enhancing norms at the international level. It was suggested in Chapter 4 that instruments that are less formal than treaties are advantageous as they may be formulated through processes based on broad consensus and through the assistance of IOs that facilitate negotiations and foster agreement.[217] Similarly, the decisions of international tribunals can be a means of creating international law, bypassing the need for consent. Such decisions may be influential and authoritative, affecting the understanding of international norms and the expectations of countries, even when decisions are only binding in the specific case and do not create formal precedents.[218] Economic analyses have also emphasized delegation

---

[212] See the discussion of the merits and problems of forum shopping in sections 5.3.1 and 5.3.2.2.

[213] van Aaken, 'Behavioral International Law and Economics' (n 6) 463. See also SK Schmidt et al, 'Internationalizing Law against the Odds: The Power of Courts and Their Limits' in H Rothgang and S Schneider (eds), *State Transformations in OECD Countries: dimensions, driving forces, and trajectories* (Palgrave Macmillan 2015).

[214] RH Thaler and C Sunstein, *Nudge: Improving Decisions about Health, Wealth and Happiness* (Penguin 2008), and Chapter 2 section 2.6.

[215] M Quintyn, 'Independent Agencies—More than a Cheap Copy of Independent Central Banks?' (2009) 20 Const Polit Econ 267.

[216] van Aaken, 'Behavioral International Law and Economics' (n 6) 432 (noting the example of the international human rights courts).

[217] Chapter 4, section 4.3.4.

[218] Guzman, 'Against Consent' (n 16) 784–87 (providing the example of the North American Free Trade Agreement's (NAFTA) investment chapter under which an investor can seek arbitration of a dispute, yet the decision is only binding between the disputing parties with respect to the particular case). See also generally AT Guzman and TL Meyer, 'International Common Law: The Soft Law of International Tribunals' (2009) 9 Chi J Intl L 515; H Thirlway, *The Sources of International Law* (OUP 2014) 121.

to enhance compliance. Specifically, the existence of IOs and dispute settlement mechanisms as part of an international framework (eg a treaty regime) may increase the reputational effects of non-compliance.[219] Such mechanisms have been used in various international contexts and subsystems, a notable example being the World Trade Organization (WTO), which is an IO with the authority to interpret laws, resolve disputes, and impose disciplinary measures.[220]

It has been suggested by the promoters of a treaty regime for cross-border insolvency that such an instrument choice would be particularly beneficial because a treaty may create dispute resolution mechanisms as a matter of state contract and can be used to establish an international bankruptcy court.[221] However, while delegation to external institutions may bridge capacity gaps and address other compliance constraints, including certain bounds on decision-making, there are also economic and behavioural *costs* to consider. The process of establishing an international institution as well as its maintenance incurs certain costs, although these may be minimized when such bodies may not necessarily operate through physical sessions but by virtual hearings. Importantly, however, delegation to external bodies might increase sovereignty costs significantly, as countries seem to be particularly resistant to the large-scale empowerment of international institutions.[222] As discussed in Chapter 4, countries are often reluctant to constrain their ability to address issues independently and make their own decisions.[223] Behavioural insights further reinforce the significance of sovereignty costs in view of loss aversion and the endowment effect.[224] While treaties are typically used to establish institutions and create dispute settlement mechanisms, such an attempt at delegation also often increases transaction and sovereign costs and makes participation in treaties less probable.[225]

Attempts at delegation might therefore risk compliance with the regime generally, and thus much like attempts at the harmonization of laws, delegation may be *targeted*. Furthermore, a delegation that entails the replacement of national authorities may not fit with the way in which international business operates and the

---

[219]   van Aaken, 'Behavioral International Law and Economics' (n 6) 432.

[220]   P Dumberry, 'Are BITs Representing the "New" Customary International Law in International Investment Law?' (2010) 28(4) Penn State International Law Review 675, 679. See also in another context, BC Matthews, 'Emerging Public International Banking Law? Lessons from the Law of the Sea Experience' (2010) 10 Chi J Intl L 539, 556–57 (noting the example of the codification of the law of the sea customary law into conventions allocating rights and responsibilities and creating dispute resolution standards).

[221]   Note by the IBA Insolvency Section Delegation to UNCITRAL Working Group V based on an article by Gregor Baer, Insolvency Section Co-Chair, published in *Business Law International* (January 2016): 'International Insolvency Convention: Issues, Options and Feasibility Considerations' (with the publisher's permission), paras 38 and 63 <https://www.ibanet.org/LPD/Insolvency_Section/Insolvency_Section/Projects.aspx#uninsolvencyconvention>. See also Matthews, 'Emerging Public International Banking Law?' (n 220) 556 (arguing that 'dispute avoidance and dispute resolution are key reasons for attempting the arduous process of negotiating an international agreement or treaty. It becomes unavoidable when cross-border enforcement issues start generating friction').

[222]   Guzman, 'Against Consent' (n 16) 785.   [223]   See Chapter 4, section 4.3.3.

[224]   ibid section 4.3.4.   [225]   ibid section 4.3.3.

various ways of addressing their default. Delegation is justified when it takes account of that reality and where it can enhance compliance without overcomplicating the cross-border insolvency system or increasing sovereignty concerns to the point where compliance is undermined.

Targeted delegation may therefore kick in if the case entails a certain complexity, conflict, or uncertainty, and thus an independent, impartial (less biased) interpretation of norms or texts can promote consistency in the application of international norms and instruments. Under such a regime, domestic courts are not replaced. Instead, they have the means to refer issues to an international body (much like the way in which the Court of Justice of the European Union (CJEU) functions in EU cross-border insolvencies), including questions about competing claims regarding jurisdiction, applicable law, recognition and enforcement, or the application of relief.[226] The international body would base its interpretive rulings on the norms set out in the applicable international instrument as well as of modified universalism. This form of delegation of disputes can then enhance the consistent interpretation of instruments such as model laws and avoid divergent interpretive tendencies over time.[227]

An international body to which certain implementation functions may be delegated would need to reflect the various legal traditions and cultures to maintain its legitimacy, and, importantly, representation in it should not be confined to the 'big and powerful' countries.[228] It may operate under the auspices of organizations such as UNCITRAL and the FSB that can maintain and foster continuous expertise and specialization in cross-border insolvency and resolution.[229] It may also include arbitration and mediation tools for resolving issues arising during a cross-border insolvency process[230] or for contemplating coordinated solutions based on recognized norms and the applicable framework to both increase the

---

[226] For example, in circumstances such as those arising in the *Rubin* case where it was not clear whether a foreign insolvency-related judgment emanating from the main forum should be enforced under the MLCBI (Chapter 1, n 282) or in *Nortel* where it was questionable whether a form of substantive consolidation should apply to the global group (Chapter 1, n 96).

[227] It would also contribute to the establishment, as well as the continued guarding and development, of CIL (see Chapter 3, section 3.6.1).

[228] I thank Ian Fletcher for this point.

[229] See also, in the context of proposals for a sovereign debt arbitration tribunal under the auspices of the UN, CG Paulus and ST Kargman, 'Reforming the Process of Sovereign Debt Restructuring: A Proposal for a Sovereign Debt Tribunal' (International Insolvency Institute, 2008) 6–7 <http://www.un.org/esa/ffd/wp-content/uploads/2008/10/20081010_KargmanPaulus_SovereignDebtTribunal.pdf>.

[230] Mediation is a negotiation process aimed at a consensual resolution while arbitration is an adjudicative process. It has been increasingly the case that mediation, at least in some jurisdictions, has been used to resolve complex issues including multi-party undertakings involving claimants from all levels of a debtor's capital structure; examples include the chapter 11 restructuring of Residential Capital, LLC and Cengage Learning, Inc. (see <http://www.bankruptcylawinsights.com/2015/09/energy-future-holdings-another-major-success-for-chapter-11-mediation/>). It is also increasingly recognized that arbitration can be useful and a legitimate way to resolve insolvency problems including cross-border insolvencies (see eg A Gropper, 'The Arbitration of Cross Border Insolvencies' (2012) 18 ABLJ 201).

system's efficiency[231] and to address the problems of local incapacity and institutional biases.[232]

The rulings of the international body may be binding and create precedents or their bindingness may be limited to the specific case.[233] In any event, the implementation of rulings and solutions is at the domestic level in the relevant jurisdictions and thus local bankruptcy tribunals and local enforcement mechanisms are not replaced. At the minimum, a committee of experts may be formed to perform certain interpretative or dispute settlement functions, although with powers limited to considering the case and making recommendations as well as ensuring adherence to norms consistently but not compelling compliance.[234] Such a committee could similarly operate under the auspices of key IOs or even through an NGO, complementing other advisory functions that such an expert committee could perform, as discussed in section 5.2.2, such as monitoring information about compliance and assisting countries in providing evidence about adherence. In this way, sovereignty concerns are significantly mitigated.[235] The committee may also summarize the issues arising in the case and provide a report on its conclusions, which could, even if not binding, inform parties and institutions in future cases.[236]

5.4 Conclusion

This chapter focused on the problem of compliance, which is a major concern in international law. The system of international insolvency is benefiting from multiple initiatives focused on cooperation and communication as well as from

---

[231] See, however, the failed settlement talks in the cross-border insolvency case of *Nortel*. In this case, over 7 billion dollars of sale proceeds were in dispute resulting in years of hugely expensive litigation (see DJ Miller and M Shakra, 'Nortel: The Long and Winding Road' in JP Sarra and Justice B Romaine (eds), *Annual Review of Insolvency Law* (Carswell 2015) 281, 288–89). See also JL Westbrook, 'International Arbitration and Multinational Insolvency' (2011) 29(3) Penn State International Law Review 635, 641 (noting that international arbitration might be more expensive than a court process).

[232] See also, in the context of proposals for a sovereign debt arbitration tribunal, Paulus and Kargman, 'Reforming The Process of Sovereign Debt Restructuring' (n 229) 4 (noting the advantage of elevating disputes to a neutral international forum thus providing 'for what may be called a "de-emotionalization" of each individual dispute'); The United Nations Conference on Trade and Development (UNCTAD), Sovereign Debt Workouts: Going Forward, Roadmap and Guide (April 2015) 4 <http://unctad.org/en/PublicationsLibrary/gdsddf2015misc1_en.pdf> (recommending the formation of a debt workout institution and noting 'impartiality' as a key objective that 'requires that actors, institutions, and information involved in debt workouts are free from bias and undue influence. While it is natural for creditors and debtors to pursue their self-interest, debt workouts require a neutral perspective, particularly with regard to sustainability assessments and decisions about restructuring terms').

[233] See eg the arrangement in the NAFTA's investment chapter that, as mentioned in n 218, includes an arbitration mechanism where the resulting award is binding only between the parties.

[234] See generally on soft methods of international dispute settlements E Boyle, 'Some Reflections on the Relationship of Treaties and Soft Law' (1998) 48(4) ICLQ 901, 909–12.

[235] Modest forms of international dispute resolution mechanisms are common in international law and have proliferated in recent decades (Guzman, 'Against Consent' (n 16) 786; PS Berman, 'Dialectical Regulation, Territoriality, and Pluralism' (2006) 38 Conn L Rev 929, 950).

[236] Such types of mechanisms are included in various treaties, including human rights treaties, described in J Galbraith, 'Treaty Options: Towards a Behavioral Understanding of Treaty Design' (2013) 53 Va J Intl L 309, 337–38.

extensive work on capacity building and standard setting. Yet, the interaction between these initiatives and the problem of compliance with cross-border insolvency frameworks has not been systematically examined. The lack of clear rationalization creates uncertainties, including concerning the extent to which other strategies such as harder forms of the harmonization of substantive laws, are required, going forward, at the global level.

The conclusions from the analysis in this chapter are largely supportive of the current system. Specifically, it was suggested that the tools, such as communication guidelines and the creation of discussion forums for insolvency judges, initiated by leading domestic and international institutions, are likely to (continue to) induce compliance in important ways, reinforcing other-regarding inclinations and positive group pressure. It was proposed to embrace mutual trust as a cornerstone of the global system, recognized, however, as a compliance force that requires regular development, rather than as an imposed principle. The chapter proposed various additional ideas to foster cooperation and trust, such as by publicizing leading judgments or by using expert groups to highlight information about participants' leadership.

Beyond this, it is possible to consider certain additional tailored incentives, specifically where such measures could reinforce reputation as a driver of compliance. Informed by behavioural law and economics insights, it was suggested to utilize impactful rating reports and emphasize the loss of reputation from non-compliance with cross-border insolvency frameworks and norms, in addition to utilizing mechanisms for monitoring information about compliance and for assisting countries in providing evidence about adherence. Other sanctions, such as blacklisting, should be considered with caution, as they might have a detrimental effect on cooperation and mutual trust.

This chapter also considered the link between the issues of institutional capacity and the problem of compliance. It suggested that the work on capacity building led by IOs, while primarily targeted at the development of domestic regimes, also provides critical support to the cross-border insolvency system, ensuring that all countries can become meaningful participants, including by overcoming biases, emphasizing the gains from compliance. Piggybacking on existing development initiatives also minimizes costs for the cross-border insolvency system. Capacity building may also entail general support in the enactment and implementation of mechanisms developed by the international community that at various times can be regarded as new and with which legal systems may be unfamiliar.

The chapter also supported the general approach so far undertaken at the global level with regard to the harmonization of insolvency laws and processes. In theory, comprehensive, top-down, harmonization could create an efficient global system with no conflicts; however, in reality, such a degree of uniformity is unlikely. Hard harmonization also entails costs, highlighted by economic analyses and supported by behavioural insights, in terms of the expected quality of the harmonized laws and the ability to maximize innovation across legal systems, including through good forum shopping. Instead, it was suggested that only limited harmonization is justified as a cross-border insolvency compliance tool. Harmonization must first be targeted at the development of jurisdictions for them to become meaningful participants in the cross-border insolvency system, even if often as host rather than home jurisdictions. Second, it must be targeted at creating standards for all legal systems, against the backdrop of widely recognized general principles, to ensure a standardized application of safeguards enshrined in a cross-border insolvency system based on modified universalism. Finally, harmonization should be targeted towards providing tools to operationalize the cross-border insolvency framework, especially regarding global entities for which tools are often missing in domestic systems. Thus far, the global insolvency system has embraced such a cautious approach to harmonization. This chapter provided the rationale for this approach. Furthermore, in addition to targeted harmonization, it proposed considering limited forms of the delegation of authority to external bodies that could assist in interpreting cross-border insolvency laws, resolving uncertainties, and dealing with a certain subset of cases, without replacing local authorities or creating a fully fledged supranational court system.

In summary, tailored incentives that reinforce concerns about reputation, co-operation measures that strengthen trust, capacity building initiatives, targeted harmonization, and moderate forms of delegation can further close gaps in the system and promote compliance.

6

Assessment of International Instruments

6.1 Introduction

This chapter is devoted to assessing the key international instruments for cross-border insolvency,[1] primarily the UNCITRAL Model Law on Cross-Border Insolvency (MLCBI), and Insolvency Standard (the Legislative Guide and the World Bank Principles) where it addresses certain cross-border aspects of insolvency. It also discusses additional developments of instruments regarding enterprise groups and the enforcement of insolvency-related judgments.[2] The discussion does not intend to be a detailed commentary of international instruments,[3] but rather a more targeted audit against the backdrop of the normative framework proposed in previous chapters. That framework encompasses various aspects of a cross-border regime, beyond the use of international instruments. It is built on the emerging norms of modified universalism and offers a range of measures to strengthen the cross-border insolvency system, including the conceptualization of the norms as binding customary international law (CIL) and the use of tools to incentivize compliance with the system, in view of expected constraints on choices and decisions by countries and implementing institutions. However, the framework also stresses that the effective governance of cross-border insolvency relies on uniform regulation that covers the various technical aspects of the cross-border aspects of insolvency, through agreement in international instruments.

---

[1] I have been involved in the development of some of the instruments discussed in this chapter as a participant in UNCITRAL Working Group V deliberations (since 2005), a senior counsel at the World Bank Group (2013–15), and an expert member of the FSB Resolution Legal Expert Group (2014–15). The views expressed are, however, solely my own and do not represent the views of any of these organizations.

[2] The work on these instruments was still ongoing at the time this book went to print, yet it was at an advanced stage.

[3] For commentary on the MLCBI see LC Ho, *Cross-Border Insolvency, A Commentary on the UNCITRAL Model Law* (4th edn, Global Law and Business 2017). See also IF Fletcher, *Insolvency in Private International Law* (OUP 2005) ch 8; J Clift, 'The UNCITRAL Model Law on Cross-Border Insolvency—A Legislative Framework to Facilitate Coordination and Cooperation in Cross-Border Insolvency' (2004) 12 Tul J Intl & Comp L 307.

The Future of Cross-Border Insolvency: Overcoming Biases and Closing Gaps. Irit Mevorach. © Irit Mevorach 2018. Published 2018 by Oxford University Press.

This chapter considers how the MLCBI, which is the leading cross-border insolvency instrument to date, and complementary instruments fit into the normative framework. It asks to what extent the instruments follow modified universalism norms,[4] thus also contributing to the crystallization and development of CIL.[5] It further assesses: the choice of instrument (specifically whether the instrument chosen is sufficiently 'hard' in the sense that it promotes high levels of precision and obligation);[6] whether there are any issues with the design of the instruments, taking into account the bounds on decision-making;[7] and whether the instruments support the required levels of targeted harmonization to incentivize compliance.[8] The focus is on the global instruments; however, this chapter also refers for comparison to the EU cross-border insolvency regime that has influenced global developments significantly.

This chapter also assesses international instruments and measures that attempt to separately address the resolution of multinational financial institutions (MFIs) including the cross-border aspects, particularly the Key Attributes, supporting principles, and contractual solutions. These instruments, too, are considered against the backdrop of the normative framework, but with lessons also drawn from experience gained in developing the UNCITRAL instruments that were primarily targeted at commercial entities. Although the development of instruments for MFIs has facilitated important advances, thus far no agreement on a comprehensive international instrument for uniform application has been reached that addresses the peculiarities of the financial sector. Generally, the chapter shows that certain gaps remain in the instruments for cross-border insolvency, including extant risks of deviations from optimal solutions when adopting or implementing the international instruments. It also proposes solutions for closing the gaps to make the regime more robust.

The chapter proceeds as follows. Section 6.2 focuses on the instruments for global cross-border insolvency primarily designed for commercial entities. It notes the approach of the Insolvency Standard to cross-border aspects, and it considers the schemes provided by the MLCBI and the instruments that are being developed for groups and for judgments enforcement. In the process, it shows how the instruments fit with relevant aspects of the normative framework. It then considers whether gaps remain, and highlights challenges related to those gaps. Section 6.3 shifts to MFIs. It reviews the main instruments and solutions developed thus far and considers how the regime for MFIs may be advanced further and the extent to which a more comprehensive instrument for cross-border insolvency of MFIs can be designed. Section 6.4 provides summary conclusions.

---

[4] Namely: efficient levels of centralization; application of the law of the main forum with limited exceptions; universal effect through recognition, assistance, and cooperation; and duties and safeguards that ensure a global approach and no discrimination. See the detailed discussion in Chapter 1, section 1.3.2.

[5] See Chapter 3 for the discussion of customary international law (CIL) and its use as a legal source for the cross-border insolvency system.

[6] See Chapter 4 for the discussion of soft and hard law for cross-border insolvency.

[7] ibid section 4.5.   [8] See Chapter 5, section 5.3.2.

6.2 UNCITRAL Model Law and Related Instruments

Following the financial crisis of the 1990s, leading international organizations (IOs), in particular UNCITRAL in coordination with the World Bank, took on the task of developing best practice standards for insolvency systems as well as a framework for cross-border insolvency in the form of a model law. The latter framework addresses key cross-border aspects within a structured and uniform scheme. The experience of using the MLCBI exposed certain important gaps in the regime, notably the lack of provisions for groups and uncertainty concerning the enforcement of judgments related to insolvency. Thus, subsequent efforts on the international level have focused on closing these gaps through the design of additional instruments. This section argues that the choice and focus on model provisions in model laws for the core cross-border regime have been adequate. The overall scheme for global insolvency is relatively comprehensive and precise, although it still retains certain gaps and challenges that require addressing.

6.2.1 The Insolvency Standard supporting cross-border insolvency

By the mid-2000s, two main international products related to insolvency have become available to the international community—the Insolvency Standard (encompassing the Legislative Guide and the World Bank Principles),[9] and the MLCBI. The Insolvency Standard delineates the key objectives of insolvency regimes. It also provides non-binding principles and recommendations on core provisions for effective and efficient insolvency laws, including concerning the commencement of the proceedings, the treatment and use of assets, the treatment of contracts, rules regarding set off, financial contracts, and netting, and rules regarding priorities and reorganization procedures.[10] Subsequent additions to the Standard provided recommendations on the treatment of enterprise groups in insolvency[11] and on directors' obligations when insolvency is approaching.[12] As such, the Insolvency Standard guides legislators when reforming and renovating insolvency laws. It is also used as a basis for the assessment of countries' insolvency regimes.[13] The Insolvency Standard is therefore primarily a tool for standardization, which, as suggested in Chapter 5, is an aim independent from the governance of cross-border insolvency,

---

[9] See Chapter 1, section 1.4.4.

[10] Legislative Guide, pts one and two. See also World Bank Principles, Principles B2 and C1-14.

[11] Legislative Guide, pt three; World Bank Principles, C16-17.

[12] Legislative Guide, pt four; World Bank Principles, Principle B2. This standard will also be expanded to include recommendations on directors' obligations in the period approaching insolvency in an enterprise group context, a topic which is subject to ongoing deliberations by Working Group V (see United Nations Commission on International Trade Law, A/CN.9/WG.V/WP.139, 23 February 2016, Directors' Obligations in the Period Approaching Insolvency: Enterprise Groups (New York, 2–6 May 2016) <https://documents-dds-ny.un.org/doc/UNDOC/LTD/V16/011/57/PDF/V1601157.pdf?OpenElement).

[13] See Chapter 5, n 34.

but one that is essential for the operationalization of and compliance with a cross-border insolvency regime based on modified universalism.[14]

Furthermore, certain recommendations in the Insolvency Standard address cross-border aspects, and while they do not proclaim that they follow a universal norm based on modified universalism, the recommendations conform with important aspects of modified universalism. Thus, the Insolvency Standard provides that insolvency jurisdiction should be based on sufficient connection to a country, though it does not proclaim the specific international ambit and role of such proceedings.[15] It also notes the need to coordinate a process in circumstances where the debtor has such connections to more than one jurisdiction and more than one proceeding is opened.[16] According to the Standard, and in line with the modified universalist norm concerning choice of law,[17] the insolvency law of the country in which insolvency proceedings are commenced should apply in those proceedings (the *lex fori concursus*). The Standard provides a rather comprehensive, though non-exhaustive, list of such insolvency issues that may be subject to the law of the forum and states that exceptions to this rule should be limited.[18] The part of the Guide concerning enterprise groups contains certain cross-border aspects as well, mainly concerning cooperation in enterprise groups' insolvencies.[19]

The World Bank Principles provide additional high-level elements of a cross-border regime, stressing the need for a clear and speedy process for obtaining recognition of foreign insolvency proceedings, for granting relief upon recognition, and for granting access to courts and other relevant authorities. The World Bank Principles also stress the need to include measures for cooperation between courts and insolvency representatives and to ensure non-discrimination between foreign and domestic creditors in international insolvency proceedings.[20] Thus, these principles, too, generally follow the norms of modified universalism,[21] and together with the Legislative Guide, they contribute to the emergence of aspects of the norms as CIL, which as explained earlier requires a demonstration that the general practice is accepted as law, evidenced, inter alia, from countries' actions and agreements in international forums.[22]

6.2.2 The model law for cross-border recognition, assistance, and cooperation

The Insolvency Standard explicitly recognizes the need for a global cross-border insolvency framework, and it provides that countries should enact rules on cross-border insolvency by adopting the MLCBI.[23] The MLCBI is, as well, a

---

[14] ibid section 5.3.2.
[15] Legislative Guide, pt two, recs 10–12. cf Chapter 1, section 1.3.2.1.
[16] Legislative Guide, pt two, paras 14 and 18.   [17] See Chapter 1, section 1.4.3.2.
[18] The Legislative Guide notes only two standard exceptions concerning obligations of participants in regulated financial markets and the effects of insolvency on labour contracts (Legislative Guide, pt two, recs 31–34).
[19] Legislative Guide, pt three, recs 239–54.   [20] World Bank Principles, Principle C15.
[21] See Chapter 1, sections 1.3.2.3–1.3.2.4.   [22] See Chapter 3, section 3.2.1.
[23] See Chapter 1, section 1.4.4.

non-binding instrument. Its Guide to Enactment and Interpretation (the MLCBI GEI) also acknowledges that the MLCBI is a form of instrument which does not amount to a treaty and that it provides room for adaptation of the law into the local regime.[24] However, it is designed as a complete framework for adoption in domestic legislation, and it specifically recommends that: 'States make as few changes as possible in incorporating the Model Law into their legal systems'.[25] It also explicitly requires that its provisions be interpreted while having regard to the international origin of the regime,[26] and it provides a guide to help promote a harmonized application.[27] As discussed in Chapter 4, the use of a model law that is intended for uniform application and implementation can overcome biases, specifically tendencies to maintain a territorialist status quo and aversion to loss of sovereignty and control, that might affect decisions in regard to cross-border insolvency. Where a model law provides a uniform framework, it creates a regime like a treaty that is, however, less costly and less threatening to sovereignty. Thus, it is more likely to achieve greater precision and completeness as well as wider adoption and greater universality of the regime.[28] The MLCBI, as well, does not envisage that the application of its provisions be contingent on reciprocity: that is, that it would apply only between countries that adopted its regime. Instead, it is intended for use in enacting countries, by relevant bodies from any jurisdiction, whether a party to the MLCBI or not. As such, the MLCBI promotes what was earlier called 'broad reciprocity', expanding the possible coverage of and participation in its framework.[29]

The preamble to the MLCBI states that its purpose is to 'provide effective mechanisms for dealing with cases of cross-border insolvency'.[30] There is no specific reference to modified universalism, namely to a regime that aims to provide a global approach to multinational default, modified to fit business structures.[31] The reason for this 'omission' is that, even though the MLCBI followed the trend or general approach of modified universalism, the drafting of the MLCBI was not necessarily seen as a process involving the enactment of certain universal norms. Thus, the preamble is quite 'neutral' where there is limited reference to the approach of the MLCBI to global insolvency, namely how it aims to advance these general objectives of insolvency on the global level.[32] It merely mentions, in addition to general objectives concerning certainty, fairness, efficiency, value maximization, and promotion of rescues, the objective of promoting cooperation between courts and other authorities and the protection of interests of all creditors.[33] Yet, the scheme

---

[24] MLCBI GEI, para 20. cf the EU Regulation on Insolvency Proceedings (2000) (EIR), replaced by the Recast EU Regulation (2015) (Recast EIR), which is binding and is directly applicable in all EU member states' regimes, except Denmark. There is no need for ratification or implementation by domestic legislation.

[25] MLCBI GEI, para 20.   [26] MLCBI, art 8.   [27] Namely, the MLCBI GEI.

[28] See Chapter 4, section 4.4.

[29] ibid section 4.2.2.2. Not all countries that adopted the MLCBI have followed this approach (see Chapter 1, n 299, Chapter 4, n 202, and accompanying texts).

[30] MLCBI, Preamble.   [31] See Chapter 1, section 1.3.2.

[32] cf recitals 22 and 23 of the Recast EIR, replacing recitals 11 and 12 of the EIR.

[33] As well as 'other interested persons, including the debtor'; (MLCBI, Preamble (c)).

that the MLCBI prescribes is generally in line with modified universalism, and it provides necessary technical detail on important aspects of its emerging norms.

Some outbound aspects of modified universalism are addressed.[34] The MLCBI recognizes the need for the insolvency proceedings to have regard for and reach out to the debtor's affairs outside the territory. Regarding any debtor,[35] it grants authority to insolvency representatives appointed in the jurisdiction (in the 'enacting State') to act in other jurisdictions ('foreign States') as permitted by the applicable foreign law.[36] There is also some specification regarding participation in proceedings in the enacting State, including the duties of the enacting State in term of due process and non-discrimination of foreign creditors.[37]

The focus of the MLCBI is, however, on the inbound effect of proceedings opened elsewhere:[38] the recognition and relief that may be granted by host jurisdictions, as well as cooperation and coordination, including in cases of concurrent processes. It envisages the circumstances where a collective process is opened abroad against a debtor who has some business presence in the enacting State—and attempts to ensure that the necessary support will be provided by the enacting State to achieve 'an orderly and fair cross-border insolvency proceeding'.[39] It further attempts to promote cooperation in the full range of scenarios where cooperation is needed to achieve a coordinated approach.

Thus, under the MLCBI, a foreign representative appointed in any foreign State where a collective insolvency proceeding was opened has access to the enacting State's court,[40] can apply to commence proceedings in the enacting State,[41] and may seek recognition of foreign proceedings.[42] The court in the enacting State may or may not recognize the foreign proceedings.[43] Yet, the decision whether to recognize the foreign proceedings is 'quasi automatic', as it is based on objective criteria,

---

[34] See Chapter 1, sections 1.3.2.1–1.3.2.2 for the discussion of the outbound aspects of modified universalism.

[35] MLCBI, art 1. The MLCBI applies 'independently of the nature of the debtor or its particular status under national law' (MLCBI GEI, para 55), though consumers and certain types of entities, such as banks or insurance companies, may be excluded by the enacting States (see section 6.3.1). It also applies to any form of foreign proceeding—the intention is 'to refer broadly to proceedings involving debtors that are in severe financial distress or insolvency' (MLCBI GEI, para 65), which also include 'the laws that prevent or address the financial distress of those debtors' (MLCBI GEI, para 67). Proceedings must be collective, but: 'A proceeding should not be considered to fail the test of collectivity purely because a class of creditors' rights is unaffected by it' (MLCBI GEI, para 70; MLCBI, art 2).

[36] MLCBI, art 5. When proceeding is opened in the enacting State, assistance and cooperation may also be sought abroad pursuant to arts 25–27.

[37] MLCBI, arts 12–14 and 24.

[38] See Chapter 1, section 1.3.2.3 for the discussion of the inbound aspects of modified universalism.

[39] MLCBI GEI, para 178.

[40] MLCBI, art 9. A foreign representative is 'a person or body, including one appointed on an interim basis, authorized in foreign proceeding to administer the reorganization or the liquidation of the debtor's assets or affairs or to act as a representative of the foreign proceeding' (MLCBI, art 2(d)). Creditors also have a right to participate in local proceedings (art 13).

[41] MLCBI, art 11.

[42] ibid art 15. Again, the meaning of foreign proceeding is intended to be broad and encompass both judicial and administrative proceedings including interim proceedings (MLCBI, art 2(a)).

[43] cf the mandatory recognition under the EU regime, subject to refusal based on public policy (Recast EIR arts 19 and 33, replacing EIR arts 16 and 26).

which, if met, require that recognition be granted, subject only to a limited safe-guard of public policy.[44]

That objective criteria is based primarily on whether a foreign collective proceeding exists and a foreign representative appointed, and whether the proceeding was opened in the proper jurisdiction for insolvency.[45] The MLCBI employs the debtor's centre of main interests (COMI), presumed to be at the registered office in the case of companies and at the habitual residence in the case of individuals,[46] as the test for recognition of 'foreign main proceeding'.[47] Recognition of 'foreign non-main proceeding' is based on a location of an establishment.[48] The inclusion of a specific test, particularly one which is based on the main seat of the debtor, promotes uniformity as well as efficiency and transparency of main proceedings.[49] COMI entails a degree of flexibility, which at various stages generated some inconsistencies in practice,[50] but uncertainties were later addressed and, in the revised version of the MLCBI GEI, it was clarified that COMI refers mainly to the place of central administration as ascertainable by third parties.[51] This revision also recognizes that the COMI may move prior to the commencement of proceedings. The MLCBI, in line with modified universalism,[52] does not preclude such movements; it only directs courts to scrutinize more carefully the conditions of COMI in circumstances where the move took place in close proximity to the opening of proceedings.[53] As

[44] MLCBI, arts 6 and 17. The MLCBI GEI notes that 'article 6 is only intended to be invoked under exceptional circumstances concerning matters of fundamental importance for the enacting State' (para 104).

[45] MLCBI, art 17.   [46] ibid art 16.

[47] ibid art 2(b). The MLCBI GEI, para 81, notes in this respect that: 'This corresponds to the formulation in article 3 of the EC Regulation (based upon the formulation previously adopted in the European Union Convention on Insolvency Proceedings (the European Convention)), thus building on the emerging harmonization as regards the notion of a "main" proceeding'.

[48] Namely, 'any place of operations where the debtor carries out a non-transitory economic activity with human means and goods or services' (MLCBI, art 2(c) and (f)).

[49] See Chapter 1, section 1.3.2.1.

[50] Inconsistency in the application of the COMI test was apparent even within the same enacting State. See in particular in the United States: *In re Bear Stearns High-Grade Structured Credit Strategies Master Fund, Ltd*, No 07-12383, 374 BR 122 (Bankr SDNY 2007), aff'd 389 BR 325 (Bankr SDNY 2008) (US); *In re Basis Yield Alpha Fund (Master)*, No 07-12762, 381 BR 37 (Bankr SDNY 2007) (US); *In re British American Insurance Company Ltd* 425 BR 884 (Bankr SD Fla 2009) (US), compared with the decision in *SPhinX, Ltd*, No 06-11760 (RDD), 351 BR 103 (Bankr SDNY 2006), aff'd 371 BR 10 (SDNY 2007).

[51] MLCBI GEI, para 145 (the Recast EIR, art 3, also clarifies that COMI refers to the place of administration which is ascertainable by third parties). See also paras 146–47 providing additional factors for determining COMI where the 'principal factors do not yield a ready answer'. The updated and revised MLCBI GEI usefully clarifies various aspects related to COMI. cf Ho, *Cross-Border Insolvency* (n 3) 317 ff (criticizing the revised MLCBI GEI noting that: 'the Revised Guide's rationale and signature recommendations seem misconceived and the Revised Guide might hinder the Model Law's cause').

[52] See Chapter 1, section 1.3.2.1.

[53] MLCBI GEI, para 148. See also paras 161–62. cf the Recast EIR recital 4 and art 3, which attempt to curtail forum shopping only to a limited extent where they provide that for companies, COMI is presumed to be at the registered office but the presumption will not apply if the registered office has been moved to another member state within three months prior to the opening of insolvency proceedings. Regarding individuals engaged in business or professional activity, COMI is presumed to be at the principal place of business unless this place has been moved to another member state in the three months before applying to open insolvency proceedings.

aforementioned, a proceeding that does not originate from a debtor's COMI will also be recognized if the debtor has an 'establishment' in the originating jurisdiction.

This additional basis for recognition via reference to establishments also establishes a limit. It minimizes recognition of additional concurrent proceedings that are opened on even more attenuated bases. Thus, the MLCBI does not stop countries from opening unnecessary multiple proceedings,[54] but at least it limits their recognition elsewhere.[55] Proceedings may be opened in the enacting State, however, after recognition of main proceedings based on the location of assets. Yet, the effect of such proceedings will be limited to these assets.[56]

The need for immediate regard and universal effect of foreign proceedings is also stressed.[57] It is mandatory that the decision to recognize a foreign proceeding is expeditious ('shall be decided at the earliest possible time');[58] that the enacting State's court can grant interim relief upon the application for recognition when relief is urgently needed;[59] and that for cases originating at the debtor's COMI, relief automatically ensues following recognition of main proceedings in the form of a stay of proceedings and executions against the debtor's assets as well as the right to transfer, encumber, or dispose of the assets.[60] The court in the enacting State may also provide additional relief to the foreign main or to non-main proceedings upon request. Such relief is discretionary,[61] and with regard to non-main proceedings should be granted only if the relief relates to assets that should be administered in such proceeding or concerns information that is required for this proceeding.[62] Again, the MLCBI does not stop countries from opening multiple proceedings or require that they do so on the basis of a global approach.[63] Still, it attempts to constrain the extraterritorial effect of additional territorial proceedings, thus promoting centralization to achieve a global collective process.

The court in the enacting State is given authority to grant any relief appropriate based on the circumstances, for example extending the stay of proceedings beyond the basic moratorium, providing information to the foreign representative, and providing for the examination of witnesses.[64] Most importantly for enabling a global

---

[54] See Chapter 1, section 1.3.2.1.

[55] cf the EU regime where proceedings may only be opened based on the presence of a COMI or an establishment (Recast EIR, art 3, replacing EIR, art 3). Under the Recast EIR, it is also possible to prevent the opening of secondary proceedings where the insolvency representative may provide an undertaking regarding the respect of creditors' rights according to local laws (art 36, codifying the practice in cases such as *Re Collins & Aikman Europe SA, [2006] EWHC (Ch) 1343; Re Nortel Networks SA & ORS*, [2009] EWHC (Ch) 206)).

[56] MLCBI, art 28.

[57] The MLCBI GEI explains that the automatic consequences of recognition of a main proceeding reflects 'a basic principle underlying the Model Law according to which recognition of foreign proceedings by the court of the enacting State produces effects that are considered necessary for an orderly and fair conduct of a cross-border insolvency' (para 178). In this regard, the MLCBI does not purport to import the foreign law into the insolvency system but rather to give the foreign proceedings the necessary effect in the enacting State.

[58] MLCBI, art 17(3).   [59] ibid art 19.   [60] ibid art 20.   [61] ibid art 21.

[62] ibid art 21(3).

[63] cf the jurisdiction norm of modified universalism discussed in Chapter 1, section 1.3.2.1.

[64] MLCBI, art 21(d), (f), and (g). The enacting State can also assist the foreign proceedings in other ways under other laws, and even where no recognition process takes place (MLCBI, art 7).

collective process at a main proceeding, discretionary relief includes the entrustment of 'the administration or realization of all or part of the debtor's assets located in this State to the foreign representative or another person designated by the court',[65] as well as entrusting 'the distribution of all or part of the debtor's assets located in this State to the foreign representative or another person designated by the court'.[66] The consequence of such relief is that all assets may become part of the insolvency estate and will be distributed, unless other conditions apply, according to the laws of the foreign State, home of the collective proceeding.[67]

Yet, the granting of such relief is subject to safeguards, in addition to the public policy exception. Granting any of the discretionary relief, as well as the interim relief, requires that the court in the enacting State is 'satisfied that the interests of the creditors and other interested persons, including the debtor, are adequately protected'.[68] Entrusting the distribution of assets to the foreign process further requires that the court is satisfied that the interests of creditors in the enacting State are adequately protected.[69] Thus, although this type of relief is paramount to the idea of a single worldwide distribution,[70] it is subject to significant discretion and provides leeway for local favouritism. The term 'adequate protection' is un-defined. It could refer to adequate process protection, realization of a distribution that is no worse than what could be realized in a stand-alone local proceeding as a practical matter, or a formal identity of entitlements. Thus, 'adequate protection' could, but need not, be interpreted in a manner, contrary to modified univer-salism norms.[71]

To maximize cross-border assistance and coordination, in all stages of the pro-cess, including before recognition, and regarding all types of proceeding (main, non-main, or other), the MLCBI requires that courts and other persons or bodies administering the proceeding cooperate and communicate with foreign courts and foreign representatives.[72] Thus, cooperation is mandatory, though quali-fied by noting that it should take place 'to the maximum extent possible'.[73] The MLCBI further details the possible forms of cooperation, which may include the appointment of persons to act at the direction of the court, communication

---

[65] MLCBI, art 21(e).   [66] ibid art 21(2).

[67] See also Fletcher, *Insolvency in Private International Law* (n 3) 469.

[68] The court may also subject the relief to additional conditions (MLCBI, art 22). cf the regime in the EU where the opening of main proceedings generates automatic effects in other member states (Recast EIR, art 19, replacing EIR, art 17) and the insolvency representative 'may exercise all the powers con-ferred on it, by the law of the State of the opening of proceedings, in another member state, as long as no other insolvency proceedings have been opened there and no preservation measure to the contrary has been taken there further to a request for the opening of insolvency proceedings in that State' (Recast EIR art 21, replacing EIR art 18).

[69] MLCBI, art 21(2).   [70] See Chapter 1, sections 1.3.2.1–1.3.2.2.

[71] ibid, section 1.3.2.3–1.3.2.4. See also section 1.4.5 indicating some inconsistency in the granting of relief by countries that adopted the MLCBI.

[72] MLCBI, arts 25–26.

[73] ibid art 25(1). cf the duty of cooperation between courts and insolvency representatives in main and secondary proceedings under the Recast EIR which applies 'to the extent such cooperation is not incompatible with the rules applicable to the respective proceedings' (arts 41 and 42, replacing and expanding the scope of art 31 of the EIR).

of information, coordination of the proceeding, the use of protocols, and co-ordination of concurrent proceedings.[74] Even where modified universalism is recognized as CIL, such concretization of the cooperation norm is important,[75] especially with regard to countries less familiar with transnational cooperation in this field.[76] As discussed in Chapter 5, cooperation, in addition to enabling effective solutions in the specific case, is also a means for developing trust between actors through repeated interactions. Such experiences can be self-reinforcing and may promote the positive, other-regarding biases, which in turn enhance compliance with the system.[77]

Overall, the MLCBI provides a significant degree of detail of a uniform scheme for addressing cross-border insolvency cases, including the sequence of steps of the process. It attempts to promote the worldwide effect of and support to a main collective proceeding, subject to concrete safeguards. It concretizes important elements of the emerging norms of modified universalism, which is critical for its successful implementation. The use of a model law that is intended for uniform adoption and interpretation, assisted by a guide for the enactment and interpretation of the model provisions, promotes universal application of the norms and can overcome territorial biases.

As noted in Chapter 1, the MLCBI has already demonstrated effectiveness as it has been adopted by more than forty jurisdictions, often with limited deviations from the scheme it provides. It has also been used quite successfully by courts in different jurisdictions, at least regarding single entities (enterprise groups are discussed in section 6.2.4). Moreover, recognition has generally been a rather smooth process.[78] As noted above, the test of COMI generated some debate and litigation, but the issue was clarified in amendments to the MLCBI GEI. Significant inconsistencies and uncertainties arose, however, regarding the scope and extent of the relief provisions, especially regarding deference to foreign laws and enforcement of foreign judgments.[79] Beginning in 2014, as next discussed, UNCITRAL commenced efforts to address this gap.

---

[74] MLCBI, art 27. See also arts 29–32 specifying how to coordinate concurrent proceedings and ensure consistency of relief provided.

[75] And certainly in the absence of CIL, especially as reliance on concepts such as comity has significant limitations (see Chapter 3, section 3.4). See also MLCBI GEI, para 214, acknowledging that in some countries cooperation may be based on the notion of 'comity among nations' and noting that the enactment of the MLCBI's provisions on cooperation 'offers an opportunity for making that principle more concrete and adapting it to the particular circumstances of cross-border insolvencies'.

[76] See also MLCBI GEI, para 213, which notes that: 'Enactment of such a legal basis would be particularly helpful in legal systems in which the discretion given to judges to operate outside areas of express statutory authorization is limited', and para 220, which notes regarding the cooperation techniques that: 'Such an indicative listing may be particularly helpful in States with a limited tradition of direct cross-border judicial cooperation and in States where judicial discretion has traditionally been limited . . .'.

[77] See Chapter 5, section 5.2.5.   [78] See Chapter 1, section 1.4.4.

[79] ibid section 1.4.5.

6.2.3 A model law to facilitate enforcement of insolvency-related judgments

The decision in *Rubin v Eurofinance*[80] revealed uncertainty regarding the scope of the relief and assistance provisions under the Model Law, specifically whether they allow enforcement of insolvency-related judgments. It is recalled that in *Rubin*, the UK Supreme Court rejected the claim that a judgment concerning a voidable transaction given by the New York court during the insolvency proceeding can be enforced under the MLCBI, even though this proceeding was recognized as a foreign main proceeding. Concluding that the foreign judgment could not be enforced under domestic general private international law rules, the UK Supreme Court analysed whether the court has power to grant relief, recognizing and enforcing the judgment under the MLCBI as implemented in the United Kingdom.[81] Article 21 of the MLCBI authorizes the court to grant certain forms of additional discretionary relief—that the court may tailor to the case at hand.[82] However, the court concluded that this did not provide an independent basis for enforcing a judgment originating in a foreign avoidance action. The Supreme Court also considered the possibility of granting relief pursuant to the provisions concerning cooperation and direct communication—specifically, the requirement to cooperate to the maximum extent possible with foreign courts and representatives.[83] It assessed the instruction in Article 27 of the MLCBI—that cooperation may be implemented 'by any appropriate means' and the examples of cooperation techniques that it provides.[84] However, the conclusion was that this did not provide an independent basis for enforcing a judgment originating in a foreign avoidance action.

The Supreme Court acknowledged the arguments that Article 21 in theory allows granting any type of relief, that the means of cooperation noted in Article 27 are mere examples, and that 'the recognition and enforcement of the judgments of a foreign court is the paradigm means of co-operation with that court'.[85] However, it concluded that none of these provisions allows for the enforcement of the insolvency-related judgment against third parties, explaining that:

the CBIR (and the Model Law) say nothing about the enforcement of foreign judgments against third parties. As Lord Mance pointed out in argument, recognition and enforcement are fundamental in international cases. Recognition and enforcement of judgments in civil and commercial matters (but not in insolvency matters) have been the subject of intense international negotiations at the Hague Conference on Private International Law, which ultimately failed because of inability to agree on recognised international bases of jurisdiction ...

It would be surprising if the Model Law was intended to deal with judgments in insolvency matters by implication. Articles 21, 25 and 27 are concerned with procedural matters. No doubt they should be given a purposive interpretation and should be widely construed in the

---

[80] *Rubin and another v Eurofinance SA and others* and *New Cap Reinsurance Corporation (in Liquidation) and another v AE Grant and others* [2012] UKSC 46.
[81] ibid para 133 ff.   [82] ibid para 138 (referring to the MLCBI GEI, paras 154 and 156).
[83] ibid para 139.   [84] ibid para 140.   [85] ibid para 141.

light of the objects of the Model Law, but there is nothing to suggest that they apply to the recognition and enforcement of foreign judgments against third parties.[86]

This narrow application, particularly of the relief and assistance provisions, although not shared by all jurisdictions that have adopted the MLCBI,[87] has not been exclusive to the United Kingdom. Other jurisdictions have also considered that recognition and enforcement of orders or judgments in cross-border insolvency cases may need to be addressed under the domestic civil procedure rules and have not considered cross-border insolvency to be exceptional. The prevailing view regarding the Japanese approach, for example, is that recognition of a foreign discharge following an insolvency proceeding should be subject to the conditions under the Japanese Civil Procedure Code rather than under the recognition and relief procedure of the MLCBI as enacted in Japan.[88] In the case of *Azabu Tatemono*,[89] in which the Japanese court recognized the foreign US Chapter 11 proceedings, a request to give effect to the debt discharge granted by the US court might have been suitable, thus giving a universal effect to the foreign proceedings, but was not pursued by the parties, probably because of uncertainty regarding the availability of such relief. This eventually led to the opening of concurrent local proceedings in Japan to assess and adjudicate the local claims.[90]

Furthermore, the MLCBI's instruction that its international origin be taken into account when applying its provisions means that decisions concerning its application should be considered by courts in other enacting States.[91] An uncertainty identified by courts in some jurisdictions thus becomes a more universal issue that requires a response on the international level. Specifically, regarding recognition and enforcement of judgments, the more general concern was that there is no global regime (eg no convention) for enforcement of civil and commercial judgments.[92]

---

[86] ibid paras 142–43.

[87] See eg *In re Metcalfe & Mansfield Alternative Investments*, 421 BR 685 (Bankr SDNY 2010) 694 where the US court enforced a foreign (Canadian) plan consisting of a broad third-party non-debtor release and injunction even though 'the Second Circuit imposes significant limitations on bankruptcy courts ordering non-debtor releases and injunctions in confirmed chapter 11 plans'. The court recognized and enforced the foreign plan implementation order as a matter of additional assistance under the MLCBI as enacted in the United States where the court is directed to consider whether additional assistance is consistent with the principles of comity (s 1507 of Chapter 15 of the US Bankruptcy Court). The court also noted that the relief provision is largely discretionary and embodies the principle of comity, citing *In re Bear Stearns High-Grade Structured Credit Strategies Master Fund, Ltd*, 389 BR 325, 333 (SDNY 2008); *Atlas Shipping*, 404 BR 738. See also Ho, *Cross-Border Insolvency* (n 3) 167 (referring to *In re Metcalfe* and noting that: 'This case demonstrates that the Model Law is not against the enforcement of foreign judgments').

[88] Law for Recognition and Assistance to Foreign Insolvency Proceedings 2001.

[89] *Azabu Tatemono*, Tokyo District Court, 3 February 2006.

[90] This note concerning Japan is a close paraphrase of I Mevorach, 'On the Road to Universalism: A Comparative and Empirical Study of UNCITRAL Model Law on Cross-Border Insolvency' (2011) 12 EBOR 517, 546. See also the approach of the Republic of Korea Courts explained in M Han, 'Recognition of Insolvency Effects of a Foreign Insolvency Proceeding: Focusing on the Effect of Discharge' in MP Ramaswamy and J Ribeiro (eds), *Trade Development Through Harmonization of Commercial Law* (New Zealand Association for Comparative Law 2015).

[91] See section 6.2.2.

[92] The Hague Conference on Private International Law has been working on a 'Judgment Project' since 1992, that aims to create an international regime for the recognition and enforcement of judgments, replacing the 1971 Hague Convention on the Recognition and Enforcement of Foreign

Additionally, to the extent that such work on a global regime for enforcement of judgments, which has been ongoing for some time, will be concluded, it will likely exclude insolvency-related judgments from its scope.[93]

For these reasons, UNCITRAL, in 2014, mandated that the Insolvency Working Group[94] develop a model law (or model legislative provisions) on the recognition and enforcement of insolvency-related judgments (MLJ).[95] The instrument that is being developed is not aimed at replacing a global instrument for enforcement of judgments beyond insolvency, instead it is aimed at addressing the gap in the global insolvency regime where the extent to which judgments, including in adversary proceedings linked to the insolvency process, can be recognized and enforced has been unclear. More specifically, the goal is to create greater certainty, avoid duplication of proceedings, promote timeliness and cost efficiency, comity, and cooperation regarding insolvency-related judgments, and maximize value.[96] Like the MLCBI, the draft MLJ refers to general goals of insolvency, as well as to comity, rather than to the more universal emerging norm of modified universalism.

The choice of instrument is a separate model law, devoted to recognition and enforcement of insolvency-related judgments. The use of a model law generally fits with the normative framework proposed in this book that advocates the supremacy of model laws over treaties or other forms of instruments where the model laws are sufficiently detailed and precise, creating an obligation to apply the provisions uniformly.[97] Inclusion of the measures for enforcement in a dedicated, separate, model law also gives prominence to this relief, and therefore this design choice can

Judgments in Civil and Commercial Matters that was ratified by only three countries (see Chapter 4, n 117). A proposed new draft convention was completed by an expert group in 2015, followed by Special Commission preparatory work on a draft convention held in 2016 and in 2017. This work was still on-going at the time this book went to print (see <https://www.hcch.net/en/projects/legislative-projects/judgments>). cf the EU regime, where jurisdiction, recognition, and enforcement of judgments in civil and commercial matters, excluding bankruptcy, is subject to the Brussels I Regulation (Regulation (EU) No 1215/2012 of the European Parliament and of the Council of 12 December 2012 on the jurisdiction and the recognition and enforcement of judgments in civil and commercial matters).

[93] Indeed, insolvency is excluded from the scope of the new draft Hague Convention on the Recognition and Enforcement of Foreign Judgments (see art 2; <https://www.hcch.net/en/projects/legislative-projects/judgments/special-commission/>). Insolvency is typically considered exceptional where it is linked to issues of public interest and may require a special regime. See eg the exclusion of bankruptcy judgments from the EU regime for enforcement of judgments in civil and commercial matters (n 92). Bankruptcy matters were also excluded from the Hague Convention of 1 February 1971 on the Recognition and Enforcement of Foreign Judgments in Civil and Commercial Matters and from the Convention of 30 June 2005 on Choice of Court Agreements (chapter 4, n 117).

[94] Working Group V.

[95] United Nations Commission on International Trade Law, A/69/17, Report of the United Nations Commission on International Trade Law, Official Records of the General Assembly, Sixty-ninth Session, Supplement No 17 (7–8 July 2014), para 155 <http://www.uncitral.org/pdf/english/texts/arbitration/transparency-convention/A-69-17-E.pdf>. The analysis of the draft MLJ is tentative and is based on the latest working papers and documents, which were available by September 2017 on the UNCITRAL website. The work was still in progress but at quite an advanced stage at the time the book went to print.

[96] United Nations Commission on International Trade Law, A/CN.9/903, 26 May 2017, Report of Working Group V (Insolvency Law) on the work of its fifty-first session (New York, 10–19 May 2017) Annex, Preamble <http://www.uncitral.org/uncitral/en/commission/working_groups/5Insolvency.html> (A/CN.9/903 Annex).

[97] See Chapter 4, section 4.4.

promote compliance.[98] As discussed earlier, the salience bias has a strong impact on choices and may affect decisions on the international level as well.[99] Indeed, the relatively vague legislative framing of the relief provisions under the MLCBI might have contributed to the more constrained (territorial) choices made by courts and the inconsistent application of the framework in different jurisdictions.[100]

Enforcement, however, is only one element of a cross-border insolvency regime, largely linked to the other private international aspects concerning jurisdiction, choice of law, recognition, and relief.[101] Therefore, an amendment to the existing MLCBI, explicitly and distinctly addressing this form of relief (namely, the recognition and enforcement of insolvency-related judgments), might have more prominently highlighted it, making the cross-border insolvency regime generally clearer, more precise, more complete and, therefore, on the whole, adequately hard.[102] Working on revising the MLCBI could address the risk of inconsistencies between separate instruments, and advance the need for adopting nations to bring conformity to their laws. For example, in a jurisdiction (such as the United States) that has interpreted the MLCBI provisions concerning relief as including enforcement of judgments, any 'additional relief' would be subject to the 'adequate protection' safeguard, but this may not be the requirement for all insolvency-related judgments under the new instrument.

There is nonetheless another potential advantage to providing a new stand-alone instrument as it may be enacted not only by countries that already adopted the MLCBI or that intend to adopt it in the future but also by other countries that have not considered adopting it. Even though the MLCBI is beneficial for all, and more so when it is sufficiently universal, it is still prone to territorial biases and thus to non-adoption.[103] A more limited instrument that addresses enforcement of judgments without subscribing to other aspects of modified universalism may be appealing to some countries. This advantage might be undermined if the availability of this instrument will induce countries to adopt the MLJ at the expense of adopting the MLCBI, which is the more general regime for cross-border insolvency (indeed, the preamble of the draft MLJ stresses that it is not intended to replace legislation based on the MLCBI). A stand-alone document may also be less effective if potential inconsistencies between instruments are not addressed. Importantly, rules concerning recognition and enforcement of judgments should conform with the underlying approach of the MLCBI, and in accordance with modified universalism allow the recognizing and enforcing of judgments emanating from the main proceedings, overcoming private international law restrictions.

The MLJ is important, as it will provide the means to seek recognition and enforcement of insolvency-related judgments, including key decisions such as the recognition of restructuring plans and debtor discharge.[104] It will explicitly

---

[98] ibid section 4.5.2.   [99] ibid.
[100] See the examples from the United Kingdom, Japan, and the Republic of Korea noted above (nn 80, 88–90 and accompanying texts).
[101] See Chapter 1, section 1.3.2.   [102] See Chapter 4, section 4.4.
[103] See Chapter 2, section 2.5.
[104] The intention is that the instrument will apply to all judgments emanating from insolvency proceedings (the Working Group has not finalized the definition of insolvency-related judgments at the

authorize courts to grant this form of relief as a matter of course, subject to technical requirements concerning the effectiveness and enforceability of the judgment and the provision of certain documents, prohibiting further considerations regarding the merits of the foreign court's decision.[105] It will also provide concrete safeguards, including for circumstances which raise public policy concerns.[106] It may also remove some of the excessive safeguards currently enshrined in the MLCBI. It is recalled that the MLCBI allows refusal of relief not only on the basis of public policy but also to protect creditors.[107] The MLJ may restrict the 'adequate protection' safeguard to enforcement of the types of judgments that directly affect the rights of creditors,[108] limiting the scope of this protection and making the enforcement process more efficient and predictable.[109] Yet, grounds to refuse recognition and enforcement may also include such general constraints where the foreign court did not exercise jurisdiction on the basis of the explicit consent of the party against whom the judgment was issued, or the submission of that party, or on a basis on which a court in the enacting country could have exercised jurisdiction, or that was not inconsistent with the law of the enacting country.[110] Such a regime, which is to some extent separate from the MLCBI scheme, might not seem to provide the clear and explicit authority to recognize and enforce judgments emanating from the main insolvency court. Yet, because it may be sufficient that one of the bases is established for recognition/enforcement not to be denied, in circumstances where proceedings were opened in the COMI jurisdiction, and where COMI is a recognized jurisdictional basis in the circumstances, judgments emanating from these proceedings may indeed be enforced, even in the absence of submission or consent to the jurisdiction.

The draft MLJ also includes a provision that seeks to clarify that in any event, notwithstanding prior interpretation to the contrary, the relief that is available under the MLCBI includes recognition and enforcement of judgments.[111] Such clarification may contribute as well to addressing the '*Rubin* uncertainty'. It might be the case, however, that post-enactment clarification of what was intended in a different

---

time this book goes to print; see (A/CN.9/903 Annex, art 2). It is not, however, intended to apply to a judgment commencing the insolvency proceeding. The explanatory materials may provide examples of such judgments, and may include in that regard: judgments concerning directors' liability in the period approaching insolvency; avoidance transactions; and orders concerning plans, debtor discharge, and approval of restructuring agreements (United Nations Commission on International Trade Law, A/CN.9/WG.V/WP.145, 1 March 2017, Recognition and enforcement of insolvency-related judgments: draft model law (New York, 10–19 May 2017), fn 9 <http://www.uncitral.org/uncitral/en/commission/working_groups/5Insolvency.html>). cf the Recast EIR art 32 (replacing EIR, art 25), which, regarding recognition and enforcement of judgments, includes references to judgments 'deriving directly from the insolvency proceedings and which are closely linked with them'.

[105] A/CN.9/903 Annex, art 12.   [106] ibid arts 7 and 13.   [107] See section 6.2.2.
[108] eg judgments concerning plans, discharge, and approvals of restructuring agreements (A/CN.9/903 Annex, art 13(f)).
[109] See Chapter 1, section 1.3.2.3.   [110] A/CN.9/903 Annex, art 13(g).
[111] ibid art X (the provision is drafted as an option for consideration by countries that have enacted the MLCBI as indeed it may not be relevant to all countries). The preamble may also stress that the MLJ complements the MLCBI (ibid Preamble).

instrument may not be sufficient, and an actual amendment of the MLCBI providing direct authority to enforce judgments of the COMI court (specifying which safeguards might apply for this purpose) may be needed. Certainly, though, even a clarification is important as it amplifies the modified universalist norm where relief to the central forum should be granted to ensure a fair and effective cross-border insolvency, thus also contributing to its crystallization as CIL. Furthermore, to ensure that the new instrument would not inadvertently require recognizing judgments emanating from proceedings that do not 'deserve' such worldwide effect, the draft MLJ provides that recognition and enforcement may be refused if they would interfere with the debtor's insolvency proceedings.[112] Such a provision may prevent conflicts between parallel proceedings, even though it does not make a distinction in this regard between main and other types of proceedings.[113]

Thus, the new MLJ may require careful analysis at the stage of implementation. Implementation and interpretation will be usefully assisted by a guide to enactment, which is being drafted to accompany the MLJ. The aim at the enactment and implementation stage should be to ensure that the cross-border insolvency regime as a whole is consistent and all its elements, taken together, enhance the necessary levels of centralization and universal effect of the process and the judgments it generates. It should be remembered that in cross-border insolvency, all pieces of the regime should fit and create a uniform and universal approach, avoiding discrepancies and cherry picking of elements.[114]

6.2.4 Model provisions addressing the insolvency of multinational enterprise groups

A major gap in the MLCBI has been the absence of specific provisions for groups, especially as the enterprise group is such a prevalent business structure for international businesses.[115] The EIR, which was based on the earlier convention and influenced the work of UNCITRAL, also neglected the enterprise group.[116] Addressing the fundamental aspects of cross-border insolvency in uniform and

---

[112] A/CN.9/903 Annex, art 13(e).

[113] For countries that enacted the MLCBI, the MLJ may include an optional provision that would allow refusing recognition where the judgment originated from a country whose proceeding would not be recognized by the enacting country under its version of the MLCBI, subject to certain exceptions (ibid art 13(h)).

[114] See Chapter 4, section 4.4. cf JAE Pottow, 'International Insolvency Law's Cross-Roads and the New Modularity' (UNCITRAL Congress, 4–6 July 2017) <http://www.uncitral.org/uncitral/en/com­mission/colloquia/50th-anniversary.html>.

[115] I Mevorach, *Insolvency within Multinational Enterprise Groups* (OUP 2009) 10–11.

[116] See M Virgos and E Schmit, 'Report on the Convention on Insolvency Proceedings' (Brussels, 3 May 1996) para 76 <http://aei.pitt.edu/952/1/insolvency_report_schmidt_1988.pdf> ('The Convention offers no rule for groups of affiliated companies (parent-subsidiary schemes). The general rule to open or to consolidate insolvency proceedings against any of the related companies as a principal or jointly liable debtor is that jurisdiction must exist according to the Convention for each of the concerned debtors with a separate legal entity. Naturally, the drawing of a European norm on associated companies may affect this answer').

detailed instruments has been already taxing, and the specific issues raised by the use of the group structure could not have been dealt with simultaneously.[117]

The key dilemma with groups is whether to give effect to the economic reality of integrated businesses operating through separate entities thus referring to the group as a whole, or to strictly adhere to the corporate form and address each group member separately. In international insolvency, that dilemma is intertwined with the indeterminacy concerning universalism or territorialism as the proper approach for cross-border insolvency.[118] Modified universalism resolves the dilemma by prescribing a global approach and accommodating different group structures. Through cooperation and centralization of group proceedings as appropriate for the group at hand, modified universalism facilitates group-wide solutions, usually without interfering with the corporate form, coordinating the process procedurally, and, in circumstances of heavier integration, supporting more complex solutions such as pro rata distribution and substantive consolidation.[119]

The MLCBI and the EU cross-border insolvency regime did not exclude groups from their scope, however, and groups could have been and have been addressed under these regimes.[120] In fact, many of the cross-border insolvency cases decided under the MLCBI and the EIR have been cases of groups.[121] These instruments refer to debtors—individuals and legal entities—in insolvency proceedings, and groups are compositions of entities, they are not separate bodies. Thus, for example, the rules concerning recognition, relief, or cooperation enshrined in the MLCBI can apply to the debtors within the group. The question is, however, whether a debtor-by-debtor application of the rules could result in the necessary levels of cooperation and centralization in group cases.

Practice demonstrated that often the professionals and courts implementing the MLCBI or the EIR could achieve such solutions through a 'pragmatic' approach,[122] paving the way for the emergence of the modified universalist norm concerning groups by applying the jurisdiction and recognition rules expansively to accommodate these more complex structures. Thus, even though the MLCBI refers to single debtors, and the report concerning the EU regime explained that 'jurisdiction must exist ... for each of the concerned debtors with a separate legal entity',[123] frequently insolvency professionals attempted to open a proceeding against several group members in a single jurisdiction and courts accepted this approach, finding

[117] Mevorach, *Insolvency within Multinational Enterprise Groups* (n 115) 97.
[118] I Mevorach, 'Towards a consensus on the treatment of multinational enterprise groups in insolvency' (2010) 18 Cardozo J Intl & Comp L 359, 379 ff.
[119] See Chapter 1, section 1.3.2.1.
[120] Mevorach, 'On the Road to Universalism' (n 90) 537 ff; I Mevorach, 'Jurisdiction in Insolvency: A Study of European Courts' Decisions' (2010) 6(2) J Priv Intl L 327, 342.
[121] Mevorach, 'On the Road to Universalism' (n 90) 537 ff; Mevorach, 'Jurisdiction in Insolvency' (n 120) 342.
[122] G Moss, 'Group Insolvency—Choice of Forum and Law: the European Experience under the Influence of English Pragmatism' (2007) 32 Brook J Intl L 1005. See also I Mevorach, 'The Home Country of a Multinational Enterprise Group Facing Insolvency' (2008) 57 ICLQ 427, 444–45.
[123] See n 116.

a mutual COMI for all relevant members of the group by focusing on the place of central administration and control of the group as a whole.[124]

However, the absence of explicit rules for groups created difficulties and uncertainties, and provided leeway for territorial biases. Globally, although centralizations were common, they have been mostly associated with Canadian or US groups and with Canadian or US courts' decisions, and have been less frequent in other parts of the world.[125] Within Europe too, under the EIR regime, at least initially, centralizations were led by the UK professionals and courts.[126] In addition, more often in group cases, recognition was less smooth and involved a process of dealing with objections or appeals. One example involves the proceedings concerning the Canadian group, Main Knitting Inc.[127] In this case, a Canadian representative sought recognition as main proceedings of proceedings opened in Canada against the Canadian registered parent company and two US registered subsidiaries, as they were all centrally controlled in Canada. Creditors in the United States objected, arguing that the United States subsidiaries had a significant presence in the United States. Eventually, the parties reached a settlement which safeguarded certain rights of the US creditors regarding their claims against US assets to which the recognition order was subject.[128] Moreover, group centralizations have not always been successful, and in some cases courts denied recognition to some, or all, of the affiliates. In Stanford,[129] a UK court denied recognition of the US receivership, finding the COMI of the Stanford subsidiary to be in Antigua and not the United States, which was the centre of the fraudulent activities of the Stanford Group. In another case,[130] creditors objected to the inclusion of a separate US corporate entity in French liquidation proceedings, arguing that such approach would contravene public policy. The US court's recognition order excluded this entity, and eventually the parties agreed to dismiss the petition regarding this entity and to coordinate between the French liquidation and US reorganization proceedings.[131] Furthermore, in the United States, Canada, and elsewhere, there were other group insolvencies where proceedings were not opened in the same jurisdiction. Consequently, in these cases there

---

[124] Mevorach, 'On the Road to Universalism' (n 90) 537 ff; Mevorach, 'Jurisdiction in Insolvency' (n 120) 345 ff.

[125] Mevorach, 'On the Road to Universalism' (n 90) 540 ff.

[126] See notably, *In re Daisytek-ISA Ltd*, [2003] BCC 562, which created some turmoil and discomfort, yet has thereafter been followed in various other cases, eg *In re Energotech SARL* [2007] BCC 123; *Hettlage-Austria*, [2004], *AG Munchen Beschl v* 4.5.2004-1501 IE 1276/04; *PIN group SA* (Luxembourg) Court Cologne [19 February 2008]; *Energotech SARL* Tribunal de Grande Instance Lure 29 March 2006, [2007] BCC 123, notwithstanding the more conservative approach expressed by the CJEU in Case C–341/04 *In re Eurofood IFSC Ltd* [2006] ECR I–03813. See also Moss, 'Group Insolvency' (n 122).

[127] *In re Main Knitting Inc.* et al, Nos 08 (11272, 11273, 274) (Bankr NDNY 2008). This discussion is a close paraphrase of Mevorach, 'On the Road to Universalism (n 90) 541–42.

[128] *In re Main Knitting Inc.* et al, Nos 08 (11272, 11273, 274), Order Granting Recognition of Canadian Proceedings under 11 USC S 1515 (Bankr NDNY June 18, 2008); Stipulation and Order Resolving Objection of HSBC Bank USA, National Association to Petition for Recognition of Canadian Proceedings under 11 USC.

[129] *In re Stanford International Bank Limited* [2009] EWHC 1441 (Ch) [2010] EWCA Civ 137.

[130] *In re SNC Summersun et cie*, et al, No 06-10955 (SMB) (Bankr SDNY).

[131] Stipulation and Order in Aid of Chapter 11 and Chapter 15 Cases, 2 May 2007.

was no recognition process concerning all relevant group members under the MLCBI or otherwise such a process encompassed only parts of the insolvent group. For example, in the case of *Spansion*,[132] it was mentioned that separate US reorganization proceedings were opened against affiliates of the Japanese company; in *Mecharcome*,[133] recognition of Canadian proceedings was sought in the United States, while a restructuring process against subsidiaries was ongoing in France; and in *Nortel*, proceedings regarding part of the group were opened in Canada and regarding another part in the United Kingdom.[134] The absence of a clear approach concerning group centralizations might have influenced the path undertaken by professionals and parties involved in proceedings concerning members of enterprise groups.[135]

In 2006, UNCITRAL took on the task of addressing the treatment of enterprise groups in insolvency, including both the domestic and the international aspects, which resulted in the issuing of an additional part to the Legislative Guide.[136] The recommendations concerning domestic groups provide innovative solutions, including the notion of procedural coordination where two or more group members file jointly and their proceedings are coordinated, and the possibility of applying the doctrine of full or partial substantive consolidation, merging some aspects of the estates or the liabilities, in specific circumstances. Other recommendations address intra-group voidable transactions, intra-group finance, and group reorganization plans.[137] As briefly noted in section 6.2.1, these recommendations concerning the international aspects of group insolvencies in the Legislative Guide focused mainly on promoting cooperation. Thus, the Legislative Guide did not address all the cross-border aspects concerning groups and, in particular, did not provide mechanisms for centralization of such proceedings. Problematically, the international aspects were not provided in the type of instrument that is most effective for a cross-border insolvency regime, namely a hard model law that is detailed, precise, and intended for uniform implementation.[138]

The global financial crisis revealed the impact of this gap, pronouncedly when the significant and large Lehman Brothers group collapsed in 2008.[139] The other major collapse of *Nortel*[140] in 2009, further exposed the difficulties in addressing the cross-border insolvency of large groups, especially where they were heavily integrated.[141] Thus, UNCITRAL Working Group V concluded in 2013, following an international colloquium, that its work on this topic should continue. This time, it resolved to address the problem of groups' insolvency (particularly the cross-border

---

[132] *In re Spansion Japan Limited*, No 09-11480 (Bankr D Del 2009).

[133] *In re Mecachrome International Inc*, No 09-24076 (Bankr CD Cal 5 June 2009).

[134] Recognition was sought in the United States regarding both proceedings. See *In re Nortel Networks UK Limited*, No 09-11972 (Bankr D Del 8 June 2009); *In re Nortel Networks Corporation,* et al, No 09-10164 (Bankr D Del 14 Jan 2009).

[135] Mevorach, 'On the Road to Universalism' (n 90) 542.

[136] Legislative Guide, pt three.   [137] ibid.   [138] See Chapter 4, section 4.4.

[139] See Chapter 1, n 315 and accompanying text.

[140] Nortel filed bankruptcy proceedings in the United States, Canada, and the United Kingdom in January 2009.

[141] See Chapter 1, n 92 and n 96, and accompanying texts.

aspects) more completely, expanding on the MLCBI and the Legislative Guide, and to consider doing so through the design of model provisions.[142]

Thus, since 2014, in parallel to the work on model provisions regarding enforcement of judgments (discussed in section 6.2.3), UNCITRAL Working Group V resumed work on the insolvency of enterprise groups.[143] The Working Group has been facing significant challenges in this process, and in the quest for consensual understandings.[144] Yet, agreements on important concepts and approaches are emerging from the deliberations. Relevant aspects of group insolvencies previously developed as recommendations in the Legislative Guide are indeed being transformed into an international instrument containing model provisions, which may become a supplement to the existing MLCBI or a separate model law concerning groups (MLG), and which may therefore induce more uniform application.[145]

Specifically, the recommendations regarding cooperation to the maximum extent possible between courts in different jurisdictions and between insolvency representatives involved in cases concerning group members, provided in the Legislative Guide, are being developed into model provisions that offer greater granularity and precision.[146] Additionally, the draft MLG builds on concepts enshrined in the MLCBI, including the initial distinction between main and non-main proceedings, the possibility of seeking recognition and relief in enacting host countries, the duty to cooperate in cross-border insolvency, the public policy exception, and additional safeguards to creditors.[147] The two instruments, therefore, are likely

---

[142] United Nations Commission on International Trade Law, A/CN.9/798, Report of Working Group V (Insolvency Law) on the work of its forty-fourth session (Vienna, 16–20 December 2013), para 16 <http://www.uncitral.org/uncitral/en/commission/working_groups/5Insolvency.html>.

[143] The Commission supported the continued deliberations on enterprise groups (United Nations Commission on International Trade Law, A/69/17, Report of the United Nations Commission on International Trade Law, Official Records of the General Assembly, sixty-ninth Session, Supplement No 17 (7–8 July 2014), para 155 <http://www.uncitral.org/pdf/english/texts/arbitration/transparency-convention/A-69-17-E.pdf>). In parallel, recommendations have also been developed on directors' obligations in the period approaching insolvency in an enterprise group context (n 12). From 2011, the EIR has also undergone a revision process and a new chapter was designed for enterprise groups (EIR Recast Chapter V, which entered into force in June 2017).

[144] Various concepts have been vigorously debated, for example the provision of relief by host countries, which would entrust the administration, realization, or distribution of assets of group members to a group representative in a foreign main proceeding, or the possibility to stay or decline to commence territorial proceedings against group members (see United Nations Commission on International Trade Law, A/CN.9/903, 26 May 2017, Report of Working Group V (Insolvency Law) on the work of its fifty-first session (New York, 10–19 May 2017) paras 116 and 136 <http://www.uncitral.org/uncitral/en/commission/working_groups/5Insolvency.html>; the recording of the deliberations is also available on the UNCITRAL website (<http://www.uncitral.org/uncitral/audio/meetings.jsp>). The analysis of the draft instrument concerning multinational enterprise groups is tentative and based on the latest working papers and documents, which were available by September 2017 on the UNCITRAL website. The work was still in progress but at quite an advanced stage at the time this book went to print.

[145] The current draft refers to 'legislative provisions' and to 'law' interchangeably, but the exact form the instrument may take has not been ultimately decided at the time this book went to print. See United Nations Commission on International Trade Law, A/CN.9/WG.V/WP.146, 2 March 2017, Facilitating the cross-border insolvency of multinational enterprise groups: draft legislative provisions (New York, 10–19 May 2017), para 1 <http://www.uncitral.org/uncitral/en/commission/working_groups/5Insolvency.html>

[146] ibid ch 2.   [147] See section 6.2.2.

to eventually fit well together as complementary frameworks, making the overall regime more complete and precise.

New innovative concepts are contemplated in the draft MLG to ensure that the
cross-border insolvency regime is fit for group structures. At the core of the draft instrument is the concept of a 'group insolvency solution', which essentially means
the proposal of a solution, either involving liquidation or reorganization (including
a sale), for the group as a whole or for a relevant part thereof, that can thus preserve and maximize value.[148] The group solution would be designed in a 'planning
proceeding'. This proceeding may take place at the main (COMI) forum of an enterprise group member which is a necessary and integral part of the group solution,[149] and in which other group members participate and a group representative
is appointed.[150]

The development and implementation of a group solution may be assisted
by cooperation methods, including the communication of information, approval, and implementation of protocols or the use of mediation.[151] In other
circumstances, cooperation may be the only method used to coordinate concurrent proceedings without attempting to commence a group planning process.[152]
Indeed, in some instances, commencing group planning proceedings may not
be necessary, and even generate additional costs (or no added benefits).[153] In
any event, cooperation does not depend on planning proceedings having been
commenced. Rather, the provisions provide the means for facilitating early pre-
planning and a period of cooperation even before the opening of group planning
proceedings.[154]

The planning proceeding may be recognized in host countries where group
members had presence (eg the COMI or an establishment), if the group representative can provide evidence of their appointment.[155] The draft provisions note potential
additional prerequisites for recognition, including the provision of information concerning the participation of other members and of statements regarding the added
benefit of a planning proceeding.[156] The group representative may also seek relief to
assist in the development of a group solution.[157] This relief includes interim relief
before recognition is granted and relief that may be granted upon recognition of
the planning proceeding.[158] The relief provisions, as currently drafted, largely mirror
those provided in the MLCBI, accommodated to group circumstances and to the
notion of participation in a group solution. Thus, for example, host countries may
entrust to the group representative 'the administration or realization of all or part of
the enterprise group member's assets' located in the country, either in the interim or
upon recognition, in order to protect and preserve the assets' value.[159] This way, all

---

[148] A/CN.9/WG.V/WP.146, art 2.
[149] ibid arts 2 and 11.
[150] ibid arts 2 and 12.   [151] ibid ch 2.   [152] ibid.
[153] See Chapter 1, section 1.3.2.1.
[154] As envisaged by modified universalism norms (see ibid section 1.3.2.3).
[155] A/CN.9/WG.V/WP.146, ch 4.   [156] ibid.   [157] ibid.   [158] ibid art 15.
[159] ibid art 15(e) and 17(f).

assets can be controlled and administered centrally, taking a global approach and promoting a global, group solution, without undermining the corporate form.[160]

Another innovation is the provision for relief in the country of the planning proceedings. Thus, in addition to introducing the concept of a group representative,[161] it is specifically provided in the draft that the representative may seek to stay executions attempted in the country of the planning proceeding against group members' assets, to stay proceedings against participating members, to administer or realize assets located in the country where the planning proceeding takes place, ask to examine witnesses, to recognize arrangements concerning funding of enterprise group members, or seek any other additional relief that may be available.[162] The instrument may, therefore, ensure that once a group proceeding is commenced, the country, home to this proceeding, would possess certain mechanisms to coordinate a group process.[163] The draft provisions do not explicitly speak to procedural coordination, but they do provide the means to achieve such an approach through participation in a joint process and the appointment of a joint representative, who can take actions concerning all the participating members. Therefore, even if, domestically, countries are lacking measures to administer group insolvencies effectively, the enactment of the MLG, once it is finalized, can close this gap, through some level of harmonization of tools for groups. The provisions also refrain from mentioning the possibility of substantive consolidation, a notion on which it is even more difficult to reach an international consensus.[164] Yet, the draft instrument does not prohibit forms of substantive consolidation,[165] as it allows the courts in the country where the planning proceeding takes place to provide any additional relief available under local law. The relief that may be granted by host jurisdictions also includes the possibility of entrusting the distribution of group members' assets to the group representative.[166]

When a group solution is finalized, it is required that the solution is submitted for approval and implementation in the host countries where affected participating members have a COMI or an establishment, if proceedings have commenced in these countries.[167] However, the draft MLG also contemplates the possibility that additional proceedings will be avoided and that host courts will defer to the planning proceeding and confirm the solution if creditors were adequately protected, which should mean that the corporate form was not unduly ignored. Local courts may stay or decline to commence non-main or main proceedings concerning group members, especially where a commitment is made regarding the treatment of foreign claims in accordance with the local law (the law of the entity's COMI or establishment).[168]

---

[160] See Chapter 1, sections 1.3.2.1 and 1.3.2.3.   [161] A/CN.9/WG.V/WP.146, art 12.

[162] ibid art 13.

[163] cf the MLCBI where the outbound aspects, namely the extent of the jurisdiction of and measures that can be taken in the main or non-main proceeding, are more limited (see section 6.2.2).

[164] Though some agreement has been previously achieved (see Legislative Guide, pt three, recs 219–31).

[165] Except if such relief contradicts the public policy or adequate protection safeguards (A/CN.9/WG.V/WP.146, arts 2 ter and 19).

[166] A/CN.9/WG.V/WP.146, art 17(2). This approach can be contrasted with the Recast EIR, which explicitly notes that no form of consolidation, procedural or substantive, is allowed in a group coordination process (Recast EIR art 72(3): 'The plan … shall not include recommendations as to any consolidation of proceedings or insolvency estates').

[167] A/CN.9/WG.V/WP.146, art 20.   [168] ibid ch 5 and pt B, arts 22 and 23.

The enactment and implementation of such model provisions can promote effective proceedings for multinational groups. In line with the emerging norms of modified universalism, which new instruments such as the MLG help shape and contribute to in their possible transformation to CIL,[169] the draft instrument provides mechanisms for cooperation, coordination of a group solution, and a degree of centralization. The choice of instrument and the issues it covers also conforms with other aspects of the normative framework, where, through model provisions (especially if these will indeed eventually form a model law or an annexe to the existing MLCBI), the MLG will unify key cross-border issues,[170] as well as harmonize tools for administering groups in a targeted manner. As noted earlier, targeted harmonization of laws is especially important regarding more sophisticated structures, such as groups, where solutions often emerge from cross-border practices.[171]

Under the framework envisaged in the draft MLG, in future cases similar to *Nortel*, for example, proceedings may be opened, and participation in them sought regarding all relevant group members, in one jurisdiction that could be designated as the planning process where a group representative may be appointed. That place would be the location of the COMI of one of the entities (under the current draft, an entity that is an integral part of the group solution: eg Canada in the circumstances of *Nortel*).[172] The group representative could seek relief in the country of the planning process, which may allow the central administration and realization of the group assets, and in circumstances like those of *Nortel* (i.e. heavy integration and blur in assets ownership within the group), also possibly their handling as one pool and their pro rata distribution.[173] The representative could then seek recognition and approval of the solution in host countries of the group members. Communication and cooperation with local courts can promote this solution. The representative may also make commitments concerning the recognition of priorities of creditors under local laws, where such an approach can result in greater centralization of the process, avoiding multiple proceedings, thus maximizing value and minimizing costs. In circumstances such as those of *Lehman Brothers*, instead of each subsidiary seeking recognition separately,[174] a group planning process could be opened usefully at the location of the parent jurisdiction (in the United States in Lehman's circumstances), and a group representative appointed, who could seek cooperation and coordination of a group solution. Courts in the host jurisdictions may recognize this process, provide relief, and may confirm the proposed solution.[175]

---

[169] As noted earlier, the development of regional and international frameworks can further define and develop CIL rules. See Chapter 3, section 3.6.1.

[170] See Chapter 4, section 4.4.1.   [171] See Chapter 5, section 5.3.2.4.

[172] Nortel was founded and was headquartered in Canada, though it had presence and subsidiaries in multiple jurisdictions.

[173] See Chapter 1, n 96 and accompanying text.

[174] eg the representative of the US subsidiary (Lehman Brothers Inc) sought recognition of the proceeding as a foreign main proceeding in the United Kingdom. The parent company (Lehman Brothers Holdings Inc) did not seek recognition for all its subsidiaries (see JM Edwards, 'A Model Law Framework for The Resolution of G-SIFIs' (2012) 7 Cap Mkts LJ 122, 135 ff).

[175] In Lehman Brothers, at least it was possible to agree on a Protocol that governed certain aspects of the process, though not all subsidiaries cooperated (the UK insolvency representatives refused to become a party and to provide information to the US representative as provision of the information was not considered to be in the interest of the local stakeholders of the UK subsidiary; see *In the Matter of*

Participation in a group solution under the draft MLG is, however, discretionary.[176] The risk is, therefore, that certain group members and their stakeholders will hold out, ring fence assets, and refuse to cooperate or participate where they are in a relatively strong position (eg are needed for the group solution, but could also be restructured separately), and that local courts may tend to overprotect local stakeholders and refrain from surrendering control to the home jurisdiction of the planning proceedings. A group solution should result in a 'no worse off' treatment of group members' stakeholders than would be realized if group members were to 'go it alone'. Nevertheless, group members and their stakeholders may attempt—and local courts might allow—exploitative leverage to extort value beyond what is realizable separately. Even in circumstances where there is less room for such manoeuvring, group members and their stakeholders, protected by local authorities, may resent cooperation, due to a lack of trust and the other territorial inclinations already discussed.

In the EU, the Recast EIR, too, contemplates a group approach based on voluntary participation of group members, where a group solution may be developed centrally, but group members may opt in or out, and local courts retain full autonomy. The approach in the Recast EIR envisions even lesser centralization compared with the draft MLG because, although the possibility of opening coordination proceedings exists, multiple decentralized cases are maintained and there is no specific measure for deference to the central forum through commitments to take account of local priorities.[177] In any event, the decisions of the coordinating forum are not binding, and each such case remain autonomous. It has been observed by the head of Germany's Federal Ministry of Justice and Consumer Protection (speaking in his personal capacity)[178] that this approach is, therefore, only a modest step and that the non-binding nature of the coordinating forum's solutions may hamper coordination and render the process ineffective. Apparently, 'more of a focus went on keeping the proceedings independent than to achieving workable rules' and '[a]ny model for truly centralised decision-making was "politically unfeasible" '.[179]

Globally, the risk of insufficient cooperation and centralization exists as well, and is exacerbated where emphasis is put on the sovereign control retained by host countries. The draft MLG includes various provisions stressing the jurisdiction of host countries where the COMI of group members is located,[180] their ability to prohibit participation of group members in a planning proceeding,[181] and the need to ensure that relief in the planning proceeding does not interfere with the administration of

---

Lehman Brothers International (Europe) (in administration) [2011] EWHC 2022 (Ch); S Di Sano, 'The Third Road to Deal with the Insolvency of Multinational Enterprise Groups' (2011) 26(1) JIBLR 15).

[176] A/CN.9/WG.V/WP.146, art 11(4) ('Participation in a proceeding ... by any enterprise group member is voluntary. The group member may commence its participation or opt out of participation at any stage of such a proceeding').

[177] Although through cooperation it is possible to agree to defer to a centralized process.

[178] *Global Restructuring Review,* 'European Academy of Law, Trier: The Need to Regroup on Groups' (5 July 2017).

[179] ibid. See also S Madaus, 'Insolvency Proceedings for Corporate Groups under the New Insolvency Regulation' [2015] IILR 235.

[180] A/CN.9/WG.V/WP.146, art 2 ter.   [181] ibid art 11(2).

proceedings in group members' COMI jurisdictions.[182] Furthermore, the default under the draft MLG is commencement of multiple main proceedings rather than a centralized administration subject to limited safeguards.[183] The option of deferring to the planning process and avoiding opening a proceeding in host countries where the COMI is located is currently drafted as an option, provided in a supplement.[184] Notably, though, it is provided in the draft MLG that it is not intended to create an *obligation* to open proceedings in the group members' host countries.[185]

Reaching agreements on deference to a planning forum by countries that may otherwise be able to control the debtor because of the location of its COMI appears challenging, and the solution of providing options for legislators is certainly a way to achieve a suitable compromise and move forward. Furthermore, in any event the MLG is intended as a non-binding instrument and none of its provisions will be mandatory (at the enactment stage). As noted earlier, however, the way options are presented can influence choices. Specifically, default (opt out) mechanisms tend to be followed, as well as provisions that are emphasized (salient) in instruments.[186] The risk is, therefore, that even though the draft instrument is designed generally in ac-cordance with the norms of modified universalism, the ultimate legislative framing might result in deviations from optimal solutions. Thus, legislators might not opt in to the option of deferring to the planning process, and implementing authorities might be inclined to retain excessive control over group members during the cross-border insolvency process, where such a possibility is highlighted in the instrument.

It should also be noted that the option that centralization be achieved by com-mencing and recognizing proceedings opened regarding several group members having their COMI in the *same* jurisdiction is not explicitly highlighted. Instead, it is assumed that the possibility of identifying a mutual COMI is available under the existing MLCBI.[187] Neither the MLCBI nor the draft MLG speak of this op-tion prominently or state how the factors for identifying COMI can be usefully considered in a group context. This option is certainly available, though, and has been used in practice. The risk is, however, of insufficient compliance where the tendency, at least in some jurisdictions, might be to open a proceeding against, and attempt to retain control over, local entities even if it is not the most efficient ap-proach. The revision in the 2014 reissue of the MLCBI GEI is useful as it emphasizes central administration as the main factor for determining COMI.[188] The place of central administration provides a single point of entry for the administration of a

---

[182] ibid arts 13(2) and 15(5).   [183] cf Chapter 1, sections 1.3.2.1 and 1.3.2.4.

[184] A/CN.9/WG.V/WP.146, pt B, arts 22 and 23. Such deference is also subject to additional safeguards (before granting additional relief under draft art 23 the court needs to be satisfied that 'the interests of the creditors of affected enterprise group members would be adequately protected in the planning proceeding').

[185] ibid art 2 ter.   [186] See Chapter 4, section 4.5.

[187] See also the Recast EIR where the possibility of identifying a mutual COMI is noted in recitals only (recital 53). For critique see I Mevorach, 'The New Proposed Regime for EU Corporate Groups in Insolvency: A Critical Note' [2013] Corporate Rescue and Insolvency 89, 90.

[188] See n 51 and accompanying text. See also the CJEU decision of *Interedil* (*Interedil Srl* (Case C-396/09) [2011] ECR) that firmly established the predominance of central administration/head office functions in determining COMI, and its codification in the Recast EIR art 3.

centrally controlled group, and thus greater scope for identifying mutual COMI for several group members, attempting full centralizations in appropriate cases.

6.2.5 Remaining gaps and decision challenges

Overall, the MLCBI and complementary—including forthcoming—instruments will provide quite a comprehensive regime for governing many aspects of cross-border insolvency and harmonize certain tools for addressing complex business structures, in line with modified universalism. The usefulness of these instruments relies heavily on their universal adoption. Importantly, at the core of the framework envisaged by the draft MLG is the development of a group solution that can encompass all aspects of the integrated multinational enterprise group. If the final MLG is not enacted widely, such solutions may be undermined; for example, where a group representative needs to develop a group-based solution but entities critical for the solution operate in countries that did not enact the MLG. Success of the envisaged solution might then depend on the application of the often inconsistent and territorial approaches under domestic private international laws applicable to insolvency of groups. The development of the MLG, however, also contributes to the emergence of relevant modified universalism norms as CIL, which if conceptualized and utilized as binding norms, rather than an interim approach, becomes mandatory in all countries whether they adopted the instrument or not, bridging gaps in legal systems and improving consistency.[189]

As highlighted in the preceding sections, there will also likely be additional decision challenges concerning the enactment of the final MLG, where certain legislators or implementing authorities might be inclined to follow the more entity-based/territorial aspects of the regime. Regarding the MLJ, issues of potential inconsistency with the existing MLCBI might pose challenges. Generally, it is important to appreciate the fact that some of the provisions in the instruments and the approaches adopted may be nuanced as designers attempt to accommodate concerns of many different jurisdictions. Such understanding and awareness can overcome, at least to some extent, bounds on decisions and choices and advance the system.[190] Sometimes, to provide clear assurances for countries, instruments must highlight the availability of territorial control; the preferred method, however, is to take a global approach and from that perspective support a global, centralized process. Specifically, in considering whether to enact the final MLJ, and how to implement it, it will be important that legislators analyse how it fits with the existing MLCBI, if enacted in the country, and generally how it can assist in supporting the needed levels of centralization in cross-border insolvency cases pursuant to modified universalism.

In addition to enactment and implementation challenges, even a wide and proper adoption of the instruments will still leave certain gaps. The MLJ will address enforcement of insolvency-related judgments, but it might not fully deal with the

---

[189] See Chapter 3, section 3.2.3.   [190] See Chapter 2, section 2.6.

uncertainty regarding deference to foreign laws.[191] The MLCBI does not contain explicit rules on choice of law in cross-border insolvency.[192] The assistance and relief provisions in the MLCBI are broad in scope, however, and courts may defer to foreign laws of the main forum.[193] Yet, the openness and lack of precision and prominence of this option creates room for territorial biases and thus inconsistent application of the relief provisions.[194]

There is room, therefore, for addressing the choice of law gap explicitly.[195] Choice of law issues have been identified by Working Group V of UNCITRAL as requiring further deliberation.[196] Various proposals have been set forth for global rules on choice of law.[197] When this topic is adopted as a working task, the approach preferably followed will be generally consistent with the Insolvency Standard,[198] where the law of the main forum prevails regarding most insolvency-related issues, subject to limited exceptions, in line with modified universalism.[199] The actual exceptions noted in the Standard might not be set in stone. Modified universalism is flexible, as it accommodates changing conditions.[200] When transforming the recommendations into concrete model provisions in a model law, the general approach should be deferential to the law of the forum unless it is necessary to carve out certain rights due to policy considerations or special protections to vulnerable parties.[201] Provisions applying the emerging norm concerning choice of law ought

[191]   As mentioned in section 6.2.2, the implementation of the MLCBI revealed uncertainty regarding deference to foreign laws. See also the examples noted in Chapter 1, n 301.

[192]   cf the Recast EIR arts 8–18 (replacing EIR arts 4–15) under which the law of the forum applies, subject, however, to many exceptions (concerning: voidable transactions, rights in rem, set-off, payment systems, and financial markets, reservation of title, immovable property, ship, aircraft, and securities, contracts of employment, patents and trademarks, pending lawsuits, and arbitral proceedings).

[193]   Ho, *Cross-Border Insolvency* (n 3) 250 ff. See also R Bork, *Principles of Cross-Border Insolvency Law* (Intersentia 2017) 34, 103 (noting that, although the MLCBI is silent on applicable law, it is likely because it was presumed that countries' official bodies will apply national law, including regarding foreign elements of the debtor. It was similarly presumed that official bodies will apply national choice of law, which may lead to deference to foreign law. However, that silence has led to unpredictable results).

[194]   See Chapter 4, sections 4.4 and 4.5. See also Ho, *Cross-Border Insolvency* (n 3) 255, 274 (pointing to 'xenophobia', 'fear', and 'the distraction of territoriality' that have prevented deference to foreign law), and generally on the territorial biases Chapter 2, section 2.5.

[195]   See also Ho, *Cross-Border Insolvency* (n 3) 250 ff (arguing in favour of developing principled choice of law rules).

[196]   In a colloquium held in 2013 (United Nations Commission on International Trade Law, A/CN.9/798, 8 January 2014, Report of Working Group V (Insolvency Law) on the work of its forty-fourth session (Vienna, 16–20 December 2013), para 24 <http://www.uncitral.org/uncitral/en/commission/working_groups/5Insolvency.html>).

[197]   See eg the Global Rules noted in Chapter 1, n 128; JAE Pottow, 'Beyond Carve-Outs and Toward Reliance: A Normative Framework for Cross-Border Insolvency Choice of Law' (2014) 9(1) Brook J Corp Fin & Com L 197; Ho, *Cross-Border Insolvency* (n 3) 264 ff; EJ Janger, 'Silos: Establishing the Distributional Baseline in Cross-Border Bankruptcies' 9(1) Brook J Corp Fin & Com L 179; I Mevorach, 'Cross-Border Insolvency of Enterprise Groups: The Choice of Law Challenge' (2014) 9(1) Brook J Corp Fin & Com L 225.

[198]   See section 6.2.1.

[199]   For the details of the choice of law emerging norm under modified universalism see Chapter 1, section 1.3.2.2.

[200]   It has been noted, for example, how exceptions concerning tax priorities have become less relevant over time (Pottow, 'Beyond Carve-Outs and Toward Reliance' (n 197) 217).

[201]   See Chapter 1, section 1.3.2.2.

to also accommodate group structures, allowing a group main process to apply its tools while taking account of local rights regarding separate entities pursuant to the law of their home jurisdiction.[202] This approach is already reflected in supplemental provisions in the draft MLG.[203] It will also be guided by modified universalism and insolvency objectives rather than by general private international law justifications.

There is also room for addressing jurisdiction issues directly, enhancing the outbound aspects of the regime. Currently, the MLCBI implicitly embraces certain jurisdictional bases (COMI, establishment) through the provisions concerning recognition of and relief to foreign main and non-main proceedings.[204] Yet, it does not provide direct competence on the same bases, and thus does not create a clear hierarchy between main and other types of processes. The draft MLG, on the other hand, does pronounce explicitly in which forum a planning, group proceeding may be opened. Similar provisions concerning the jurisdiction of, primarily, the main forum, including the possibility that such forum will preside over proceedings of group members that were centrally controlled in the jurisdiction having a mutual COMI there, may be included in a revised MLCBI.

A more general future review of cross-border insolvency instruments may take up the task of creating an overall framework within a single rule book that includes the core regime for single entities including the rules on jurisdiction and choice of law, the additional provisions for groups, and those related to enforcement of judgments. Such a framework may also refer to modified universalism norms more explicitly, pronouncing their universal eminence, promoting their crystallization as CIL and amplifying their binding nature. Future revisions may also address some of the excess prominence given to local protections, including the requirement that local creditors are protected before certain relief is provided or even that cooperation is to the maximum extent possible. Instead, the requirement may be that a global approach must be taken, and adequate relief provided, if there is no breach of home country duties or circumstances where the governing law or processes applied fall short of universally accepted principles and standards.[205] Closing the choice of law gap should make such streamlining simpler, as some of the concerns reflected in the more territorial protections can be addressed in acknowledged exceptions to the *lex fori concursus* rule.[206] In all, these modifications and enhancements can make the international instruments quite comprehensive and fit for the present challenges of cross-border insolvency.

---

[202] ibid.   [203] See section 6.2.4.

[204] Bork, *Principles of Cross-Border Insolvency Law* (n 193) 33–34. cf the Recast EIR where the regime applies from the beginning of the case and thus governs international jurisdiction explicitly.

[205] See Chapter 1, section 1.3.2.4.

[206] It has been argued that a choice of law analysis should inform the notions of 'sufficient protection' and 'additional assistance' in the US version of the MLCBI (AL Gropper, 'The Curious Disappearance of Choice of Law as an Issue in Chapter 15 Cases' (2014) 9(1) Brook J Corp Fin & Com L 151). It is argued here that it may be possible, as well, to agree to remove the undefined and vague protections in the MLCBI, once the choice of law gap is addressed.

6.3 The Key Attributes and Supporting Initiatives

The MLCBI does not specifically address the cross-border insolvency of MFIs. The absence of an international framework that responded effectively to the insolvency of financial institutions, especially the resolution of global systemically important financial institutions (G-SIFIs), was apparent during the global financial crisis,[207] most pronouncedly when Lehman Brothers collapsed. As a complex and large MFI group, it was difficult to minimize the number of proceedings that were opened throughout the world and to cooperate across borders.[208] Generally, tendencies in situations of general default of MFIs are often to ring-fence assets, and territorial manoeuvring is not unusual, resulting in coordination problems.[209] Post-crisis, there have been calls to develop international approaches to the cross-border insolvency of MFIs that will address the problem of value loss resulting from multiple and disjointed proceedings and unilateral actions.[210] Important initiatives have ensued through, in particular, extensive work of IOs.[211] This section reviews the key instruments developed since the crisis, namely the Key Attributes that were introduced in 2011, and updated in 2014,[212] and additional guiding principles and contractual solutions endorsed between 2014 and 2016. It is argued that these instruments are largely in line with the normative framework proposed in this book. There are gaps remaining, however, especially in the level of precision and obligation (hardness) of the instruments. Lessons can be learned in this respect from the design and operation of the UNCITRAL instruments.

6.3.1 The international standard for resolution regimes (Key Attributes)

The Key Attributes were endorsed by the G20 in 2011, as the international standard for resolution regimes.[213] They contain non-binding best practices that countries are encouraged to implement and comply with over time, providing the overall umbrella standard that can guide domestic legislation in the design of resolution laws.[214] Thus, the Key Attributes do not address only cross-border issues. The instrument is similar in nature to the Insolvency Standard,[215] though its primary focus is the large

---

[207] In Europe, too, prior to the global financial crisis, the EU Winding-up Directive did not cover the more complex institutions' structures and the recognition of sophisticated resolution tools (see Chapter 1, nn 247–49 and accompanying texts).

[208] See Chapter 1, section 1.4.5, and Chapter 2, section 2.5.2.

[209] See Chapter 2, sections 2.5.1 and 2.5.2 where it was noted that territorial and short-termism tendencies may be particularly strong in MFI insolvencies.

[210] See Chapter 1, section 1.4.4.   [211] ibid.   [212] ibid.

[213] Key Attributes, 1 (referring to: Communiqué G20 Leaders Summit—Cannes—3–4 November 2011, Section 13).

[214] Resolution laws in this context refer to providing for a broad range of powers, including both stabilization and liquidation options (Key Attributes, 3–4).

[215] See United Nations Commission on International Trade Law, Insolvency Law: Insolvency of Large and Complex Financial Institutions, Note by the Secretariat, A/CN.9/WG.V/WP.109 (2012) para 63 <http://www.uncitral.org/uncitral/en/commission/working_groups/5Insolvency.html> (noting regarding the Key Attributes that they 'may be viewed as performing to some extent a function with respect to bank and financial institution resolution regimes similar to the function performed by

and complex institutions that operate across borders (the G-SIFIs).[216] The preamble to the Attributes proclaims the general objectives of resolution regimes, which are similar in scope to the general shared objectives in the Insolvency Standard, but specific to G-SIFIs.[217] The preamble also includes specific objectives on the cross-border aspects of resolution. Yet, unlike the Insolvency Standard, these do not refer to a uniform framework (eg a model law) for adoption in domestic laws, rather the standard itself purports to provide the cross-border insolvency international framework.

Like the MLCBI, the Key Attributes do not proclaim an explicit approach to cross-border resolution in terms of the level of universality or territoriality endorsed. However, there is a clear emphasis on cooperation and coordination in cross-border resolutions, in line with modified universalism. Thus, the preamble of the Key Attributes states that resolution regimes should 'provide a mandate in law for cooperation, information exchange and coordination domestically and with relevant foreign resolution authorities before and during a resolution'.[218] It also stresses the importance of convergence of resolution laws,[219] which is indeed vital for compliance with a cross-border regime. As discussed earlier, such a regime requires that safeguards are based on universal standards and that certain essential tools are in place.[220] Particularly, targeted harmonization is crucial regarding complex entities and complicated scenarios such as the stabilization of SIFIs.[221] The Key Attributes delineate such standards and tools by specifying the key elements of resolution regimes,[222] which range from the type of entities subject to the regime, the roles and responsibilities of resolution authorities, the type of resolution powers that should be available in the regime, and safeguards for creditors.[223]

Specific attributes delineate main elements that the resolution regime should adopt to enhance the effectiveness of cross-border resolution.[224] These cover significant and important portions of modified universalism norms. Although the focus of the preamble is on cooperation, the Attributes in fact go beyond it, suggesting that legal systems provide a framework for recognition and support to foreign resolutions. Like the MLCBI, the focus is on the inbound aspects of modified universalism. Yet,

---

the Legislative Guide on Insolvency Law with respect to commercial insolvency law, addressing key objectives, core principles and other elements that should be addressed in an effective and efficient insolvency regime, albeit in somewhat less detailed manner').

[216] The Key Attributes address global financial institutions of all types that could be systemic in failure. The Attributes are relevant, however, to cross-border institutions that may not be systematically important, though not all elements and high standards may be relevant to all entities in all countries in the same manner. See International Monetary Fund, 'Cross-Border Bank Resolution: Recent Developments' (2 June 2014) 21 <https://www.imf.org/external/np/pp/eng/2014/060214.pdf>.

[217] These include ensuring continuity of systematically important services and functions, protecting depositors, respecting claims priorities in loss allocation, avoiding the need for public support, avoiding value destruction and losses to creditors, ensuring orderly liquidation of non-viable firms and providing incentives for market-based solutions (Key Attributes, 3–4).

[218] Key Attributes, Preamble.

[219] ibid ('In order to facilitate the coordinated resolution of firms active in multiple countries, jurisdictions should seek convergence of their resolution regimes through the legislative changes needed to incorporate the tools and powers set out in these Key Attributes into their national regimes').

[220] See Chapter 5, section 5.3.2.   [221] ibid.   [222] Key Attributes 5 ff.
[223] ibid 1.   [224] ibid ss 7–9.

the Key Attributes, too, to some extent assume that the home jurisdiction of a financial institution may take action to resolve the institution and attempt to ensure recognition and support in host countries to enable a degree of centralized control. Thus, it is explained that recognition and support:

> would enable a foreign home resolution authority to gain rapid control over the firm (branch or shares in a subsidiary) or its assets that are located in the host jurisdiction, as appropriate, in cases where the firm is being resolved under the law of the foreign home jurisdiction.[225]

For this purpose, host countries should, swiftly and transparently, give effect to home country measures, through a recognition process or by applying domestic measures that support and are consistent with the home country actions.[226] Key Attributes concerning resolution planning also provide that at least with regard to G-SIFIs, the home resolution authority should lead the development of group resolution plans.[227] Thus, although norms concerning jurisdiction, centralization, control, and choice of law are not fully specified, central control is encouraged through the framework for recognition and support.[228] That support and the process of providing it (or for recognizing foreign measures) is not stated and detailed, though it is noted that, for example, the host jurisdiction may order 'a transfer of property located in its jurisdiction to a bridge institution established by the foreign home authority'.[229]

In addition, national resolution regimes 'should empower and strongly encourage the authority wherever possible to act to achieve a cooperative solution with foreign resolution authorities'.[230] National laws should also empower the resolution authorities to share relevant information with their foreign counterparts, subject to confidentiality requirements.[231] Cooperation should also take place through establishment of crisis management groups that include relevant authorities of home or host jurisdictions and through institution-specific cooperation agreements.[232] Thus, regimes that follow the Key Attributes would need to provide a toolbox of ways to address multinational default of financial institutions that fit the specific scenario and structure of the firm. The Key Attributes also do not narrowly focus on single entity institutions; in addition, they note the need to coordinate solutions where countries host subsidiaries.[233]

The Key Attributes also ensure that host countries retain a degree of sovereign control and can safeguard the rights of creditors and the public interest. The safeguards are concrete and intended for circumstances where standards of fairness and duties of home countries are breached or cannot be pursued. Thus, discrimination of creditors is explicitly prohibited.[234] But, if creditors are nonetheless

---

[225] ibid s 7.5.   [226] ibid s 7.5.   [227] ibid s 11.8.
[228] cf the home country rule under the EU Winding-up Directive and the Bank Recovery and Resolution Directive (BRRD) which prescribes a universal effect to the measures taken by the home member state, including regarding obligations governed by foreign law (EU Winding-up Directive, arts 3 and 9; BRRD, art 66), and the regime for joint decisions in cross-border group resolutions, led and chaired by the group-level resolution authority (BRRD, art 87 ff).
[229] Key Attributes, s 7.3.   [230] ibid s 7.1.   [231] ibid ss 7.6, 7.7, and 12.
[232] ibid ss 8 and 9.   [233] ibid s 7.5.   [234] ibid s 7.4.

treated inequitably in the foreign proceeding, recognition or support to foreign measures may be denied.[235] The duties envisaged regarding those taking resolution actions also reach beyond the home jurisdiction, as authorities should 'undertake best efforts to avoid taking actions that could reasonably be expected to trigger instability elsewhere in the group or in the financial system'.[236] Local authorities may also take a separate initiative. Such action should be reserved, however, to 'exceptional cases' where the home jurisdiction 'is not taking actions or acts in a manner that does not take sufficient account of the need to preserve the local jurisdiction's financial stability',[237] and it is also required that national action is taken following due notification and consultation with the home authority.[238] Host countries too, when taking local action, 'should consider the impact on financial stability in other jurisdictions'.[239]

Thus, the duties and safeguards contemplated in the Key Attributes envisage a regime that requires taking a global approach and considering interests beyond those of domestic stakeholders, which is in line with modified universalism. As a rule, host countries are not supposed to protect local interests and grab assets where the resolution process takes due regard of interest of all entities worldwide. Recognition and support may not be automatic, but they are not open to unlimited discretion. They should be based on objective criteria and denial of them accepted only by reference to universally accepted safeguards.[240]

These cross-border aspects are complemented by the TLAC standard,[241] which applies to global significantly important banks (G-SIBs).[242] TLAC stands for total loss absorbance capacity. The TLAC standard requires that the financial institution retain sufficient capital and or contractually or structurally subordinated (bail-in) debt to implement a resolution that pays all creditors of the operating entities in a way that avoids instability and the need for public funds.[243] As such, it enhances the likelihood that countries will comply with the envisioned cross-border framework. As discussed in Chapter 5, compliance is largely reliant on trust in foreign system's capacity and regulation and specifically the ability of home jurisdictions to deal adequately with insolvencies.[244] Regarding G-SIBs, this depends on adequate

---

[235] ibid s 7.5.   [236] ibid s 3.9. See also s 2.3.   [237] ibid s 7.3.   [238] ibid s 7.3.

[239] ibid s 7.2. cf the EU regime, where under the Winding-up Directive, member states may open winding up proceedings (widely defined) in relation to branches of third-country institutions and there are no provisions for the prevention of multiple proceedings and the recognition and enforcement of a foreign home proceeding (EU Winding-up Directive, art 19).

[240] In this respect and although prescribed through high level concepts, the Key Attributes envisage a regime which is even more constrained in terms of territorial intervention compared with the MLCBI. As noted above, the MLCBI allows denying relief based on protection of local interests, and does not explicitly link this safeguard to a breach of a global approach, discrimination, or other aspects of public policy. See also the rather broad safeguard under the EU regime for financial institutions applicable to third countries that allows, in addition to other considerations, refusal of recognition and enforcement where it would be 'contrary to national law' (BRRD, art 95).

[241] Chapter 1, n 231.   [242] ibid.

[243] Financial Stability Board, Principles on Loss-absorbing and Recapitalisation Capacity of G-SIBs in Resolution, Total Loss-absorbing Capacity (TLAC) Term Sheet (9 November 2015) Principle (i) <http://www.fsb.org/wp-content/uploads/TLAC-Principles-and-Term-Sheet-for-publication-final.pdf>.

[244] See Chapter 5, section 5.3.1.

pre-planning and that institutions are subject to and comply with loss absorption requirements. Importantly, such requirements should take sufficient account of the needs of branches and subsidiaries in host jurisdictions. In the absence of such trust, as observed in the TLAC standard: 'host authorities could demand extra resources to be ring-fenced in their own jurisdictions either ex ante or ex post in a resolution'.[245] The result would then be 'global fragmentation of the financial system, and disorderly resolutions of failed cross-border firms...'.[246] The standard, therefore, aims to ensure that host countries have the confidence that there are sufficient resources in the global firm to address the distress situation of the subsidiaries in their jurisdictions.[247] It also provides that there should be some flexibility in the manner in which the capacity is used across-jurisdictions within the G-SIB.[248]

6.3.2 Complementary guiding principles and contractual approaches

Implementation of the Key Attributes in domestic systems has proved challenging, particularly the cross-border aspects.[249] The FSB, therefore, undertook to improve the cross-border resolution regime, specifically enhancing legal certainty in cross-border resolution.[250] From 2013, efforts focused mainly on implementing solutions that would enhance certainty that bail-in measures[251] and temporary stays on early termination of financial contracts will be recognized and enforced across jurisdictions.[252] The main concern in this regard has been how to avoid bail-outs (government rescues) in future insolvencies and how to prevent large-scale termination of contracts that could render a value-maximizing resolution impossible, as happened when Lehman Brothers entered insolvency proceedings.[253]

---

[245] Financial Stability Board, Principles on Loss-absorbing and Recapitalisation Capacity of G-SIBs (n 243) Principle VI.

[246] ibid.   [247] ibid.   [248] ibid.

[249] See Financial Stability Board, 'Cross-Border Recognition of Resolution Action: Consultative Document 7' (29 September 2014) 3, 11 <http://www.fsb.org/2014/09/c_140929/>; Financial Stability Board, 'Resilience through resolvability—moving from policy design to implementation', 5th Report to the G20 on progress in resolution (18 August 2016) 21–22 <http://www.fsb.org/wp-content/uploads/Resilience-through-resolvability-%E2%80%93-moving-from-policy-design-to-implementation.pdf>. Some aspects of the discussion in this section draw on I Mevorach, 'Beyond the Search for Certainty: Addressing the Cross-Border Resolution Gap' (2015) 10(1) Brook J Corp Fin & Com L 183.

[250] An FSB Report to the G20 identified legal uncertainties about the cross-border effectiveness of resolution measures as one of the main obstacles to the resolution of SIFIs that operate across borders. See Financial Stability Board, 'Progress and Next Steps towards Ending "Too-Big-To-Fail"', Report of The Financial Stability Board to the G20 (2 September 2013) 13–15 <http://www.financialstabilityboard.org/publications/r_130902.pdf>.

[251] Mechanisms such as write-down, cancellation, or conversion of debt instruments, designed to enable a restructuring of failing bank without having to resort to a state rescue. The temporary stay on termination rights in financial contracts and the bail-in are some of the resolution measures contemplated in the Key Attributes, s 3.2 (ix) and (x)).

[252] 'Progress and Next Steps towards Ending "Too-Big-To-Fail"', Report of The Financial Stability Board to the G20 (2 September 2013) 14–16 <http://www.financialstabilityboard.org/publications/r_130902.pdf>.

[253] The early termination of many of Lehman's assets that were considered financial contracts precluded a resolution of the failed international financial group through a going concern sale to another bank (EJ Janger, RJ Mokal, and R Phelan, 'Treatment of Financial Contracts in Insolvency—Analysis of the ICR

Thus, in 2015, the FSB introduced a set of principles (FSB Principles)[254] that comprise both statutory and contractual measures 'that jurisdictions should consider including in their legal frameworks to give cross-border effect to resolution actions in accordance with the *Key Attributes*'.[255] These principles, like the Key Attributes, are not binding and do not provide a comprehensive cross-border law for adoption in legal systems.[256] Instead, they enhance parts of the general policy framework of the Key Attributes, specifically the cross-border aspects. The scenario the FSB Principles address is one in which a firm is in resolution proceedings in a home country, but has a branch, subsidiary, assets, liabilities, or contracts in other jurisdictions.[257] In that regard, the FSB Principles attempt to enhance the recognition and support measures contemplated in the Key Attributes.

The FSB Principles elaborate on what recognition or support entails and what the legislation would need to include to comply with that aspect of the Key Attributes. In addition, the FSB Principles stress the need to follow the Key Attributes generally— to make recognition possible as a matter of law or policy and minimize inconsistencies between measures available in home and host jurisdictions.[258] Thus, the FSB Principles explain that recognition means local acceptance of the commencement of foreign resolution proceedings and the enforcement of foreign resolution measures or other granted relief (eg a stay on proceedings), to give effect to the measures adopted by the home jurisdiction.[259] Supportive measures are measures taken locally to support the foreign process, either pursuant to a request by the foreign authority or taken independently. The FSB Principles acknowledge that absent greater uniformity of available measures, such supportive measures may be limited to what is available locally and may not be fully consistent with the home resolution process.[260]

More specifically, the FSB Principles explain that recognition and support measures are complementary.[261] Their implementation requires that legislation grants authority to domestic authorities to give effect to foreign proceedings, through recognition or support or a combination of recognition and supportive measures, supported by either an administrative or judicial framework. The framework should

---

Standard: For Discussion at World Bank Insolvency and Creditor/Debtor Regimes Task Force Meeting' (World Bank Discussion Paper, 24 October 2014) <http://siteresources.worldbank.org/EXTGILD/Resources/WB_ICR_TaskForce_2014_FinancialContractsInInsolvency_DiscussionPaper.pdf>). Lehman's financial contracts portfolio was also subject to different regimes, and different systems attempted to apply their laws regarding the same contracts, ending with conflicting decisions regarding the validity of the termination clauses included in the contracts (see eg *Perpetual Tr Co v BNY Corp Tr Servs Ltd* [2009] EWCA (Civ) 1160 (Eng); *Lehman Bros Special Fin Inc v BNY Corp Tr Servs Ltd*, 422 BR 407 (Bankr SDNY 2010)).

[254] Financial Stability Board, Principles for Cross-border Effectiveness of Resolution Actions (3 November 2015) <http://www.fsb.org/2015/11/principles-for-cross-border-effectiveness-of-resolution-actions/>.

[255] ibid 5. The Principles focus on banks, but acknowledge that many of them may be relevant to other financial institutions as well.

[256] ibid. It is also noted that: 'The Principles are not intended to be comprehensive, and each jurisdiction will need to consider what is required in the context of its own legal environment for such a legal framework to be effective'.

[257] ibid.   [258] FSB Principles 6, 11; Principle 1.   [259] ibid 5–6.   [260] ibid 6.
[261] ibid 6.

also allow access to foreign authorities to request recognition and enforcement.[262] The Principles further stress that recognition and enforcement may be 'quasi automatic',[263] 'should in principle not be contingent on reciprocity',[264] and grounds for refusing to give effect to foreign measures should be 'clearly defined' and limited to infringement of public policy, including where such effect will undermine local financial stability or have material fiscal implications.[265] Supportive measures may be based on the local resolution framework and the conditions for taking local measures as well as conditions for cooperation with foreign authorities.[266] Processes for giving effect to foreign resolutions should be expedited,[267] and should be guided by the principles of non-discrimination and equitable treatment of creditors.[268]

The FSB Principles do not go further than that in terms of providing a more coherent model framework for adoption. They are confined to guiding principles. The instrument does acknowledge the importance of implementing statutory frameworks and the need for uniformity across jurisdictions, but it also considers such an approach as a long-term, more complex endeavour.[269] Therefore, to enhance certainty more rapidly, the FSB Principles also contemplate contractual approaches to cross-border recognition.[270] Regarding some of the resolution tools—those that affect contractual rights in the event of resolution—recognition and enforcement may be achieved through contracts. The focus of the contractual approach is, therefore, on such contract-related tools, specifically on bail-in and the stay on early termination of financial contracts, which, as noted above, have also been major resolution tools for avoiding future bailouts. Thus, the Principles state that firms should be required or incentivized by regulatory authorities to include cross-border recognition clauses concerning temporary stays on termination rights and bail-in in their financial contracts and debt instruments that are in line with the conditions described in the Key Attributes.[271] The idea is to ensure that such contractual clauses are sufficiently widespread and the solution is truly global.[272] For this purpose, the FSB also collaborated with the International Swaps and Derivatives Association (ISDA)[273] to implement such solutions through standardized protocols.[274]

---

[262] ibid Principle 2.   [263] ibid Principle 3.   [264] ibid.   [265] ibid.

[266] ibid.   [267] ibid Principle 5.

[268] ibid Principle 4. Additionally, legislation should include mechanisms to protect authorities and their officials when providing, in good faith, support to foreign resolution proceeding (Principle 6).

[269] ibid 5, 8. See also the preceding consultative document of the FSB Expert Group, which noted that: 'Statutory frameworks of the kind detailed in section 1 are the preferred longer term solution to the cross-border recognition of resolution actions. However, very few jurisdictions currently have such frameworks in place. Given the time required to implement the necessary statutory changes, which are likely to be complex …' (Financial Stability Board, 'Cross-border Recognition of Resolution Action' (n 249) 11.

[270] FSB Principles 5, and Principles 7–9.

[271] ibid Principle 7. The Principle also provides examples of such official measures that can incentivize inclusion of contractual provisions recognizing temporary stays and bail-in measures.

[272] Noting that: 'The impact of contractual solutions on aiding the cross-border enforceability of resolution actions depends on a sufficiently widespread adoption of appropriate contractual language by market participants' (FSB Principles 8).

[273] The dominant trade association for over-the-counter derivatives.

[274] ISDA published a series of 'Stay Protocols'. The first Protocol from 2014 amends standard ISDA master agreements and contractually opts adhering parties into provisions within specific qualifying

The FSB Principles describe the way such clauses should be framed so that parties adhering to the clauses would be bound by stays or bail-in measures under eligible resolution regimes, no matter where the firm or counterparty is located or what is otherwise the governing law of the contract.[275] The contractual solutions are in line with modified universalism as they attempt to reach a result where the home country process and measures (indeed only certain types) apply. The idea is to avoid situations where, for example, a stay might not apply to foreign counterparties or to counterparties trading under agreements governed by foreign laws. Thus, for example, regarding early termination rights in financial contracts, this approach 'brings the contract within the scope of the relevant statutory regime' where 'all parties, domestic and foreign, would be subject to the same stay'.[276] Aspects of modified universalism are therefore addressed through contracts, supported by regulation and supervision, enhancing certainty about the cross-border application (recognition and enforceability) of bail-in measures and stays on early termination rights in financial contracts.

6.3.3 Remaining gaps, decision challenges, and lessons from UNCITRAL

The umbrella policies and the specification of principles as well as contractual solutions concerning the cross-border insolvency of MFIs are thus generally in line with modified universalism where they envisage coordinated solutions and a global approach to the multinational default. The effort to standardize resolution regimes, including creditor protection standards in resolutions and the availability of certain minimum tools, is also critical for the operationalization of and compliance with the cross-border regime by home and host jurisdictions.[277]

The multi-faceted initiatives that include standards, principles, and contractual approaches supported by regulation, also contribute to the emergence of CIL concerning cross-border insolvency of MFIs by increasing the evidence of general practice accepted as law.[278] These initiatives all follow a rather consistent, modified universalist approach and manifest growing agreements regarding the norms by different bodies and players, including the support of the industry. The contractual approach, in particular, is being followed by major banks pursuant to regulatory

---

special resolution regimes that limit the exercise of termination rights (ISDA, International Swaps and Derivatives Association, Inc, ISDA 2014 Resolution Stay Protocol (4 November 2014) <http://assets.isda.org/media/f253b540-25/958e4aed-pdf/>). This Protocol was relaunched in 2015, expanding the type of financial contracts covered (ISDA, International Swaps and Derivatives Association, Inc, ISDA 2015 Universal Resolution Stay Protocol (4 November 2015) <http://assets.isda.org/media/ac6b533f-3/5a7c32f8-pdf/>). Another Stay Protocol from 2016 assists in complying with regulation that require entities to obtain recognition of stays from counterparties and provides modules that fit with different regulatory requirements in different jurisdictions (ISDA, International Swaps and Derivatives Association, Inc, ISDA Resolution Stay Jurisdictional Modular Protocol (3 May 2016) <http://assets.isda.org/media/f253b540-95/83d17e3d-pdf/>).

[275] FSB Principles, Principles 8–9.   [276] ibid Principle 8.
[277] Including through capacity building work by IOs. See Chapter 5, sections 5.3.1 and 5.3.2.
[278] See Chapter 3, section 3.2.1.

requirements adopted in different jurisdictions and is also implemented by industry bodies and by regulators in a way that promotes broad adoption by counterparties on the buy side as well,[279] again demonstrating growing adherence to the norms and thus the evolution of binding international law.

The limitations of CIL have been identified in previous chapters.[280] In particular, in the context of MFI insolvency, enforcement of norms might be more difficult in the absence of concrete international agreements. Recognition via contracts also entails inevitable limitations. The FSB has recognized that the contractual approach may not cover all contracts and all counterparties.[281] Enforceability of recognition clauses is also uncertain, especially when they might contradict applicable law or could be undermined by the application of local notions of public policy, which may not be aligned with international standards.[282] Even where the recognition clauses are widespread, they cover only a limited aspect of a cross-border regime, addressing recognition of specific resolution measures: bail-in and the stay of early termination rights in financial contracts. Contractual solutions cannot address the whole spectrum of resolution powers and their cross-border effects.[283]

The Key Attributes and supporting guidance for legislators in the FSB Principles, also do not provide a fully satisfactory solution. They are not sufficiently precise and complete, failing to create a strong enough obligation to adhere to a uniform regime.[284] First, they are the type of instrument that generates more room for inconsistent implementation and fragmentation. Because they allow significant flexibility regarding the manner of enactment, there is limited obligation to adhere to the regime in its entirety.[285] Influenced by the status quo bias, endowment effect, and loss aversion,[286] when given such an open choice, implementing institutions might apply standards in a way that largely correspond with the existing local system and avoid surrendering control to foreign jurisdictions or to external authorities.

[279] See Allen & Overy, 'Cross-border Recognition of Resolution Stays—Significant Compliance Challenges on the Horizon' <http://www.allenovery.com/publications/en-gb/lrrfs/continental%20 europe/Pages/Cross-border-recognition-of-resolution-stays.aspx>.

[280] See Chapter 3, section 3.2.4.

[281] Financial Stability Board, 'Cross-border Recognition of Resolution Action' (n 249) 11; FSB Principles 8.

[282] SL Schwarcz et al, 'Comments on the September 29, 2014 FSB Consultative Document, "Cross-Border Recognition of Resolution Action" ' Ctr for Intl Governance Innovation, CIGI Paper No 51, 3 December 2014 <https://www.cigionline.org/sites/default/files/no.51.pdf> (arguing that the contractual approach adopted by ISDA and the FSB has limited utility because it only binds the parties to the contract and even then, its enforceability is questionable).

[283] Mevorach, 'Beyond the Search for Certainty' (n 249) 208. See also B Wessels, 'Giving Legal Effect to Foreign Resolution Measures in the Financial Sector' (2015) 28(3) Insolv Int 44 ('I think the FSB is right in submitting that these contractual solutions should not be considered a substitute for statutory regimes').

[284] See Chapter 4, section 4.4.

[285] cf the EU Winding-up Directive and BRRD regime that prescribes minimum harmonization of resolution tools in addition to a regime for cross-border insolvency of financial institutions. As noted in Chapter 4, a directive is a less optimal instrument for cross-border insolvency compared with directly applicable regulation, still, the cross-border aspects in the EU regime for financial institutions are detailed and comprehensive and their implementation is mandatory.

[286] See Chapter 2, section 2.3.

Second, attributes or principles cannot provide a complete scheme for cross-border insolvency that can be followed uniformly.[287] Full harmonization based on such instruments providing standards for resolution regimes is not expected, as it is acknowledged that implementation should be adjusted to very different market conditions across systems.[288] Such variation, however, is incompatible with the requirements concerning the cross-border aspects including the core private international law-related rules, which cannot operate properly unless the same rules are followed.

Thus, there is still a major gap in the international infrastructure for cross-border insolvency where financial entities may not be subject to a uniform regime of mandatory international recognition and related cross-border effects.[289] Whilst the MLCBI could potentially address financial institutions—and thus the recognition, relief, and cooperation concerning their insolvency proceedings—it provides that it does not apply to proceedings concerning 'types of entities, such as banks or insurance companies, that are subject to a special insolvency regime' (if the enacting State wishes to exclude such entities from the law that enacts the MLCBI).[290]

Typically, domestic financial institutions or foreign institutions with local branches are not subject to the MLCBI.[291] Furthermore, the MLCBI does not specifically cover the types of restructuring measures, such as bail-in, or the types of tools that may be required to support MFI resolutions.[292] The draft MLG also refers to enterprises 'engaged in economic activities' that 'may be governed by the insolvency law'.[293] The definition of an enterprise group is based on the one developed in the Legislative Guide, which explains that the part in the Guide on

[287] See Chapter 4, section 4.4.1.
[288] Especially considering the application of the Standard beyond the globally systemic institutions. See International Monetary Fund, 'Cross-Border Bank Resolution' (n 216) 21–23. Surveys show significant divergence existing between different systems. See, for example, Financial Stability Board, 'Key Attributes of Effective Resolution Regimes for Financial Institutions, Second Thematic Review on Resolution Regimes Peer Review Report' (18 March 2016) 20–21 <http://www.fsb.org/2016/03/second-thematic-review-on-resolution-regimes/> (noting significant variations in conditions for use of resolution powers).
[289] The situation is different within the EU which created a banking union and where comprehensive directives govern the cross-border regime (see Chapter 1, section 1.4.4).
[290] MLCBI, art 1(2).
[291] See eg the UK Cross-Border Insolvency Regulation 2006, Sch 1, art 1(2)(h) and (i) and the US Chapter 15, Sec 1501(c)(1). The MLCBI may apply in less complex circumstances. See eg *International Bank of Azerbaijan OJSC*, Re Chancery Division, 06 June 2017 where recognition was granted regarding proceedings opened against a foreign bank to block creditors in the enacting State (the United Kingdom) from pursuing claims under loan agreements governed by UK law; *Flynn v Wallace* (*In re Irish Bank Res Corp Ltd*), 538 BR 692, 696 (D Del 2015) where a US court granted recognition to Irish liquidation proceeding for a failed bank, determining that this proceeding were not excluded from recognition since the bank had no branch or agency in the United States when the Chapter 15 petition was filed.
[292] See C Bates and S Gleeson, 'Legal Aspects of Bank Bail-ins' (2011) 5(4) Law and Financial Markets Review 264, 273. For example, if a single point of entry (SPOE) strategy is employed and a bail-in tool utilized, confined to the holding company, cross-border issues are minimized. Still, support by host countries may be needed, for example to operationalize a transfer of control in local subsidiaries to a bridge entity while maintaining relevant licenses and authorizations (see Financial Stability Board, 'Cross-border Recognition of Resolution action' (n 249) 3, 11; Financial Stability Board, 'Resilience through Resolvability' (n 249) 21–22.
[293] A/CN.9/WG.V/WP.146, art 2(a).

enterprise groups focuses on 'the conduct of economic activities by entities' and 'it is not intended to include consumers or other entities of a specialized nature (eg banks and insurance companies) that would not be governed by insolvency law'.[294]

Both before and pronouncedly after the global financial crisis, this gap in the cross-border regime has been identified and highlighted; and, in response, various suggestions have been made, including proposals to develop model laws or a treaty on cross-border insolvency of MFIs.[295] There have also been calls by UNCITRAL to address this gap.[296] Yet, thus far the international regulatory efforts have fallen short of attempting a comprehensive instrument.[297] This overly humble approach may be attributed to extant scepticism regarding the feasibility of such a project in view of countries' inclinations to focus on local interests. The political biases and bounds on decision-making concerning adherence to and implementation of a universalist regime are strong in the context of financial institutions.[298] Against this backdrop, treaties on MFI cross-border insolvency might entail significant costs and consequently risk becoming too hollow or, worse, unratified.[299] A model law, on the other hand, can achieve a regime which is de facto similar to a treaty relationship, and even harder in terms of levels of precision and obligation, while overcoming bounds on decisions.[300] A model law

---

[294] Legislative Guide, pt three, Glossary, para 4(b). Recommendation 8 of the Legislative Guide also refers to debtors engaged in economic activity as debtors governed by insolvency law.

[295] See eg EHG Hüpkes, 'Insolvency: Why a Special Regime for Banks?' (2005) 3 Current Dev in Monetary and Fin L, International Monetary Fund 1, 30; RM Lastra, 'Northern Rock, UK Bank Insolvency, and Cross-Border Bank Insolvency' (2008) 9 J Banking Reg 165, 175–77; Basel Committee on Banking Supervision, Report and Recommendation of the Cross-Border Bank Resolution Group (March 2010), paras 70–73 <http://www.bis.org/publ/bcbs169.pdf>; International Monetary Fund, 'Resolution of Cross-Border Banks—A Proposed Framework for Enhanced Coordination' (11 June 2010) 32–33 <https://www.imf.org/external/np/pp/eng/2010/061110.pdf>; RM Lastra, 'International Law Principles Applicable to Cross-Border Bank Insolvency' in RM Lastra (ed), *Cross-Border Bank Insolvency* (OUP 2011) 184; Bates and Gleeson, 'Legal Aspects of Bank Bail-ins' (n 292) 264; Edwards, 'A Model Law Framework' (n 174); Schwarcz et al, 'Comments on the FSB Consultative Document, "Cross-Border Recognition of Resolution Actions"' (n 282); Wessels, 'Giving Legal Effect to Foreign Resolution Measures' (n 283).

[296] Following proposals by the Swiss delegation (United Nations Commission on International Trade Law, Insolvency Law: Possible Future Work: Addendum, Proposal by the Delegation of Switzerland for Preparation of a Study on the Feasibility of an Instrument Regarding the Cross-Border Resolution of Large and Complex Financial Institutions, A/CN.9/WG.V/WP.93/Add.5, 1 (2010); United Nations Commission on International Trade Law, Insolvency Law: Possible Future Work: Further Proposal by the Delegation of Switzerland for Preparation by the UNCITRAL Secretariat of a Study on the Feasibility and Possible Scope of an Instrument Regarding the Cross-Border Resolution of Large and Complex Financial Institutions, A/CN.9/709, 3 (2010); United Nations Commission on International Trade Law, Insolvency Law: Insolvency of Large and Complex Financial Institutions, Note by the Secretariat, A/CN.9/WG.V/WP.109, 2 (2012); United Nations Commission on International Trade Law, Insolvency Law: Background Information on Topics Comprising the Current Mandate of Working Group V and Topics for Possible Future Work, Note by the Secretariat, A/CN.9/WG.V/WP.117, 8 (2013); United Nations Commission on International Trade Law, Insolvency Law: Recent Developments Concerning the Global and Regional Initiatives Regarding the Insolvency of Large and Complex Financial Institutions, A/CN.9/WG.V/WP.118, 2 (2013) <http://www.uncitral.org/uncitral/en/commission/sessions/43rd.html>).

[297] This discussion draws on Mevorach, 'Beyond the Search for Certainty' (n 249) 212 ff.

[298] See also Edwards, 'A Model Law Framework' (n 174) 140 ('Developing a cross-border resolution regime for G-SIFis is an uphill battle in part because countries must relinquish state sovereignty and control').

[299] See Chapter 4, sections 4.3.3 and 4.3.4.   [300] ibid section 4.4.

does not require a cumbersome adoption process, as enactment and enforcement are based on usual domestic procedures, and, additionally, such an instrument may be considered less threatening to sovereignty control.[301]

The process of developing a model law can still be potent, as has been the case with the MLCBI, where negotiations take place between representatives of many countries and organizations.[302] This process increases legitimacy,[303] which likely contributed to the success of the MLCBI in terms of adoption and implementation.[304] This is the first lesson that can be learned from the process of developing and implementing the MLCBI: deliberations should aim to be inclusive and involve interaction and negotiation among a wide range of representatives. This inclusivity turns such deliberations into mechanisms that not only allow for the development of an instrument but also allow for the education of representatives from a broad range of jurisdictions, which helps build consensus and impacts buy-in and adherence.

Another possible reason for the reluctance to proceed to harder instruments in relation to MFIs is path dependency, where the Key Attributes had already established a way to address the resolutions of these institutions, including the cross-border aspects, at least regarding G-SIFIs. Thus, redesigning the method for addressing resolutions in a different instrument format is now more difficult as this path has already been chosen.[305] Here, however, another lesson can be gleaned from the work on the MLCBI and additional model laws in conjunction with the Legislative Guide and parallel developments of the World Bank Principles forming the Insolvency Standard. The Key Attributes instrument is largely equivalent to the Insolvency Standard, as both provide an international standard for resolution/insolvency, respectively. The Legislative Guide and World Bank Principles continued to develop standards for insolvency issues (eg guidance regarding enterprise groups in insolvency), while ultimately 'delegating' to model laws the creation of a cross-border insolvency regime and transforming standards on cross-border aspects into model provisions.[306] The same approach can be applied to MFIs, where the development of a model law can be linked to and be in line with the Key Attributes and the supporting principles. Designing a harder instrument is even more important in the MFI context where territorial biases may be more pronounced, and CIL, and certainly notions such as comity, may be ignored or interpreted narrowly with standards being implemented partially or inconsistently.

The scepticism surrounding hard instruments, including a model law, may also be driven by concerns regarding the adequacy of the MLCBI for MFIs. The MLCBI had arguably been designed with corporate non-bank enterprises and single entities in mind and therefore does not fit with the more complex group structures

---

[301] ibid. It was also suggested in previous chapters, that choosing a model law for cross-border insolvency does not preclude entry into additional agreements, such as memoranda of understanding (MOUs), or treaties, that contain certain, even if limited, understandings (Chapter 4, section 4.4.2.3 and Chapter 5 section 5.3.3).

[302] See Chapter 4, section 4.4.2.1. [303] ibid section 4.3.2.

[304] See Chapter 1, section 1.4.4. [305] See Chapter 4, section 4.4.2.1.

[306] See sections 6.2.1–6.2.3.

that dominate MFIs.[307] It has also been noted that even if countries adopted the MLCBI and applied it to financial institutions, this would not eliminate persisting problems, as its provisions do not extend to enforcement of foreign judgments and other orders.[308] There have been important developments, however, since UNCITRAL's adoption of the MLCBI. First, it is true that the MLCBI focused on single debtors; however, in practice it accommodated cases of enterprise groups as well.[309] Importantly, the insolvency of multinational groups as well as the enforcement of insolvency-related judgments[310] is being addressed in additional work of UNCITRAL.[311] Thus, the UNCITRAL regime is becoming a rather sophisticated set of model laws that cover complex group structures as well. A model law for MFIs can take into account the peculiarities of the financial sector, falling in line with modified universalism norms that accommodate different entity types and circumstances.[312] Yet, much can be learned from the provisions, structure, and design of the MLCBI and related instruments, which, as discussed above, already cover significant portions of a modified universalist regime. Their application in MFI contexts may, at this stage, not be so complex and far-fetched, and thus it is possible to use the model law regime as a platform.

Building on the UNCITRAL work would prevent the reinvention of the wheel, increasing the efficiency and effectiveness of international law-making by drawing lessons from the design of closely related instruments. Insolvency of multinational commercial enterprises and MFIs are not only close in nature but also possess overlaps whereby enterprises may be comprised of financial and non-financial entities, and banks may be part of an enterprise group.[313] In substance, too, the problems specific to groups, especially how to respect the corporate form while giving effect to group economic realities, arise in both (commercial entities and financial institutions) contexts.[314] Thus, following the UNCITRAL instruments' scheme and accommodating their application to MFIs can ensure greater consistency across the different types of entities, including in circumstances where the same group includes both commercial and financial aspects. Complementing the UNCITRAL models may also ensure that all gaps are closed, and entities do not fall between instruments. Thus, a model law for MFIs could apply in circumstances not covered by the MLCBI as adopted locally, including to insolvency and resolution measures concerning institutions that are subject to special insolvency regimes and to banks and other financial institutions whose 'home' or branches are located in enacting countries.

---

[307] See eg Edwards, 'A Model Law Framework' (n 174) 124–25, 135 (noting the failure of the MLCBI to address groups and to satisfy the universalist benefits). The FSB also noted that the MLCBI is generally not applicable to financial firms and does not include specific rules regarding enterprise groups (Financial Stability Board, 'Cross-border Recognition of Resolution Action' (n 249) 7). See also: International Monetary Fund, 'Resolution of Cross-Border Banks' (n 295) 32–33 (noting the great relevance of the MLCBI, but also the fact that it does not address groups).

[308] See A Zacaroli and M Arnold, 'Banking on Brexit' South Square Digest (June 2017) 8, 15.

[309] See section 6.2.4.   [310] See section 6.2.3.   [311] ibid.

[312] See Chapter 1, section 1.3.2.   [313] See also Legislative Guide, pt three, para 9.

[314] See Chapter 1, section 1.2.3.

Following the UNCITRAL instruments' scheme and key features, in the MFIs context too, the regime may be based primarily on the notion of proper jurisdiction as an objective basis for swift recognition and relief.[315] In the MLCBI, it is COMI and establishment that determine the form of recognition and relief that should be granted. Proceedings opened at the COMI should be recognized as main proceedings, resulting in certain automatic relief, while proceedings opened in establishments may be recognized as non-main proceedings and may be granted various discretionary relief.[316] In the MFI context, the notions of home and host jurisdictions (head offices vs branches) are even more straightforward, and the uncertainty associated with COMI can be avoided.[317] Also, as noted above, to more tightly align the MLCBI with modified universalist norms, the concept of non-main proceedings should be utilized primarily to proclaim the role and duties of such proceedings as supplemental or secondary to the main proceedings.[318]

The notion of automatic relief that is provided to main proceedings, in the form of a general stay on proceedings and executions, may be less relevant in resolution contexts whereby a stay may be one of a number resolution options.[319] Thus, instead of speaking of COMI and establishment, and main and non-main proceedings as bases for automatic or discretionary relief, the distinction in a model framework for MFIs may be between home and host jurisdictions, where the primary role is given to a home proceeding, and this proceeding or resolution measures taken by the home jurisdiction should be recognized in other countries. It should also be provided that recognition and relief may be sought in jurisdictions other than those hosting branches, namely where the institution has assets or other operations.[320]

As also required under the MLCBI regime, host countries should provide access to the home country bodies so that they are able to seek recognition or relief and participate in local proceedings. Reciprocity should not be a requirement, as also stressed by the FSB Principles.[321] The relief that may be granted may depend on the circumstances of the case, and a model law can list the types of support that may be requested and should be provided regarding different resolution measures. Some of the relief delineated in the MLCBI can be similarly relevant in MFI contexts, importantly 'entrusting the administration or realisation of all or part of the debtor's assets' located in the host country to the foreign authority in the home country, allowing it to take control over the local branch or assets.[322]

Additional relief that should be specified for the MFI context include the enforcement of bail-in, the stay on exercise of early termination rights, and the transfer of property located in the enacting country to a bridge institution

---

[315] See section 6.2.2.   [316] ibid.
[317] Edwards, 'A Model Law Framework' (n 174) 141–43. See also Chapter 1, n 110.
[318] See section 6.2.5.
[319] M Marcucci, World Bank, Law, Justice and Development Week (October 2014) (unpublished presentation notes, on file with author).
[320] Under the MLCBI, as well, there is no restriction to the destination of recognition or relief requests. See also Edwards, 'A Model Law Framework' (n 174) 143 ('A "Host Country" is any country, other than the Home Country, in which a Group Member has assets or operations').
[321] See section 6.3.2.   [322] See section 6.2.2.

established by the home authority. Support and assistance should also include financial support by the host jurisdiction.[323] As in the MLCBI, relief should include interim support where urgent assistance is needed in the foreign jurisdiction, and a model law could sequence the provisions and clarify the time line for requesting relief at different stages.[324] Relief provisions should also explicitly include enforcement of orders and judgments provided in the home jurisdiction to avoid narrowly interpreting the model provisions and reverting to the territorial inclinations.[325]

In line with the Key Attributes and modified universalism, host proceedings may be opened in support of the home proceedings or as a separate process, if more efficient or necessary.[326] Recognition and support should be subject to safeguards,[327] which may be confined to matters of public policy, and adapted to MFI circumstances in a manner sufficiently concrete so as not to open the door to ring-fencing and territorial biases.[328] Public policy concerns should encompass breach of a home jurisdiction's duties concerning non-discrimination and due process, as well as incompatibility with recognized standards—namely, the standards and safeguards provided in the Key Attributes concerning the operation of resolution tools. Furthermore, in the MFI context, issues of stability and fiscal implications should be an additional specified reason for declining support, or for opening independent proceedings regarding domestic branches.[329]

In group circumstances, specifically in decentralized structures, which would be typical in cases of G-SIFIs, provisions in the draft MLG discussed above allow the opening of coordination proceedings where one of the members that is an integral part of the process has its COMI.[330] In the MFI context, again the notion of group home jurisdiction in the place of consolidated supervision is more established[331] and, thus, can be used as a basis for recognition and support to allow for a coordinated process to take place on the group level. The group home proceeding may contemplate a solution for the entire institution, and such proceedings could seek various relief in countries hosting subsidiaries. Subsidiary-host proceedings may be opened in order to support the group process, or recognition of that process may suffice. Here too, specific relief can be delineated; for example, when a single point of entry

---

[323] The home country may be responsible for the bulk of the funding and additional financial burden may be allocated according to an agreed formula. See JL Westbrook, 'SIFIs and States' (2014) 49(2) Tex Intl L J 329, 351 (noting that: 'Ideally, some formula, perhaps related to asset size, would allocate financial protection for each branch or subsidiary in advance'); Edwards, 'A Model Law Framework' (n 174) 144 (suggesting that: 'Host Countries will contribute to the Home Country's losses based on their failures before and during the crisis').

[324] See section 6.2.2.

[325] See the draft MLJ, discussed in section 6.2.3, that attempts to address the inconsistent application of the MLCBI relief provisions regarding enforcement of judgments.

[326] See Chapter 1, section 1.3.2.1.

[327] See the discussion of safeguards under the MLCBI in section 6.2.2.   [328] ibid.

[329] See Chapter 1, section 1.3.2.4. cf BRRD, art 95 (which allows resolution authorities to refuse recognition or enforcement of third-country resolution proceedings if it considers that 'the effects of such recognition or enforcement would be contrary to the national law').

[330] Section 6.2.4.   [331] See Chapter 1, section 1.3.2.1.

(SPOE) strategy is employed the relief may be specified such that only the holding company is subject to the insolvency process.[332]

Coordinated solutions may alternatively be achieved through cooperation; thus, a model law for MFIs can largely follow the MLCBI and the cooperation provisions in the draft MLG, including the use of protocols, while adding specific cooperation mechanisms and relevant safeguards, such as conditions for information sharing and the modes of cooperation envisaged for G-SIFIs via crisis management groups and institution-specific cooperation agreements.[333]

The regime for MFIs can also more explicitly and comprehensively address the outbound aspects of modified universalism.[334] The jurisdiction rule can be specified, based on the notions of home/host jurisdictions and group home/subsidiary-host jurisdictions. The home country/group coordination rule would give the enacting country the primary or ancillary role in the insolvency of the MFI, depending on whether it is the home or host country and on the level of control and concentration adequate in the circumstances. As the home process, the relevant authority may employ a liquidation or reorganization strategy and decide on the measures appropriate in the circumstances, as available under applicable law; furthermore, a model law can delineate such relief that should be available in the home country.[335] The home jurisdiction may also carry the main financial burden and be responsible for coordinating burden-sharing solutions. The choice of law rule, as well, can be specified and, as a rule, should be the law of the home jurisdiction with limited exceptions.[336] It should also allow adjustments for a group home jurisdiction to apply resolution measures centrally, while taking account of rights emanating from the law of subsidiaries' home countries.[337]

Ideally, a model law for MFIs would contain all the above features concerning jurisdiction, choice of law, recognition, relief, and cooperation. It would require a global approach as a matter of course, and swift assistance and recognition based on objective criteria and subject to concrete safeguards that would not leave much room for territorial biases to come into play. To the extent that negotiations would require accommodating differing approaches and as a result provide more discretion, options, or other forms of flexibility—as may be expected if deliberations are inclusive and based on broad representation—it would be preferable that the design of the instrument highlight the approach closest to modified universalism.[338] Such approach may also be presented as the default solution. As noted earlier, default rules—as well as framing and the manner in which options are presented—matter.[339] A careful design that accounts for bounds on decisions can affect choices and align them with the more optimal solutions.

---

[332] In such a case, support of host countries may be required for the transfer of ownership in local subsidiaries (see Financial Stability Board, 'Resilience through Resolvability' (n 249) 21–22).

[333] See section 6.3.1.

[334] See also the proposal to address this gap in the MLCBI (section 6.2.5).

[335] Similar to the relief that may be available in a group planning proceeding under the draft MLG (see section 6.2.4).

[336] ibid.   [337] See the regime developed in the draft MLG, discussed in section 6.2.4.

[338] See eg the potential decision challenges highlighted in section 6.2.4 regarding the application of a forthcoming MLG.

[339] See Chapter 2, section 2.4.3, and Chapter 4, section 4.5.

6.4 Conclusion

The assessment of the key international instruments reveals that many of the cross-border aspects of insolvency are addressed in detailed instruments that aim for uniform adoption and are formed in ways that make them conducive to widespread, universal application. The leading instrument is the MLCBI. It addresses mainly the inbound aspects of the cross-border insolvency, namely access, recognition, relief, and cooperation, emphasizing the role of host jurisdictions in facilitating a global collective process in a main forum. The MLCBI uses a proper instrument form, and its provisions are generally in line with, and have influenced, the emerging norms of modified universalism, thus also contributing to their transformation into binding international norms. The MLCBI is also supported by the Legislative Guide and the World Bank Principles that recommend that the MLCBI be adopted in legal systems and that provide universal standards against which safeguards in the cross-border regime can be applied more consistently.

Important gaps in the MLCBI, including where the application of provisions revealed uncertainties and inconsistencies, have been addressed in later revisions of the MLCBI GEI, especially regarding aspects concerning the criteria for recognition (aspects concerning COMI). Additional gaps are being addressed in ongoing efforts by UNCITRAL, specifically regarding groups and the enforcement of judgments. This work largely follows and builds on the MLCBI approach, in terms of the instrument choice and the key features of the model, yet it provides explicit and salient treatment of these important aspects of the regime.

This chapter also highlighted remaining gaps and potential challenges going forward. The MLCBI still does not explicitly address choice of law issues, and its approach to basic outbound aspects, namely rules on international jurisdiction, is also only implied. Addressing these gaps can make the regime more complete and less prone to territorial biases. It may also be possible in the process to generally streamline aspects of the regime—including the newer instruments for groups and for facilitating enforcement—removing excessive territorial protections and ensuring general consistency across the instruments. Such revisions should be informed by and refer to the norms of modified universalism, ensuring a principled and consistent approach and promoting the widespread application of the norms.

The UNCITRAL instruments have also focused largely on commercial entities, and thus the cross-border insolvency of MFIs is not fully addressed, except in high level standards, principles, and certain contractual solutions. The completion of the international regulatory landscape for cross-border insolvency requires that these institutions are covered fully in instruments, transforming general principles into model provisions intended for uniform application and targeted harmonization. Lessons from the UNCITRAL instruments can be learned, and the MLCBI and related newer instruments can provide a platform for the design of a model law for MFI cross-border insolvency.

It is likely that implementation challenges remain, especially where the development of instruments requires compromises, such as providing options for enacting provisions in domestic laws or in applying the provisions in cross-border insolvency cases. This chapter highlighted specific aspects of the instruments that carry the risk that policymakers and implementing institutions may deviate from optimal solutions. Awareness of these risks and challenges can increase compliance by legal systems with the instruments' objectives and allow for continued improvements in their design going forward.[340] Finally, it should be emphasized that it was not argued in this chapter that once existing gaps are addressed, the international instruments will be forever complete. Instead, modified universalism requires that instruments are regularly monitored to ensure that they fit with changing market conditions.

---

[340] See also additional compliance-inducing tools discussed in Chapter 5.

7

Conclusion

The Future of Cross-Border Insolvency

The analysis in this book shows that a bright future of cross-border insolvency is on the horizon. A regime that fits current market conditions and increases global and local welfare is within reach. It is founded on the emerging norms of modified universalism. These norms evolved from the theory of pure universalism—the idea that cross-border insolvencies should be unitary and universal. Against this backdrop, modified universalism provides concrete guidance for real-world cases. It is shaped by a reality in which cross-border insolvency cases take place within a large market, across distinct legal systems, or in regions with different levels of pooled sovereignty. Insolvency affects a range of diverse types and forms of enterprises and institutions. Thus, modified universalism's emerging norms prescribe efficient, and therefore varying, levels of centralization in cross-border insolvency proceedings that involve multinational entities, group enterprises, or multinational financial institutions (MFIs). The law and processes of a central forum should apply in principle, subject to concrete exceptions related to special policy considerations and to circumstances where the choice of law norm needs to accommodate the flexibility of the jurisdiction norm. This allows, for example, opening a coordinating process for certain enterprise structures in a forum other than that of the separate entities' home countries. The norms contemplate a universal effect of the centralized proceedings. They also require a global approach and global responsibility, with defined duties concerning all stakeholders and implicated entities. These emerging norms envisage a significant surrender of control and deference to foreign proceedings in cases when, from a global perspective, this represents the desired approach. Modified universalism also allows local courts in countries that host aspects of a multinational business or institution to retain residual control in the form of concrete safeguards.

A system based on modified universalism is attractive and has gained prominence in recent decades, both in theory and in practice. Nevertheless, it has been weakened by the fact that some nations have not enacted laws or adopted international instruments that follow modified universalism, as well as by instances where countries and their implementing institutions do not address cross-border insolvency cases in a way that reflects modified universalist norms. Modified universalism is fragile because it is often considered a trend or interim approach. Especially during the global financial crisis, there have been notable instances of territorial approaches in the form of discrimination against foreign stakeholders, non-cooperation with

The Future of Cross-Border Insolvency: Overcoming Biases and Closing Gaps. Irit Mevorach. © Irit Mevorach 2018. Published 2018 by Oxford University Press.

foreign proceedings, and a reluctance to defer to a foreign main proceeding, even without public policy justifications.

The book explored whether territorial approaches or deviations from modified universalism necessarily reveal what countries and their implementing institutions prefer, and whether countries give lip service to universalism but in fact favour territorialism, as proponents of territorialism have argued. It drew insights from the psychology of decision-making and its possible application to international law contexts to understand the factors that affect choices and decisions in international insolvency. Importantly, decision-making scholarship shows how choices and decisions are strongly biased and often deviate in predictable ways from economically optimal behaviour. Behavioural international law provides further theoretical grounds and indicative studies that show that bounds on decision-making may operate when actors in international law make decisions concerning international law issues.

A well-established phenomenon in decision-making research is the impact of loss aversion on individuals' real-life choices. People tend to give exaggerated weight to losses, in comparison with gains, even when this approach does not produce the highest yields. We even tend to take more risks to avoid losses than to increase gains. Importantly, for our purposes, losses need not be limited to assets but can encompass sovereignty, control over resources, control over lawmaking, and control over locally registered companies and local constituencies. Similarly, people tend to avoid action that they think may lead to a loss. This may be an obstacle to achieving a modified universalist system, which requires such loss-related actions. Adopting a global instrument on cross-border insolvency, for example, may represent a potential loss of sovereignty. Thus, countries' reluctance to cooperate in the cross-border insolvency realm and their low enthusiasm for proactively adopting a cross-border instrument may be driven (to some degree) by loss aversion biases, even though this approach is less likely to yield actual benefits.

Loss aversion is also linked to the endowment effect—people are reluctant to give up an asset that is theirs or under their control; they tend to ask for more to agree to give it up than they would be willing to pay to obtain it. Choices and decisions are also affected by the status quo bias—a preference for things to stay as they are and an aversion to change. Changes, as well as losses and gains, are apparently measured against perceptions of the current state of affairs. In cross-border insolvency, these perceptions are likely to differ among jurisdictions that have more, or less, experience of cross-border insolvency. Thus, territorial inclinations may be strongly affected by the status quo bias, especially where the traditional approach has been territorialism, even when it is not the ideal solution.

The way options are framed, including in legislation, can also affect decision-making. One of the strongest framing techniques that has been shown to affect decisions, including those regarding adherence to options in international treaties, is the use of default rules. The option presented as the default (status quo) is substantially more likely to be selected than the same option presented as a new choice. Thus, universal or territorial choices can be affected by the way options are presented. Finally, short-termism is another strong tendency that may affect choices in international law: for example, where policies focus on short-term political benefits at the expense of long-term commitments and gains.

It is plausible, therefore, to presume that territorial approaches are influenced by such biases and do not necessarily reflect the best options or most desirable choices. It is also possible to explain the relative success of modified universalism by looking at 'positive' tendencies and biases that may help to overcome the challenges of cooperating among multiple participants in complex cross-border scenarios. The presumption of standard economic theory is that international frameworks, such as treaties, might fail to address global problems effectively because participants may rationally pursue their own self-interests while disregarding those of others. Experiments show, however, that people can develop other-regarding and fairness preferences and gain social and psychological benefits from meeting the expectations of the group. Such preferences are strongly influenced by peer pressure; an indication of the force of the peer effect has been discussed in treaty studies. In cross-border insolvency, a significant number of countries and their implementing institutions have had substantial experience in regional and global multinational defaults. They have had opportunities to interact with peers and to see how international insolvencies are handled in other countries; this has likely contributed to a favourable approach to universalism.

Persisting territorial inclinations should not cast a shadow over the desirability of modified universalism. Rather than yielding to territorialist habits, international actors should strengthen modified universalism by attempting to close gaps in the system to reflect agreed norms and by working to overcome negative biases in favour of positive ones, thus aligning decisions and choices with optimal solutions. Actors who are aware of constraints on decision-making can counteract biases. It is also possible to choose strategies and design the system to account for bounds on optimal decisions.

Specifically, it was suggested that modified universalism can crystallize into binding law in the form of customary international law (CIL), which is a key source of public international law. It has limitations but also important advantages. CIL emerges from the general and consistent practice of countries, where that practice is based on a belief that the practice conforms to international law. What is interesting about CIL is that it is a gap-filling source—operating in parallel to treaties and soft law—as well as a debiasing tool. CIL can help to overcome loss aversion and status quo bias, which impede action, because it operates as a default system. Countries do not need to actively consent to it, and they are bound by its norms unless they actively object. Conceptually, it was shown that reaching the point where the norms become CIL requires modified universalism to transform from an interim concept into a stand-alone norm. In addition, the elevation of modified universalism to CIL requires an emphasis on the international role of cross-border insolvency and the fact that state actors and implementing institutions, including courts dealing with cross-border insolvency cases, operate in the international realm and can create and influence international law.

It was also stressed that norms concerning cross-border insolvency must be translated into technical rules within international instruments, and that here, the choice of instrument is important. The general view, in this field, has been that a treaty is the ultimate, ideal, and long-term regime, reflecting the aspiration to ultimately reach a purely universalist system. Other 'softer' instruments, such as model laws, are therefore viewed as interim, incremental measures. Yet, a broader analysis of instrument choice, informed by international law theory and practice, shows that the assumption that treaties are hard and binding, while non-treaty instruments are soft and non-binding, requires unpacking. So-called 'soft law' may in fact be harder than a treaty in its degree of precision and the credible obligations it generates. In cross-border insolvency, a hard instrument is needed, but instruments other than treaties are more likely to achieve the desired results. Economic analysis of international law, reinforced by behavioural perspectives, highlights the disadvantages of treaties, especially where they attempt to regulate complex problems among multiple participants. Treaties are costly to negotiate and to ratify. They are also associated with greater loss of sovereignty. Concerns about sovereignty can be exaggerated, making it more difficult for countries operating in a 'loss frame' to act, especially when a treaty requires greater action, in comparison with adopting a non-treaty text. Agreements concerning cross-border insolvency (in line with modified universalism) entail sovereignty loss and require coordination between multiple negotiators and ratifiers regarding complex issues. It is, therefore, more likely that a model law which is less formal can achieve greater precision through provisions that are less hollow and have greater uniformity and the potential for universal adoption. Model laws are therefore proper tools for the long term. They can close gaps and overcome biases. Moreover, and regardless of the choice of instrument, any instrument for cross-border insolvency can be further hardened through proper instrument design, which is especially important in circumstances where negotiations require concessions or the provision of options. Considering the effect of legislative framing, and particularly of default rules and the salience bias (the tendency to focus on information that is prominent and ignore what is less visible), when optimal solutions are presented prominently as a default, implementation is likely to come closer to an optimal approach.

It was observed, however, that even where the system appears complete at any given point in time—based on a strong, binding norm and accompanied by instruments that cover all issues and entities—compliance with the system is not guaranteed. Compliance is a challenge, especially in international law, where enforcement is largely decentralized. In cross-border insolvency, compliance raises a host of issues; again, certain strategies are available to the system. As a start, the disciplinary force of reputation is not limited to traditional public international law—it is equally important within the cross-border insolvency system, and reputation as a driver of compliance can be strengthened further by taking decision-making constraints into account. Thus, it was suggested that the system may use various mechanisms to induce compliance: for example, piggybacking on the reports that international organizations (IOs) use to rate insolvency systems. These can provide salient information about compliance with cross-border insolvency instruments, while emphasizing how non-compliance may result in a loss of rating. More negative sanctions, such as blacklisting or naming-and-shaming, may have a limited positive effect. Generally, measuring and sanctioning violations are not straightforward tasks. Such measures might even do more harm than good when they may undermine multilateral, voluntary cooperation.

It was, therefore, acknowledged that the cross-border insolvency system rightly (already) uses other types of mechanisms to highlight the compliance of participants and foster cooperation, such as forums where regulators or judges can meet to discuss relevant issues. These measures are paramount for developing mutual trust, which is not presumed under modified universalism (it can also be challenged by political events affecting the composition of integrated regions and the inclination to participate in frameworks and cooperate) but should be recognized and reinforced as a driver of compliance. Trust, as well as a readiness to comply with a modified universalist system, also requires the closing of capacity and regulatory gaps in legal systems, because without access to certain tools, legal systems cannot deal effectively with cross-border insolvency cases that land within their borders, or assist home and foreign countries properly. While forum shopping can address capacity and regulatory gaps to some extent, by moving cases to countries that have the tools and capacity to deal with cross-border insolvency, it is not a fully satisfactory solution. Compliance must be linked to the development of systems, including through external assistance; it can be achieved by taking advantage of existing IOs' development initiatives.

Beyond institutional capacity gaps, the actual insolvency laws vary across jurisdictions and are evolving at different rates in different countries. Yet, it was argued that only a limited form of harmonization would promote the cross-border insolvency system; a harmonization of laws can be justified when it targets standardization, the closure of regulatory gaps in less developed systems, and the development of measures to govern sophisticated entities, for which effective regulation is often missing domestically. This has generally been the approach taken at the global level thus far. Beyond this scope, it was argued, harmonization could undermine development and limit the exploitation of innovation across borders.

Finally, it was suggested that delegating part of the regime's implementation aspects—importantly, the handling of disputes and the resolution of certain cross-border insolvency cases—to international bodies may be an additional way of dealing with capacity gaps. It can also serve as a debiasing tool, with delegation reducing the risk that compliance will be undermined by a lack of willpower (short-termism) or inconsistent interpretations of international commitments. At the same time, delegation to external authorities can significantly increase sovereignty concerns, risking compliance at the stage when nations agree to participate in a global framework. Yet, delegation can be targeted. International bodies can be used to perform specific functions or to handle a subset of cases, rather than fully replacing the role of local courts or other authorities.

Together, these tools and strategies form a normative framework that can guide future reform and inform the debate about cross-border insolvency. Importantly, this framework suggests that the desired regime can be achieved without attempting a purist solution for the unforeseeable future. Instead, the framework contemplates concrete ways to create a complete, sufficiently widespread system based on modified universalism.

A close inspection of existing instruments, especially the model laws developed by the United Nations Commission on International Trade Law (UNCITRAL), shows that cross-border insolvency is already governed by proper instruments that are helping modified universalism evolve into a binding norm, while creating a uniform scheme for handling cross-border insolvency cases in pursuance of the goals of international insolvency. Gaps remain, as the instruments do not cover all the cross-border aspects of insolvency explicitly or comprehensively. Decision challenges are also expected, given that certain countries and implementing institutions may choose to follow the more territorial protectionist aspects highlighted in the instruments. Notably, the instruments do not comprehensively cover the cross-border insolvency of MFIs, which is currently largely informed by international standards and principles and supported by contractual approaches. These instruments are not sufficiently hard to properly address cross-border insolvency. However, the development of a model law covering these institutions more comprehensively is an achievable task; lessons can be learned from the way UNCITRAL instruments were developed, while accommodating the specialness of MFIs.

There is, therefore, room for additional work on the instruments and generally on strengthening the cross-border insolvency system. Future reform and development should continue to be multifaceted, with different roles assigned to different actors. IOs may prioritize addressing some of the most evident gaps and challenges, including developing a comprehensive cross-border insolvency regime for MFIs, developing uniform choice of law rules, and bridging capacity gaps through continued capacity-building work. For domestic legislators, the main effort should be to ensure that the national regime conforms to standards, that the country is party to cross-border insolvency instruments, and that such instruments are enacted consistently in pursuance of modified universalist solutions. To contribute to its transformation to CIL, courts and other authorities engaged in cross-border insolvency cases should seek to utilize modified universalism as the practised international law in this field. In particular, insolvency hubs and leading jurisdictions should continue to push modified universalism forward by explaining the ways in which choices and decisions are consistent with, and follow, its norms. Academics can assist, including by revealing the state of modified universalism across jurisdictions and in regions, going forward and as experience accumulates following the further development and adoption of international instruments.

Bibliography

Abbott KW and Snidal D, 'Hard and Soft Law in International Governance' (2000) 54 Intl Org 421

Abdelal R, *Capital Rules: The Construction of Global Finance* (Harvard University Press 2007)

Allen & Overy, 'Cross-border Recognition of Resolution Stays—Significant Compliance Challenges on the Horizon' <http://www.allenovery.com/publications/en-gb/lrrfs/continental%20europe/Pages/Cross-border-recognition-of-resolution-stays.aspx>

Anderson K, 'The Cross-border Insolvency Paradigm: A Defence of the Modified Universal Approach Considering the Japanese experience' (2000) 21 U Pa J Intl Econ L 679

Andreoni J, 'Cooperation in Public Goods Experiments: Kindness or Confusion' (1995) 85 Am Econ Rev 891

Armstrong Panuska T, 'The Chaos of International Insolvency—Achieving Reciprocal Universality under Section 304 or MIICA' (1993) 6 Transnat L 373

Arrow KJ, 'Gifts and Exchanges' (1972) 1(4) Phil & Publ Affairs 343

Asch A, 'Effects of Group Pressure upon the Modification and Distortion of Judgments' in H Guetzkow (ed), *Groups, Leadership and Men: Research in Human Relations* (Carnegie Press 1951)

Asian Development Bank, 'Technical Assistance Completion Report' (TA 5975-REG: Promoting Regional Cooperation in the Development of Insolvency Law Reforms' (2009) <https://www.adb.org/sites/default/files/project-document/64987/34496-reg-tcr.pdf>

Avi-Yonah RS, 'National Regulation of Multinational Enterprises: An Essay on Comity, Extraterritoriality, and Harmonization' (2003) 42 Colum J Transnatl L 5

Axelrod R and Keohane RO, 'Achieving Cooperation Under Anarchy: Strategies and Institutions' in KA Oye (ed), *Cooperation under Anarchy* (Princeton University Press 1986)

Ayres I et al, 'Evidence from Two Large Field Experiments that Peer Comparison Feedback Can Reduce Residential Energy Usage' [2009] Natl Bureau of Econ Research, Working Paper No 15386

Baker RB, 'Customary International Law: A Reconceptualization' (2016) 2 Brook J of Intl L 439

Balz M, 'The European Union Convention on Insolvency Proceedings' (1996) 70 Am Bankr L J 485

Bank for International Settlements, Basel Committee on Banking Supervision, 'Report and Recommendations of the Cross-Border Bank Resolution Group' (March 2010) <www.bis.org/publ/bcbs169.pdf>

Bates C and Gleeson S, 'Legal Aspects of Bank Bail-ins' (2011) 5(4) Law and Financial Markets Rev 264

Bebchuk LA, 'The Debate on Contractual Freedom in Corporate Law, Forward to Symposium, Contractual Freedom in Corporate Law' (1989) 89 Colum L Rev 1395

Bebchuk LA and Guzman AT, 'An Economic Analysis of Transnational Bankruptcies' (1999) 42 JL & Econ 775

Becker GS, *The Economic Approach to Human Behavior* (University of Chicago Press 1976)

Beckering KJ, 'United States Cross-Border Corporate Insolvency: The Impact of Chapter 15 on Comity and the New Legal Environment' (2008) 14 L & Bus Rev of the Americas 281

Ben-Shahar O and Pottow JAE, 'On the Stickiness of Default Rules' (2006) 33 Fla St U L Rev 651

Berg J, Dickhaut J, and McCabe K, 'Trust, Reciprocity and Social History' (1995) 10 Games Econ Behav 122

Berman HJ, 'The Law of International Commercial Transactions' (1998) 2 Emory J Intl Dispute Resolution 235

Beshears J et al, 'The Importance of Default Options for Retirement Saving Outcomes: Evidence from the United States' in J Brown et al (eds), *Social Security Policy in a Changing Environment* (University of Chicago Press 2009)

Block-Lieb S and Halliday TC, 'Harmonization and Modernization in UNCITRAL Legislative Guide on Insolvency Law' (2007) 42 Tex Intl L J 475

Block-Lieb S and Halliday TC, 'Incrementalism in Global Lawmaking' (2007) 32 Brook J Intl L 851

Bodgan M, Chapter 31, in JS Ziegel (ed), *Current Developments in International and Comparative Corporate Insolvency Law* (OUP 1994)

Boraine A, 'Elements of Bankruptcy law and Business Rescue in South Africa', unpublished note (2015) (on file with author)

Bork R, *Principles of Cross-Border Insolvency Law* (Intersentia 2017)

Bornschier V and Stamm H, 'Transnational Corporations' in S Wheeler (ed), *The Law of the Business Enterprise* (OUP 1994)

Boshkoff DG, 'Some Gloomy Thoughts Concerning Cross-Border Insolvencies' (1994) 72 Wash U L Q 931

Boyle AE, 'Soft Law in International Law Making' in MD Evans (ed), *International Law* (4th edn, OUP 2014)

Boyle AE, 'Some Reflections on the Relationship of Treaties and Soft Law' (1999) 48 ICLQ 901

Bradley CA and Gulati M, 'Withdrawing from International Custom' (2011) 120 Yale L J 202

Brewster R, 'Reputation in International Relations and International Law' in JL Dunhoff and MA Pollack (eds), *Interdisciplinary Perspectives on International Law and International Relations: The State of the Art* (CUP 2013)

Brewster R, 'Withdrawing from Custom: Choosing Between Default Rules' (2010) 21 Duke J Comp & Intl L 47

Brierly JL, *The Law of Nations: An Introduction to the International Law of Peace* (6th edn, OUP 1963)

Briggs A, 'Rubin and New Cap: Foreign Judgements and Insolvency' (10 April 2013) Singapore Management University School of Law Research Paper No. 7/2013 Available at SSRN: <https://ssrn.com/abstract=2248422> or <http://dx.doi.org/10.2139/ssrn.2248422>

Bromley JL and Phillips T, 'International Lessons from Lehman's Failure: A Cross-Border No Man's Land' in RM Lastra (ed), *Cross-Border Bank Insolvency* (OUP 2011)

Broude T, 'Behavioral International Law' (2015) 163 U Pa L Rev 1099

Brownlie I, *Principles of International Law* (OUP 2008)

Brummer C, *Soft Law and the Global Financial System: Rule Making in the 21st Century* (CUP 2015)

Bruner CM, 'States, Markets and Gatekeepers: Private-Public Regulatory Regimes in an Era of Economic Globalisation' (2009) 30 Mich J Intl L 125

Burman HS, 'Harmonisation of International Bankruptcy Law: United States Perspective' (1996) 64 Fordham L Rev 2543

Burton LA, 'Toward an International Bankruptcy Policy in Europe: Four Decades in Search of a Treaty' (1999) 5 Annual Survey of International and Comparative Law 205

Campbell A, 'Issues in Cross-Border Bank Insolvency: The European Community Directive on the Reorganisation and Winding-Up of Credit Institutions' <https://www.imf.org/external/np/leg/sem/2002/cdmfl/eng/campb.pdf>

Castel JG, *Canadian Conflict of Laws* (3rd edn, Butterworths (Canada) Toronto 1994)

Cataldi G, 'Italy' in D Shelton (ed), *International Law and Domestic Legal Systems* (OUP 2011)

Chandra Mohan S, 'Cross-Border Insolvency Problems: Is the UNCITRAL Model Law the Answer?' (2012) 21 Intl Insolv Rev 199

Charlesworth H, 'International Law: A Discipline of Crisis' (2002) 65(3) MLR 377

Chaudhuri A, 'Sustaining Cooperation in Laboratory Public Goods Experiments: A Selective Survey of the Literature' (2011) 14 Experimental Econ 47

Chayes A and Handler Chayes A, *The New Sovereignty: Compliance with International Regulatory Agreements* (Harvard University Press 1995)

Cheng B, *General Principles of Law as Applied by International Courts and Tribunals* (CUP 2006)

Cheng B, 'Custom: The Future of General State Practice in a Divided World' in R MacDonald and DM Johnston (eds), *The Structure and Process of International Law: Essays in Legal Philosophy Doctrine and Theory* (Martinus Nijhoff Publishers 1983)

Chinkin CM, 'The Challenge of Soft Law: Development and Change in International Law' (1989) 38 ICLQ 850

Cho S and Kelly CR, 'Promises and Perils of New Global Governance: A Case of the G20' (2012) 12 Chi J Intl L 491

Chung JJ, 'In Re Qimonda AG: The Conflict Between Comity and the Public Policy Exception in Chapter 15 of the Bankruptcy Code' (2014) 32 Boston U Intl L J 89

Chung JJ, 'The New Chapter 15 of the Bankruptcy Code: A Step Toward Erosion of National Sovereignty' (2007) 27 Nw J Intl L & Bus 89

Chung W, 'Hanjin Shipping: From the Eye of the Storm and Back' (2017) <http://www.marinelog.com/index.php?option=com_k2&view=item&id=25323:hanjin-shipping-from-the-eye-of-the-storm-and-back&Itemid=230>

Clapham A, *Human Rights Obligations of Non-State Actors* (OUP 2006)

Clark LM and Goldstein K, 'Sacred Cows: How to Care for Secured Creditors' Rights in Cross-Border Bankruptcies' (2011) 46 Tex Intl LJ 513

Clift J, 'The UNCITRAL Model Law on Cross-Border Insolvency—A Legislative Framework to Facilitate Coordination and Cooperation in Cross-Border Insolvency' (2004) 12 Tul J Intl & Comp L 307

Clift J, 'UNCITRAL Model Law—Alive and Well in 43 Jurisdictions and Counting!' *Global Turnaround* (May 2016)

Coase RH, 'The Problem of Social Cost' (1960) 3 J L & Econ 1

Collins L, 'Comity in Modern Private International Law' in J Fawcett (ed), *Reform and Development of Private International Law: Essays in Honour of Sir Peter North* (OUP 2002)

Collins L (ed), *Dicey and Morris on The Conflict of Laws* (13th edn, Sweet & Maxwell London 2000)

Colombo G et al, 'Potential Reforms to Brazilian Bankruptcy Law—Getting Closer to UNCITRAL Model Law on Cross-Border Insolvency' <http://www.insol.org/emailer/July_2017_downloads/Doc1.pdf>

Cook DC, 'Prospects for a North American Bankruptcy Agreement; Les Prospects Pour une Convention de la Faillite en Amerique du Nord; Los Prospectos Para un Convenio de Quiebra de Norte America' (1995) 2 Sw J L & Trade in the Americas 81

Crawford J, *Brownlie's Principles of Public International Law* (8th edn, OUP 2012)

Crawford J, ' "Single Point of Entry": The Promise and Limits of the Latest Cure for Bailouts' (2014) 109 Nw U L Rev Online 103

Culmer DH, 'The Cross-Border Insolvency Concordat and Customary International Law: Is it Ripe Yet' (1999) 14 Connecticut J Intl L 563

Cutler AC, 'Artifice, Ideology and Paradox: The Public/Private Distinction in International Law' (1997) 4 Rev Intl Pol Econ 261

D'amato A, *The Concept of Custom in International Law* (Cornell University Press 1971)

Davies PL, 'Resolution of Cross-Border Banking Groups' in M Haentjens and B Wessels (eds), *Research Handbook on Crisis Management in the Banking Sector* (Research Handbooks in Financial Law Series 2015)

Dawes RM, 'Social Dilemmas' (1980) 31(1) Annu Rev Psych 169

Dawson A, 'Offshore Bankruptcies' (2009) 88 Neb L Rev 317

De Martino B et al, 'Frame, Biases, and Rational Decision-Making in the Human Brain' (2006) 313 Science 684

Denza E, 'The Relationship between International and National Law' in MD Evans (ed), *International Law* (4th edn, OUP 2014)

Di Sano S, 'The Third Road to Deal with the Insolvency of Multinational Enterprise Groups' (2011) 26(1) JIBLR 15

Dicey AV, *Digest of the Law of England with Reference to the Conflict of Laws* (Stevens and Sons 1896)

Dolzer R and von Walter A, 'Fair and Equitable Treatment-Lines of Jurisprudence on Customary Law' in F Ortino (ed), *Investment Treaty Law: Current Issues II* (British Institute of International and Comparative Law 2007)

Drobnig U, 'Secured Credit in Cross-Border Insolvency Proceedings' (1998) 33 Tex Intl L J 27

Dumberry P, 'Are BITs Representing the "New" Customary International Law in International Investment Law?' (2010) 28(4) Penn St Intl L Rev 675

Dworkin R, *Sovereign Virtue: The Theory and Practice of Equality* (Harvard University Press 2000)

Easterbrook FH, 'The Race for the Bottom in Corporate Governance' (2009) 95 Va L Rev 685

Easterbrook FH and Fischel DR, 'The Corporate Contract' (1989) 89 Colum L Rev 1416

Edwards JM, 'A Model Law Framework for The Resolution of G-SIFIs' (2012) 7 Cap Mkts L J 122

Eichengreen B, 'Not a New Bretton Woods but a New Bretton Woods Process' (6 November 2008) <https://eml.berkeley.edu/~eichengr/not_new_bretton_woods.pdf>

Eidenmüller H, 'Abuse of Law in the Context of European Insolvency Law' (2009) 6 Eur Company and Financial L Rev 1

Eidenmüller H, 'Contracting for a European Insolvency Regime' University of Oxford and ECGI, Law Working Paper No 341/2017

Eidenmüller H, 'Free Choice in International Company Insolvency Law in Europe' (2005) 6 EBOR 423

Eidenmüller H and van Zwieten, K, 'Restructuring the European Business Enterprise: The EU Commission Recommendation on a New Approach to Business Failure and Insolvency' (2015) 16 EBOR 625

Einhorn HJ and Hogarth RM, 'Decision Making under Ambiguity' (1986) 59(4) J Bus 225

Ellsberg D, 'Risk, Ambiguity and the Savage Axioms' (1961) 75 Q J Econ 643

Engel C, 'The Behavior of the Corporate Actors: How Much Can We Learn from the Experimental Literature?' (2010) 6 J Inst Econ 445

Engel C, 'The Emergence of a New Rule of Customary Law: An Experimental Contribution' (2011) 7 Rev L Econ 767

Engel C and Kurschiligen M, 'The Coevolution of Behavior and Normative Expectations: An Experiment' (2013) 15 Am L Econ Rev 578

Enriques L and Gatt M, 'The Uneasy Case for Top-Down Corporate Law Harmonization in the European Union' (2006) 27 U Pa J Intl Econ L 939

EU Cross-Border Insolvency Court-to-Court Cooperation Principles and Guidelines (2014) <http://www.tri-leiden.eu/uploads/files/EU_Cross-Border_Insolvency_Court-to-Court_Cooperation_Principles.pdf>

European Commission, Action Plan on Building a Capital Markets Union, COM(2015) 468 final, 30 September 2015 <http://eur-lex.europa.eu/legal-content/EN/TXT/PDF/?uri=CELEX:52015DC0468&from=EN>

European Commission, 'Proposal for a Directive of the European Parliament and of the Council on preventive restructuring frameworks, second chance and measures to increase the efficiency of restructuring, insolvency and discharge procedures and amending Directive 2012/30/EU' COM(2016) 723 final <http://ec.europa.eu/information_society/newsroom/image/document/2016-48/proposal_40046.pdf>

European Commission, Recommendation of 12 March 2014 on a new approach to business failure and insolvency, COM(2014) 1500 final <http://ec.europa.eu/justice/civil/files/c_2014_1500_en.pdf>

European Parliament, DG for Research Working Paper, 'The Private Law Systems in the EU: Discrimination on Grounds of Nationality and the Need for a European Civil Code' Legal Affairs Series, JURI 103 EN, <http://www.europarl.europa.eu/workingpapers/juri/pdf/103_en.pdf>

Executive Summary and Working Papers for International Insolvency Convention Discussion, December 2015 <https://www.ibanet.org/LPD/Insolvency_Section/Insolvency_Section/Projects.aspx>

Fagbayibo B, 'Towards the Harmonisation of Laws in Africa: Is OHADA the Way to Go?' (2009) 42 Comp & Intl L J of Southern Africa 309

Falk A and Fischbacher U, 'A Theory of Reciprocity' (2006) 54 Games & Econ Behav 293

Falk A et al, 'Appropriating the Commons: A Theoretical Explanation' in E Ostrom et al (eds), *The Drama of the Commons* (The National Academies Press 2002)

Falk A et al, 'Testing Theories of Fairness—Intentions Matter' (2008) 62 Games & Econ Behav 287

Farber DA 'What (if Anything) Can Economics Say about Equity?' (2003) 101 Mich L Rev 1791

Farmer D, 'Chapter 15 Ancillary and Other Cross-Border Insolvency Cases' (2015) 19 Hawaii Bar J 14

Fed Deposit Ins Corp & the Bank of England, 'Resolving Globally Active, Systemically Important, Financial Institutions' (2012) <https://www.fdic.gov/about/srac/2012/gsfi.pdf>

Fehr E and Falk A, 'Psychological Foundations of Incentives' (2002) 46 Eur Econ Rev 687

Fehr E, Kirchsteiger G, and Riedl A, 'Does Fairness Prevent Market Clearing?' (1993) 108(2) Q J Econ 437

Fehr E and Rockenbach B, 'Detrimental Effect of Sanctions on Human Altruism' (2003) 422 Nature 137

Fehr E and Schmidt KM, 'The Economics of Fairness, Reciprocity and Altruism- Experimental Evidence and New Theories' in S Kolm and JM Ythier (eds), *Handbook of the Economics of Giving, Altruism and Reciprocity* (Science Direct 2006)

Felsenfeld C, *International Insolvency: A Treatise on The Law Of International Insolvency* 1, 3–8 (Juris Publishing 2000)

Financial Stability Board, 'Cross-Border Recognition of Resolution Action: Consultative Document 7' (29 September 2014) <http://www.fsb.org/2014/09/c_140929/>

Financial Stability Board, 'Key Attributes of Effective Resolution Regimes for Financial Institutions' (2011), revised in FSB, 'Key Attributes of Effective Resolution Regimes for Financial Institutions' (2014) <http://www.fsb.org/what-we-do/policy-development/effective-resolution-regimes-and-policies/key-attributes-of-effective-resolution-regimes-for-financial-institutions/>

Financial Stability Board, 'Key Attributes of Effective Resolution Regimes for Financial Institutions, Second Thematic Review on Resolution Regimes Peer Review Report' (18 March 2016) <http://www.fsb.org/2016/03/second-thematic-review-on-resolution-regimes/>

Financial Stability Board, 'Principles for Cross-Border Effectiveness of Resolution Actions' (3 November 2015) <http://www.fsb.org/wp-content/uploads/Principles-for-Cross-border-Effectiveness-of-Resolution-Actions.pdf>

Financial Stability Board, 'Principles on Loss-absorbing and Recapitalisation Capacity of G-SIBs in Resolution, Total Loss-absorbing Capacity (TLAC) Term Sheet' (9 November 2015) <http://www.fsb.org/wp-content/uploads/TLAC-Principles-and-Term-Sheet-for-publication-final.pdf>

Financial Stability Board, 'Progress and Next Steps towards Ending "Too-Big-To-Fail"', Report of The Financial Stability Board to the G-20 (2 September 2013) <http://www.financialstabilityboard.org/publications/r_130902.pdf>

Financial Stability Board, 'Resilience through Resolvability—Moving from Policy Design to Implementation' 5th Report to the G20 on Progress in Resolution (18 August 2016) <http://www.fsb.org/wp-content/uploads/Resilience-through-resolvability-%E2%80%93-moving-from-policy-design-to-implementation.pdf>

Finch V, *Corporate Insolvency Law* (CUP 2002)

Fischel DR, 'The "Race to the Bottom" Revisited: Reflections on Recent Developments in Delaware's Corporate Law' (1982) 76 Nw U L Rev 913

Fitzmaurice G, 'The General Principles of International Law Considered from the Standpoint of the Rule of Law' (1957) 92 *Receuil de cours* 7

Fletcher IF, *Insolvency in Private International Law* (OUP 2005)

Folz HP, 'Germany' in D Shelton (ed), *International Law and Domestic Legal Systems* (OUP 2011)

Franck TM, *Fairness in International Law and Institutions* (Clarendon Press 1995)

Franck TM, *The Power of Legitimacy Among Nations* (OUP 1990)

Franken S, 'Cross-border Insolvency Law: A Comparative Institutional Analysis' (2014) 34 OJLS 97

Gaa TM, 'Harmonization of International Bankruptcy Law and Practice: Is it Necessary? Is It Possible?' (1993) 27 Intl L 881

Galbraith J, 'Treaty Options: Towards a Behavioral Understanding of Treaty Design' (2013) 53 Va J Intl L 309

Garcimartin F, 'Universal Effects of European Pre-Insolvency Proceedings: A Case Study' in R Parry and P Omar (eds), *Re-imagining Rescue* (INSOL Europe Technical Series 2016)

Gardella A, 'The Court of Appeal Rules in Favor of Mutual Recognition and Rescues Cross-Border Resolution' (2016) <https://www.law.ox.ac.uk/business-law-blog/blog/2016/11/court-appeal-rules-favor-mutual-recognition-and-rescues-cross-border>

Gigerenzer G and Goldstein DG, 'Reasoning the Fast and Frugal Way: Models of Bounded Rationality' (1996) 103 Psychol Rev 650

Gigerenzer G and Selten R, *Bounded Rationality: The Adaptive Toolbox* (MIT Press 2002)

Gigerenzer G and Todd PM, *Simple Heuristics that Make Us Smart* (OUP 1999)

Gintis H, 'Strong Reciprocity and Human Sociality' (2000) 206(2) J Theor Biol 169

Gitlin RA and Flaschen ED, 'The International Void in the Law of Multinational Bankruptcies' (1987) 42 Bus Lawyer 307

Global Restructuring Review, 'Chapter 11 Update Makes Bank Resolution in Court "Credible", but Doubts Linger' (21 April 2017)

Global Restructuring Review, 'Electronics Group swaps Hong Kong for Bermuda's "More Flexible" Regime' (24 February 2017)

Global Restructuring Review, 'European Academy of Law, Trier: The Need to Regroup on Groups' (5 July 2017)

Global Restructuring Review, 'Hong Kong Court Sets Standard Order for Recognition Applications' (27 September 2016)

Global Restructuring Review, 'Indian Committee Clears New Bankruptcy Law after Overseas Provisions Added' (29 April 2016)

Global Restructuring Review, 'International Debt Restructuring: Can Other Jurisdictions Compete with London and New York' (1 March 2017)

Global Restructuring Review, 'Is the Common Law Gibbs Rule Outdated?' (3 February 2017)

Global Restructuring Review, 'Regulatory Round-up: Hungary Snubs the Model Law' (20 April 2017)

Gneezy U and Rustichini A, 'A Fine is a Price' (2000) 29 J Legal Stud 1

Godwin A, Howse T, and Ramsay I, 'The Inherent Power of Common Law Courts to Provide Assistance in Cross-Border Insolvencies: From Comity to Complexity' (2017) 26 Intl Insolv Rev 5

Goldmann M, 'We Need to Cut Off the Head of the King: Past, Present, and Future Approaches to International Soft Law' (2012) 25(2) Leiden J Intl L 335

Goldsmith JL and Posner EA, *The Limits of International Law* (OUP 2005)

Gong X, 'To Recognise or Not to Recognise? Comparative Study of Lehman Brothers Cases in Mainland China and Taiwan' (2013) 10(4) ICR 240

Goode R, *Principles of Corporate Insolvency Law* (Sweet & Maxwell 2011)

Goodman R and Jinks D, 'How to Influence States: Socialization and International Human Rights Law' (2004) 54 Duke L J 621

Goodman R and Jinks D, *Socializing States: Promoting Human Rights through International Law* (OUP 2013)

Gopalan S and Guihot M, 'Cross-Border Insolvency and Multinational Enterprise Groups: Judicial Innovation as an International Solution' (2016) 48 Geo Wash Intl L Rev 549

Gopalan S and Guihot M, 'Recognition and Enforcement in Cross-Border Insolvency Law: A Proposal for Judicial Gap-Filling' (2015) 48 Vand J Transnatl L 1225

Gordon JN et al, 'Financial Scholars Oppose Eliminating 'Orderly Liquidation Authority' As Crisis-Avoidance Restructuring Backstop' 5 (23 May 2017 letter to Congress) <https://www.law.columbia.edu/sites/default/files/microsites/law-economics-studies/scholars_letter_on_ola_-_final_for_congress.pdf>

Greene J, 'Bankruptcy Beyond Borders: Recognizing Foreign Proceedings in Cross-Border Insolvencies' (2005) 30 Brooklyn J Intl L 685

Gropper A, 'The Arbitration of Cross Border Insolvencies' (2012) 18 ABLJ 201

Gropper AL, 'The Curious Disappearance of Choice of Law as an Issue in Chapter 15 Cases' (2014) 9(1) Brook J Corp Fin & Com L 151

Gross Stein J, 'Psychological Explanations of International Conflict' in W Carlsnaes et al (eds), *Handbook of International Relations* (Sage Publishing 2002)

Guanawardana ADZ, 'The Inception and Growth of Bilateral Investment Promotion and Protection Treaties' (1992) 86 Proc Am Socy Intl L 544

Guidelines for Communication and Cooperation between Courts in Cross-Border Insolvency Matters (as promulgated by the Judicial Insolvency Network Conference 10–11 October 2016) <https://www.gov.uk/government/uploads/system/uploads/attachment_data/file/612376/JIN_Guidelines.pdf>

Guttel E and Harel A, 'Matching Probabilities: The Behavioral Law and Economics of Repeated Behavior' (2005) 72 U Chi L Rev 1197

Guzman AT, 'A Compliance-Based Theory of International Law' (2000) 90 Cal L Rev 1823

Guzman AT, 'Against Consent' (2012) 52 Va J Intl L 747

Guzman AT, *How International Law Works: A Rational Choice Theory* (OUP 2008)

Guzman AT, 'International Bankruptcy: In Defence of Universalism' (2000) 98 Mich L Rev 2177

Guzman AT, 'Reinvigorating Customary International Law' in CA Bradley (ed), *Custom's Future, International Law in a Changing World* (CUP 2016)

Guzman AT, 'Saving Customary International Law' (2005) 27 Mich J Intl L 115

Guzman AT and Meyer TL, 'International Common Law: The Soft Law of International Tribunals' (2009) 9 Chi J Intl L 515

Guzman AT and Meyer TL, 'International Soft Law' (2010) 2 J Leg Analysis 171

Hafner-Burton EM et al, 'Decision Maker Preferences for International Legal Cooperation' (2014) 68 Intl Org 845 <http://fowler.ucsd.edu/decision_maker_preferences_for_international_legal_cooperation.pdf>

Hague Conference on Private International Law (HCCE), The Judgments Project https://www.hcch.net/en/projects/legislative-projects/judgments

Hall S, 'The Persistent Spectre: Natural Law, International Order and the Limits of Legal Positivism' (2001) 12 Eur J Intl L 269

Halliday TC and Carruthers BG, 'The Recursivity of Law: Global Norm Making and National Lawmaking in the Globalization of Corporate Insolvency Regimes' (2007) 112 AJS 1135

Han M, 'Recognition of Insolvency Effects of a Foreign Insolvency Proceeding: Focusing on the Effect of Discharge' in MP Ramaswamay and J Ribeiro (eds), *Trade Development Through Harmonization of Commercial Law* (New Zealand Association for Comparative Law 2015)

Hardin G, 'The Tragedy of the Commons' (1968) 162 Science 1243

Harner M, 'The Corporate Governance and Public Policy Implications of Activist Distressed Debt Investing' (2008) 77 Fordham L Rev 703

Hathaway OH, 'Path Dependency in the Law: The Courts and Pattern of Legal Change in a Common Law System' (2001) 86 Iowa L Rev 601

Hatzimihail N, 'On Mapping the Conceptual Battlefield of Private International Law' (2000) 13 Hague Y B Intl L 57

Helleiner E, *The Status Quo Crisis: Global Financial Governance after the 2008 Financial Meltdown* (OUP, 2014)

Henkin L, *How Nations Behave* (Columbia University Press 1979)

Henrich J et al, 'Group Report: What Is the Role of Culture in Bounded Rationality?' in G Gigerenzer and R Selten (eds), *Bounded Rationality, The Adaptive Toolbox* (The MIT Press 2001) 343)

Ho LC, *Cross-Border Insolvency, A Commentary on the UNCITRAL Model Law* (4th edn, Global Law and Business 2017)

Ho LC, *Cross-Border Insolvency: Principles and Practice* (Sweet & Maxwell 2016)

Ho LC, 'Recognising Foreign Insolvency Discharge and Stare Decisis' (2011) 26 JIBLR 266

Honsberger J, *The Negotiation of a Bankruptcy Treaty*, reprinted in 1985 Meredith Memorial Lectures (McGill University 1985)

Hüpkes EHG, 'Allocating Costs of Failure Resolution: Shaping Incentives and Reducing Moral Hazard' in RM Lastra (ed), *Cross-Border Bank Insolvency* (OUP 2011)

Hüpkes EHG, 'Insolvency: Why a Special Regime for Banks?' (2005) 3 Current Dev in Monetary and Fin L, International Monetary Fund 1

INSOL Europe (2010), *Harmonisation of insolvency law at EU level*, European Parliament, Directorate General for Internal Policies, Policy Department C: Citizens' Rights and Constitutional Affairs, Legal Affairs, PE 419.633 <http://www.eesc.europa.eu/sites/default/files/resources/docs/ipol-juri_nt2010419633_en.pdf>

INSOL International, Statement of Principles for a Global Approach to Multi-Creditor Workouts II, INSOL International, Second Edition, 2017

Institute of International Finance, 'Making Resolution Robust- Completing The Legal And Institutional Frameworks For Effective Cross-Border Resolution of Financial Institutions' (June 2012) <https://www.iif.com/system/files/Making_Resolution_Robust_20120607.pdf>

International Law Association, London Conference (2000), Committee on Formation of Customary (General) International Law, 'Final Report of the Committee' <https://www.law.umich.edu/facultyhome/drwcasebook/Documents/Documents/ILA%20Report%20on%20Formation%20of%20Customary%20International%20Law.pdf >

International Law Commission, Identification of Customary International Law, Text of the draft conclusions provisionally adopted by the Drafting Committee, A/CN.4/L.872, (30 May 2016) ,http://legal.un.org/docs/index.asp?symbol=A/CN.4/L.872>

International Law Commission, 'Summaries of the Work of the International Law Commission' <http://legal.un.org/ilc/summaries/1_13.shtml>

International Monetary Fund, 'Cross-Border Bank Resolution: Recent Developments' (2 June 2014) https://www.imf.org/external/np/pp/eng/2014/060214.pdf

International Monetary Fund, IMF Staff, 'The Role of Capacity-building in Poverty Reduction' (March 2002) <https://www.imf.org/external/np/exr/ib/2002/031402.htm>

International Monetary Fund, 'Resolution of Cross-Border Banks—A Proposed Framework for Enhanced Coordination' (11 June 2010) <https://www.imf.org/external/np/pp/eng/2010/061110.pdf>

International Swaps and Derivatives Association, Inc, ISDA 2014 Resolution Stay Protocol (4 November 2014) <http://assets.isda.org/media/f253b540-25/958e4aed-pdf/>

International Swaps and Derivatives Association, Inc, ISDA 2015 Universal Resolution Stay Protocol (4 November 2015) <http://assets.isda.org/media/ac6b533f-3/5a7c32f8-pdf/>

International Swaps and Derivatives Association, Inc, ISDA Resolution Stay Jurisdictional Modular Protocol (3 May 2016) <http://assets.isda.org/media/f253b540-95/83d17e3d-pdf/>

Jackson TH, *The Logic and Limits of Bankruptcy Law* (Harvard University Press 1986)

Jackson TH, 'Translating Assets and Liabilities to the Bankruptcy Forum' (1985) 14 J Legal Stud 73

Jackson TH and Scott RE, 'On the Nature of Bankruptcy: An Essay on Bankruptcy Sharing and the Creditors' Bargain' (1989) 75(2) Vand L Rev 155

Janger EJ, 'Reciprocity Comity' (2011) 46 Texas Intl L J 441

Janger EJ, 'Silos: Establishing the Distributional Baseline in Cross-Border Bankruptcies' 9(1) Brook J Corp Fin & Com L 179

Janger EJ, 'Universal Proceduralism' (2007) 32 Brook J Intl L 819

Janger EJ, Mokal RJ, and Phelan R, 'Treatment of Financial Contracts in Insolvency— Analysis of the ICR Standard: For Discussion at World Bank Insolvency and Creditor/ Debtor Regimes Task Force Meeting' (World Bank Discussion Paper, 24 October 2014) <http://siteresources.worldbank.org/EXTGILD/Resources/WB_ICR_TaskForce_ 2014_FinancialContractsInInsolvency_DiscussionPaper.pdf>

Jansen N and Michaels R, 'Private Law and the State Comparative Perceptions and Historical Dimensions' (2007) 71 *RabelsZ* 345

Jennings R and Watts A, (eds), *Oppenheim's International Law* (9th edn, Longman Harlow 1992)

Jervis R, *Perception and Misperception in International Politics* (Princeton University Press 1976)

Johnson EJ and Goldstein D, 'Do Defaults Save Lives' (2003) 302 Science 1338

Jolls C and Sunstein CR, 'Debiasing Through Law' (2006) 35 J Legal Stud 199

Jolls C et al, 'A Behavioral Approach to Law and Economics' (1998) 50 Stan L Rev 1471

Kahneman D, 'A Perspective on Judgment and Choice: Mapping Bounded Rationality' (2003) 58 Am Psychol 697

Kahneman D, 'Maps of Bounded Rationality: Psychology for Behavioral Economics' (2003) 93 Am Econ Rev 1449

Kahneman D, Knetch JL, and Thaler RH, 'Anomalies: The Endowment Effect, Loss Aversion and Status Quo Bias' (1991) 5(1) J Econ Perspectives 193

Kahneman D, Knetch JL, and Thaler RH, 'Experimental Tests of the Endowment Effect and the Coase Theorem' (1990) 98 J Pol Econ 1325

Kahneman D and Tversky A, 'Choices, Values and Frames' (1984) 39 American Psychologist 341

Kahneman D and Tversky A, 'Prospect Theory: An Analysis of Decisions Under Risk' (1979) 47 Econometrica 263

Kahneman D et al, 'Experimental Tests of the Endowment Effect and the Coase Theorem' (1990) 98 J Pol Econ 1325

Kalensky P, *Trends of Private International Law* (Martinus Nijhoff Publishers 1971)

Kannan R, Supreme Court of Singapore, 'The Cross-border Project—A "Dual-track" Approach' INSOL International Group of 36 Meeting in Singapore (30 November 2015) <http://www.supremecourt.gov.sg/Data/Editor/Documents/Insol%2036_Speech_khb_ upload%20version.pdf>

Kannan R, 'The Gibbs Principle: A Tether on the Feet of Good Forum Shopping' (2017) 29 Singapore Academy L J 42

Kargman S, 'Emerging Economies and Cross-Border Insolvency Regimes: Missing BRICS in the International Insolvency Architecture (Part II)' (2013) 7(1) Insolv & Restructuring Intl 8

Kipnis AM, 'Beyond UNCITRAL: Alternatives to Universality in Translational Insolvency' (2008) 36 Denv J Intl L & Pol'y 155

Kishoiyan B, 'The Utility of Bilateral Investment Treaties in the Formulation of Customary International Law' (1994) 14 Nw J Intl L & Bus 327

Klissouras C, 'Promoting Global Solutions against Fundamental Inefficiencies of National Laws: A Case for International Harmonization of Civil Procedure Laws' Law, Justice and Development Week, World Bank Group (20–24 October 2014) <http://siteresources. worldbank.org/EXTGILD/Resources/Klissouras_Insolvency_PanelDiscussionPaper. pdf>

Knetsch JL and Sinden JA, 'Willingness to Pay and Compensation Demanded: Experimental Evidence of an Unexpected Disparity in Measures of Value' (1984) 99 Q J Econ 507

Korobkin R, 'The Endowment Effect and Legal Analysis' (2003) 97 Nw U L Rev 1227

Korobkin R, 'The Status Quo Bias and Contract Default Rules' (1998) 83 Cornell L Rev 608

Korobkin R and Guthrie C, 'Heuristics and Biases at the Bargaining Table' (2004) 87 Marq L Rev 795

Korobkin R and Ulen TS, 'Law and Behavioral Science: Removing the Rationality Assumption from Law and Economics' (2000) 88 Calif L Rev 1051

Koskenniemi M, 'Formalism, Fragmentation, Freedom: Kantian Themes in Today's International Law' (2007) 4 No Foundations: Journal of Extreme Legal Positivism 7

Koskenniemi M, 'Global Governance and Public International Law' (2004) 37 Kritische Justiz 241

Kotuby Jr CT, 'General Principles of Law, International Due Process, and The Modern Role of Private International Law' (2013) 23 Duke J Comp & Intl L 411

Kritsiotis, D, 'On the Possibilities of and for Persistent Objection' (2010) 21 Duke J Comp & Intl L 121

Kuran T and Sunstein CR, 'Availability Cascades and Risk Regulation' (1999) 51 Stan L Rev 683

Laffont JJ and Martimort D, *The Theory of Incentives* (Princeton University Press 2002)

Langevoort DC, 'Behavioral Theories of Judgement and Decision Making in Legal Scholarship: A Literature Review' (1998) 51 Vand L Rev 1499

Lastra RM, 'International Law Principles Applicable to Cross-Border Bank Insolvency' in RM Lastra (ed), *Cross-Border Bank Insolvency* (OUP 2011)

Lastra RM, 'Northern Rock, UK Bank Insolvency, and Cross-Border Bank Insolvency' (2008) 9 J Banking Reg 165

Leno ND, 'Development of a Uniform Insolvency Law in SADC: Lessons from OHADA' (2013) 57 J African L 259

Leong J, 'Is Chapter 15 Universalist or Territorialist? Empirical Evidence from US Bankruptcy Court Cases' (2011) 29(1) Wisconsin Intl L J 110

Lepard BD, *Customary International Law: A New Theory with Practical Applications* (CUP 2010)

Lim CL, 'The Strange Vitality of Custom in the International Protection of Contracts, Property, and Commerce' in CA Bradley (ed), *Custom's Future, International Law in a Changing World* (CUP 2016)

Lipson C, 'Why Are Some Agreements Informal?' (1991) 45 Intl Org 495

Lipstein K, Chapter 14 in IF Fletcher (ed), *Cross-Border Insolvency: Comparative Dimensions: the Aberystwyth Insolvency Papers* (United Kingdom National Committee of Comparative Law 1990)

Lipstein K, *Principles of the Conflict of Laws: National and International Perspectives* (Martinus Nijhoff Publishers 1981)

LoPucki LM, 'Cooperation in International Bankruptcy: A Post-Universalist Approach' (1999) 84 Cornell L Rev 696

LoPucki LM, 'Global and Out of Control?' (2005) 79 Am Bankr L J 79

LoPucki LM, 'The Case for Cooperative Territoriality in International Bankruptcy' (2000) 98 Mich L Rev 2216

Lord CG et al, 'Biased Assimilation and Attitude Polarization: The Effects of Prior Theories on Subsequently Considered Evidence' (1979) 37 J Personality & Soc Psychol 2098

Lowe V, *International Law* (Clarendon Law Series 2007)

Madaus S, 'Insolvency Proceedings for Corporate Groups under the New Insolvency Regulation' [2015] IILR 235

Malanczuk P, *Akehurst's Modern Introduction to International Law* (7th edn, Routledge 1997)

Manga Fombad C, 'Some Reflections on the Prospects for the Harmonization of International Business Laws in Africa: OHADA and Beyond' (2013) 59 Africa Today 50

Marcucci M, World Bank, Law, Justice and Development Week (October 2014) (unpublished presentation notes, on file with author)

Mason R, 'Cross-Border Insolvency and Legal Transnationalisation' (2012) 21 Int Insolv Rev 105

Matthews BC, 'Emerging Public International Banking Law? Lessons from the Law of the Sea Experience' (2010) 10 Chi J Intl L 539

Matthews BC, 'Prospects for Coordination and Competition in Global Finance' (2010) Proceedings of the Annual Meeting (American Society of International Law) Vol 104, International Law in a Time of Change (2010) 289

McCormack G, 'Control and Corporate Rescue—An Anglo-American Evaluation' (2007) 56(3) Intl Comp LQ 515

McCormack G, 'Jurisdictional Competition and Forum Shopping in Insolvency Proceedings' (2009) 68(1) CLJ 169, 196

McCormack G, 'Universalism in Insolvency Proceedings and the Common Law' (2012) 32(2) OJLS 325

McCormack G, 'US Exceptionalism and UK Localism? Cross-border Insolvency law in Comparative Perspective' (2016) 36(1) Legal Stud 136

McCorquodale R, 'The Individual and the International Legal System' in MD Evans (ed), *International Law* (4th edn, OUP 2014)

McInerney TF, 'The Emerging Developmental Approach to Multilateral Treaty Compliance' (2005) <http://treatyeffectiveness.org/wp-content/uploads/2012/05/McInerney_Developmental_Approach.pdf>

McLachlan C, 'Investment Treaties and General International Law' (2008) 57(2) ICLQ 361

Meier N and Rodriguez R, 'Recast of the Swiss International Insolvency Law' (2015/2016) *Yearbook of Private International Law*, Vol 17

Mellers BA et al, 'Group Report: Effects of Emotions and Social Processes on Bounded Rationality,' in G Gigerenzer and R Selten (eds), *Bounded Rationality, The Adaptive Toolbox* (The MIT Press 2001) 263

Mendelson MH, 'The Formation of Customary International Law' (1998) 272 Recueil Des Cours 155

Menezes A and Paterson W, 'One Insolvency Law, Seventeen Countries: A Brief Overview of the Revised OHADA Uniform Act on Insolvency' (2016) 1 INSOL World 28

Menski WF, 'Comparative Law in a Global Context: *The Legal Systems of Asia and Africa*' (2nd edn, CUP 2006)

Meron T, 'The Continuing Role of Custom in the Formation of International Humanitarian Law' (1996) 90 Am J Intl L 238

Mevorach I, 'Beyond the Search for Certainty: Addressing the Cross-Border Resolution Gap' (2015) 10(1) Brook J Corp Fin & Com L 183

Mevorach I, 'Centralizing Insolvencies of Pan-European Corporate groups: A Creditor's Dream or Nightmare?' [2006] JBL 468

Mevorach I, 'Cross-Border Insolvency of Enterprise Groups: The Choice of Law Challenge' (2014) 9(1) Brook J Corp Fin & Com L 105

Mevorach I, 'Forum Shopping in Times of Crisis: A Directors Duties Perspective,' (2013) 10(4) ECFR 523

Mevorach I, *Insolvency within Multinational Enterprise Groups* (OUP 2009)

Mevorach I, 'Jurisdiction in Insolvency: A Study of European Courts' Decisions' (2010) 6(2) J Priv Intl L 327

Mevorach I, 'On the Road to Universalism: a Comparative and Empirical Study of UNCITRAL Model Law on Cross-Border Insolvency' (2011) 12 EBOR 517

Mevorach I, 'The Home Country of a Multinational Enterprise Group Facing Insolvency' (2008) 57 ICLQ 427

Mevorach I, 'The New Proposed Regime for EU Corporate Groups in Insolvency: A Critical Note' [2013] Corporate Rescue and Insolvency 89

Mevorach I, 'Towards a Consensus on the Treatment of Multinational Enterprise Groups in Insolvency' (2010) 18 Cardozo J Intl & Comp L 359

Meyerowitz J et al, 'A Dodd-Frank Living Wills Primer: What you Need to Know Now' (2012) 31 Am Bankr Inst J 34

Michaels R, 'Private and Public International Law: German View on Global Issues', (2008) 4 J Priv Intl L 121

Miller DJ and Shakra M, 'Nortel: The Long and Winding Road' in JP Sarra and Justice B Romaine (eds), *Annual Review of Insolvency Law* (Carswell 2015)

Mills A, *The Confluence of Public and Private International Law, Justice, Pluralism and Subsidiarity in the International Constitutional Ordering of Private Law* (CUP 2009)

Mills A, 'The Private History of International Law' (2006) 55 Intl & Comp L Q 1

Mokal RJ, *Corporate Insolvency Law: Theory and Application* (OUP 2005)

Mokal RJ, 'Liquidity, Systemic Risk, and the Bankruptcy Treatment of Financial Contracts' (2015) 10(1) Brook J Corp Fin & Com L 15

Mokal RJ, 'On Fairness and Efficiency' [2003] MLR 452

Morales SA and Deutcsh BA, 'Bankruptcy Code Section 304 and U.S. Recognition of Foreign Bankruptcies: The Tyranny of Comity' (1984) 39 Bus Lawyer 1573

Moss G, 'Group Insolvency—Choice of Forum and Law: the European Experience under the Influence of English Pragmatism' (2007) 32 Brook J Intl L 1005

Moss G, '"Modified universalism" and the Quest for the Golden Thread' (2008) 21(10) Insolv Int 145

Murphy DS, *Principles of International Law* (Thomson/West 2006)

Murphy PJ, 'Why Won't The Leaders Lead? The Need for National Governments to Replace Academics and Practitioners in the Effort to Reform the Muddled World of International Insolvency' (2002) 34 U Miami Interam L Rev 121

Nadelmann K, 'Bankruptcy Treaties' (1944) 93 U Pa L Rev 58

Neuberger DE, Lord, President of the Supreme Court, The Supreme Court, the Privy Council and International Insolvency, Keynote speech at the International Insolvency Institute Annual Conference 2017, London (19 June 2017)

Neuberger DE Lord, 'The International Dimension of Insolvency' [2010] Insolv Int 42

Nielsen A et al, 'The Cross-Border Insolvency Concordat: Principles to Facilitate the Resolution of International Insolvencies' (1996) 70 Am Bankr L J 533

Norman G and Trachtman J, 'The Customary International Law Game' (2005) 99 Am J Intl L 541

Note by the IBA Insolvency Section Delegation to UNCITRAL Working Group V based on an article by Gregor Baer, Insolvency Section Co-Chair, published in *Business Law International* (January 2016): 'International Insolvency Convention: Issues, Options and Feasibility Considerations' (with the publisher's permission) <https://www.ibanet.org/LPD/Insolvency_Section/Insolvency_Section/Projects.aspx#uninsolvencyconvention>

O'Connell DP, *International Law*, Vol 1 (Stevens 1970)

O'Donoghue T and Rabin M, 'Doing it Now or Later' (1999) 89 Am Econ Rev 103

Oh S, 'An Overview of the New Korean Insolvency Law' (2007) 16 Norton J Bankr L & Practice 5

Omar PJ, 'The European Insolvency Regulation 2000: A Paradigm of International Insolvency Cooperation' (2003) 15 Bond L Rev 215

Ostrom E, 'A Behavioral Approach to the Rational Choice Theory of Collective Action' (1998) 92(1) Am Pol Sci Rev 1

Parisi F and Smith VL, 'Introduction' in F Parisi and VL Smith (eds), *The Law and Economics of Irrational Behavior* (Stanford University Press 2005)

Paterson S, 'Rethinking Corporate Bankruptcy Theory in the Twenty-First Century' (2016) 36(4) OJLS 697

Paul JR, 'Comity in International Law' (1991) 32 Harv Intl L J 1

Paulus CG, 'The ECJ's Understanding of the Universality Principle' (2014) 27(5) Insolv Int 70

Paulus CG and Kargman ST, 'Reforming the Process of Sovereign Debt Restructuring: A Proposal for a Sovereign Debt Tribunal' (International Insolvency Institute, 2008) <http://www.un.org/esa/ffd/wp-content/uploads/2008/10/20081010_KargmanPaulus_SovereignDebtTribunal.pdf>

Paulus CG et al, 'Insolvency Law as a Main Pillar of Market Economy—A Critical Assessment of the Greek Insolvency Law' (2015) 24(1) Intl Insolv Rev 1

Payne J, 'Cross-border Schemes of Arrangement and Forum Shopping' (2013) 14 EBOR 563

Peck, JM, 'Cross-Border Observations Derived from My Lehman Judicial Experience' (2013) 30 Butterworths J Intl Banking & Fin L 131

Peihani M, 'Crisis Management and Orderly Resolution of Banks in Canada and Internationally: A Perspective on Reforms and Challenges' in JP Sarra and Justice B Romaine (eds), *Annual Review of Insolvency Law* (Carswell 2015)

Petersen N, 'Customary Law Without Custom? Rules, Principles, and the Role of State Practice in International Norm Creation' (2007) 23(2) Am U Intl L Rev 275

Posner EA and Sykes AO, *Economic Foundations of International Law* (Harvard University Press 2013)

Pottow JAE, 'Beyond Carve-Outs and Toward Reliance: A Normative Framework for Cross-Border Insolvency Choice of Law' (2014) 9(1) Brook J Corp Fin & Com 197

Pottow JAE, 'Greed and Pride in International Bankruptcy: The Problems of and Proposed Solutions to "Local Interests"' (2006) 104 Mich L Rev 1899

Pottow JAE, 'International Insolvency Law's Cross-Roads and the New Modularity' (UNCITRAL Congress, 4–6 July 2017) <http://www.uncitral.org/uncitral/en/commission/colloquia/50th-anniversary.html>

Pottow JAE, 'Procedural Incrementalism: A Model for International Bankruptcy' (2005) 45 Va J Intl L 935

Pottow JAE, 'Two Cheers for Universalism: Nortel's Nifty Novelty' in JP Sarra and Justice B Romaine (eds), *Annual Review of Insolvency Law* (Carswell 2015)

Poulsen LNS, 'Bounded Rationality and the Diffusion of Modern Investment Treaties' 58(1) (2013) Int Stud Q 1

Poulsen LNS and Aisbett E, 'When the Claim Hits: Bilateral Investment Treaties and Bounded Rational Learning' (2013) 65 k, World Pol 273

Quintyn M, 'Independent Agencies—More than a Cheap Copy of Independent Central Banks?' (2009) 20 Const Polit Econ 267

Rajak H, 'Modified Universalism in International Insolvency and the Rubin Case: One Step Backwards?' (2014) 350 Company Law Newsletter 1

Rammeloo SFG, 'EU Law Reform: Cross-Border Civil and Commercial Procedural Law and Cross-Border Insolvency Law' [2014] DQ 44

Ramsay I, 'The Inherent Power of Common Law Courts to Provide Assistance in Cross-Border Insolvencies: From Comity to Complexity' (2017) 26 Int Insolv Rev 5

Rasmussen R, 'A New Approach to Transnational Insolvencies' (1997) 19 Mich J Intl L 1

Raustiala K, 'Form and Substance in International Agreement' (2005) 99 Am J Intl L 581

Restelli E (ed), *Actas y Tratados del Congreso Sud-americano de Derecho Internacional Privado* (Montevideo 1888–1889)

Rickford J, 'Legal Approaches to Restricting Distributions to Shareholders: Balance Sheet Tests and Solvency Tests' (2006) 7 EBOR 135

Ringe WG, 'Forum Shopping under the EU Insolvency Regulation' (2008) 9(4) EBOR 580

Roberts AE, 'Traditional and Modern Approaches to Customary International Law: A Reconciliation' (2001) 95 Am J Intl L 757

Roberts A and Sivakumaran S, 'Lawmaking by Non-State Actors: Engaging Armed Group in the Creation of International Humanitarian Law' (2012) 37 Yale J Intl L 107

Rona P, Section Subcommittee Update, Legislation and Policy Subcommittee Update, 'The Next Law Reform Frontier—A UN Insolvency Convention' (2015) 9(2) Insolv & Restructuring Intl 42 <https://www.ibanet.org/LPD/Insolvency_Section/Insolvency_Section/Projects.aspx>

Samuelson W and Zechhauser R, 'Status Quo Bias in Decision Making' (1988) 1 J Risk and Uncertainty 7

Sarra J, 'Northern Lights, Canada's version of the UNCITRAL Model Law on Cross-Border Insolvency' (2007) 16 Intl Insolv Rev 19

Sarra, J, 'Oversight and Financing of Cross-Border Business Enterprise Group Insolvency Proceedings' (2009) 44 Tex Intl L J 547

Schachter O, *International Law in Theory and Practice* (Martinus Nijhoff Publishers 1991)

Schmidt SK, et al, 'Internationalizing Law against the Odds: The Power of Courts and Their Limits' in H Rothgang and S Schneider (eds), *State Transformations in OECD Countries: Dimensions, Driving Forces, and Trajectories* (Palgrave Macmillan 2015)

Schreuer C and Dolzer R, *Principles of International Investment Law* (OUP 2008)

Schwarcz SL et al, Comments on the September 29, 2014 FSB Consultative Document, 'Cross-Border Recognition of Resolution Action' Ctr for Intl Governance Innovation, CIGI Paper No 51 (3 December 2014) <https://www.cigionline.org/sites/default/files/no.51.pdf>

Scott R and Stephan P, *The Limits of Leviathan Contract Theory and The Enforcement of International Law* (CUP 2006)

Segundo Congreso Sudamericano de Derecho Internacional Privado, Acta Final, Seguinda Edicion (Montevideo 1940)

Sender O and Wood M, 'Custom's Bright Future: The Continuing Importance of Customary International Law' in CA Bradley (ed), *Custom's Future, International Law in a Changing World* (CUP 2016)

Shaw MN, *International Law* (CUP 2014)

Shelton D, 'Soft Law' in D Armstrong (ed), *Handbook of International Law* (Routledge Press 2008)

Simma B and Alston P, 'The Sources of Human Rights Law: Custom, Jus Cogens, and General Principles' (1988) 12 Austl Y B Intl L 82

Simon HA, 'A Behavioral Model of Rationale Choice' (1955) 69 Q J Econ 99

Skeel DA, 'European Implication of Bankruptcy Venue Shopping in the US' (2007) 54 Buff L Rev 439

Slaughter AM and Burke-White W, 'The Future of International Law is Domestic (or the European Way of Law)' (2006) 47 Harv Intl L J 327

Smith A, 'Some Aspects of Comity and the Protection of Local Creditors in Cross-Border Insolvency Law: South Africa and the United States Compared' (2002) 14 S Afr Mercantile L J 17

Smith AL and Boraine A, 'Crossing Borders into South African Insolvency Law: From the Roman-Dutch Jurists to the Uncitral Model Law' (2002) 10 ABI L Rev 138

Smith J, 'Approaching Universality: The Role of Comity in International Bankruptcy Proceedings Litigated in America' (1999) 17 B U Intl L J 396

Song FM and Li L, 'Bank Governance: Concepts and Measurements' in JR Barth et al (eds), *Research Handbook on International Banking and Governance* (Edward Elgar Publishing 2012)

Spiermann O, 'Twentieth Century Internationalism in Law' (2007) 18(5) Eur J Intl L 785

Stango V and Zinman J, 'Limited and Varying Consumer Attention: Evidence from Shocks to the Salience of Bank Overdraft Fees' (2011) Fed Res Bank of Phila Research Dept, Working Paper No 11-17 <https://www.phil.frb.org/-/media/research-and-data/publications/working-papers/2011/wp11-17.pdf>

Stern B, 'Custom at the Heart of International Law' (2011) 11 Duke J Comp & Intl L 89

Subedi SP, 'International Investment Law' in MD Evans (ed), *International Law* (4th edn, OUP 2014)

Sunstein CR, *Behavioral Law and Economics* (CUP 2000)

Takahashi S, 'The Reality of the Japanese Legal System for Cross-Border Insolvency Driven by Fear of Universalism' (2011) <https://www.iiiglobal.org/node/124>

Taylor SE, 'The Availability Bias in Social Perception and Interaction' in D Kaahneman et al (eds), *Judgement Under Uncertainty: Heuristics and Biases* (CUP 1982) 190

Thaler RH and Sunstein C, *Nudge: Improving Decisions about Health, Wealth and Happiness* (Penguin Books, 2008)

The American Law Institute (ALI), 'Principles of Cooperation Among the NAFTA Countries Transnational Insolvency' (2003)

The American Law Institute and the International Insolvency Institute, 'Transnational Insolvency: Global Principles for Cooperation in International Insolvency Cases' (2012) (Wessels B and Fletcher IF, Joint Reporters) <https://www.iiiglobal.org/sites/default/files/alireportmarch_0.pdf>

The American Law Institute (ALI) and the International Insolvency Institute, 'Transnational Insolvency: Global Principles for Cooperation in International Insolvency Cases, Annex: Global Rules on Conflict-of-Laws Matters in International Insolvency Cases' (2012) (Wessels B and Fletcher IF, Joint Reporters) <https://www.iiiglobal.org/sites/default/files/alireportmarch_0.pdf>

Thirlway H, 'The Sources of International Law' in MD Evans (ed), *International Law* (4th edn, OUP 2014)

Thirlway H, *The Sources of International Law* (OUP 2014)

Tirado I, 'An Evolution of COMI in the European Insolvency Regulation: from "Insolvenzimperialismus" to the Recast' in JP Sarra and Justice B Romaine (eds), *Annual Review of Insolvency Law* (Carswell 2015) 819

Tirado I, 'Out of Courts Debt Restructuring in Spain: A Modernised Framework' (on file with author)

Tom M et al, 'The Neural Basis of Loss Aversion in Decision-Making Under Risk' (2007) 315 Science 515

Tomasic R, 'The Sociology of Legislation' in R Tomasic (ed), *Legislation and Society in Australia* (Allen & Unwin 1980)

Torremans P, 'Coming to Terms with the COMI Concept in the European Insolvency Regulation' in PJ Omar (ed), *International Insolvency Law Themes and Perspectives* (Aldershot 2008)

Trachtman JL, *The Economic Structure of International Law* (Harvard University Press 2008)

Trautman DT et al, 'Four Models for International Bankruptcy' (1993) 41 Am J Comp L 573

Tung F, 'Fear of Commitment in International Bankruptcy' (2001) 33 Geo Wash Intl L Rev 555

Tung F, 'Is International Bankruptcy Possible?' (2002) 23 Mich J Intl L 31

Tversky A and Fox CR, 'Ambiguity, Aversion and Comparative Ignorance' (1995) 110(3) Q J Econ 585

Tversky A and Kahneman D, 'Advances in Prospect Theory: Cumulative Representation of Uncertainty' (1992) 5(4) J Risk and Uncertainty 297

Tversky A and Kahneman D, 'Availability: A Heuristic for Judging Frequency and Probability' (1973) 5(2) Cognitive Psychology 207

Tversky A and Kahneman D, 'Judgment under Uncertainty: Heuristics and Biases' (1974) 185 Science 1124

Tversky A and Kahneman D, 'The Framing of Decisions and the Psychology of Choice' (1981) 211 Science 453

Tversky A and Kahneman D, 'Rational Choice and the Framing of Decisions' (1986) 59 J Bus 251

United Nations Commission on International Trade Law, Insolvency Law: Background Information on Topics Comprising the Current Mandate of Working Group V and Topics for Possible Future Work, Note by the Secretariat, UN Doc. A/CN.9/WG.V/WP.117 (2013) <http://www.uncitral.org/uncitral/en/commission/working_groups/5Insolvency.html>

United Nations Commission on International Trade Law, Insolvency Law: Recent Developments Concerning the Global and Regional Initiatives Regarding the Insolvency of Large and Complex Financial Institutions, A/CN.9/WG.V/WP.118 (2013) <http://www.uncitral.org/uncitral/en/commission/sessions/43rd.html>

United Nations Commission on International Trade Law, 'Comments by the International Bar Association respecting proposals to consider an international convention and/or model law on cross-border enterprise group insolvency' UNCITRAL Working Group V, 38th Session (New York, April 2010) UN Doc A/CN.9/WG.V/WP.93/Add.6 <http://www.uncitral.org/uncitral/en/commission/working_groups/5Insolvency.html>

United Nations Commission on International Trade Law, A/CN.9/WG.V/WP.146, 2 March 2017, Facilitating the cross-border insolvency of multinational enterprise groups: draft legislative provisions (New York, 10–19 May 2017) <http://www.uncitral.org/uncitral/en/commission/working_groups/5Insolvency.html>

United Nations Commission on International Trade Law, Insolvency Law: Insolvency of Large and Complex Financial Institutions, Note by the Secretariat, UN Doc. A/CN.9/WG.V/WP.109 (2012) <http://www.uncitral.org/uncitral/en/commission/working_groups/5Insolvency.html>

United Nations Commission on International Trade Law, Insolvency Law: Possible Future Work: Addendum, Proposal by the Delegation of Switzerland for Preparation of a Study on the Feasibility of an Instrument Regarding the Cross-Border Resolution of Large and Complex Financial Institutions, UN. Doc. A/CN.9/WG.V/WP.93/Add.5 (2010) <http://www.uncitral.org/uncitral/en/commission/working_groups/5Insolvency.html>

United Nations Commission on International Trade Law, Insolvency Law: Possible Future Work: Further Proposal by the Delegation of Switzerland for Preparation by the UNCITRAL Secretariat of a Study on the Feasibility and Possible Scope of an Instrument Regarding the Cross-Border Resolution of Large and Complex Financial Institutions, A/CN.9/709 (2010) <http://www.uncitral.org/uncitral/en/commission/sessions/43rd.html>

United Nations Commission on International Trade Law, UNCITRAL Legislative Guide on Insolvency Law, Parts one and two, 25 June 2004; Part three, 1 July 2010; Part four, 18 July 2013 <http://www.uncitral.org/uncitral/en/uncitral_texts/insolvency/2004Guide.html>

United Nations Commission on International Trade Law, Proposal for Future Work for Working Group V by the Union Internationale des Avocats (UIA) UNCITRAL Working Group V 37th Session (November 2009) UN Doc A/CN.9/WG.V/XXXVII/ CRP.3

United Nations Commission on International Trade Law, A/CN.9/WG.V/WP.145, 1 March 2017, Recognition and enforcement of insolvency-related judgments: draft model law (New York, 10–19 May 2017) <http://www.uncitral.org/uncitral/en/commission/working_groups/5Insolvency.html>

United Nations Commission on International Trade Law, A/CN.9/686, Report of Working Group V (Insolvency Law) on the work of its thirty-seventh session (Vienna, 9–13 November 2009) <http://www.uncitral.org/uncitral/en/commission/working_groups/5Insolvency.html>

United Nations Commission on International Trade Law, A/CN.9/691, Report of Working Group V (Insolvency Law) on the work of its thirty-eighth session (New York, 19–23 April 2010) <http://www.uncitral.org/uncitral/en/commission/working_groups/5Insolvency.html>

United Nations Commission on International Trade Law, A/CN.9/798, Report of Working Group V (Insolvency Law) on the work of its forty-fourth session (Vienna, 16–20 December 2013) <http://www.uncitral.org/uncitral/en/commission/working_groups/5Insolvency.html>

United Nations Commission on International Trade Law, A/CN.9/WG.V/WP.139, 23 February 2016, Directors' obligations in the period approaching insolvency: enterprise groups (New York, 2–6 May 2016) <https://documents-dds-ny.un.org/doc/UNDOC/LTD/V16/011/57/PDF/V1601157.pdf?OpenElement>

United Nations Commission on International Trade Law, A/CN.9/903, 26 May 2017, Report of Working Group V (Insolvency Law) on the work of its fifty-first session (New York, 10–19 May 2017) <http://www.uncitral.org/uncitral/en/commission/working_groups/5Insolvency.html>

United Nations Commission on International Trade Law, A/69/17, Report of the United Nations Commission on International Trade Law, Official Records of the General Assembly, Sixty-ninth Session, Supplement No 17 (7–8 July 2014) <http://www.uncitral.org/pdf/english/texts/arbitration/transparency-convention/A-69-17-E.pdf>

United Nations Commission on International Trade Law, UNCITRAL Model Law on Cross-Border Insolvency (1997) with Guide to Enactment and Interpretation with Guide to Enactment and Interpretation (2013) <http://www.uncitral.org/uncitral/en/uncitral_texts/insolvency/1997Model.html>

United Nations Commission on International Trade Law, UNCITRAL Model Law on Cross-Border Insolvency: The Judicial Perspective (2013) <http://www.uncitral.org/uncitral/uncitral_texts/insolvency/2011Judicial_Perspective.html>

United Nations Commission on International Trade Law, UNCITRAL Practice Guide on Cooperation (2009) <http://www.uncitral.org/uncitral/en/uncitral_texts/insolvency/2009PracticeGuide.html>

United Nations Commission on International Trade Law, UNCITRAL Yearbook, Volume XXVIII: 1997, Summary Records of The United Nations Commission on International Trade Law for Meetings Devoted to the Preparation of the Draft UNCITRAL Model Law on Cross-Border Insolvency (12 May 1997) <http://www.uncitral.org/uncitral/en/publications/yearbook.html>

United Nations, A/71/17, Report of the United Nations Commission on International Trade Law, Forty-ninth session (27 June–15 July 2016) para 247 <http://www.uncitral.org/uncitral/en/commission/sessions/49th.html>

US House of Representatives, 'Bankruptcy Abuse Prevention and Consumer Protection Act of 2005: Report of the Committee on the Judiciary House of Representatives to accompany s 256 together with dissenting, additional dissenting and additional minority views' 109th Congress 1st Session' Report 109–31 Part 1 (8 April 2005) <https://www.congress.gov/congressional-report/109th-congress/house-report/31/1>

van Aaken A, 'Behavioral International Law and Economics' (2014) 55(2) Harv Intl L J 421

van Hoof GJH *Rethinking the Sources of International Law* (Kluwer Law and Taxation Publishers 1983)

Verzijl J, 'International Law in Historical Perspective' (1968) 1 A Sijthoff Leyden 190

Virgos M and Schmit E, 'Report on the Convention on Insolvency Proceedings' (Brussels, 3 May 1996) <http://aei.pitt.edu/952/1/insolvency_report_schmidt_1988.pdf>

Vondracek O, European Commission (DG Justice & Consumers), EU Insolvency Initiative, presentation at the Insolvency Law Association (ILA) Academic Forum and Annual Conference (March 2016) (on file with author)

Waldron J, 'Foreign Law and the Modern *Ius Gentium*' (2006) 119 Harv L Rev 129

Walters A, 'Giving Effect to Foreign Restructuring Plans in Anglo-US Private International Law' (2015) 3 NIBLeJ 37

Walters A, 'Modified Universalisms & the Role of Local Legal Culture in the Making of Cross-border Insolvency Law' Am Bankr L J (*forthcoming*) available at SSRN: <https://papers.ssrn.com/sol3/papers.cfm?abstract_id=3084117>

Walters A, 'United States' Bankruptcy Jurisdiction over Foreign Entities: Exorbitant or Congruent?' (2017) 17(2) J Corp L Stud 367

Walters A and Smith A, ' "Bankruptcy Tourism" Under the EC Regulation on Insolvency Proceedings: A View from England and Wales' (2010) 19(3) IIR 181

Warren E, 'Bankruptcy Policy' (1987) 54 U Chi L Rev 775

Warren E and Westbrook JL, 'Contracting out of Bankruptcy: An Empirical Intervention' (2005) 118 Harv L Rev 1197

Watters W, 'Guidelines for Cooperation and Communication between Courts on Cross-border Insolvency Matters: Too Far or Not Far Enough?' (2017) 38(6) Comp L 172

Watson A, *The Evolution of Law* (John Hopkins 1985)

Way R, 'Transnational Liftoff and Juridical Touchdown: The Regulatory Function of Private International Law in an Era of Globalization' (2002) 40 Colum J Transnatl L 209

Webber C, 'Universalism? Not in My Backyard' (2013) 47 Com Litigation J 6

Weller M, 'Mutual Trust: In Search of the Future of European Union Private International Law' (2015) 11(1) J of Priv Intl L 64

Wessels B, 'Giving Legal Effect to Foreign Resolution Measures in the Financial Sector' (2015) 28(3) Insolv Int 44

Wessels B, *International Insolvency Law* Part I (Wolters Kluwer 2015)

Wessels B, 'Is Switzerland Opening up for Cross-border Insolvency?' (7 May 7 2012) <http://leidenlawblog.nl/articles/is-switzerland-opening-up-for-cross-border-insolvency>

Wessels B, 'The Effects in the Netherlands of an Order Issued in Indian Insolvency Proceedings' *Leiden Law Blog* (25 July 2016) <http://leidenlawblog.nl/articles/the-effects-in-the-netherlands-of-an-order-issued-in-indian-insolvency-proc>

Wessels B, 'Towards a Next Step in Cross-Border Judicial Cooperation' (2014) 27 Insolv Int 100

Westbrook JL, 'A Global Solution to Multinational Default' (2000) 98 Mich L Rev 2276

Westbrook JL, 'An Empirical Study of the Implementation in the United States of the Model Law on Cross Border Insolvency' (2013) 87(2) Am Bankr L J 247

Westbrook JL, 'Avoidance of Pre-Bankruptcy Transactions in Multinational Bankruptcy Cases' (2007) 42 Tex Intl LJ 899

Westbrook JL, 'Breaking Away: Local Priorities and Global Assets' (2011) 46 Tex Intl LJ 601

Westbrook JL, 'Chapter 15 and Discharge' (2005) 13 Am Bankr Inst L Rev 503

Westbrook JL, 'Chapter 15 Comes of Age' in JP Sarra (ed), *Annual Review of Insolvency Law 2013* (Thomson Carswell 2013)

Westbrook JL, 'Choice of Avoidance Law in Global Insolvencies' (1991) 17 Brook J Intl L 499

Westbrook JL, 'Coordination in International Corporate Insolvencies' in RM Lastra (ed), *Cross-Border Bank Insolvency* (OUP 2011)

Westbrook JL, 'International Arbitration and Multinational Insolvency' (2011) 29 Penn State Intl L Rev 635

Westbrook JL, 'International Judicial Negotiations' (2003) 38 Tex Intl L J 567

Westbrook JL, 'Interpretation Internationale' (2015) 87 Temp L Rev 739

Westbrook JL, 'Locating the Eye of the Financial Storm' (2007) 32 Brook J Intl L 1019

Westbrook JL, 'Multinational Enterprises in General Default: Chapter 15, The ALI Principles, and The EU Insolvency Regulation' (2002) 76 Am Bankr L J 1

Westbrook JL, 'Theory and Pragmatism in Global Insolvencies: Choice of Law and Choice of Forum' (1991) 65 Am Bankr L J 457

Westbrook JL, 'SIFIs and States' (2014) 49(2) Tex Intl L J 329

Westbrook JL, 'Universalism and Choice of Law' (2005) 23 Penn St Intl L Rev 625

Westbrook JL, Booth CD, Paulus CG, and Rajak, H, 'A Global View of Business Insolvency System' [2010] The World Bank, Law, Justice, and Development Series

Wilkins, M, *The Emergence of Multinational Enterprises: American Business Abroad from the Colonial Era to 1914* (Harvard University Press 1970) Part Two

Wilson JQ and Abrahamse A, 'Does Crime Pay?' (1992) 9 Just Q 359

Winter RK, 'State Law, Shareholder Protection, and the Theory of the Corporation' (1977) 6 J Legal Stud 251

Woods AK, 'A Behavioral Approach to Human Rights' (2010) 51 Harv J Intl L 51

Wolfke K, *Custom in Present International Law* (2d edn, Martinus Nijhoff Publishers 1993)

World Bank Principles for Effective Insolvency and Creditor/Debtor Regimes (2016) <http://documents.worldbank.org/curated/en/518861467086038847/pdf/106399-WP-REVISED-PUBLIC-ICR-Principle-Final-Hyperlinks-revised-Latest.pdf>

Wright ND et al, 'Approach-Avoidance Processes Contribute to Dissociable Impacts of Risk and Loss on Choice' (2012) 32(20) J Neuroscience 7009

Wright ND et al, 'Manipulating the Contribution of Approach-avoidance to the Perturbation of Economic Choice by Valence' (2013) 7 Frontiers in Neuroscience 1

Yamamoto K, 'New Japanese Legislation on Cross-Border Insolvency as Compared to the UNCITRAL Model Law' (2002) 11(2) Int Insolv Rev 67

Yntema H, 'The Comity Doctrine' (1966) 65 Mich L Rev 9

Zacaroli A and Arnold M, 'Banking on Brexit' *South Square Digest* (June 2017) 8 <http://www.southsquare.com/files/DIGEST%20JUNE%202017.pdf>

Ziegel JS, 'Corporate Groups and Crossborder Insolvencies: A Canada–United States Perspective' (2002) 7 Fordham J Corp & Fin L 367

Zulman RH, 'Cross-Border Insolvency in South African Law' (2009) 21 S Afr Mercantile L J 804

Zumbro PH, 'Cross-Border Insolvencies and International Protocols—An Imperfect But Effective Tool' (2010) 11 Bus L Intl 157

Index